Brilliant Microsoft® Access 2007

Forms, Reports, and Queries

Paul McFedries

PEARSON
Prentice
Hall

Harlow, England • London • New York • Bos...
Sydney • Tokyo • Singapore • Hong Kong
Cape Town • Madrid • Mexico City • Amste...

Contents at a Glance

Pearson Education Limited
Edinburgh Gate
Harlow
Essex CM20 2JE
England

and Associated Companies throughout the world

Visit us on the World Wide Web at:
www.pearsoned.co.uk

Original edition, FORMS, REPORTS, AND QUERIES FOR MICROSOFT
OFFICE ACCESS 2007, 1st edition, 9780789736697 by PAUL MCFEDRIES.,
published by Pearson Education, Inc, publishing as Que/Sams, Copyright © 2008
Que Publishing.

ISBN: 978-0-273-71495-8

British Library Cataloguing-in-Publication Data
A catalogue record for this book is available from the British Library

10 9 8 7 6 5 4 3 2 1
11 10 09 08 07

Printed and bound by Henry Ling Ltd at the Dorset Press, Dorchester, Dorset, UK.

The publisher's policy is to use paper manufactured from sustainable forests.

Contents

III CREATING POWERFUL QUERIES

About the Author

Paul McFedries is the president of Logophilia Limited, a technical writing company. Now primarily a writer, Paul is well known as a teacher of Microsoft Office and Microsoft Windows, and has worked as a programmer, consultant, database developer, and website developer. He has written more than 50 books that have sold more than three million copies worldwide. These books include *Brilliant Microsoft Office 2007 Tips and Tricks* (Prentice Hall, 2008), *Brilliant Microsoft Access 2007 Forms, Reports and Queries* (Prentice Hall, 2008), *VBA for Microsoft Office 2007* (Prentice Hall, 2008), and *Windows Vista Unleashed* (Sams, 2006).

Dedication

To Karen and Gypsy.

Acknowledgments

When people ask me what I do for a living, I tell them that I write technical books. However, if my ego was just a tad smaller, what I'd really say is that I *collaborate* on technical books. Yes, it's my name on the front cover (there's that ego thing again), and the text you're about to read was written by me, but a book like this comes together with the hard work and dedication of *lots* of people. My heartfelt thanks go out to all of them. I'd also like to pass along extra thanks to those hard-working souls who I worked with directly: Acquisitions Editor Loretta Yates, Development Editor Todd Brakke, Project Editor Andy Beaster, Copy Editor Chuck Hutchinson, and Technical Editor Scott Diamond.

Introduction

Microsoft Access is a large, intimidating program.
Unlike Word or Excel, where you can perform
basic tasks without much in the way of training,
Access presents challenges from the outset. Most
users never progress beyond creating simple tables
and using wizards to create basic forms and reports.
At the same time, all users—from managers to
researchers to administrative assistants—need information and know that what they seek is embedded
somewhere in their Access tables. Without a more
sophisticated knowledge of how to extract and present that data, they are forced to rely on office
gurus and overworked IT people to provide canned
reports or one-size-fits-all solutions.

This book will change all that by giving you the
skills required to extract the data you need
(queries), build efficient front ends for that data
(forms), and publish the results in an attractive and
easy-to-read format (reports). To that end, this
book shuns the big Access picture and instead
focuses intently on queries, forms, and reports. This
in-depth approach gives you the skills and understanding you need to get at the data and prove the
old saying that knowledge is indeed power. And this
book does all that with no-nonsense, step-by-step
tutorials and lots of practical, useful examples aimed
directly at business users.

Even if you've never been able to get Access to do
much beyond storing data in simple tables, you'll
still find this book to your liking. I show you how
to build useful, powerful queries, forms, and reports
from the ground up, so no experience with these
aspects of Access is necessary.

INTRODUCTION

What's in the Book

This book isn't meant to be read from cover to cover, although you're certainly free to do just that if the mood strikes you. Instead, most of the chapters are set up as self-contained units that you can dip into at will to extract whatever nuggets of information you need. However, if you're a relatively new Access user, I suggest starting the first one or two chapters in each of the book's three main sections to ensure you have a thorough grounding in the fundamentals of Access queries, forms, and reports.

The book is divided into three main parts. To give you the big picture before diving in, here's a summary of what you'll find in each part:

Part I, Creating Forms: The five chapters in Part I show you how to build efficient and useful forms for inputting and editing data. Chapter 1, "Creating and Using a Form," and Chapter 2, "Working with Form Controls," give you the basic form know-how you need. From there, you learn about using data validation to ensure data entry accuracy, learn how to design forms for the business environment, and learn how to create specialized forms such as switchboards, dialog boxes, and startup screens.

Part II, Designing and Customizing Reports: The four chapters in Part II tell you everything you need to know to create attractive and practical reports. Chapter 6, "Creating and Publishing a Report," gives you the basics, and the subsequent chapters add to your knowledge by showing you the fundamentals of good report design and how to build advanced reports.

Part III, Creating Powerful Queries: The six chapters in Part III give you a thorough grounding in the features and uses of Access queries. After learning some query fundamentals in Chapter 10, "Creating a Basic Query," you move on to understanding criteria expressions; multiple-table queries; totals, parameter, and action queries; PivotTable queries; and SQL statements.

This Book's Special Features

Microsoft Office Access 2007 Forms, Reports, and Queries is designed to give you the information you need without making you wade through ponderous explanations and interminable technical background. To make your life easier, this book includes various features and conventions that help you get the most out of the book and Access itself.

Steps—Throughout the book, each Access task is summarized in step-by-step procedures.

Things you type—Whenever I suggest that you type something, what you type appears in a **bold** font.

Commands—I use the following style for Access Ribbon commands: Create, Form. This means that you click the Ribbon's Create tab and then click the Form button. For the Office menu, I use the form Office, <u>O</u>pen. This means that you pull down the Office menu and select the <u>O</u>pen command.

Dialog box controls—Dialog box controls have underlined accelerator keys: <u>C</u>lose.

This book also uses the following boxes to draw your attention to important (or merely interesting) information.

> **NOTE**
> The Note box presents asides that give you more information about the topic under discussion. These tidbits provide extra insights that give you a better understanding of the task at hand.

> **TIP**
> The Tip box tells you about Access methods that are easier, faster, or more efficient than the standard methods.

> **CAUTION**
> The all-important Caution box tells you about potential accidents waiting to happen. There are always ways to mess things up when you're working with computers. These boxes help you avoid at least some of the pitfalls.

→ These cross-reference elements point you to related material elsewhere in the book.

CASE STUDY

You'll find these case studies throughout the book, and they're designed to take what you've learned and apply it to projects and real-world examples.

The Examples Used in the Book

An old saw tells us that "a good example has twice the value of good advice." I tried to cram this book with as much good advice as I could think of, but just to make sure you get your money's worth, I've also included tons of examples. I've found over the years that examples do the most good if the reader can follow along when the mood strikes. To that end, all the examples I use in this book are based on the sample database that comes with Access 2007: Northwind 2007, a database of products, employees, invoices, and much more from Northwind Traders, a fictitious food company. If you want to use this database while learning about Access forms, reports, and queries, here's how to load it:

1. Launch Access 2007 and, in the list of template categories that appears, click Sample. (If you already have Access 2007 started, choose Office, New to see the list of template categories.)

2. Click the Northwind 2007 icon.

3. Adjust the File Name, if desired.

4. Click Download.

5. If you see the Microsoft Office Genuine Advantage dialog box, click Continue. Access 2007 downloads and installs the database.

6. If you see the Security Warning message bar, click Options, click Enable This Content, and then click OK.

7. In the Login Dialog, click Login.

Creating Forms

IN THIS PART

Creating and Using a Form

1

Data entry is the unglamorous side of Access. Sure, entering a record or two isn't so bad, but entering dozens of records quickly becomes a chore you might do anything to avoid. The datasheet techniques presented later in this book in Chapter 10, "Creating a Basic Query," can help, but the datasheet isn't the most attractive way to get information into a table. You can take some of the drudgery out of data entry by using *forms*.

In the real world, we deal with forms of various descriptions all the time—application forms, registration forms, license renewals, deposit slips, and traffic tickets (one of my specialties, unfortunately). It's a rare day that goes by without some officious person tossing a form our way and telling us to fill it out in triplicate.

Paper forms, then, are documents with blank boxes that you use to fill in the required information. Each box usually has a label beside it to let you know what kind of information to enter. Access forms are basically the same as their paper counterparts. For example, compare the datasheet view of Northwind's Products table in Figure 1.1 with the same table displayed in a form in Figure 1.2. As you can see, a form is a window that displays, for each field in the table, a control such as a text box, drop-down list, or check box.

Figure 1.1
The datasheet view of the Products table.

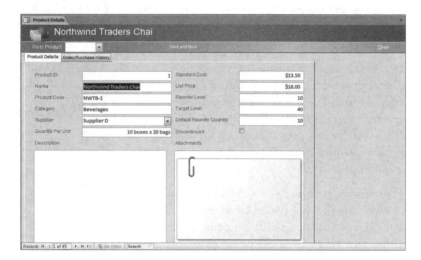

Figure 1.2
The first record of the Products table displayed in a form.

Forms bring a number of advantages to the data entry table:

- Because the form shows only one record at a time, you can almost always see all the table fields at once. In contrast, you can usually see only four or five columns at a time in a datasheet.

- Controls such as drop-down lists reduce the possibility of data entry errors by giving the users a limited set of choices for a field.

- Access gives you a number of customization options. These features let you create Access forms that look exactly like paper forms, and you can add graphics and other objects to make the forms more interesting.

- You aren't distracted by other data in the table, so you can give your full attention to the task at hand.

This isn't to say that you must always use a form whenever you want to enter data into an Access table. The datasheet is probably faster if you have just a few fields to fill in, and the datasheet is definitely the way to go if you want to refer to as many other records as possible when entering your data.

When you do need a form, however, this chapter gives you the basics for building forms and then for using them to navigate and edit data.

Building a Basic Form

NEW Form building in Access 2007 is easier than it has ever been. Yes, you can still access the Design view (as described later in this chapter) to build your forms. However, if your needs are simple or time is short, then you can build a great-looking form with just a few mouse clicks. The secret is that Access 2007 comes with three basic form layouts that you can apply to an existing table or query:

- **Form**—This standard form layout shows the data from one record at a time, as well as records from another table that are related. See "Building a Standard Form," next.

- **Split Form**—This layout has two sections: a form on top and a datasheet below. When you select a record in the datasheet, the record data appears in the form. See "Building a Split Form," later in this chapter.

- **Multiple Items**—This tabular form layout shows the records in rows with the field names at the top. See "Building a Multiple Items Form," later in this chapter.

→ To learn how to build a PivotChart form, **see** "Creating a PivotChart Form," **p. 108**. (Chapter 5)
→ To learn how to build a modal dialog box, **see** "Creating a Form Pop-Up Box or Dialog Box," **p. 103**. (Chapter 5)

Note that in all three form layouts, Access displays most text and numeric fields using a simple text box, and it displays Yes/No fields with a check box.

Building a Standard Form

Running the Form command to build a standard form requires just two steps:

> **NOTE**
> Before you can follow the steps in this section, you need to have a database open. If you want to use the sample Northwind database, choose Office, <u>N</u>ew, click the Sample category, click the Northwind 2007 icon, and then click <u>D</u>ownload.

1. In the Navigation pane, click the table or query you want to use as the form record source.
2. Choose Create, Form.

1

Figure 1.3 shows a form created from the Northwind Employees table.

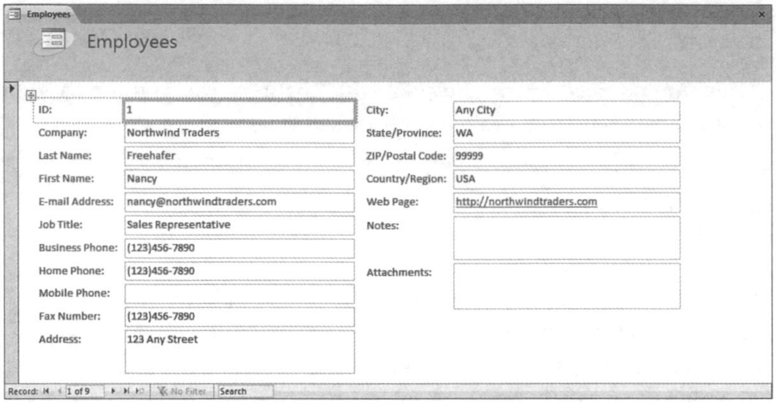

Figure 1.3
A standard form built on the Northwind database's Employees table.

ID:	1	City:	Any City
Company:	Northwind Traders	State/Province:	WA
Last Name:	Freehafer	ZIP/Postal Code:	99999
First Name:	Nancy	Country/Region:	USA
E-mail Address:	nancy@northwindtraders.com	Web Page:	http://northwindtraders.com
Job Title:	Sales Representative	Notes:	
Business Phone:	(123)456-7890		
Home Phone:	(123)456-7890	Attachments:	
Mobile Phone:			
Fax Number:	(123)456-7890		
Address:	123 Any Street		

Record: ⋈ ⋪ 1 of 9 ▸ ⋈ ⋈ No Filter Search

Sometimes when you run the Form command, the resulting form will be a bit more complex. For example, take a look at the form in Figure 1.4, which I built using the Orders table as the record source.

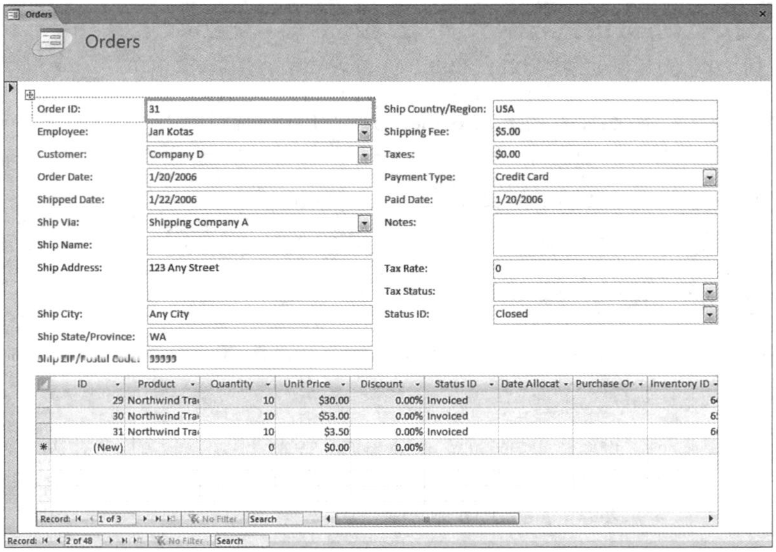

Figure 1.4
A more complex form built on the Northwind database's Orders table.

Order ID:	31	Ship Country/Region:	USA
Employee:	Jan Kotas	Shipping Fee:	$5.00
Customer:	Company D	Taxes:	$0.00
Order Date:	1/20/2006	Payment Type:	Credit Card
Shipped Date:	1/22/2006	Paid Date:	1/20/2006
Ship Via:	Shipping Company A	Notes:	
Ship Name:			
Ship Address:	123 Any Street	Tax Rate:	0
		Tax Status:	
Ship City:	Any City	Status ID:	Closed
Ship State/Province:	WA		
Ship ZIP/Postal Code:	99999		

	ID	Product	Quantity	Unit Price	Discount	Status ID	Date Allocat	Purchase Or	Inventory ID
	29	Northwind Tra	10	$30.00	0.00%	Invoiced			6
	30	Northwind Tra	10	$53.00	0.00%	Invoiced			6
	31	Northwind Tra	10	$3.50	0.00%	Invoiced			6
*	(New)		0	$0.00	0.00%				

Record: ⋈ ⋪ 1 of 3 ▸ ⋈ ⋈ No Filter Search

Record: ⋈ ⋪ 2 of 48 ▸ ⋈ ⋈ No Filter Search

In particular, notice the datasheet on the bottom of the form. This is called a *subform*, and it shows the current order's related records from the Order Details table. I discuss creating forms based on multiple, related tables later in this book. For now, however, you should know that if the table has a field that's used as the basis of a one-to-many relationship with another table and the current table is the "one" side of that relationship, the "many" table's related records are displayed in a subform.

Also notice in Figure 1.4 that some of the fields are displayed as drop-down lists instead of text boxes. In general, if the table has a field that is used as the basis of a one-to-many relationship with another table and the current table is the "many" side of that relationship, that field is displayed as a drop-down list that contains the values from the related table. For example, the Orders table is related to the Employees table, so the Employee drop-down list contains the names of all the people in the Employees table.

If you've never used multiple, related tables before, don't worry if the preceding two paragraphs don't make much sense right now. I'll explain everything in much more detail later.

→ For the details on building a form from multiple, related tables, **see** "Creating a Multiple-Table Form," **p. 95**. (Chapter 5)

Building a Split Form

One of the advantages of viewing a table or query in a datasheet is that you can quickly navigate among the records by using the scrollbars or navigation keys such as Page Down and Page Up. A standard form shows just one record at a time, so getting to the record you want (particularly if the underlying table or query has many records) can be time-consuming.

The advantage of a split form is that it combines the best of both worlds—the nicer layout of a form and the navigation speed of a datasheet. The split form accomplishes this by creating a form that's split in two: The top half is a standard form and the bottom half is a datasheet. The idea is that you use the datasheet to find the record you want, and when you click anywhere inside the record, the record's data appears in the form.

As with the Form command, wielding the Split Form command takes but two steps:

1. In the Navigation pane, click the table or query you want to use as the form record source.
2. Choose Create, Split Form.

Figure 1.5 shows a split form created from the Northwind Orders table.

Building a Multiple Items Form

The multiple items form is another form/datasheet hybrid. In this case, the form is laid out using the same tabular layout as a datasheet, with the records in rows and the fields in columns, with the field headings along the top of the form. However, unlike a datasheet, which displays only a single line of data for each record, the multiple items form displays up to three lines of data.

Here are the steps to follow to create a multiple items form:

1. In the Navigation pane, click the table or query you want to use as the form record source.
2. Choose Create, Multiple Items.

Figure 1.5
A split form built on the Northwind database's Orders table.

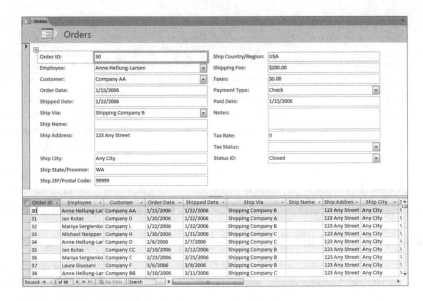

Figure 1.6 shows the multiple items layout built from the Northwind Orders table.

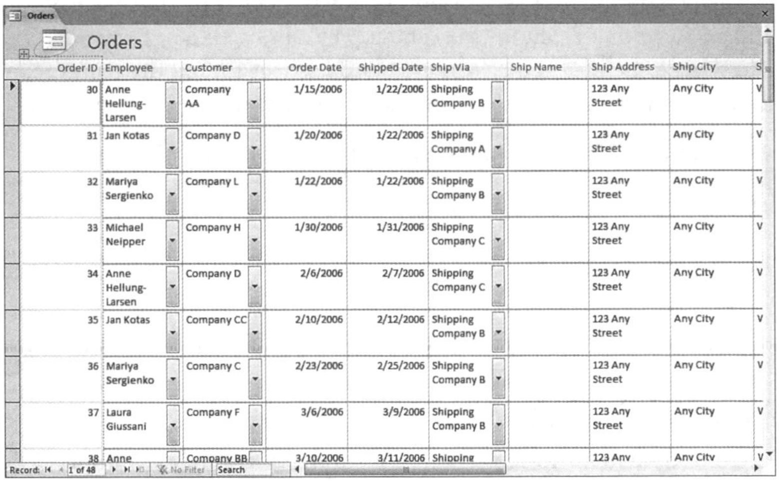

Figure 1.6
A multiple items form built on the Northwind database's Orders table.

Creating Simple Forms with the Form Wizard

The Form, Split Form, and Multiple Items commands are fast ways to create a form, but they suffer from a lack of interaction. That is, you have no way of specifying the fields you want to see or the formatting style you want to use. For a bit more control over your forms, you need to use the Form Wizard. The Form Wizard is more like a traditional

Office wizard: It displays a series of dialog boxes that take you step by step through the entire form-creation process, as described here:

→ The Form Wizard even lets you select fields from multiple tables; **see** "Creating a Form and Subform with the Form Wizard," **p. 96**. (Chapter 5)

1. In the Navigation pane, click the table or query you want to use as the form record source.

2. Choose Create, More Forms, Form Wizard. Access displays the first Form Wizard dialog box, shown in Figure 1.7.

Figure 1.7
Use this Form Wizard dialog box to select the fields you want in your form.

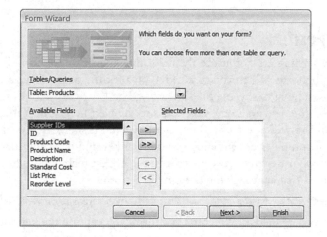

3. For each field you want to include in the form, click the field in the Available Fields list and click the > button. (If you want to select all the fields, click the >> button.) When you're done, click Next.

4. The next Form Wizard dialog box asks you to choose the layout of the fields. You have four choices (click Next after you've made your selection):

    - **Columnar**—The fields are arranged in columns, and only one record is shown at a time.

    - **Tabular**—The fields are arranged in a table, with the field names at the top and the records in rows.

    - **Datasheet**—The fields are arranged in a datasheet layout.

    - **Justified**—The fields are arranged across and down the form with the field names above their respective controls.

5. The next wizard dialog box asks you to select one of the predefined AutoFormat styles. Click the style you want to use and then click Next.

6. The fourth and last wizard dialog box lets you modify the name of the form. A suggestion is already in place in the What Title Do You Want for Your Form? text box; it's based on the name of the underlying table or query, but you can enter any name that doesn't conflict with an existing form.

7. If you want to use the form right away, leave the <u>O</u>pen the Form to View or Enter Information option activated. Alternatively, click <u>M</u>odify the Form's Design to open the form in Design view (see "Creating a Form in Design View," later in this chapter).

8. Click <u>F</u>inish to complete the form.

This is the end of the Form Wizard. You can create a sophisticated and professional data entry form in a fraction of the time needed to create the form from scratch. The wizard isn't as fast as the Form, Split Form, and Multiple Items commands, but it does allow a bit more flexibility in the customization.

Navigating a Form

Navigation in a form refers not just to the fields that appear on the form but also to the records within the form. When you're working on a form, you can navigate the form using several methods. The first is to use the Enter key. The Enter key accepts the data that the user entered into the field and moves the focus to the next field. The Tab key performs the same action, but the user doesn't need to enter any data. If shortcut keys are associated with buttons on the form, the user can hold down the Alt key and press the corresponding underlined letter. For moving between records, the easiest technique is to use the record navigation buttons that appear at the bottom of the form.

→ To learn how to specify shortcut keys for form controls, **see** "Using Labels to Create Keyboard Shortcuts for Controls," **p. 42**. (Chapter 2)

Otherwise, to navigate fields and records in a form, you can use the keys outlined in Table 1.1.

Table 1.1   Keys to Use When Navigating Fields and Records in a Form

Key	Description
Tab or right arrow	Moves to the next field to the right; from the last field, moves down to the first field in the next record.
Shift+Tab or left arrow	Moves to the previous field to the left; from the last field, moves up to the first field in the previous record.
Home	Moves to the first field.
End	Moves to the last field.
Page Down	Moves to the same field in the next record.
Page Up	Moves to the same field in the previous record.
Ctrl+Home	Moves to the first field of the first record.
Ctrl+End	Moves to the last field of the last record.

Creating a Form in Design View

Although the Form Wizard is a step up from the Form, Split Form, and Multiple Items commands in terms of control, the resulting forms still might not satisfy your needs. For example, you might want to build a custom form that mirrors as closely as possible an equivalent paper form. If the Access form resembles the paper form, the person using the form to enter data will feel more comfortable with it and will be less likely to make mistakes.

For maximum form flexibility, you need to use the form design window, which gives you total control over the form, including the positioning of the controls, the formatting of the text, the colors, and much more.

Displaying the Design View

Access forms have a Design view that you can use for your customization chores. How you display this view depends on whether you're dealing with an existing form or a new one.

To open an existing form in Design view, you have two choices:

- If the form isn't open, right-click the form in the Navigation pane and then click Design View.
- If the form is already open, choose Home, click the lower half of the View split button, and then click Design View. (Alternatively, click the Design View button on the status bar; see Figure 1.8.)

To start a new form, you have two choices:

- Choose Create, Blank Form. Then choose Format, click the lower half of the View split button, and then click Design View.
- Choose Create, Form Design.

When you create a new form, it isn't associated with a table or query, so you need to set the record source by hand. See "Changing the Record Source," next.

Figure 1.8 shows a new, blank form in Design view. Note that you place the form controls, including the table's fields and their labels, in the Detail area.

Changing the Record Source

The fields available to the form depend on the table or query that you've defined as the form's record source. If you've created a blank form, you need to specify the record source yourself. For an existing form, you might want to change the record source to a different table or query. Either way, you follow these steps to change the record source while you're in Design view:

1. Select the form by clicking the form selector button (pointed out in Figure 1.8).

2. Choose Design, Property Sheet. The Property Sheet pane appears.

3. Click the Data tab.

4. Pull down the Record Source list and then click the table or query you want to associate with the form.

5. Choose Design, Property Sheet. The Property Sheet pane disappears.

Click here to select the form   Detail area

Figure 1.8
Use the Design view to design and customize all aspects of your form.

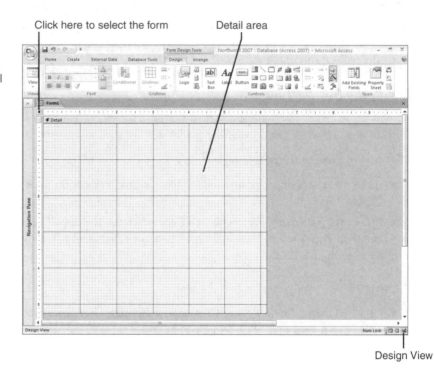

Design View

Understanding Form Controls

An Access form can contain one of three types of controls: bound, unbound, or calculated. The following sections discuss the differences between these types.

Bound Controls (Fields)

You use bound controls to display and edit data from the form's underlying record source. The term *bound* refers to the fact that the control is tied to a field of a table, query, or SQL SELECT statement. The most common type of bound control is the text box, but many other types of controls can operate as bound controls.

A bound control inherits many of its formatting and text properties from the field to which it is bound (for example, Caption, Description, Input Mask, and Default Value). You can change these properties on the form by using the control's property sheet, which you display as follows:

- Click the control (the data control, not the associated label) and then choose Design, Property Sheet (or press Alt+Enter).
- Right-click the control and then click Properties.

See "Adding Fields to the Form," later in this chapter, to learn how to add a bound control to the form.

Unbound Controls

An unbound control is used to convey information to the user or to receive from the user input that won't be stored in the underlying record source. In other words, *unbound* means that the control isn't associated with (bound to) any field.

Here are some examples of using unbound controls:

- A label for a text box that describes what the text box represents.
- Text boxes or drop-down list boxes that can be used to select different scenarios on a what-if form.
- A line used to separate different sections of the form.
- A company logo or other graphical effects.

When you add a control to a form when the Control Wizard is activated, the control is automatically unbound.

→ To learn about adding unbound controls and using the Control Wizard, **see** "Inserting Controls on a Form," **p. 30**. (Chapter 2)

Calculated Controls

Calculated controls use expressions to derive their data. Expressions are combinations of operators, fields, control names, functions, and constants. Although text boxes are the most common form of calculated controls, any control having the `Control Source` property can be a calculated control. A calculated control can be used to compute sales tax on an order entry form, for example.

→ To learn how to build calculated controls, **see** "Using Text Boxes as Calculated Controls," **p. 44**. (Chapter 2)

Adding Fields to the Form

Here are the steps to follow to add a field (that is, a bound control) to your form:

1. Choose Design, Add Existing Fields. Access displays the Field List pane.
2. Double-click the field you want to add to the form.
3. Repeat step 2 until you have added all the fields you need.

1

When you add a field, Access creates a control for the field as follows (see Figure 1.9):

- Most text or numeric fields use a text box.
- If the field is used as the basis of a one-to-many relationship with another table and the current table is the "many" side of that relationship, the field is displayed as a drop-down list that contains the values from the related table.
- Yes/No fields use a check box.

Also, a label control is placed beside each field. The text of the label is the Caption property for the field to which the control is bound.

Figure 1.9
Some fields from the Products table added to the form.

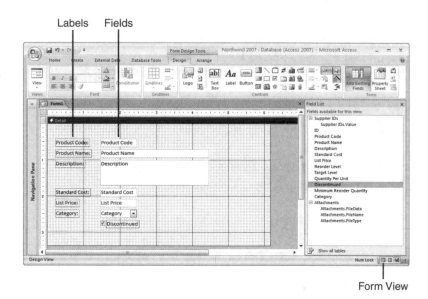

Changing the Size of the Form

If you find that your form is either too small to hold all the fields or has too much empty space, you can change the size of the form as follows:

- To adjust the form's height, move the mouse pointer to the bottom edge of the Detail area. Click and drag the edge of the form down (to make the form bigger) or up (to make the form smaller).
- To adjust the form's width, move the mouse pointer to the right edge of the Detail area. Click and drag the edge of the form right (to make the form wider) or left (to make the form thinner).

Viewing the Form

After you've added at least one field, you can display the underlying record source in the form by switching to Form view. You have two choices:

- Choose Design and then click the top half of the View split button.

- In the status bar, click Form View (see Figure 1.9).

Figure 1.10 shows the Form view of the design displayed in Figure 1.9.

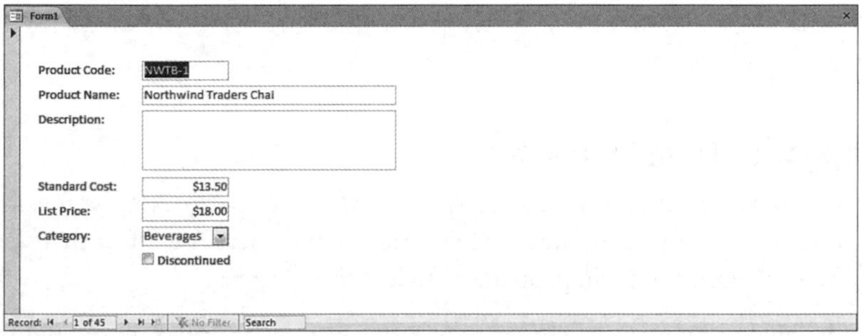

Figure 1.10
The Form view of the
form design shown in
Figure 1.9.

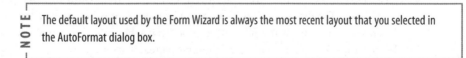

Assigning an AutoFormat in Design View

You learn how to change control fonts, colors, borders, and other formatting in Chapter 2, "Working with Form Controls." For now, you can do some quick formatting by applying one of the 20 predefined form looks, called *AutoFormats*. Choose the Arrange tab (not, surprisingly, the Design tab), click AutoFormat to display the AutoFormat gallery, and then click the look you prefer.

→ For the specifics of form formatting, **see** "Formatting Controls," **p. 31.** (Chapter 2)

For a bit more control, you can use the AutoFormat Wizard:

1. Choose Arrange, AutoFormat, Auto<u>F</u>ormat Windows to display the AutoFormat dialog box.

2. In the Form <u>A</u>utoFormats list, click the AutoFormat you want to use.

3. To control which layout attributes Access applies to the form, click <u>O</u>ptions to display the Attributes to Apply group and then activate or deactivate the following check boxes: <u>F</u>ont, Co<u>l</u>or, and <u>B</u>order.

4. Click OK.

> **NOTE**
> The default layout used by the Form Wizard is always the most recent layout that you selected in the AutoFormat dialog box.

Note, too, that you can customize these AutoFormats to suit your taste. In the AutoFormat dialog box, click the <u>C</u>ustomize button to display the Customize AutoFormat dialog box that has three options:

- **Create a New AutoFormat Based on the Form '*Form*'**—Choose this option to create a new AutoFormat template based on the formatting used in the current form.

- **Update *AutoFormat* with Values from the Form '*Form*'**—Choose this option to change the currently selected *AutoFormat* template based on the formatting used in the current form.

- **Delete *AutoFormat***—Choose this option to delete the currently selected *AutoFormat* template.

Working with Form Properties

Any form object comes with a large number of properties that you can work with. Many of these are obscure and can be safely ignored, but there are a few that you might find useful. To work with the form properties, follow these steps:

1. Select the form by clicking the form selector button, pointed out earlier in Figure 1.8.

2. Choose Design, Property Sheet (or press Alt+Enter) to display the Property Sheet pane.

3. Modify the properties you want to work with.

 TIP

If you're not sure what a property does, click inside the property and then press F1. Access loads the Help window and displays the Help topic for that property.

4. Click the Close button (X) to activate the new settings.

Working with the Form Header and Footer

The Detail section of a form is supposed to be a data-only area. That is, it's supposed to contain only controls that are directly or indirectly related to the form's underlying record source. What if you want to display a form title or the current date or some other information not related to the data? Although it's possible to put such things in the Detail area, a better choice is to take advantage of the following sections:

- **Form Header**—This section appears above and separate from the Detail area, so it's a good choice for the form title, a company logo, or any other items that you want displayed separately from the form data. Note that when you print the form, the Form Header appears only at the top of the first page.

- **Form Footer**—This section appears below and separate from the Detail area. It's a good place to add nondata items such as the current date or instructions on how to fill in the form. When you print the form, the Form Header only appears below the Detail section on the last page.

To display the Form Header and Form Footer, choose the Arrange tab and then click the Form Header/Footer button in the Show/Hide group.

Besides the Form Header and Form Footer, Access also defines separate Page Header and Page Footer sections, both of which appear only when you print the form:

- **Page Header**—This section appears at the top of each printed page (except for the first printed page, where it appears below the Form Header).
- **Page Footer**—This section appears at the bottom of each printed page.

To display the Page Header and Page Footer, choose the Arrange tab and then click the Page Header/Footer button in the Show/Hide group.

Figure 1.11 shows a form with the four header and footer sections added. Note that if you need to select a section (to format it, for example), you can do so by using either of the following techniques:

- Click the separator bar above the section you want to work with.
- Choose Design, Property Sheet and then use the Object list in the Property Sheet pane (pointed out in Figure 1.11) to choose the section you want.

Figure 1.12 shows the Form view, which displays the Form Header and Form Footer sections.

NOTE To change the height of any section, move the mouse pointer to the bottom edge of the section. Then click and drag up or down to resize the section.

Page Header/Footer

Form Header/Footer

Object list

Figure 1.11
A form with the Form Header, Form Footer, Page Header, and Page Footer.

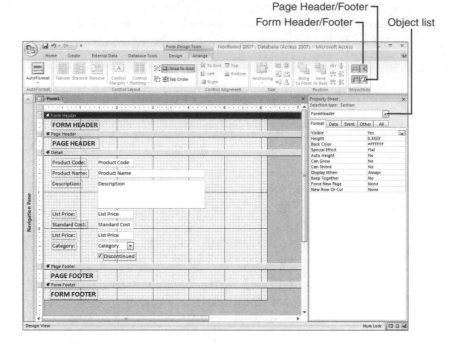

Figure 1.12
The Form view shows the Form Header and Form Footer sections.

Adding a Logo

You can add visual appeal to a form by adding a logo to the form header. This will most often be a company logo, but you might also want to use different logos for different projects, teams, or departments. In previous versions of Access, you could insert a logo using the Image control, but you usually had to spend time resizing the resulting image. Access 2007 comes with a separate Logo command that automatically inserts the image into the Form Header section and adjusts the image's dimensions to logo size (usually 0.6 inch square). The resulting image is an Auto_Logo object.

Here are the steps to follow to insert a logo:

1. Choose Design, Logo. Access displays the Insert Picture dialog box.
2. Navigate to the folder that contains the image you want to use as a logo.
3. Click the image.
4. Click OK. Access resizes the image and inserts it in the Form Header section.

Adding a Title

 Adding a title to your form is usually a good idea so that users have some idea what the form is used for. You can use a `Label` control to add a title, but Access 2007 comes with a new Title command that automatically inserts an Auto_Title object in the Form Header section.

Here are the steps to follow to insert a title:

1. Choose Design, Title (just to the right of the Logo button). Access adds the Auto_Title object to the Form Header.
2. Type your title. (Note that the Auto_Title box expands automatically as you type your text.)
3. Click outside the title.
4. Move the title to the position you want.

→ For information on moving controls, **see** "Moving Controls," **p. 34.** (Chapter 2)

Formatting the Background

Most of the formatting options apply to the controls, as you'll see in Chapter 2. For the form itself, about the only thing you can do is change the look of the background for each section: You can change the background color, or you can display an image as the background, as described in the next two sections.

Setting the Background Color

To change the background color of a form section, follow these steps:

1. Click the section's separator bar to select the section.
2. On the Design tab, click the Fill/Back Color palette (see Figure 1.13) so that it drops down.
3. Click the background color you want.

CAUTION

When choosing a background, make sure the color doesn't clash with the color of the field label text. For example, the default label text color is black, so any dark background will cause a problem. Either use a light color for the background or change the color of the label text (as described in Chapter 2).

Fill/Back Color

Figure 1.13
Click the Fill/Back Color palette and then click the background color you want.

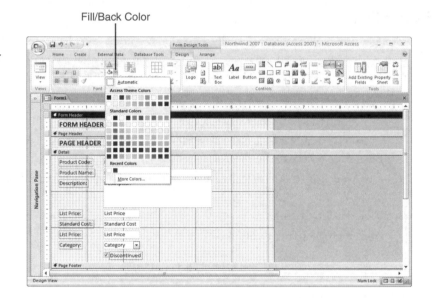

Setting the Background Picture

A simple, solid-color background that contrasts well with the form text (for example, a white or light-colored background with black or dark-colored text) is often the safest bet in a business environment. However, you might feel the need to spice up your form a bit with a more interesting background treatment: an image. Access enables you to use either a single, large image as the background or smaller images that are stretched or tiled to cover the entire form.

Follow these steps to set an image as a form's background:

1. Select the form.
2. Choose Design, Property Sheet to open the Property Sheet pane.
3. Click the Format tab.
4. Click inside the `Picture` property and then click the ellipsis … button. Access displays the Insert Picture dialog box.
5. Find the file you want to use, click it, and then click OK.

6. Use the `Picture Size Mode` property to choose one of the following settings:

- `Clip`—The image is displayed using its actual dimensions. If the image is larger than the form, the edges of the image are clipped to fit.
- `Stretch`—The image is stretched or shrunk vertically and horizontally so that it fills the entire form.
- `Zoom`—The image is enlarged or reduced until it fills the form either vertically or horizontally; the image's original proportions are maintained.
- `Stretch Horizontal`—The image is stretched or reduced horizontally so that it fills the entire form width.
- `Stretch Vertical`—The image is stretched or reduced vertically so that it fills the entire form height.

7. Use the `Picture Alignment` property to specify how you want the image aligned within the form.

8. If you selected either `Clip` or `Zoom` as the `Picture Size Mode`, use the `Picture Tiling` property to determine whether you want the image repeated (tiled) across the background so that it fills the entire form; select `Yes` for tiling; select `No` to display just a single image.

9. Close the property sheet.

> **CAUTION**
>
> As with the background color, be careful which image you choose for the background. A "busy" background can render label text unreadable.

Creating a Form Interactively in Layout View

 The major problem with creating a form in Design view is that you don't see data from the form's record source until you switch to Form view. This means that you often have to switch back and forth to get the layout you prefer and to size the controls properly.

Access 2007 helps you reduce much of this design drudgery by offering a new form view called Layout. This hybrid view shows you the data from the record source but also enables you to change many aspects of the form design. To switch to this view from Design view, choose Design, click the lower half of the View split button, and then click Layout View. (You can also click the Layout View button in the status bar.)

As you can see in Figure 1.14, the form data appears, but you also have access the Ribbon's Format and Arrange tabs, which enable you to change the font, add certain controls (such as a logo and title), add fields, apply an AutoFormat, and more.

Figure 1.14
Use Access 2007's new Layout View to modify the form and see its data at the same time.

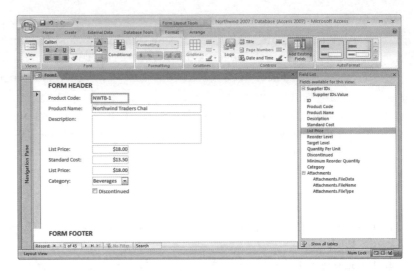

Protecting the Form and Data from Other Users

In a business environment, it's common to build forms as front ends for other users. A properly designed form gives users easier access to the data and keeps them away from fields they don't need to see (such as primary key fields and sensitive data). As you'll see in the next few chapters, building good business forms takes a bit of extra work on your part. So if you go to all that trouble, the last thing you want is for the users to either change the form design (on purpose or inadvertently) or alter the data in some unacceptable way (such as deleting records).

Access can help you protect both the form and the underlying data. The property sheet for a form contains a number of properties that enable you to restrict the actions that users can take with your form.

You can protect the form design in the following ways:

- **Preventing the form from being resized**—In the form property sheet, click the Format tab and choose any `Border Style` setting other than `Sizable` (that is, `None`, `Thin`, or `Dialog`).

- **Preventing the form from being maximized or minimized**—In the Format tab, go to the `Min Max Buttons` property and choose `None`. If you want to prevent the form only from being maximized, choose `Min Enabled`; if you want to prevent the form only from being minimized, choose `Max Enabled`.

- **Preventing the form from being moved**—In the Format tab, choose `No` for the `Moveable` property.

- **Disabling other form views**—In the Format tab, choose `No` for each of the following views you want to disable: `Allow Datasheet View`, `Allow PivotTable View`, `Allow PivotChart View`, and `Allow Layout View`.

You can protect the form data in the following ways:

→ You can also set up validation rules to ensure data integrity. **See** "Preventing Errors by Validating Data," **p. 50** (Chapter 3)

- **Preventing the user from editing data**—In the form property sheet, display the Data tab and set the `Allow Edits` property to `No`.

- **Preventing the user from deleting data**—In the Data tab, set the `Allow Deletions` property to `No`.

- **Preventing the user from adding records**—In the Data tab, set the `Allow Additions` property to `No`.

- **Preventing the user from seeing other data**—In the Data tab, set the `Data Entry` property to `Yes`. This is different from `Allow Additions` in that when this feature is turned on, the form automatically opens to a new, blank record. The user doesn't have the capability to view existing records. Note that the users cannot see existing records or add new data (in other words, they won't be able to do *anything* with the form data) if `Allow Additions` is set to `No` and `Data Entry` is set to `Yes`.

- **Making form data read-only**—In the Data tab, set the `Recordset Type` property to `Snapshot`. This is the same as setting the `Allow Edits`, `Allow Deletions`, and `Allow Additions` properties to `No`.

- **Preventing multiple users from editing the same record simultaneously**—In the Data tab, set the `Record Locks` property to `Edited Record`. (If you prefer that other users can't edit *any* record while one user has the form open, set `Record Locks` to `All Records`, instead.)

From Here

→ Unbound controls are the subject of Chapter 2, "Working with Form Controls." **See p. 29.** (Chapter 2)

→ For the specifics of form formatting, **see** "Formatting Controls," **p. 31.** (Chapter 2)

→ To learn how to specify shortcut keys for form controls, **see** "Using Labels to Create Keyboard Shortcuts for Controls," **p. 42.** (Chapter 2)

→ To learn how to build calculated controls, **see** "Using Text Boxes as Calculated Controls," **p. 44.** (Chapter 2)

→ To learn how to set up validation rules to ensure data integrity, **see** "Preventing Errors by Validating Data," **p. 50.** (Chapter 3)

→ The Form Wizard even lets you select fields from multiple tables; **see** "Creating a Form and Subform with the Form Wizard," **p. 96.** (Chapter 5)

→ To learn how to build a PivotChart form, **see** "Creating a PivotChart Form," **p. 108.** (Chapter 5)

→ To learn how to build a modal dialog box, **see** "Creating a Form Pop-Up Box or Dialog Box," **p. 103.** (Chapter 5)

→ For the specifics of working with the PivotTable view fields, **see** "Creating PivotTable Queries," **p. 311.** (Chapter 14)

Working with Form Controls

If you want a form laid out in a certain way that either mimics the arrangement of a paper form or gives the form a design that you think will make sense for the users, the techniques you've seen so far haven't given you the tools to do the job. For example, pre-fab form layouts and the Form Wizard, although easy and fast, arrange form controls in only a few basic designs. Using the Design view is better because you can at least click and drag the table fields and drop them anywhere you want on the form. However, if you've tried this, you've certainly noticed that the results are seldom perfect. The reason is that you still need to "fine-tune" the controls by moving them, sizing them, formatting them, and so on.

These fine-tuning techniques are the subject of this chapter. You learn not only how to insert and manipulate form controls, but also how to get the most out of the two most common control types: labels and text boxes.

Manipulating Form Controls

You saw in Chapter 1, "Creating and Using a Form," that when you add a field to a form, Access mostly uses text boxes, combo boxes, and check boxes to enable the user to insert and edit field data. Whether you stick with the controls that Access suggests, or you branch out to use other types of controls on your forms, your form-building duties will be much quicker and of higher quality if you get comfortable manipulating the controls to get them exactly the way you want them. To that end, in the following sections you learn quite a few useful techniques that you can apply to any control.

Inserting Controls on a Form

As you learned in Chapter 1, you add bound controls to the form by double-clicking fields in the Field List pane. For unbound controls (or controls that you want to bind to a field later), you need to use the Design tab's Controls group, which contains buttons for all the controls you can add to a form. Some of these controls—specifically, Option Group, Combo Box, List Box, Command Button, and Subform—also come with their own Control Wizard that takes you step by step through the process of creating and setting up the control. (For example, the Combo Box and List Box controls have wizards that help you define, among other things, the items that appear in each list.)

Here are the basic steps to follow to add any control to the form:

1. In the Design tab, use the Controls group to click the button you want to use.
2. If the control type has an associated wizard, click the Use Control Wizards button (pointed out later, in Figure 2.1) to toggle the wizard on or off, as preferred.
3. Move the mouse pointer into the form and position it where you want the top-left corner of the control to appear.
4. Click and drag the mouse pointer. Access displays a dashed border indicating the outline of the control.
5. When the control is the size and shape you want, release the mouse button. Access creates the control and gives it a default name (such as CheckBox*n*, where *n* signifies that this is the *n*th check box you've created on this form).
6. If the control has a wizard and you activated the Use Control Wizards button, the first wizard dialog box appears. Follow the wizard's steps. (You learn the control wizards later in this chapter when I take you through the specifics of each control.)

Note that sometimes Access also includes a label beside the control you insert. For example, when you add a text box, Access also inserts a label to the left of the text box.

> **TIP** If you want to add multiple instances of the same type of control, double-click the appropriate button in the Controls group. The button remains pressed, and you can draw as many instances of the control as you need. When you're done, click the control's button to reset the control.

Selecting Controls

Before you can work with a control, you must select it. For a single control, you select it simply by clicking it. If you prefer to work with multiple controls, Access gives you a number of techniques:

- Hold down the Ctrl key and click each control.
- You also can "lasso" multiple controls by clicking and dragging the mouse. Move the mouse pointer to an empty part of the form, hold down the left button, and click and

drag. Access displays a box with a dashed outline, and any control that falls within this box (in whole or in part) is selected.

■ To select every control, choose Design, Select All in the Controls group (or press Ctrl+A).

To exclude a control from the selection, hold down the Ctrl key and click inside the control.

After you've selected multiple controls, you can set properties for all the controls at once (choose Design, Property Sheet). Note, however, that the Property Sheet pane shows only those properties that are common to all the controls. Not only that, but if you size, move, copy, or delete one of the selected controls (as described in the next few sections), your action will apply to all the controls.

Formatting Controls

You saw in Chapter 1 that you can format all the controls on a form by applying one of the predefined AutoFormat layouts. That's an easy way to work, but if the layout isn't quite what you want, or if you want to create your own AutoFormat layout, you need to format the controls by hand.

→ To learn how to apply an AutoFormat, **see** "Assigning an AutoFormat in Design View," **p. 19**. (Chapter 1)

You can format any control by selecting it (you can work with multiple controls, if need be) and using the lists and buttons in the Design tab (see Figure 2.1):

■ Use the lists and buttons in the Font group to format the control text as well as the background color of the control.

■ Use the lists and buttons on the right side of the Controls group to format the control's outline (the Line Thickness, Line Type, and Line Color lists) and its Special Effect (Flat, Raised, Sunken, and so on).

> **TIP**
> After you apply formatting to a particular type of control, you might want Access to use the same formatting on all future controls of the same type that you add to that form. To set this up, click the control with the formatting you want to use, choose Design, and then click the Set Control Defaults button (it's in the Controls group).

Adding Conditional Formatting

Access enables you to apply a particular font automatically when a control value meets a specified condition. This is called *conditional formatting*, and it's a useful tool when you need to monitor one or more values. For example, if your form is used to input budget values, you may want to flag those values that are over a certain threshold (such as the original budget target). Similarly, if your form calculates a value—such as gross margin—you might want to flag results that come in below a target value. In both cases, you can set up the conditional formatting to display any anomalous values in, say, a red, bold font so that they stand out from the rest of the numbers.

Use Control Wizards

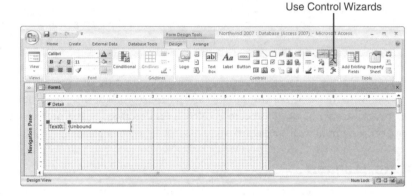

Figure 2.1
Use the lists and buttons in the Font and Controls groups to format the selected control.

You apply conditional formatting by following these steps:

1. Select the field to which you want the conditional format applied.
2. Choose Design, Conditional. Access displays the Conditional Formatting dialog box, shown in Figure 2.2.

Figure 2.2
Use the Conditional Formatting dialog box to specify font formatting to apply to a control when a specific condition is met.

3. If you want to specify the format to use when the condition is not met, use the formatting buttons in the Default Formatting group.
4. Select the type of condition you want to use:
   - **Field Value Is**—The condition is applied to the current value of the field or unbound control. In this case, you construct the condition by selecting a comparison operator (such as Between or Less Than) in the second list and then entering one or two values (depending on the operator).
   - **Expression Is**—The condition is met when the logical expression you enter returns True. For example, if you enter **Date()=#8/23/2007#**, the formatting is applied only on August 23, 2007.
   - **Field Has Focus**—The condition is met when the field or unbound control has the focus (that is, when the cursor is inside the field).

5. Click the formatting buttons to specify the font formatting to apply to the control when the condition is met.

6. If you want to apply another condition, click Add and repeat steps 4 and 5 for the new condition.

7. Click OK.

Sizing Controls

An invisible rectangular frame surrounds each control. When you select a control, Access displays selection handles at the frame's corners and midpoints, as shown in Figure 2.3.

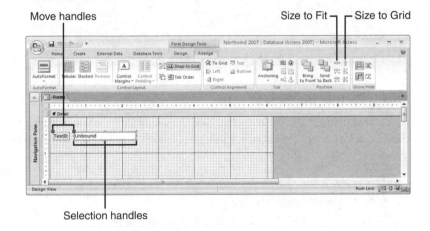

Figure 2.3
Selecting a control displays the control's selection handles.

You can resize any control to change its shape or dimensions. The following procedure outlines the steps to work through:

1. Select the object you want to size.

2. Position the mouse pointer over the selection handle you want to move. The pointer changes to a two-headed arrow. To change the size horizontally or vertically, use the appropriate handle on the middle of a side. To change the size in both directions at once, use the appropriate corner handle.

3. Click and drag the handle to the position you want.

4. Release the mouse button. Access redraws the object and adjusts the frame size.

To reduce some of the drudgery of control sizing, Access also offers a number of automatic sizing techniques. The next few sections give you a quick tour of these techniques.

Sizing to the Grid

When you draw a control on the form, Access normally sizes the control so that it automatically lines up with the nearest grid mark. You can turn off this behavior by deactivating the Arrange, Snap To Grid button.

If you turn off the Snap To Grid feature, you can still adjust a control's size to the grid by hand. To do this, follow these steps:

1. Select the control.
2. Choose Arrange, Size To Grid (see Figure 2.3). Access adjusts the control's frame to the nearest grid marks.

Sizing to the Control's Content

Access has an annoying habit of not making controls large enough to see the text they contain. This is particularly true when you click and drag fields from the Field list. Instead of sizing the fields or labels by hand, you can make a control automatically large enough to display its text by following these steps:

1. Select the control.
2. Choose Arrange, Size To Fit (see Figure 2.3).

Making Controls the Same Size

If you've added similar controls (such as command buttons), your form will look its best if these controls are the same size. Here's the easiest way to get a uniform size height and/or width:

1. Select the controls you want to make the same size.
2. Choose the Arrange tab.
3. In the Size group, click one of the following commands:
   - **Size To Tallest**—Adjusts the height of all the controls to match the height of the tallest control.
   - **Size To Shortest**—Adjusts the height of all the controls to match the height of the shortest control.
   - **Size To Widest**—Adjusts the width of all the controls to match the width of the widest control.
   - **Size To Narrowest**—Adjusts the width of all the controls to match the width of the narrowest control.

Moving Controls

You can move any control to a different part of the form by following these steps:

1. Select the control you want to move.
2. Position the mouse pointer as follows:
   - To move an individual control, place the pointer over the control's frame, although not over a selection handle. When the pointer is positioned correctly, it turns into a four-headed arrow.

- To move a *paired* control (that is, a control such as a text box or check box that also comes with a label), place the pointer over the frame of whichever control is selected (again, however, not over a selection handle).

- To move one control of a paired control, first notice that clicking any control in the pair displays a move handle in the upper-left corner of both controls, as shown earlier in Figure 2.3. Place the pointer over the move handle of the control you want to move. When the pointer is positioned correctly, it turns into a four-headed arrow.

3. Click and drag the control to the position you want.

4. Release the mouse button. Access redraws the control in the new position.

 TIP If you just need to make subtle adjustments to the position of a control, select it and then press an arrow key. Whichever key you press, Access moves the control one grid mark in the arrow's direction. For even more fine-tuned control, hold down the Ctrl key while you press an arrow key. In this case, Access moves the control one pixel in the arrow's direction.

As with sizing, Access also boasts quite a collection of commands that can adjust the position of one or more controls automatically. The next few sections give you the rundown.

Aligning to the Grid

If you've turned off the Arrange tab's Snap To Grid command (which, when activated, causes Access to align moved controls to the grid marks), you can still align to the grid by hand:

1. Select the control.

2. Choose Arrange and then click To Grid in the Control Alignment group. Access moves the control to the nearest grid marks.

Aligning Control Edges

Forms look best when the controls are neatly aligned. The simplest way to align them is to use the buttons in the Control Alignment group. These buttons are similar to Size buttons discussed earlier in that they operate on multiple controls and let you align, say, their left edges.

Note, however, that Access aligns the selected controls with a single *base control*, which is the control that is the farthest positioned in whatever direction you are aligning the controls. For example, if you want to align the controls on their right edges, the base control is the one that is farthest to the right. Here are the steps to follow:

1. Arrange the controls you want to work with so that one of them is the base control.

2. Select the controls you want to work with (including the base control).

3. Choose the Arrange tab.

4. Choose one of the following commands in the Control Alignment group:

   - **Left**—Adjusts the horizontal position of all the selected controls so that they line up on the left edge of the base control.

   - **Right**—Adjusts the horizontal position of all the selected controls so that they line up on the right edge of the base control.

   - **Top**—Adjusts the vertical position of all the selected controls so that they line up on the top edge of the base control.

   - **Bottom**—Adjusts the vertical position of all the selected controls so that they line up on the bottom edge of the base control.

Adjusting the Spacing Between Controls

If you want to make your forms easy to read, the controls shouldn't be crammed together edge to edge, nor should they be too far apart. Again, you can avoid making subtle spacing adjustments by hand thanks to a few more Access commands.

To adjust the horizontal spacing between multiple controls, follow these steps:

1. Select the controls.

2. Choose Arrange.

3. Choose one of the following commands in the Position group:

   - **Make Horizontal Spacing Equal**—If you have three or more controls selected, use this command to adjust the horizontal spacing so that it's the same between each control.

   - **Increase Horizontal Spacing**—This command increases the horizontal spacing between each control by one grid mark, relative to the base control.

   - **Decrease Horizontal Spacing**—This command decreases the horizontal spacing between each control by one grid mark, relative to the base control.

   - **Make Vertical Spacing Equal**—If you have three or more controls selected, use this command to adjust the vertical spacing so that it's the same between each control.

   - **Increase Vertical Spacing**—This command increases the vertical spacing between each control by one grid mark, relative to the base control.

   - **Decrease Vertical Spacing**—This command decreases the vertical spacing between each control by one grid mark, relative to the base control.

Creating a Control Layout

So that you don't have to fiddle with control sizes and alignments, Access 2007 gives you an easy way to arrange your form controls: the *control layout*. This simple layout acts as a kind of table, and your controls are slotted neatly into the layout's rows and columns. There are two types of control layouts:

- **Stacked**—The controls are arranged vertically in two columns, with field names in the left column and fields in the right column. (If you're working with unbound controls, the labels appear in the left column and the controls appear in the right column.) Figure 2.4 shows an example of the stacked control layout.
- **Tabular**—The controls are arranged horizontally in two rows, with field names in the top row (which appears in the Form Header section) and fields in the bottom row (which appears in the Detail section). (If you're working with unbound controls, the labels appear in the top row and the controls appear in the bottom row.) Figure 2.5 shows an example of a tabular control layout.

Figure 2.4
A stacked control layout.

Use this button to select and move the entire control layout

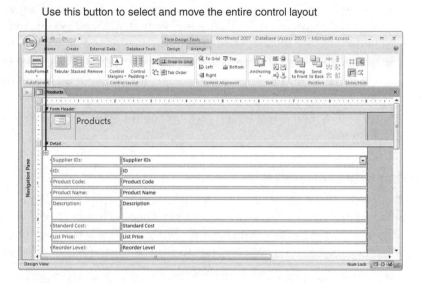

Figure 2.5
A tabular control layout.

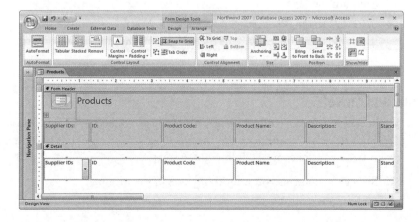

To create a control layout, follow these steps:

1. Select the controls you want to work with.
2. Choose the Arrange tab.
3. In the Control Layout group, click either Tabular or Stacked.

After you create the control layout, use any of the following techniques to work with it:

- To adjust the amount of space between controls, choose Arrange, Control Padding, and then click a padding command: None, Narrow, Medium, or Wide. (You can also choose Design, Property Sheet; click the Format tab in the Property Sheet pane; and then adjust the values (in inches) of the Top Padding, Bottom Padding, Left Padding, and Right Padding properties.)
- To display gridlines between and around the controls, choose Design, Gridlines and then click a gridline style: Horizontal, Vertical, Both, and so on. You can also use the buttons in the Gridlines group to format the gridline Width, Style, and Color.
- To move the control layout, click any control within the layout and then click and drag the move handle that appears at the upper-left corner of the layout (pointed out in Figure 2.4).
- To remove the control layout, click any control in the layout and then choose Arrange, Remove.

Working with Control Margins

 By default, Access leaves very little space between a control's text and its border. This can make controls such as text boxes cramped-looking and harder to read. To fix this, Access 2007 now allows you to specify the *control margin*, which is the space that surrounds the text inside the control. There are two ways to adjust the margins for a selected control:

- Choose Arrange, Control Margins and then click a preset value: None, Narrow, Medium, or Wide.
- Choose Design, Property Sheet; click the Format tab in the Property Sheet pane; and then adjust the values (in inches) of the Top Margin, Bottom Margin, Left Margin, and Right Margin properties.

Grouping Controls

Access lets you create control *groups*. A group is a collection of controls you can format, size, and move together, similar to the way you format, size, and move a single control. To group two or more controls, follow these steps:

1. Select the controls you want to include in the group.
2. Choose Arrange, Group.

Access treats a group as a single control with its own frame. To select an entire group, you just need to select one control from the group.

To ungroup controls, follow these steps:

1. Select the group.
2. Choose Arrange, Ungroup.

Ordering Overlapped Controls

When you're inserting controls, you'll usually want to avoid overlapping the controls so that the user doesn't become confused and so the captions don't get mixed together. However, sometimes you might want controls to overlap. For example, if you've added two or more picture controls, you might be able to produce interesting effects by superimposing one picture on another.

When you have two controls that overlap, the most recently created control covers part of the other control. The newer control is "in front" of the older one. The overlap order of these controls is called the Z-order. (Think of the Z-axis in a three-dimensional graph.)

To change the Z-order, follow these steps:

1. Select one of the overlapping controls.
2. Choose the Arrange tab.
3. In the Position group, click one of the following commands:
   - **Bring To Front**—Moves the control to the top of the Z-order, which places it in front of every other control.
   - **Send To Back**—Moves the control to the bottom of the Z-order, which places it behind every other control.

Converting an Unbound Control to a Bound Control

Unbound controls are useful for gathering information that you need only temporarily. For example, you might ask for the user's name to customize the form, or you might want to ask for a value or two that you can use to filter the records.

However, most of your form work will involve bound controls. If you've created an unbound control, you can convert it to a bound control by following these steps:

1. Select the unbound control.
2. Choose Design, Property Sheet. (You can also press Alt+Enter or double-click the control.) Access opens the control's property sheet.
3. Click the Data tab.
4. Pull down the Control Source list and click the field name to which you want to bind the control.
5. Close the control's property sheet.

┌─ C A U T I O N ───┐

The one problem with converting an unbound control to a bound control is that this won't cause
the control to inherit many of the field's properties. The exceptions are the `Default Value`,
`Validation Rule`, and `Validation Text` properties, which are always enforced for
the field.

└───┘

Changing a Control's Type

Certain controls can be changed to different control types. For example, a label can be
changed to a text box, and a text box can be changed to a label, combo box, or list box.
Follow these steps to convert a control from one type to another:

1. Right-click the control.
2. Click Change To.
3. Choose the new type for the control.

Setting the Tab Order

As you know, you can navigate a form by pressing the Tab key. The order in which the controls are selected is called the *tab order*. Access sets the tab order according to the order you
create the controls on the form. You'll often find that this order doesn't correspond to the
"natural" order of the controls, so pressing Tab causes the focus to jump haphazardly
around the form. To fix this, Access lets you control the tab order yourself. The following
procedure shows you how it's done:

1. Choose Arrange, Tab Order. Access displays the Tab Order dialog box, shown in
   Figure 2.6.
2. Use the Section list to click the form section you want to work with.
3. In the Custom Order list, select the control you want to work with by clicking the
   selection button to the left of the control.
4. Click and drag the control's selection button to move the control up or down in the
   Custom Order list.
5. Repeat steps 3 and 4 for other controls you want to move.
6. Click OK.

Selection buttons

Figure 2.6
Use the Tab Order dialog box to set the order in which the user navigates the form when pressing the Tab key.

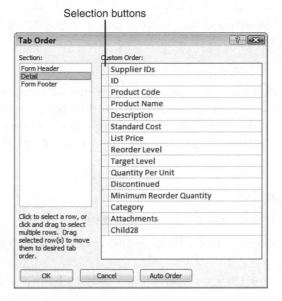

2

Adding Labels to the Form

A label is a control that displays static text (that is, text that can't be edited or copied by the user of the form). Labels are most often used to display the name of a field, but they have many other uses, as well:

- The name of an unbound control
- The form subtitle (this should go in the Form Header section, below the title)
- Explanatory text (instructions for filling out the form, shortcut keys, and so on)

➡ To learn how to add a title to the form, **see** "Adding a Title," **p. 23**. (Chapter 1)

Inserting a Label

As I mentioned earlier, controls such as text boxes, check boxes, and option buttons come with their own labels. If you want to add a label for another type of control or just to add some text to the form, follow these steps:

1. Choose the Design tab.
2. In the Controls group, click Label.
3. Draw the label on the form.
4. Type the label text.
5. Press Enter.

> **TIP** To create a label with multiple lines of text, press Ctrl+Enter at the end of one line to start a new line within the label.

Access assumes that each label must be associated with a control, so when you add a label on its own, Access displays a smart tag to warn you that the label is unassociated. (You see this smart tag only if you have at least one bound control already on the form.) If you're using the label just to display text, you can remove the smart tag by clicking it and then clicking Ignore Error.

Editing the Label Caption

If you need to change the label text, you have two choices:

- Click the label to select it and then click the label again to edit the text. Press Enter when you're done.
- Select the label; choose Design, Property Sheet; click the Format tab; and then edit the Caption property.

Using Labels to Create Keyboard Shortcuts for Controls

When you work with dialog boxes in Access and most other Windows programs, each control has a shortcut key that enables you to select the control from the keyboard by holding down Alt and pressing the key. This key is usually underlined on the control's label. For example, if you see a button named Yes and the Y is underlined, then you can select that button by pressing Alt+Y while the dialog box is displayed.

You can give your users the same convenience by defining shortcut keys for the controls on your form. Here are the steps to follow:

1. Assuming the control comes with a label automatically, insert the control. If the control already exists on the form, skip to step 2.
2. Edit the associated label text by inserting the ampersand character (&) before the letter you want to use as the shortcut key. For example, if the label has the text Name, editing the text to &Name sets up the letter N as the shortcut key (meaning that Alt+N will select the control associated with the label; see Figure 2.7).

> **TIP** If you want to associate another label with a control, first select the control's current label and delete it. Add the new label (if you haven't done so already) and then click the smart tag that appears. In the menu, click Associate Label with a Control, use the Associate Label dialog box to click the control you want to use with the label, and then click OK.

N is the underlined shortcut key

Ampersand appears before N in the Caption

Figure 2.7
Precede a letter with the ampersand character (&) to set up that letter as the control's shortcut key.

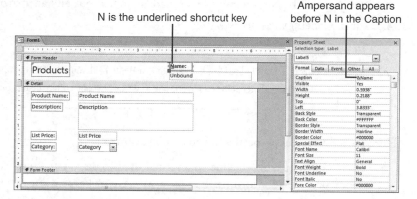

CAUTION _____

To avoid confusion, make sure each control on the form has a unique shortcut key. If you accidentally use the same shortcut on two controls, Access will display a smart tag on both labels notifying you of the problem. Click the smart tag and then click Change Caption to see some suggested alternatives for the shortcut key.

If, for some reason, it's unavoidable that two controls use the same shortcut key, note that you can navigate to the second control by pressing the shortcut key combination twice. For example, suppose you have the label &Name and &Number on the form, in that order. Pressing Alt+N first selects the Name control, and pressing Alt+N again selects the Number control.

Adding Text Boxes to the Form

Text boxes are versatile controls that let the user enter text, numbers, dates, and more. Text boxes are mostly used as input controls for entering field values, but they can also be used as unbound controls when you use a form to make calculations. Unbound text boxes can be used as follows:

- To display the results of an expression. (See "Using Text Boxes as Calculated Controls," later in this chapter.)
- To accept input values that are used as part of an expression in another text box. (See "Case Study: Creating a Mortgage Calculator," later in this chapter.)

Inserting a Text Box

To create a text box, follow these steps:

1. Choose the Design tab.
2. In the Controls group, click Text Box.

3. Draw the text box on the form. Access adds the text box and an associated label.

4. Edit the label text, as necessary.

> **TIP**
>
> If the text box is unbound or if it's bound to a Memo field, you can enter multiple lines of text by pressing Ctrl+Enter at the end of one line to start a new line within the text box.

Here are a few useful properties of the text box control:

- `Format` **(Format tab)**—Defines the format used to display the text. You can either select a predefined format (such as `General Date` or `Percent`) or enter a format string.

- `Decimal Places` **(Format tab)**—Defines the number of decimal places to display for numeric values.

- `Default Value` **(Data tab)**—Specifies text that initially appears inside the text box.

- `Name` **(Other tab)**—Specifies the name of the text box. For unbound text boxes, this property is important only if you'll be referencing the text box value as part of an expression in another calculated control.

- `Status Bar Text` **(Other tab)**—Specifies text that appears in the Access status bar when the user enters the text box.

- `Enter Key Behavior` **(Other tab)**—When this property is set to `Default`, pressing Enter moves the user to the next field; when it is set to `New Line in Field`, pressing Enter starts a new line within the text box.

Using Text Boxes as Calculated Controls

In Chapter 11, "Building Criteria Expressions," you'll see how to use an expression to build a calculated query column that, when you run the query, displays the result of the expression for each record in the query dynaset.

→ For the details on constructing calculated columns in queries, **see** "Setting Up a Calculated Column," **p. 239**. (Chapter 11)

You can do something similar in your forms by setting up a text box to display the results of an expression. This expression can use any of the Access operators, operands, and functions, and it can use the values in both bound and unbound controls.

Here are the steps to follow to create a calculated text box control:

1. Choose the Design tab.

2. In the Controls group, click Text Box.

3. Draw the text box on the form. Access adds the text box and an associated label.

4. Click the text box to select it.

5. Choose Design, Property Sheet to display the control's property sheet. (You can also press Alt+Enter or double-click the control.)

6. Choose the Data tab.

7. Type the expression in the `Control Source` property. (You can also click … to create your expression using the Expression Builder.)

→ For the details on the Expression Builder, **see** "Working with the Expression Builder," **p. 256**. (Chapter 11)

→ To learn how to use the Access built-in functions, **see** "Using the Built-In Functions," **p. 241**. (Chapter 11)

8. Close the property sheet.

For example, Figure 2.8 shows the property sheet for a text box that has the expression `=Date()` as its `Control Source` property. In the Form view in Figure 2.9, you can see that the text box displays the current date. (Note that I entered the format string `mmmm d, yyyy` in the text box's `Format` property to get the date format shown in Figure 2.9.)

> **NOTE** Users can't edit the text in a calculated text box. They can move the insertion point cursor within the control and then can select and copy the control text, but if they try to edit the text, Access beeps the speaker and displays the following in the status bar (where *expression* is the expression in the `Control Source` property):
>
>   Control can't be edited; it's bound to the expression
>   'expression'.

Calculated text box   Type the expression here

Figure 2.8
To create a calculated control, enter an expression in a text box's `Control Source` property.

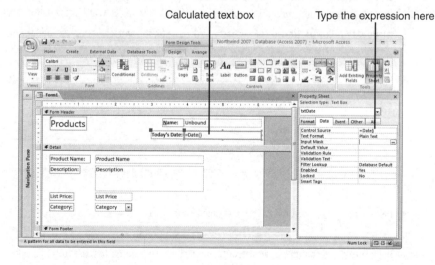

Figure 2.9
In the Form view, the
text box displays the
current date.

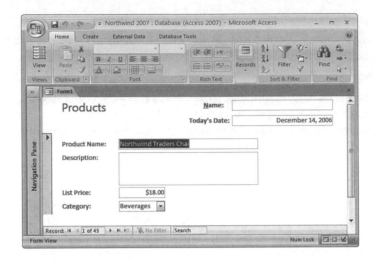

Creating a Mortgage Calculator

To demonstrate calculated text box controls, let's construct a form that uses nothing but unbound controls to implement a simple mortgage calculator.

The calculator is divided into two sections:

- **Principal Calculation**—This section asks the user for the house price and the down payment and then uses a calculated text box to display the difference between these values, which is the mortgage principal.

- **Payment Calculation**—This section asks the user for the annual interest rate and the number of years in the term and then uses a calculated text box to display the monthly payment.

> **NOTE** You can download the examples used in this book from my website:
>
>   http://www.mcfedries.com/Access2007Forms/

Figure 2.10 shows the form in Design view with the Principal Calculation section added. Here are some notes about the controls:

- The `House Price` control is a text box named `HousePrice`.

- The `Down Payment` control is a text box named `DownPayment`.

- The `Principal` control is a calculated text box named `Principal` that uses the following expression as its `Control Source` property:

  `=[HousePrice]-[DownPayment]`

Figure 2.10
The Payment Calculation section of the mortgage calculator.

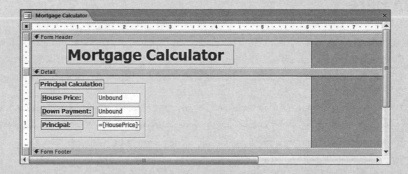

Figure 2.11 shows the form with the Payment Calculation section added. Here are some notes about the controls:

- The `Interest Rate` control is a text box named `InterestRate`.
- The `Term` control is a text box named `Term`.
- The `Monthly Payment` control is a calculated text box named `MonthlyPayment` that uses the following expression as its `Control Source` property:

```
=Pmt([InterestRate] / 12, [Term] * 12, [Principal]) * -1
```

Figure 2.11
The Payment Calculation section added to the mortgage calculator.

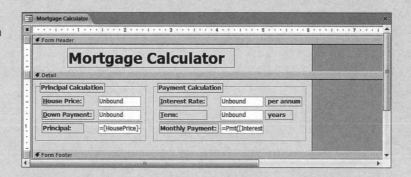

Figure 2.12 shows the result in Form view.

Figure 2.12
The running mortgage calculator.

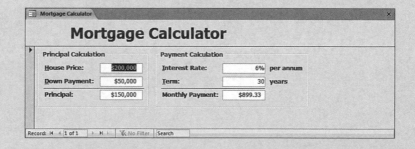

From Here

→ To learn how to apply an AutoFormat, **see** "Assigning an AutoFormat in Design View," **p. 19**. (Chapter 1)

→ For the details on adding data validation to a form control, **see** "Preventing Errors by Validating Data," **p. 50**. (Chapter 3)

→ For the specifics of check box and toggle buttons controls, **see** "Working with Yes / No Fields," **p. 56**. (Chapter 3)

→ To learn how to use option groups and option buttons, **see** "Using Option Buttons to Present a Limited Number of Choices," **p. 59**. (Chapter 3)

→ To learn how to use list and combo boxes, **see** "Using Lists to Present a Large Number of Choices," **p. 62**. (Chapter 3)

→ To learn how to use ActiveX controls for data entry, **see** "Entering Data with ActiveX Controls," **p. 67**. (Chapter 3)

→ To learn how to use the Tab control, **see** "Organizing with a Tab Control," **p. 84**. (Chapter 4)

→ For the details on using subforms, **see** "Creating a Multiple-Table Form," **p. 95**. (Chapter 5)

→ For the details on constructing calculated column in queries, **see** "Setting Up a Calculated Column," **p. 239**. (Chapter 11)

→ To learn how to use the Access built-in functions, **see** "Using the Built-In Functions," **p. 241**. (Chapter 11)

→ For the details on the Expression Builder, **see** "Working with the Expression Builder," **p. 256**. (Chapter 11)

Designing Forms for Efficient and Accurate Data Entry

3

Data entry is one of those tasks that I describe as "dangerous" because it's a chore that's both tedious and important. It's tedious because entering dozens or hundreds of records is no one's idea of fun. It's important because the data must be entered accurately; otherwise, any analysis of the data becomes at best misleading and at worst just plain wrong. The danger, then, lies in the fact that data entry is prone to errors but can't afford to have any.

As a forms designer, you can help to reduce this danger by setting up your forms so that data entry is both as efficient as possible and as accurate as possible. In some cases you can achieve both goals with a single technique. For example, asking someone to type a customer name manually is both slow and prone to misspellings. However, suppose you already have a Customers table with a CustomerName field. If you relate the current table with the Customers table (using, say, a common CustomerID field), Access adds the CustomerName field to the current form using a drop-down list that contains all the customers. This makes data entry more efficient (the users just select a name from the list instead of typing it) and more accurate (the users can't misspell the customer name).

This chapter introduces you to several techniques that serve to either make data entry less of a chore, or to reduce or eliminate data entry errors (or both).

Preventing Errors by Validating Data

If, as the cooks say, a recipe is only as good as its ingredients, a database is only as good as its data. Viewing, summarizing, and analyzing the data are meaningless if the table you're working with contains erroneous or improper data. For basic data errors (for example, entering the wrong date or transposing a number's digits), there's not a lot you can do other than exhorting yourself or the people who use your forms to enter data carefully. Fortunately, you have a bit more control when it comes to preventing improper data entry. By "improper," I mean data that falls in either of the following categories:

- Data that is the wrong type. For example, entering a text string in a cell that requires a number.

- Data that falls outside an allowable range. For example, entering 200 in a cell that requires a number between 1 and 100.

> **NOTE**
>
> To stress the importance of data entry, consider the story told to me by computer book author Greg Perry. Greg used to work for a large Fortune 500 company, and he says that the company made its data entry clerks enter all data *twice*: One clerk would enter the data in a file and then, when finished, another clerk would enter the same data. Then a comparison would be run to find exceptions where data didn't match, and that would then be reconciled. The lesson, he says, is that to the company, accuracy was far less costly than paying its employees to do the same job twice.

The next few sections show you several techniques that can help you reduce these types of errors.

Helping Users with Text Prompts

You can prevent improper entries to a certain extent by adding text that provides details on what is allowable inside a particular cell. You have two choices:

- Add status bar text. This is a string that appears in the Access status bar when users enter the field. You specify this text by opening the field's property sheet, displaying the Other tab, and then entering the string in the `Status Bar Text` property.

- Add a label. Place a `Label` control near the field and use it to enter text that describes the field's data requirements or shortcut keys. For example, if the field requires a date, the label might say `Press Ctrl+; to enter today's date`.

For example, Figure 3.1 shows the Mortgage Calculator form. Notice the labels added beside the Interest Rate and Term text boxes that specify to the users that they must enter the interest rate per annum and the term in years. Note, too, the status bar text that appears when the users enter the Interest Rate field.

Figure 3.1
Use form labels and status bar text to give the users text prompts about the data they must enter.

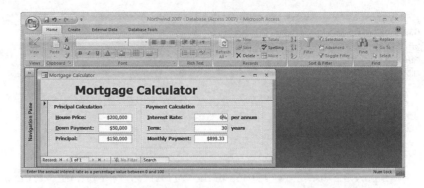

Preventing Errors with Data Validation Expressions

The problem with text prompts is they require other people to both read *and* act on the text. The better solution for preventing data entry errors is the Access data validation feature. With data validation, you create *rules* that specify exactly what kind of data can be entered and in what range that data can fall. You can also specify pop-up input messages that appear when a cell is selected, as well as error messages that appear when data is entered improperly.

Follow these steps to define the settings for a data validation rule:

1. Display the property sheet of the field to which you want to apply the data validation rule.
2. Click the Data tab.
3. Click inside the Validation Rule property.
4. Enter a formula that specifies the validation criteria. You can either enter the formula directly into the property box, or you can click the ellipsis (...) button and enter the formula using the Expression Builder.
5. If you want a dialog box to appear when the users enter invalid data, click inside the Validation Text property and then specify the message that appears.
6. Close the property sheet to apply the data validation rule.

For example, suppose you want the users to enter an interest rate. This quantity should be positive, of course, but it should also be less than 1. (That is, you want users to enter 6% as 0.06 instead of 6.) Figure 3.2 shows the property sheet for a field named InterestRate that meets these criteria by defining the following expression in the Validation Rule property:

```
>0 And <1
```

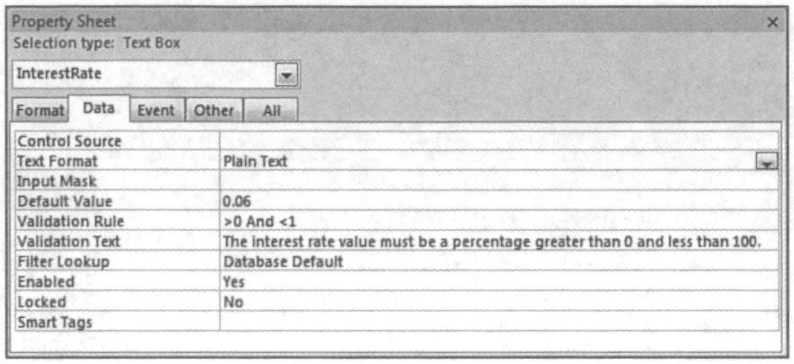

Figure 3.2
Use the Validation
Rule property to
enter a data validation
expression for a field.

Figure 3.2 also shows a string in the Validation Text property. If the users enter invalid data (that is, any value for which the Validation Rule expression returns False), the Validation Text appears in a dialog box, as shown in Figure 3.3.

3

Figure 3.3
If the users enter invalid
data in the field, Access
displays a dialog box
such as this one, which
uses the string entered
into the Validation
Text property.

Microsoft Office Access
(i) The interest rate value must be a percentage greater than 0 and less than 100.
OK

Using Input Masks for Consistent and Accurate Data Entry

One of the major headaches that database administrators have to deal with is data entered in an inconsistent way. For example, consider the following phone numbers:

```
(123)555-6783
(123)  555-6783
(123)5556783
123555-6783
1235556783
```

These sorts of inconsistencies might appear trivial, but they can cause all kinds of problems, from other users misreading the data to improper sorting to difficulties analyzing or querying the data. And it isn't just phone numbers that cause these kinds of problems. You also see them with Social Security numbers, ZIP codes, dates, times, account numbers, and more.

One way to avoid such inconsistencies is to add a label or status bar message that specifies the correct format to use. As with data validation, however, these prompts are not guaranteed to work every time (or even most of the time).

A better solution is to apply an *input mask* to the field. An input mask is a kind of template that shows the users how to enter the data and prevents them from entering incorrect characters (such as a letter where a number is required). For example, here's an input mask for a phone number:

Each underscore (_) acts as a placeholder for (in this case) a digit, and the parentheses and dash appear automatically as the user enters the number.

Using the Input Mask Wizard

The easiest way to create an input mask is to use the Input Mask Wizard. Here are the steps to follow:

1. Display the property sheet of the field to which you want to apply the input data.
2. Click the Data tab.
3. Click inside the Input Mask property.
4. Click the ellipsis (…) button to start the Input Mask Wizard, shown in Figure 3.4.

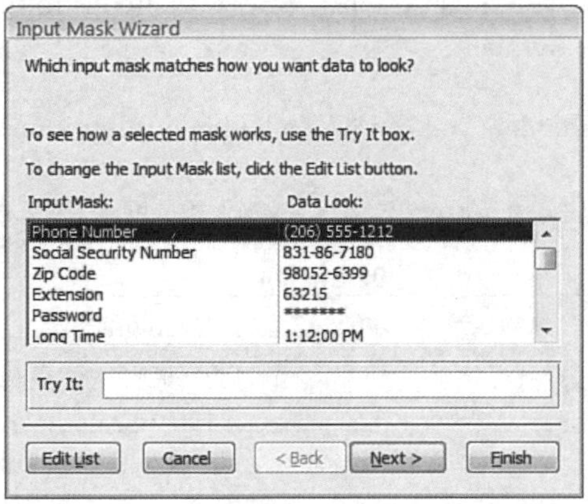

Figure 3.4
Use the Input Mask Wizard to choose a pre-defined input mask or to create your own input mask.

5. In the Input Mask list, click the input mask you want (or that's close to what you want) and then click Next.
6. Use the Input Mask box to make changes to the mask (see "Creating a Custom Input Mask Expression," next, for the specifics of which symbols to use); use the Placeholder Character list to choose the character you want to appear in the input mask as a placeholder; click Next.
7. Click the option that matches how you want the field data stored in the table (click Next after you've made your choice):
   - **With the Symbols in the Mask**—Click this option if you want the extra symbols (such as the parentheses and dash in a phone number mask) stored along with the data.
   - **Without the Symbols in the Mask**—Click this option to store only the data.
8. Click Finish.

Creating a Custom Input Mask Expression

If your data doesn't fit any of the predefined input masks, you need to create a custom mask that suits your needs. You do this by creating an expression that consists of three kinds of characters:

- **Data placeholders**—These characters are replaced by the actual data typed by the users. The different placeholders specify the type of character the users must enter (such as a digit or letter) and whether the character is optional or required.
- **Modifiers**—These characters aren't displayed in the mask; instead, they're used to modify the mask in some way (such as converting all the entered characters to lowercase).
- **Literals**—These extra characters appear in the mask the same as you enter them in the expression. For example, you might use parentheses as literals to surround the area code portion of a phone number.

Table 3.1 lists the data placeholders you can use to build your input mask expressions.

Table 3.1   Data Placeholders to Use for Custom Input Masks

Placeholder	Data Type	Description
0	Digit (0–3)	The character is required; the users are not allowed to include a plus sign (+) or minus sign (–).
3	Digit or space	The character is optional; the users are not allowed to include a plus sign (+) or minus sign (–).
#	Digit or space	The character is optional; the users are allowed to include a plus sign (+) or minus sign (–).
L	Letter (*a–z* or *A–Z*)	The character is required.
?	Letter (*a–z* or *A–Z*)	The character is optional.
a	Letter or digit	The character is required.
A	Letter or digit	The character is optional.
&	Any character or space	The character is required.
C	Any character or space	The character is optional.

Table 3.2 lists the modifiers and literals you can use to build your input mask expressions.

Table 3.2   Modifiers and Literals to Use for Custom Input Masks

Modifier	Description
\	Displays the following character as a literal; for example, \ (is displayed as (.
"*text*"	Displays the string *text* as a literal; for example, "MB" is displayed as MB.
.	Decimal separator.

Modifier	Description
,	Thousands separator.
: ; - /	Date and time separators.
<	Displays all the following letters as lowercase.
>	Displays all the following letters as uppercase.
!	Displays the input mask from right to left when you have optional data placeholders on the left.
Password	Displays the characters as asterisks so that other people can't read the data.

You can enter your input mask expressions directly into the `Input Mask` property, or you can modify a predefined input mask using the Input Mask Wizard.

For example, suppose your company uses account numbers that consist of four uppercase letters and four digits, with a dash (-) in between. Here's an input mask suitable for entering such numbers:

`>aaaa\-0000`

Note, too, that input masks can contain up to three sections separated by semicolons (;):

`first;second;third`

> `first`—This section holds the input mask expression.
>
> `second`—This optional section specifies whether Access stores the literals in the table when you enter data. Use 0 to include the literals; use 1 (or nothing) to store only the data.
>
> `third`—This optional section specifies the placeholder character. The default is the underscore (_).

For example, here's an input mask for a ZIP code that stores the dash separator and displays dots (.) as placeholders:

`00000\-3333;0;.`

Using Controls to Limit Data Entry Choices

Data entry always trips over two unfortunate facts of life: Humans are fallible creatures, and typing is an error-prone activity. Expert data entry operators can't achieve 100% accuracy (although some come remarkably close), and the rest of us can only hope for the best. In short, if your form relies on other people (or yourself, for that matter) typing in field values, it's death-and-taxes certain that your table will end up with errors.

It stands to reason, then, that you can greatly reduce the number of errors by greatly reducing the amount of typing. The best way to do that is by taking advantage of controls to generate field values automatically. Here are some examples:

3

- If you have a Yes/No field that uses a text box, the users must enter the unintuitive values -1 (for Yes) and 0 (for No). A more intuitive approach is to use a check box (or toggle button) that the users either activate (for Yes) or clear (for No).

- Suppose you have a field that can take only one of a small set of values (say, two to five values). For example, an invoice form might offer the users three choices for freight or four choices for credit cards. Again, instead of having the users type the freight choice or credit card name, you can populate the form with option buttons representing the choices.

- Suppose you have a field that can take one of a relatively large set of values (more than five). For example, the field might hold a customer name or a product name. Instead of making the users look up (time-consuming) and then type (inaccurate) the value, it's both faster and more accurate to place all the possible values in a drop-down list.

The rest of this chapter shows you how to use check boxes, toggle buttons, option buttons, lists, and other controls to build faster and more accurate forms. In each case, the idea is to move the users away from typing values and toward selecting them via a familiar and easily used control.

> **TIP**
>
> Another way to ensure data accuracy is to set up a field with a default value that Access enters into the field automatically when the user starts a new record. This can be a literal value such as 0 for a numeric field, or a formula such as =Date() for a date/time field. In the control's Property Sheet, display the Data tab and type the value in the Default Value property.

> **CAUTION**
>
> This is as good a place as any to warn you against what I call "form complacency." This is the attitude (which I've succumbed to myself on more than one occasion) which assumes that once *you* are happy with your form's layout, format, and data validation, then other people will automatically be happy with those things, too. Probably not! Other people will almost certainly approach the form differently, and they'll almost always have trouble figuring out how it works and what's expected of them. In other words, *always* "test drive" your form by letting other users take their best shots at it. It only takes a little extra time, and the suggested changes they come up with (and there *will* be suggestions, believe me) will save you time in the long run.

Working with Yes/No **Fields**

You use Yes/No fields in tables when you have a quantity that you can represent in one of two states: on (Yes, True, or -1) or off (No, False, or 0).

When you create a Yes/No field in the table Design view, the Display Control property (it's in the Lookup tab) defaults to Check Box. This means that when you add a Yes/No field to a form, Access automatically represents the field with a check box control (along with a label that displays the name of the field or the field's `Caption` property). However, it's possible that the `Display Control` property has been set to `Text Box`, either by design or by accident. As I mentioned earlier, you want to avoid users having to enter `-1` or `0` into a text box, so you should never use a text box for a `Yes/No` field on your forms. Instead, you have two choices:

- If you have access to the table's design, change the `Yes/No` field's `Display Control` property to `Check Box`. After you've done that, return to the form, delete the `Yes/No` field's text box and label (if they're already on the form), and then add the field back to the form to get the check box version.

- If you can't change the table design, use a check box or toggle button control bound to the `Yes/No` field. The next two sections show you how to do this.

Using Check Boxes

Here are the steps to follow to insert a check box and bind it to a `Yes/No` field:

1. In the Design tab's Controls group, click the Check Box button.

2. Draw the check box on the form.

3. Edit the text of the label control that Access adds to the right of the check box. (For clarity, it's best to use the name of the `Yes/No` field.)

4. Click the check box and then choose Design, Property Sheet to open the Property Sheet pane.

5. In the Data tab, use the `Control Source` property to choose the name of the `Yes/No` field you want bound to the check box.

6. In the `Default Value` property, enter the initial value for new records: `Yes`, `True`, or `-1`; or `No`, `False`, or `0`.

> ┌─ CAUTION ───
> Many form designers like to use an option group as a way of "framing" a number of related controls. This is often a good idea (I discuss it in more detail in Chapter 4, "Designing Forms for Business Use"), but you need to be careful: If you add the option group and then insert the check boxes within the group, Access treats the check boxes as mutually exclusive options. That is, the users can activate only one check box at a time. To avoid this situation, add the check boxes to the frame first and then draw the option group around them.

It's worth pointing out here that check boxes (and toggle buttons, discussed next) can insert only one of two values into a field: `-1` or `0`. You can't use a check box for other two-state choices, such as `"male"` and `"female"` or `"Pepsi"` and `"Coke"`. For fields that can take only one of two values other than `0` and `-1`, use option buttons instead (as described later in this chapter).

3

Using Toggle Buttons

A toggle button is a cross between a check box and a command button: Click it once, and the button stays pressed; click it again, and the button returns to its normal state. The button can display either a caption or a picture. Here are the steps to follow to insert a toggle button and bind it to a Yes/No field:

1. In the Design tab's Controls group, click Toggle Button.
2. Draw the toggle button on the form.
3. Choose Design, Property Sheet to open the Property Sheet pane.
4. In the Format tab, you have two choices that determine what appears on the face of the button:
   - Caption—Use this property to specify text that appears on the face of the button. (For clarity, it's best to use the name of the Yes/No field.)
   - Picture—Use this property to specify an image that appears on the button face. Click the ellipsis button (…) to display the Picture Builder dialog box, shown in Figure 3.5. Either use the Available Pictures list to click an image or click Browse to choose an image from the Select Picture dialog box (although note that Access can only use BMP or icon files).

> **CAUTION**
>
> If you want to use a custom picture, bear in mind that if the image is larger than the toggle button, Access won't shrink the image to fit inside the button—it just centers the image in the button and displays as much as will fit. Therefore, always choose a bitmap or icon that's the same size or smaller than the toggle button.

Figure 3.5
Use the Picture Builder dialog box to choose an image to appear on the face of the toggle button.

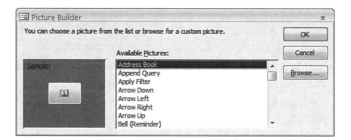

5. In the Data tab, use the Control Source property to choose the name of the Yes/No field you want bound to the toggle button.
6. In the Default Value property, enter the initial value for new records. For the "pressed" state, use Yes, True, or -1; for the "unpressed" state, use No, False, or 0.

Using Option Buttons to Present a Limited Number of Choices

Option buttons are a good choice if the underlying field accepts only a limited number of possible numbers: at least two but no more than about five or six. (If you have more possible values, use a list box or combo box, discussed later in this chapter.)

How does having multiple option buttons on a form enable you to store a single value in a field? There are two components to consider:

- **The option buttons**—You assign each option button a value from among the list of possible values that the field can take.

> **NOTE** Option button values must be numeric. Therefore, you can use option groups and option buttons only with numeric fields.

- **The option group**—This is a separate control that you use to organize the option buttons. That is, if you insert multiple option buttons inside a group, Access allows the users to activate only one of the options at a time. (You can also use check boxes or toggle buttons, but option buttons are best because most users are familiar with them and know how to operate them.)

The option group is bound to the field in the underlying table. Therefore, when you activate an option button, the value assigned to that button is stored in the field. This form of data entry brings many advantages to the table (literally!):

- **It's quick.** The users don't have to look up the possible values elsewhere.
- **It's accurate.** The field value is stored "behind the scenes," so the users can't enter the wrong value.
- **It's intuitive.** The option button captions can be as long as you like (within reason), so you can provide users with a helpful description or title for each option.
- **It's familiar.** All Windows users know how to operate option buttons, so no extra training is required.

The next two sections show you how to create option buttons using a wizard and by hand.

Running the Option Group Wizard

The easiest way to create an option group and its associated option buttons is to use the Option Group Wizard, as described in the following steps:

1. In the Design tab's Controls group, make sure the Control Wizards button is activated and then click the Option Group button.
2. Draw the option group on the form. Access launches the Option Group Wizard.

3. For each option button you want, type the label in the Label Names list and press Tab. When you're done, click <u>N</u>ext.

4. To select a default choice (the option that Access activates automatically when the user starts a new record), leave the <u>Y</u>es, The Default Choice Is option activated and then choose the option label from the list. Click <u>N</u>ext.

5. Use the Values column to assign a numeric value for each option, as shown in Figure 3.6. Note that each value must be unique. Click <u>N</u>ext when you're done.

Figure 3.6
Use this Option Group Wizard dialog box to assign a unique numeric value to each option.

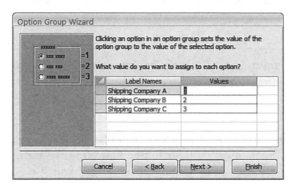

6. Specify where you want the option group value stored (click <u>N</u>ext when you're done):

   - **<u>S</u>ave the Value for Later Use**—Click this option to have Access save the option group value. This is mostly used by VBA programmers—the current value of the option group is stored in the Frame object's Value property.

   - **Store the <u>V</u>alue in This Field**—Click this option and then select a field from the list to have Access store the option group value in the field.

7. Click the type of control you want to use in the option group: <u>O</u>ption Buttons, <u>C</u>heck Boxes, or Toggle Buttons. You can also select the special effect used by the option group border (<u>E</u>tched, F<u>l</u>at, and so on). Click <u>N</u>ext to continue.

8. Edit the option group caption (the text that the users see along the top border of the option group frame; use the field name or something similar) and then click <u>F</u>inish to complete the wizard.

 TIP | If you already have an "unframed" option button on your form, you can still insert it into an option group. Select the button, cut it to the Clipboard, select the option group (by clicking its frame), and paste. Access adds the button to the option group.

Creating an Option Group By Hand

If you'd rather create the option group yourself, here are the steps to follow:

1. In the Design tab's Controls group, make sure the Control Wizards button is deactivated and then click the Option Group button.

2. Draw the option group on the form.

3. In the Design tab's Controls group, click Option Button.

4. Draw the option button inside the option group.

5. Choose Design, Property Sheet to display the option button's property sheet.

6. In the Data tab, use the Option Value property to specify the numeric value associated with the option.

7. Use the drop-down list to choose the label associated with the option button. (It's the control that is one number greater than the option button. For example, if the option button name assigned by Access is Option10, the associated label will be named Label11.)

8. In the Format tab, use the Caption property to specify text that appears alongside the option button.

9. Repeat steps 3–8 for the other option buttons you want to add to the option group.

10. Use the drop-down list to choose the option group (it's named Frame*n*, where *n* means it was the *n*th control added to the form).

11. In the Data tab, use the Control Source property to choose the field in which you want the value of the selected option button stored.

12. If you want one of the option buttons to be activated when the users start a new record, use the Default Value property to enter the value of the corresponding option button.

13. Close the property sheet.

3

CASE STUDY

Using an Option Group to Select the Shipper

In the Northwind 2007 database, the Orders table has a Shipper ID field that specifies which shipping company to use. There are three shipping companies that the users can select: Shipping Company A, Shipping Company B, and Shipping Company C. (The person at Microsoft who put together the Northwind 2007 database was singularly uncreative when it came to names.) Option buttons can take only numeric values, so you can't use them to assign a text value such as "Shipping Company A" to the Shipper ID field. That's not a problem because the Shipper ID field is designed to store a number: 1 for Shipping Company A, 2 for Shipping Company B, and 3 for Shipping Company C. These numbers correspond to the ID field in the Shippers table. The Shipper and Orders tables have a one-to-many relation based on the ID and Shipper ID fields.

A field that takes one of three numeric choices is perfect for an option group. You set things up as follows:

- Create an option group and bind it to the `Shipper ID` field.
- Add three option buttons for Shipping Company A, Shipping Company B, and Shipping Company C, and assign them the values 1, 2, and 3, respectively.

Figure 3.7 shows the resulting option group in the form.

Figure 3.7
This form uses an option group to choose the shipping method for each order.

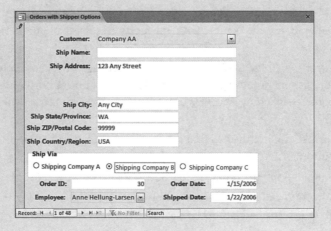

Using Lists to Present a Large Number of Choices

Option buttons have three main disadvantages:

- If a field can take more than about five or six values, option buttons become too unwieldy and confusing for the users.
- Option buttons can't work with non-numeric values.
- Users can't enter unique values. This is normally a good thing, but in some instances you might want to give the users the flexibility to choose either a predefined value or to enter a different value.

To solve all these problems, Access offers two different list controls that enable you to present the users with a list of choices:

- A list box presents a list of choices. These choices are *static*, meaning that users can't enter any different values.
- A combo box enables users to either select a value from a drop-down list or (optionally) enter a different value using the associated text box.

> **NOTE** Another consideration you need to bear in mind when deciding between a list box and a combo box is the size of each control on the form. A list box is usually large enough to show at least three or four items in the list, whereas a combo box always shows only a single item (the users click the list to choose another). Therefore, the list box always takes up quite a bit more room than the combo box, so keep that in mind when designing your form. If you don't have much room, but you don't want the users to be able to add different values to the field, you'll see later that it's possible to restrict the combo box to just the values in the list.

In both cases, the item the users choose from the list (or the item the users enter in the combo box) is the value that is stored in the bound field. This means that you can use list and combo boxes for any type of value, including numeric, string, and date values.

It's important to note that Access defaults to a combo box when you add to the form a field that is used as part of a relationship with another table. Specifically, if the relationship is one-to-many and the current table is the "many" side, adding the field that corresponds to the common field on the "one" side creates a list that contains all the values from that field.

For example, the Products table has a one-to-many relationship with the Order Details table via the common ID and Product ID fields, respectively. If you're putting together a form based on the Order Details table and you add the Product ID field, Access creates a combo box list and populates it with the values from the Products table's Product Name field. Why Product Name and not Product ID? The reason is that in the design for the Order Details table, the Product ID field's Row Source property (in the Lookup tab) specifies an SQL statement that selects the Product Name field from the Products table:

```
SELECT ID, [Product Name] FROM Products ORDER BY [Product Name]
```

The next few sections show you various ways to work with both controls.

Starting the List Box or Combo Box Wizard

The List Box Wizard and Combo Box Wizard make it easy to create a bound list control. Here are the steps to follow to get started with these wizards:

1. In the Design tab's Controls group, make sure the Control Wizards button is activated.
2. Click either Combo Box or List Box.
3. Draw the box on the form. Access starts either the List Box Wizard or the Combo Box Wizard.

These wizards work identically, but the steps you take vary dramatically depending on which option you choose in the initial dialog box. The next three sections take you through the details of each option.

Getting List Values from a Table or Query Field

The most common list scenario is to populate the list box or combo box with values from a field in a specified table or query. For example, if you're putting together an orders form, you'll probably want to include a list that contains all the customer names, so you'll populate the list with the values from the Customers table's Company field.

The following steps show you how to continue with the List Box or Combo Box Wizard to populate a list with values from a table or query field:

1. In the first wizard dialog box, click the I Want the List Box to Look Up the Values in a Table or Query option and then click Next.
2. Click the table or query that contains the field you want to use for the list and then click Next.
3. In the Available Fields list, select the field you want to use and then click > to add it to the Selected Fields list. Click Next.
4. If you want the list sorted, use the drop-down list to choose the field you selected, click the Ascending (or Descending) toggle button, and then click Next.
5. Click and drag the right edge of the column header to set the width of the list column and then click Next.
6. To create a bound list box or combo box, select the Store That Value in This Field option, choose the field you want to use from the drop-down list, and then click Next.
7. In the final wizard dialog box, use the text box to edit the label text that appears above the list and then click Finish.

Specifying Custom List Values

If the items you want to appear in your list don't exist in another table or query, you need to specify them by hand. Here are the steps to follow to continue with the List Box or Combo Box Wizard and populate a list with custom values:

1. In the first wizard dialog box, click the I Will Type in the Values That I Want option and then click Next.
2. For each value you want to add, type the item text and press Tab. Click Next when you're done.
3. To create a bound list box or combo box, select the Store That Value in This Field option, choose the field you want to use from the drop-down list, and then click Next.
4. In the final wizard dialog box, use the text box to edit the label text that appears above the list and then click Finish.

Getting List Values from the Current Table

Sometimes the values you want in your list already exist in the form's underlying table or query. For example, if your form uses the Customers table, you might want to set up a list for the Job Title field and use the unique values in that to populate the list. (This example illustrates when you might want to use a combo box, because a new customer contact could have a title other than the ones in the list.) Note, however, that the list you create using this method will always be an *unbound* control.

The following steps show you how to continue with the List Box or Combo Box Wizard to populate a list with values from a field in the form's current data source:

1. In the first wizard dialog box, click the Find a <u>R</u>ecord on My Form Based on the Value I Selected in My Combo Box option and then click <u>N</u>ext.

2. In the Available Fields list, select the field you want to use and then click > to add it to the Selected Fields list. Click <u>N</u>ext.

3. Click and drag the right edge of the column header to set the width of the list column and then click <u>N</u>ext.

4. In the final wizard dialog box, use the text box to edit the label text that appears above the list and then click <u>F</u>inish.

Creating a Multiple-Column List

Sometimes displaying a single column of values in a list might not be enough. For example, if you're working with data from the Northwind 2007 Products table, displaying just the Product Name field might not give the users enough information. Instead, you might also want to show the users the corresponding Category or Supplier value (using an inner join query for the latter) for each product.

➜ To learn about inner joins, **see** "Establishing Table Relationships," **p. 267**. (Chapter 12)

You can do this by adding one or more columns to the list and then specifying which of those columns contains the value you want to store in your form's bound field. Here are the steps to follow:

1. Draw a list box or combo box on the form to launch the List Box or Combo Box Wizard.

2. In the first wizard dialog box, select the I Want the List Box to <u>L</u>ook Up the Values in a Table or Query option and then click <u>N</u>ext. (Note that you can also display multiple columns using the Find a <u>R</u>ecord on My Form Based on the Value I Selected in My Combo Box option.)

3. Select the table or query that contains the field you want to use for the list and then click <u>N</u>ext.

4. In the Available Fields list, for each field you want to display in the list, select the field and then click > to add it to the Selected Fields list. Click <u>N</u>ext.

5. You sort the list on multiple fields by using separate drop-down lists to choose each field and its sort order. Click <u>N</u>ext.

6. Click and drag the right edge of each column header to set the width of the list columns. Note, too, that you can also change the column order by clicking and dragging the column headers left or right. Click <u>N</u>ext.

7. To create a bound list box or combo box, select the <u>S</u>tore That Value in This Field option, choose the field you want to use from the drop-down list, and then click <u>N</u>ext.

8. In the final wizard dialog box, use the text box to edit the label text that appears above the list and then click <u>F</u>inish.

Figure 3.8 shows a form that uses a two-column combo box to display both the `Product Name` field and the `Category` field from the Products table.

Figure 3.8
This combo box uses multiple columns to display both the `Product Name` field and the corresponding `Category` field.

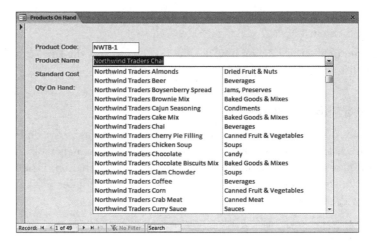

Modifying List Box and Combo Box Properties

If you want a bit more control over the list layout and data, you need to tweak the control properties. Here's a list of the properties to work with:

- `Control Source` **(Data tab)**—The field in which the selected list item will be stored.

- `Row Source Type` **(Data tab)**—Choose `Table/Query` for values that come from a table or query field; choose `Value List` for values that you enter by hand; choose `Field List` to populate the list with field names from a table or query.

- `Row Source` **(Data tab)**—This value depends on the `Row Source Type` value:

  - `Table/Query`—Enter an SQL `SELECT` statement that specifies the field you want to use to populate the list (along with any criteria you want to use). Alternatively, click the ellipsis button (…) and use the Query Builder to specify the table, field, and criteria. When you close the Query Builder, Access converts your selections into an SQL `SELECT` statement.

  - `Value List`—Enter the values with which you want to populate the list, separated by semicolons.

- `Field List`—Enter the name of the table or query that contains the field names with which you want to populate the list.

> **NOTE** If you want to display a multiple-column list, specify each field that you want to include in the list after the `SELECT` verb in the SQL statement, as in this example:
>
>   SELECT CategoryName, Description FROM Categories;
>
> Alternatively, use the Query Builder to add each field to the criteria grid.

- `Bound Column` (**Data tab**)—If `Row Source Type` is `Table/Query` and the `Row Source` `SELECT` statement specifies only a single field, the `Bound Column` value should always be 1. If the `Row Source` proeprty specifies two or more fields (for a multiple-column list), set `Bound Column` to the number of the field that contains the value you want to store in the current table (1 is the first field, 2 is the second field, and so on).
- `Limit To List` (**Data tab**)—This is a combo box-only property. When the value is `Yes`, the users can only select values from the list; when the value is `No`, the users can enter new values.
- `Column Count` (**Format tab**)—The number of columns in the list box.
- `Column Heads` (**Format tab**)—If this property is `Yes`, the list columns are displayed with headers, whereby each header contains the name of the field.
- `Column Widths` (**Format tab**)—The width, in inches, of each column, separated by semicolons.
- `List Rows` (**Format tab**)—This is a combo box-only property, and it specifies the number of items the users see when they click the list.
- `Multi Select` (**Other tab**)—This is a list box-only property. If this property is `None`, users can select only one item at a time; if this value is `Simple`, users can select multiple items by clicking them; if this value is `Extended`, users must hold down the Ctrl key to select multiple items (or hold down Shift to select multiple items that appear consecutively in the list).

Entering Data with ActiveX Controls

The controls you see in the Design tab's Controls group will likely satisfy most of your form needs. However, you might have noticed that some controls that are commonly seen in Windows dialog boxes aren't available in the Controls group. For example, many Windows programs use spin buttons for entering numeric values, whereas others use a "calendar" control to enable users to choose dates via the mouse.

These and many other controls are available on your system as separate components that either come with the default Windows installation or are added to the system when you install Microsoft Office. (Other programs might also add their own controls to the system.) There are dozens of these so-called ActiveX controls, although only a few are suitable to be used on an Access form. The next three sections show you how to use three of them: a spin button, a scrollbar, and a calendar control.

Entering Numbers Using a Spin Button

A spin button comes with up and down arrows that the users can click to increment or decrement a value. Most spin buttons have a text box control beside them to show the current value. In most cases, the text box also gives users the choice of entering the number directly or selecting the number by using the spin button arrows. However, as you'll see, to use a spin button on an Access form, you can't make the text box editable, so the users must use the spin button arrows. Therefore, this control is useful only for fields that require relatively small numbers (to minimize the amount of clicking the users must do to get the required value).

Here are the steps required to add a spin button and companion text box to a form:

1. In the Design tab's Controls group, click the Insert ActiveX Control button. Access displays the Insert ActiveX Control dialog box.

2. In the Select an ActiveX Control list, click Microsoft Forms 2.0 SpinButton and then click OK.

3. Adjust the dimensions of the control as needed. Note that if you make the control taller than it is wide, you get up and down arrows; if you make the control wider than it is tall, you get left and right arrows.

4. In the Design tab's Controls group, click the Text Box button.

5. Draw the text box on the form beside the spin button. Access adds the text box and an associated label. Make a note of the text box name because you need it later in these steps.

6. Edit the text box label, as necessary.

7. Click the spin button and choose Design, Property Sheet to display the control's property sheet.

8. In the Data tab, use the `Control Source` property to specify the field in which you want the spin button value stored.

9. In the Other tab, customize the spin button using the following properties:

   - `Min`—Sets the minimum value of the spin button.
   - `Max`—Sets the maximum value of the spin button.
   - `SmallChange`—Sets the amount that the spin button value changes when the users click one of the arrows.

10. Ensure that the text box gets updated with the new spin button value whenever the users click an arrow. To do this, right-click the spin button, click Build Event, click

Code Builder, and then click OK. Access opens the Visual Basic Editor and adds a stub for the Updated event, which you can delete. In the procedure list (the one on the right at the top of the module), click Change.

11. Inside the Change procedure, type the following statement, where *TextBox* is the name of the text box you added in step 6 (see Figure 3.9):

```
TextBox.SetFocus
```

Figure 3.9
Use a simple Visual Basic for Applications statement to keep the text box updated with the current spin button value.

12. Choose File, Close and Return to Microsoft Office Access (or press Alt+Q or Alt+F11).

13. Use the Property Sheet pane's drop-down list to choose the text box.

14. In the Data tab, set the text box value equal to the spin button value by using the Control Source to add the following expression (where *SpinButton* is the name of the spin button control):

```
=SpinButton
```

15. Close the property sheet.

Figure 3.10 shows a form with a spin button and associated text box.

Figure 3.10
When you click the spin button arrows, the value displayed inside the text box changes accordingly.

Entering Numbers Using a Scrollbar

Scrollbars are normally used to navigate windows, but by themselves you can use them to enter values between a predefined maximum and minimum. In this context, they are very similar to spin buttons, so the procedure for adding them to your form is more or less the same:

1. In the Design tab's Controls group, click the Insert ActiveX Control button. Access displays the Insert ActiveX Control dialog box.

2. In the Select an ActiveX Control list, click Microsoft Forms 2.0 ScrollBar and then click OK.

3. Adjust the dimensions of the control as needed. Note that if you make the control taller than it is wide, you get a vertical scrollbar; if you make the control wider than it is tall, you get a horizontal scrollbar.

4. In the Design tab's Controls group, click the Text Box button, draw the text box on the form beside the scrollbar, and edit the label. Remember to make note of the text box name.

5. Click the scrollbar and choose Design, Property Sheet to display the control's property sheet.

6. In the Data tab, use the `Control Source` property to specify the field in which you want the scrollbar value stored.

7. In the Other tab, customize the scrollbar using the following properties:
   - `Min`—Sets the minimum value of the scrollbar.
   - `Max`—Sets the maximum value of the scrollbar.
   - `SmallChange`—Sets the amount that the scrollbar value changes when the users click one of the scroll arrows.
   - `LargeChange`—Sets the amount that the scrollbar value changes when the users click between the scroll box and one of the scroll arrows.

8. Right-click the scrollbar, click Build Event, click Code Builder, and then click OK. Access opens the Visual Basic Editor and adds a stub for the `Updated` event, which you can delete. In the procedure list (the one on the right at the top of the module), click Change.

9. Inside the `Change` procedure, type the following statement, where *TextBox* is name of the text box you added in step 4:

   `TextBox.SetFocus`

10. Choose File, Close and Return to Microsoft Office Access (or press Alt+Q or Alt+F11).

11. Use the property sheet drop-down list to choose the text box.

12. In the Data tab, set the text box value equal to the scrollbar value by using the `Control Source` property to add the following expression (where *ScrollBar* is the name of the scrollbar control):

    `=ScrollBar`

13. Close the property sheet.

Figure 3.11 shows a form with a scrollbar and associated text box.

Figure 3.11
When you click the
scrollbar arrows or drag
the scroll box, the value
displayed inside the text
box changes accordingly.

Entering Dates Using a Calendar

Entering dates can be problematic because users might not use the proper format. For
example, they might reverse the month and day, they might use an unrecognizable month
abbreviation, they might leave out a date separator, and so on. To avoid these common data
entry scenarios, you can add a calendar control to your form. The users enter a date by
selecting the month and year and then just clicking the day of the month.

Follow these steps to add a calendar control to your form:

1. In the Design tab's Controls group, click the Insert ActiveX Control button. Access
   displays the Insert ActiveX Control dialog box.

2. In the Select an ActiveX Control list, click Calendar Control 12.0 and then click OK.

3. Adjust the size and position of the control to ensure that the calendar is displayed
   properly.

4. Click the calendar and choose Design, Property Sheet to display the control's property
   sheet.

5. In the Data tab, use the `Control Source` property to specify the date field in which you
   want the calendar value stored.

6. In the Other tab, use properties such as `DayFontColor` and `GridCellEffect` to format
   the calendar.

7. Close the property sheet.

Figure 3.12 shows a form with a calendar control added.

Figure 3.12
With the calendar con-
trol, use the drop-down
lists to select a month
and year and then click
the date you want.

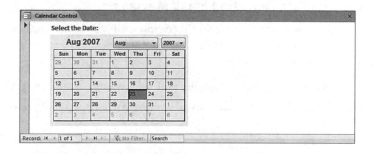

Collecting Form Data via Email

 Although small databases are often managed by a single person, larger databases require input from multiple people. If those people are on your network, such collaboration is most easily achieved either by placing the database in a shared network location or by moving some or all of the data to a SharePoint site. However, what do you do if your collaborators don't have network access? One solution would be to export the necessary tables and forms into another database and then email that database to the collaborators. When the data is returned, you could then import it back into your database.

Such a solution is workable, but a little too unwieldy to be practical. Fortunately, Access 2007 comes with a new feature called Access Data Collection (ADC) that makes email-based data collection much easier. With this feature, you create a form that includes fields for the data you want to collect, place that form in an HTML email message, and then send that message to every person from whom you want to collect the data. Each person fills in the form and returns the message, which is then saved in a special Outlook folder called Access Data Collection Replies. You then synchronize Access (by hand or automatically) with those replies, and the data is added to the underlying table.

CAUTION

Many people set up their email clients to read messages in plain text, and that's not good for ADC. First, viewing the ADC message in plain text prevents the user from seeing the form at all. Second, even if the user converts the message to HTML (by clicking the Information bar and then clicking Display as HTML), Access will perceive this as a "change" to the form, and it won't process the reply. That is, in the Access Data Collection Replies folder, the Data Collection Status column for the reply will say the following:

```
Failure: Cannot process this e-mail message. The form in
this e-mail message is either corrupt or has been modified.
```

The user must turn off the Outlook option to read messages in plain text (choose Tools, Trust Center, click E-mail Security, and then click to deactivate the Read All Standard Mail in Plain Text check box), reply to and fill in the ADC form, and then reset the plain text option.

Sending the Access Data Collection Email Message

Unlike the other forms you've seen in this chapter, an ADC form cannot be created by hand. Instead, Access runs a wizard that builds the form step by step, as shown in the following procedure:

1. Use the Navigation pane to click the table you want to use to store the collected data.
2. Choose External Data, Create E-mail. Access starts the ADC Wizard.

3. In the initial wizard dialog box, click <u>N</u>ext. The wizard asks whether you want to use an HTML form or an InfoPath form.

4. Click <u>H</u>TML Form and then click <u>N</u>ext.

5. If the table already contains data, the wizard asks whether you want to collect new information or update existing information. Click one of the following options and then click <u>N</u>ext:

- **Collect Ne<u>w</u> Information Only**—Click this option to send a blank form for new data.

- **<u>U</u>pdate Existing Information**—Click this option to send existing data for the recipient to edit. The record that contains the recipient's address is the record the recipient will edit.

6. For each field you want to include in the form, click the field and then click > (or click >> to add all the fields). Click <u>N</u>ext.

7. If you want Access to synchronize with Outlook automatically when the replies arrive, click to activate the Automatically <u>P</u>rocess Replies and Add Data to *Table* check box (where *Table* is the name of the table you chose in step 1) and then click <u>N</u>ext.

8. Choose how you want to specify the message recipients (click <u>N</u>ext after you've made your choice):

- **Enter the E-mail Addresses in Microsoft Office <u>O</u>utlook**—Click this option to enter the recipients by hand in the Outlook message window that appears later. Skip to step 10.

- **Use the E-mail Addresses Stored in a Field in the <u>D</u>atabase**—Click this option if you have the recipients' addresses stored in the current database. Proceed to step 9.

9. Specify the addresses in the database using one of the following options (click <u>N</u>ext when you are done):

- **The <u>C</u>urrent Table or Query**—Click this option if the email addresses are stored in the table you're using with ADC. Use the associated list to click the field that contains the addresses.

- **An <u>A</u>ssociated Table**—Click this option if the addresses reside in another table that's related to the current table. First, use the associated list to click the field in the current table upon which the relationship is based. Second, when Access displays a list of fields in the related table, use the list to click the field that contains the email addresses.

10. Edit the message <u>S</u>ubject and <u>I</u>ntroduction, as needed. If the addresses came from the Access database, click where you want the addresses added: the To Field, Cc Field, or Bcc Field. Click <u>N</u>ext.

3

11. You now have two ways to proceed:

- If you choose an Access field for the recipient addresses, click Next. Access displays a list of the recipients with check boxes for each address. Leave the check boxes activated for the recipients you want to receive the message. When you are done, click Send.

- If you will be specifying recipients via Outlook, click Create to create the message, select the recipients, and then click Send.

Replying to an Access Data Collection Email Message

If you receive an ADC message, you need to fill in the fields and return the message. Here are the steps to follow:

1. Click the Access Data Collection message and then click Reply. Access displays the message window.

2. Scroll down the message body until you see the form, as shown in Figure 3.13.

Figure 3.13
When you reply to an ADC message, fill in each form field in the body of the reply.

3. Click inside a form field and type the data.

4. Repeat step 3 for each field.

5. After you've filled in each field, click Send.

Managing the Access Data Collection Replies

As I mentioned earlier, when you receive replies to your messages, they are automatically routed to the Access Data Collection Replies folder in Outlook. (This is a subfolder of the Inbox folder.) If you didn't set up Access to handle the replies automatically, follow these steps to handle a reply manually:

1. In Outlook, open the reply.
2. Click Export to Access. Outlook asks you to confirm.
3. Click OK. Outlook exports the data.
4. Click OK.

From Here

→ To learn how to work with the Label control, **see** "Adding Labels to the Form," **p. 41**. (Chapter 2)

→ To learn how to work with the Text Box control, **see** "Adding Text Boxes to the Form," **p. 43**. (Chapter 2)

→ For the specifics of the Expression Builder, **see** "Working with the Expression Builder," **p. 256**. (Chapter 11)

→ To learn about inner joins, **see** "Establishing Table Relationships," **p. 267**. (Chapter 12)

→ For the details on building SQL SELECT statements, **see** "Using SQL to Perform a Select Query," **p. 342**. (Chapter 15)

3

Designing Forms for Business Use

4

You've seen so far that designing a basic form is not hard, whether you use a default form layout, the Form Wizard, or the Design view. And certainly if you're the only person who will use the form, a quick-and-dirty job might be all that you need or have time to build.

However, if other people are going to use the form, quick-and-dirty almost certainly won't be good enough. You need to take a bit of extra time to build certain design elements into the form that make it easy to use, attractive, familiar, and, above all, conducive to accurate input. Taking the extra time to get the form just right might seem burdensome now, but you'll save time in the long run because you'll spend less time training users, answering their questions, troubleshooting problems, and dealing with data entry errors.

And the good news is that knocking a basic form into shape doesn't take all that long. With the concepts and techniques you learn in this chapter, you'll be able to build attractive and usable forms without spending all day tweaking controls and fussing with formatting.

Using Forms in a Business Context

If you use Access in a business environment, forms are a necessity for one simple reason: They're better than datasheets for entering, editing, and even analyzing data. A form is faster, easier, more flexible, less error-prone, less tiring, and less intimidating than a datasheet. Moreover, Access users generally *expect* to use a form to work with data.

So you need to add "Form Designer" to the list of hats you wear at work. But before you dive in, you need to take a step or two back and survey the scene. You need, in short, to ask yourself three simple questions to help get your bearings: Why collect the data in the first place? What exactly *is* the data you're collecting? And who are the people collecting it?

Why Collect the Data?

An increasing percentage of Fortune 500 companies pay a hefty salary to someone they call the chief knowledge officer, or CKO. The ascendancy of the CKO is a reflection of the relative importance that business is putting on knowledge over mere information. The CKO is, in the simplest terms, the overseer of a company's knowledge management—that is, the way the company creates, organizes, and shares its institutional knowledge. The CKO takes to heart the maxim of former Hewlett-Packard CEO Lew Platt: "If HP knew what HP knows, we would be three times as profitable." The CKO finds out what his corporation knows by setting up "knowledge mining expeditions" where managers and "knowledge engineers" codify corporate know-how using technology such as—you guessed it— Microsoft Access. That's why corporations collect data: to turn it into knowledge.

But knowledge management isn't solely the province of Fortune 500 behemoths. Even small- and medium-sized companies need to know what they know. And it's this quest for knowledge that can have a subtle effect on your form design.

For example, if the data is collected for business analysis, a PivotChart form will probably display the data in the best and most analytically flexible light. If the data is collected for marketing purposes, you'll want your form to emphasize key areas such as addresses and demographic data.

➔ To learn how to work with PivotChart forms, **see** "Creating a PivotChart Form," **p. 108**. (Chapter 5)

What Is the Data?

The content of the data is another important factor in form design. For example, a form that collects order data should almost certainly show extended subtotals for each item (units ordered multiplied by the price per unit), freight charges, taxes, the order total, and other calculated form fields. Similarly, if the data relies on existing information that sits in other tables—such as customer or product data—you need to populate your form with lists that enable the users to choose the correct data. Or if the underlying form table is the "one" side of a one-to-many relationship, you might want to add a subform that shows the related records from the "many" table.

➔ For the details of subforms, **see** "Creating a Multiple-Table Form," **p. 95**. (Chapter 5)

Who Are Your Users?

Finally, and perhaps most importantly, you need to consider who will be using the form. Are they novice users? If so, you might need to add extra explanatory labels and take extra care with data validation. Are the users experienced data entry operators? If so, you need to design your form for speed, including making each field accessible via the keyboard. Will the form be used by people throughout the company? If so, you might have to build your form according to corporate design guidelines. Managers probably want forms that aid in data analysis (such as a PivotChart form or a form with calculated fields), whereas clerks probably want forms that let them enter data with a minimum of fuss.

Ten Design Guidelines for Business Forms

Answering the three questions from the previous sections is only the first step toward creating a usable business form. The following sections offer a set of 10 guidelines that help you build usable and attractive forms for easy and accurate data entry and editing.

1. Make Forms Fast

Most, perhaps all, users of business forms are busy people with long to-do lists, and working with your form is only one item on those lists. These people don't want to spend precious minutes trying to determine how to use a form or what a particular field is supposed to represent. Make your control names clear, but not verbose; for tricky fields, add an explanatory label.

2. Make Forms Foolproof

Be sure to take advantage of list boxes, combo boxes, option buttons, and other controls that minimize typing. These tools are not only faster, but they reduce strain and increase accuracy, as explained in detail in Chapter 3, "Designing Forms for Efficient and Accurate Data Entry."

3. Mimic Paper Forms When Practical

If your Access form replaces or is used in addition to a paper form, try to make the electronic version mimic its counterpart. At the very least, the fields should be in the same order so that people used to filling out the paper form will feel comfortable with the Access version. Size text boxes to match the original and use fonts, colors, boxes, and lines to make the Access form a carbon copy of the original, if that's practical within the confines of the computer screen (see the discussion of screen resolution that follows).

4. Give Users What They Need and Then Stop

After you've learned the ins and outs of form design, the temptation is to put your hard-won knowledge to good use by building in all kinds of bells and whistles to each form. Resist this temptation at all costs because nobody likes to use an overdesigned form. Don't use a combo box for a two-state field; avoid toggle buttons that use ambiguous images instead of plain caption text; don't use pop-up boxes or dialog boxes needlessly.

➔ To learn how to build pop-up boxes and dialog boxes, **see** "Creating a Form Pop-Up Box or Dialog Box," **p. 103**. (Chapter 5)

Also, don't show the users fields that they'll never need to fill in. This is certainly true of most AutoNumber fields, and it goes without saying that sensitive data should be displayed only to those with the authorization to see it.

5. Don't Neglect the Keyboard

We tend to assume that Windows users are primarily mouse users and that therefore they prefer to select form fields and control values by clicking. That might be true some of the time, but many form users are in "typing mode," so it's faster and easier to keep their hands poised over the keyboard instead of making forays over to the mouse. This is particularly true for order takers and other professional data entry operators who are keyboarding exp erts. Therefore, be sure to edit labels to set up shortcuts for each field. Also, if a field recognizes a particular key combination (such as Ctrl+; for today's date or Ctrl+: for the current time), add a label to the form that lets the users know.

6. Watch the Field Order (and the Tab Order, Too)

I mentioned earlier that an Access form based on a paper form should display the fields in the same order as they appear in the paper version. Even if you're not using a paper form as a model, form fields often have an internal logic. For example, an order form should always take the customer information before the order details. Similarly, address fields should always follow the standard street-city-region-country-postal code order. Always examine the underlying data to look for these "natural" field orders and then set up your form accordingly.

After you've gone to this trouble, be sure to check the tab order (in Design view, choose Arrange, Tab Order). Few things are as frustrating to the users as pressing Tab and moving to some field other than the one that appears to be next on the form.

7. Watch Your Screen Resolution

It's a common design mistake to build a form on a screen with the resolution set at 1,280×1,024 or even 1,600×1,200 and then realize that only part of the form shows up on a 1,024×768 display. You need to determine the lowest screen resolution that is used by a significant portion of your users and then build your form with your own screen set to that screen area. In most offices today, 1,024×768 is a good design resolution (few people still run at 800×600).

Finally, if your users have a uniform screen type—for example, 14-inch laptop screens or 17-inch monitor sizes—be sure to test your form on this screen before deploying it, particularly, if your own computer has a significantly larger screen size.

8. Make Form Text Readable

Few things are as frustrating as screen text that is unreadable. This is particularly true for Access forms where the text is usually there for an important reason (such as naming a field or providing explanatory text). Therefore, take care when you apply font formatting to your forms. See "Enhancing Form Text," later in this chapter, for some pointers on using fonts.

9. Go Easy on the Extras

You see later in this chapter that you can spruce up a drab form with extras such as colors, images, and various special effects. When used judiciously, these goodies can add visual interest to a form. Watch out, though: if you overdo it, your form can easily become a hard-to-read, hard-to-navigate mess that distracts the users and either slows down data entry or causes data entry errors (or both). When it comes to form extras, moderation is always the key.

10. Organize Your Form Controls

Most forms have groups of related controls. For example, on an order form, one group might be the customer's name and address data, another might be overall order data such as the shipping method and payment info, and another might be the order details. You can make data entry much easier if you use visual aids to emphasize these groupings. As you see in the next section, you can use lines, borders, option groups, and tab controls to achieve this.

Organizing Controls on the Form

A form that holds just three or four fields doesn't require much in the way of organization. You can more or less just plop the fields onto the form, pretty them up a bit, and then move on. However, it's a rare form that contains so few fields. It's much more common for a form to contain 10, 15, even 20 controls, all vying for the user's attention. Tossing all those controls onto the form willy-nilly is definitely not a good idea: Inexperienced form users are likely to get confused; busy users will resent the time it takes to determine what's what; and expert operators will get frustrated by the inefficient and tiring layout.

Proper control organization doesn't imply anything elaborate. It just means three things:

- Grouping related controls together.
- Putting individual controls in a natural order and adjusting the tab order so that moving through the fields using the Tab key reflects this natural order.
- Making it clear which controls belong to which groups.

The first two are a product of the underlying data, as described in the previous section. In the following sections, you learn a few visual aids that can help enclose controls into groups and separate these groups so that users can easily see the overall organization of the form.

Making Good Use of Lines and Rectangles

The Form Design view's Design tab contains two buttons in the Control group that create graphic elements on the form: Line and Rectangle. Here's how you use these tools to organize a form's controls:

■ Use a rectangle to organize a set of related controls into a group. Place the controls together on the form and then draw the rectangle around them.

■ Use a line to separate groups and individual controls. Add a bit of extra space between the bottom (or right) of one control or group and the top (or left) of the next control or group. Then draw the line in this extra space.

> **TIP** Most people find it a bit tricky to draw a straight line using the standard click-and-drag technique. To ensure a perfectly straight line every time, hold down the Shift key and then click and drag.

In both cases, you click the button in the Controls group and then click and drag on the form to draw the line or rectangle.

Figure 4.1 shows a sample form that uses these techniques. Note, too, the use of two lines to represent the double line that often appears above a total.

Figure 4.1
Use rectangles to organize related controls into groups and use lines to separate individual controls and groups.

After you've drawn your line or rectangle, you can use the following Design tab lists to format the graphic:

■ **Fill/Back Color (Font group)**—Click a color swatch in this list to set the color of the rectangle's background.

> **TIP** If you add a rectangle around a set of existing controls and then set the rectangle's background color, the controls will be obscured by the nontransparent background. To fix this, select the rectangle and then choose Arrange, Send to Back. This changes the Z-order so that the rectangle is now "behind" the other controls.

- **Line Thickness (Controls group)**—Click an item in this list to set the width of the line or the rectangle's border.

- **Line Type (Controls group)**—Click an item in this list to set the style (such as dotted or dashed) of the line or the rectangle's border.

- **Line Color (Controls group)**—Click a color swatch in this list to set the color of the line or the rectangle's border.

- **Special Effect (Controls group)**—Click this list and then choose the effect you want to apply to the line or the rectangle's border: Flat, Raised, Sunken, Etched, Shadowed, or Chiseled.

Organizing with Option Groups

You saw in Chapter 3 that you can use an option group control to create a set of mutually exclusive choices using option buttons (or, less often, check boxes or toggle buttons). You use an option group to define the set because any option button within the group becomes one of the mutually exclusive options.

→ For the details on creating option buttons within an option group, **see** "Using Option Buttons to Present a Limited Number of Choices," **p. 59.** (Chapter 3)

However, the option group itself is really just a rectangle with a label in the upper-left corner. That label is a handy thing because it enables you to supply the group with a name or short description, which adds to the readability and ease-of-use of the form. Not only that, but there are no rules against using option groups to organize other kinds of controls such as text boxes and lists.

Here are the steps to follow to create an option group for organizing controls:

1. Adjust the controls that form the group so that they reside in the same part of the form, with no other controls nearby.

2. In the Design tab's Controls group, deactivate the Use Control Wizards button.

3. In the Controls group, click the Option Group button.

4. Draw the option group around the controls.

5. Format the option group's background color, and color, width, and special effect of its border, as necessary. (If you set the background color, choose Design, Send to Back to bring the other controls on top of the option group.)

6. Choose Design, Property Sheet to display the option group's property sheet.

7. In the Other tab, change the Tab Stop property to No. (This prevents Access from selecting the option group when users are pressing Tab to navigate the form.)

8. Close the property sheet.

Figure 4.2 shows the Mortgage Calculator form that uses two option groups to organize the form's text boxes.

4

Figure 4.2
Use an option group to
organize related controls
and include a label
to name or describe
the group.

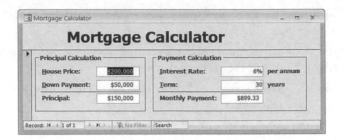

--- CAUTION ---

After you add the option group to the form, don't cut two or more check boxes or toggle buttons
from elsewhere in the form and then paste them inside the option group. If you do that, Access will
think you're creating a true option group and will set up the check boxes or toggle buttons as mutually exclusive choices.

Organizing with a Tab Control

Rectangles and option groups are simple methods for organizing related controls visually
and thus helping users make sense of the form. However, there are two situations in which
these methods fall down on the job.

The first situation is when you need the form to show multiple sets of the same (or similar)
data. For example, suppose you have a form that shows values for sales and expense categories. You might want the form to be capable of showing separate data for various company divisions. One solution is to create separate option groups for each division and
populate each group with the same controls, but this is clearly inefficient. A second solution
is to use a list or a set of option buttons. This approach works, but it might not be obvious
to the users how they are supposed to display different sets of data, and these extra controls
just serve to clutter the frame.

The second situation is when you have a lot of controls. In this case, even the judicious use
of option groups won't be enough to keep your form from becoming difficult to navigate
and understand.

In both of these situations, the solution is to create a form that looks and acts like the
tabbed dialog boxes you work with in Windows, Office, and other modern programs:

- When you have multiple sets of similar data, create a tabbed form where each tab represents a different set of data.

- When you have a large number of controls, you're better off creating a tabbed form
  that spreads the controls over several tabs, with each tab containing a set of related
  controls.

You create a tabbed form using the tab control. Here are the steps to follow:

1. In the Design tab's Controls group, click the Tab Control button.
2. Draw the tab control on the form.
3. If you already had controls on the form, choose Arrange, Send to Back to bring the other controls on top of the tab control.

Here's a list of techniques you can use to adjust and format the tab control to get the setup you want:

- **To add another page**—The default tab control comes with two tabs, or *pages* as Access calls them. To add another page, right-click the tab control and then click Insert Page.

- **To move a page**—Right-click the tab control and then click Page Order to display the Page Order dialog box. Click the page you want to adjust and then click either Move Up or Move Down until the page is in the position you want.

- **To delete a page**—Right-click the page and then click Delete Page.

- **To change the caption of a page**—Double-click the page caption to display its property sheet, choose the Format tab, and then change the Caption property.

- **To add a control to a page**—Click the page caption to display the page and then draw the control inside the page.

- **To move an existing control to another page**—Select the control; choose Home, Cut; click the caption of the page to which you want to move the control; and then choose Home, Paste.

Figure 4.3 shows the Order Details form that uses a tab control to divide the fields into three pages: Order Details (such as products ordered, quantities, unit prices, and discounts), Shipping Information (such as shipping company, ship date, and the ship-to address), and Payment Information (payment type, payment date, and payment notes).

Figure 4.3
Use a tab control to divide a form's fields into separate pages that contain related controls.

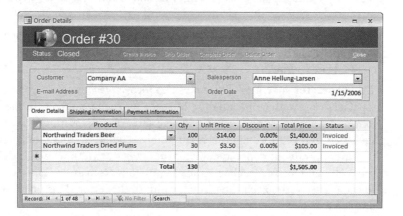

Enhancing Form Text

Most form builders seem not to think too much about the text that appears in a form's labels, text boxes, and other controls. They usually accept the Access defaults and move on to seemingly more important duties such as getting the fields placed just so. But the text should be an integral part of the overall form design. After all, nicely formatted characters make the form readable and easy on the eyes, whereas slapdash text formatting can ruin an otherwise successful form.

Text is important because its readability and visual appeal are centered around four characteristics that define what might be called the "architecture" of each character:

- **The typeface**—This is a distinctive design that is common to any related set of letters, numbers, and symbols. This design gives each character a particular shape and thickness that is unique to the typeface and difficult to classify. However, three main categories serve to distinguish all typefaces:
  - **Serif**—This style of typeface contains fine cross strokes (called *feet*) at the extremities of each character. These subtle appendages give the typeface a traditional, classy look that's most often used for long stretches of text. Times New Roman is an example of a serif typeface.
  - **Sans serif**—This style of typeface doesn't contain these cross strokes. As a result, sans serif typefaces usually have a cleaner, more modern look that works best for headings and titles. Calibri is an example of a sans serif typeface.
  - **Decorative**—This style of typeface is usually a special design that is supposed to convey a particular effect. So, for example, if your document needs a fancy, handwritten effect, something like French Script MT is perfect.
- **The type size**—This measures how tall a font is. The standard unit of measurement is the *point*, and there are 72 points in an inch. So, for example, the letters in a 24-point font are twice as tall as those in a 12-point font. Technically, type size is measured from the highest point of a tall letter, such as *f*, to the lowest point of an underhanging letter, such as *g*. (In case you're wondering, this book is laid out in a 9.5-point Janson text font.)
- **The type style**—This refers to extra attributes added to the typeface, such as **bold**, *italic*, and <u>underlining</u>. These styles are normally used to highlight or add emphasis to elements of a form.
- **The character spacing**—This takes two forms: *monospaced* or *proportional*. Monospaced typefaces reserve the same amount of space for each character. In the Courier New font, for example, skinny letters such as *i* and *l* take up as much space as wider letters such as *m* and *w*. Although this is admirably egalitarian, these fonts tend to look like they were produced with a typewriter (in other words, they're ugly). By contrast, in a proportional typeface, such as Arial, Times New Roman, or Tahoma, the space allotted to each letter varies according to the width of the letter. This gives the text a more natural look.

See Figure 4.4, in the next section, to view some examples of typefaces, type sizes, and character spacing.

Formatting Text

To format a control's text, select it and then use either of the following:

- **The Ribbon**—As pointed out in Figure 4.4, the Design tab's Font group offers six controls for formatting text: Font (that is, the typeface), Font Size, Bold, Italic, Underline, and Font Color. You can also use the Align Left, Center, and Align Right buttons to align the text within the control.

- **The property sheet**—In a control's property sheet, the Format tab has six text-related properties: Font Name (typeface), Font Size, Font Weight (varieties of boldness), Font Italic, Font Underline, and Fore Color. You can also use the Text Align property to choose the alignment within the control.

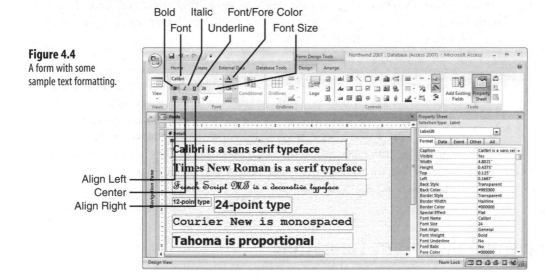

Figure 4.4
A form with some sample text formatting.

Text Formatting Tips and Guidelines

Access makes it easy to add unique and eye-catching fonts to all your forms. However, some restraint is called for here. Nothing looks worse than—or is as confusing as—a form with too many fonts crammed together. This is known in the trade as the *ransom note look*, and it's to be avoided at all costs. Here are a few pointers for keeping your form text looking good:

- Don't make the type size too small. Access defaults to 11-point type, which is usually fine, but anything smaller is usually too small.

■ Use a larger type size for titles and headings. Form titles (which should be placed in the Form Header section) should stand out from the rest of the text, so use a relatively large type size for them.

■ Use a plain, unadorned typeface. A form is no place for fancy, decorative typefaces. A plain typeface, particularly a sans serif typeface such as Arial, displays best onscreen.

■ Don't mix typefaces. Try to restrict your typefaces to one, or at most two, per form. If you need various looks, use larger sizes or different styles of the same typeface.

■ Make use of bolding. You can make field names and other labels stand out from the form background by formatting them as bold (see "Enhancing Form Text," earlier in this chapter). However, you rarely have to make the text inside a control (particularly a text box or list box) bold because the white control background provides enough contrast. Other text effects such as italics and underlining should be avoided.

■ Watch the background. For maximum readability, there should be significant contrast between the text color and the form's background color. Dark text on a light background is best. Don't use a background image unless it is relatively faint and the text stands out well against it (you might have to use bolding, a larger type size, or a darker text color to achieve this effect).

> **NOTE** A given typeface covers not only the letters, numbers, and symbols you can see on your keyboard, but dozens of others as well—for example, the pound sign (£), the copyright symbol (©), and the trademark symbol (™). If you need to add these or other nonkeyboard characters to your form text, an easy way to go about it is to use Windows' Character Map program. Choose Start, All Programs, Accessories, System Tools, Character Map. In the Character Map window, double-click the character you want and then click Copy. Return to your form, position the cursor where you want the character to appear, and then choose Home, Paste.

Applying Fancier Form Formatting

Business forms don't need to be fancy. In fact, in most cases forms should *not* be fancy because a garish or overdone design can distract users. However, that doesn't mean your forms need to be drab, dull affairs. As long as you wield a relatively light touch, there's no reason why you can't use colors, images, and other effects to add visual interest to the form or to apply your company's color scheme or logo to give the form an official feel. The rest of this chapter takes you through these nonessential form-beautification techniques.

Working with Colors

You've already seen three ways to adjust form colors:

■ To adjust the background color of a control, select it and then use the Design tab's Fill/Back Color list (in the Fonts group) to choose a new color. You can also open the control's property sheet and adjust the Back Color property on the Format tab.

- To adjust the text color of a control, select it and then use the Design tab's Font Color list (in the Fonts group) to choose a new color. You can also open the control's property sheet and adjust the `Fore Color` property on the Format tab.

- To adjust the line color or the border color of a control, select it and then use the Design tab's Line Color list (in the Controls group) to choose a new color. You can also open the control's property sheet and adjust the `Border Color` property on the Format tab.

Creating a Custom Color

The Design tab lists give you a selection of nearly 100 colors. However, you can use the Colors dialog box to create a custom color. Follow these steps to get started:

1. Select the control you want to work with.

2. In the Design tab, pull down the color list you want to work with and then choose <u>M</u>ore Colors. Access displays the Color dialog box.

3. Click the Custom tab, shown in Figure 4.5.

Figure 4.5
Use the Custom tab of the Color dialog box to create custom colors.

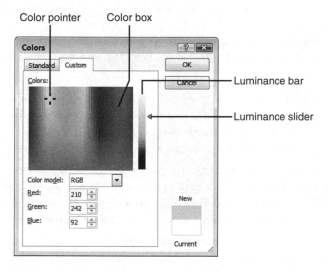

To create your own color, you can use one of two methods. The first method uses the fact that you can create any color in the spectrum by mixing the three primary colors: red, green, and blue. The Color dialog box lets you enter specific numbers between 0 and 255 for each of these colors, by using the <u>R</u>ed, <u>G</u>reen, and <u>B</u>lue spin buttons. (Make sure that RGB is selected in the Color Mo<u>d</u>el list.) A lower number means the color is less intense, and a higher number means the color is more intense.

To give you some idea of how this works, see Table 4.1, which lists eight common colors and their respective red, green, and blue numbers.

Table 4.1	The Red, Green, and Blue Numbers for Eight Common Colors		
Color	**Red**	**Green**	**Blue**
Black	0	0	0
White	255	255	255
Red	255	0	0
Green	0	255	0
Blue	0	0	255
Yellow	255	255	0
Magenta	255	0	255
Cyan	0	255	255

> **NOTE** Whenever the Red, Green, and Blue values are equal, you get a grayscale color. Lower numbers produce darker grays, and higher numbers produce lighter grays.

The second method for selecting colors involves setting three attributes—hue, saturation, and luminance. Use the Color Model list to click HSL and then adjust the following spin buttons:

- **Hue**—This number (which is more or less equivalent to the term *color*) measures the position on the color spectrum. Lower numbers indicate a position near the red end, and higher numbers move through the yellow, green, blue, and violet parts of the spectrum. As you increase the hue, the color pointer moves from left to right.

- **Sat**—This number is a measure of the purity of a given hue. A saturation setting of 255 means that the hue is a pure color. Lower numbers indicate that more gray is mixed with the hue until, at 0, the color becomes part of the grayscale. As you increase the saturation, the color pointer moves toward the top of the color box.

- **Lum**—This number is a measure of the brightness of a color. Lower numbers are darker, and higher numbers are brighter. The luminance bar to the right of the color box shows the luminance scale for the selected color. As you increase the luminance, the slider moves toward the top of the bar.

To create a custom color, you can either enter values in the text boxes, as just described, or you can use the mouse to click inside the color box and luminance bar. The New box shows the custom color. When you're done, click OK.

Using Color Effectively

Now you know how to apply colors to your forms, but that's only half the battle. Colors that are poorly matched or improperly applied can make a form look worse, not better. This section examines a few basics for effectively using colors in your forms.

With so many colors available, the temptation is to go overboard and use a dozen different hues on each page. However, using too many colors can confuse your users and even cause eye fatigue. Try to stick to two or three colors at most. If you must use more, try to use different shades of two or three hues.

Before finalizing your color scheme, you need to make sure the colors you've selected work well together. For example, blue and black are often difficult to distinguish and green/red combinations clash. Other color combinations to avoid are red/blue, green/blue, and brown/black. On the other hand, color combinations such as red/yellow, gray/red, and blue/yellow go well together, as do contrasting shades of the same color, such as black and gray.

> **CAUTION**
>
> Another good reason to avoid using too much green and red in your worksheets is that approximately 8% of the male population suffers from red-green color blindness.

When selecting colors, think about the psychological impact that your scheme will have on your users. Studies have shown that "cool" colors such as blue and gray evoke a sense of dependability and trust. Use these colors for a more business-like appearance. For forms that require a little more excitement, "warm" colors such as red, yellow, and orange can evoke a festive, fun atmosphere. For a safe, comfortable ambiance, try using brown and yellow. For an environmental touch, use green and brown.

Adding Images to Your Forms

A nice way to spruce up a form is to add an unbound image. This can be a company, department, or project logo; clip art related to the form's purpose; or an image related to the form's underlying data.

Follow these steps to add an image to the form:

1. In the Design tab's Controls group, click the Image button.
2. On the form, click and drag to draw a rectangle to contain the image. When you release the mouse button, Access displays the Insert Picture dialog box.
3. Open the folder containing the image you want, click the image file, and then click OK.

4. Resize the image control, as needed.

5. Choose Design, Property Sheet to display the image control's property sheet.

6. Display the Format tab.

7. Use the Size Mode property to choose one of the following settings:

   - Clip—The image is displayed using its actual dimensions. If the image is larger than the control, the edges of the image are clipped to fit.
   - Stretch—The image is stretched or shrunken vertically and horizontally so that it fills the entire control.
   - Zoom—The image is enlarged or reduced until it fills the control either vertically or horizontally; the image's original proportions are maintained.

8. Use the Picture Alignment property to specify how you want the image aligned within the control.

9. If you selected either Clip or Zoom as the Size Mode, use the Picture Tiling property to determine whether you want the image repeated (tiled) across the background so that it fills the entire control. Select Yes for tiling; select No to display just a single image.

10. Close the property sheet.

Creating a Shadow Effect for Text

In the Design tab's Control group, the Special Effects list includes a Shadow effect, which applies a shadow to the control borders. What if you want the same effect with the text in a label? You can do this by following these steps:

1. Add the label to the form, edit the text, and set up the text formatting as needed.

2. With the label selected, choose Design, Line Color, Transparent.

3. Press Ctrl+C to copy the label and then press Ctrl+V to paste a copy of the label.

4. Move the copy of the label so that it is offset slightly from the original (slightly below and slightly to the right is the usual shadow position).

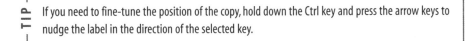
TIP — If you need to fine-tune the position of the copy, hold down the Ctrl key and press the arrow keys to nudge the label in the direction of the selected key.

5. Choose Design, Font Color and then click a relatively light color for the shadow label (such as light gray).

6. Choose Arrange, Send to Back. Access places the shadow label behind the original label.

Figure 4.6 shows an example of shadowed text.

Figure 4.6
Use a duplicate of a label to create a text shadow effect.

From Here

→ For the basics of form design, **see** "Creating a Form in Design View," **p. 15** (Chapter 1)

→ To learn some techniques for protecting a form and its data, **see** "Case Study: Protecting the Form and Data from Other Users," **p. 26**. (Chapter 1)

→ For a number of techniques for working with controls, **see** "Manipulating Form Controls," **p. 29**. (Chapter 2)

→ To get the details on form data validation, **see** "Preventing Errors by Validating Data," **p. 50**. (Chapter 3)

→ For other ways to ensure accurate data entry, **see** "Using Controls to Limit Data Entry Choices," **p. 55**. (Chapter 3)

→ For the details on creating option buttons within an option group, **see** "Using Option Buttons to Present a Limited Number of Choices," **p. 59**. (Chapter 3)

→ For the details of subforms, **see** "Creating a Multiple-Table Form," **p. 95**. (Chapter 5)

→ To learn how to build pop-up boxes and dialog boxes, **see** "Creating a Form Pop-Up Box or Dialog Box," **p. 103**. (Chapter 5)

→ To learn how to work with PivotChart forms, **see** "Creating a PivotChart Form," **p. 108** (Chapter 5)

4

Creating Specialized Forms

5

Most of the forms you'll build and use will have data entry as their main purpose. However, Access forms are versatile enough to take you well beyond straightforward data input. For example, in Chapter 2, "Working with Form Controls," I showed you a form designed to be used as a mortgage calculator, meaning it had no data entry duties at all.

You'll see some similar forms in this chapter, including forms that enable you to display startup splash screens, dialog boxes, and "switchboard" forms that give the users easy ways to open tables, reports, and other forms. You'll start by learning how to build forms that incorporate multiple tables.

Creating a Multiple-Table Form

After you set up a query that includes two or more tables, as explained in Chapter 12, "Working with Multiple-Table Queries," using this query as the underlying data source in a form is straightforward. However, there's another way that you can use multiple tables with forms: by creating subforms. The next few sections show you various ways to create and work with subforms to build a multiple-table form.

➔ For the specifics of multiple-table queries, **see** "Working with Multiple Tables in a Query," **p. 271**. (Chapter 12)

Understanding Subforms

One of the handiest uses for related tables is to create a form that displays the related data from both tables simultaneously. For example, the form shown in Figure 5.1 contains data from two sources. The bulk of the form's fields displays data from the Orders table, and the datasheet in the bottom part of the form contains data from the Order Details table. Because the Orders and Order Details tables are related by the `Order ID` field, the order details shown are just those for the displayed order; when you move to a different order, the order details change accordingly.

Figure 5.1
A form showing data from two related tables.

Subform

This type of form is actually a combination of two separate forms. The regular form fields (in the example, the ones showing the Orders table data) are part of the *main form*, and the datasheet (the Order Details table data) is called the *subform*. A form/subform combination can be thought of as a main/detail form or a parent/child form.

Subforms are especially effective at showing dependent records from tables or queries participating in one-to-many relationships. In the preceding example, each item in the Orders table can have many related records in the Order Details table. Because of this, most subforms are viewed in datasheet mode, but this isn't a requirement (you can also view the subform in tabular or columnar mode). However, the main form can't be viewed in datasheet mode when a subform is present.

Creating a Form and Subform with the Form Wizard

→ **See** "Building a Standard Form," **p. 9**. (Chapter 1)

In Chapter 1, "Creating and Using a Form," you learned that, given a table that has a one-to-many relationship with another table, you can create a standard form/subform by selecting the main table (the "one" side of the one-to-many relationship) in the Navigation pane and then choosing Create, Form.

→ **See** "Creating Simple Forms with the Form Wizard," **p. 12**. (Chapter 1)

The problem with creating a standard form using this method is that Access adds *every* field to the form and subform. If you want to include only a subset of the field in your multiple-table form, then you need more control over the creation process. In Chapter 1, you also learned how to use the Form Wizard to create basic forms step by step. The Form Wizard is also an easy way to create a form/subform combination when you're working with multiple tables. Here are the steps to follow:

→ When using multiple tables and queries, you must have the relationships between those tables and queries established. For more information, **see** "Establishing Table Relationships," **p. 267**. (Chapter 12)

1. In the Navigation pane, click the table or query you want to use for the main form.

2. Choose Create, More Forms, Form Wizard.

3. In the first of the wizard's dialog boxes, for each field you want to include in the form, click the field in the Available Fields list and click the > button. (If you want to include all the fields, click the >> button.)

4. To add another table or query to the form, click it in the Table/Queries list and then repeat step 3.

5. When you're done adding data sources, click Next.

6. Use the next wizard dialog box (shown in Figure 5.2) to click the table or query that contains the data to be displayed in the main form. Also, make sure the Form with Subform(s) option is activated. Click Next.

Figure 5.2
Use this Form Wizard dialog box to select which data source is displayed in the main form.

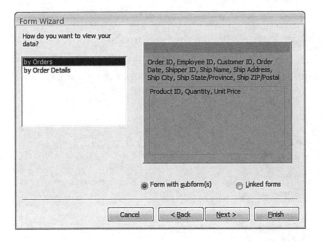

7. The next Form Wizard dialog box asks you to choose the layout of the subform. You have two choices (click Next after you've made your selection):

   • **Tabular**—The fields are arranged in a table, with the field names at the top and the records in rows.

   • **Datasheet**—The fields are arranged in a datasheet layout.

8. The next wizard dialog box asks you to select one of the predefined themes. Click the theme you want to use and then click Next.

9. The last wizard dialog box lets you modify the name of the form and subform. Suggestions are already in place in the Form and Subform text boxes; these suggestions are based on the names of the underlying tables or queries, but you can enter any names that don't conflict with an existing form.

10. If you want to use the form right away, leave the Open the Form to View or Enter Information option activated. Alternatively, click Modify the Form's Design to open the form in Design view.

11. Click Finish to complete the form.

Creating a Subform in the Form Design View

If you've already started your form, you can still add a subform in Design view by using the Subform control. Access even comes with a handy Subform Wizard that takes you step by step through the process of setting up the subform. The next two sections show you how to create a subform from a table or query and from an existing form.

Creating a Subform Using Another Table or Query

If you want to base your subform on the fields from another table or query, here are the steps to follow to add the subform using the Subform Wizard:

1. In the Form Design View, click the Design tab, make sure the Use Control Wizards button is activated, and then click the Subform/Subreport button in the Controls group.

2. Draw the subform on the form. Access launches the Subform Wizard, as shown in Figure 5.3.

Figure 5.3
The Subform Wizard makes it easy to add a subform to an existing form.

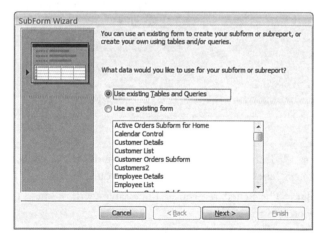

3. Activate the Use Existing Tables and Queries option and click Next.

4. Use the Table/Queries list to choose the underlying data source for the subform. Then, for each field you want to include in the subform, highlight the field in the Available Fields list and click the > button. (If you want to select all the fields, click the >> button.) Click Next.

5. Use the next wizard dialog box to choose the field that links the main form and the subform. As long as the tables are related (which they should be for this to work), Access will establish the correct linking field automatically. (If not, you can always activate the Define My Own option and set up the link fields yourself.) Click Next.

6. Enter a name for the subform and click Finish to complete your work.

Creating a Subform Using Another Form

Access also enables you to use an existing form as a subform. That is, you can draw the subform control on your form and then embed the existing form within that control. This capability is useful if you have a specific subform layout in mind and you want to create that layout beforehand.

If you want to base your subform on an existing form, here are the steps to follow to add the subform using the Subform Wizard:

1. Create and save the other form, if you haven't done so already.

2. In the Form Design view, click the Design tab, make sure the Use Control Wizards button is activated, and then click the Subform/Subreport button in the Controls group.

3. Draw the subform on the form. Access launches the Subform Wizard.

4. Activate the Use an Existing Form option and use the list provided to select the form you want to use. Click Next.

5. Use the next wizard dialog box to choose the field that links the main form and the subform. As long as the tables are related (which they should be for this to work), Access will establish the correct linking field automatically. (If not, you can always activate the Define My Own option and set up the link fields yourself.) Click Next.

6. Enter a name for the subform and click Finish to complete your work.

Working with Form Command Buttons

As you know all too well from working with dialog boxes in Windows applications, you use a command button to launch some action. For example, you usually click an OK button to put dialog box settings into effect, and you normally use a Cancel button to close a dialog box without performing any action. Other common dialog box command buttons are Print, Close, and the Back, Next, and Finish buttons that are standard features of the Microsoft Office wizards.

Access also enables you to add one or more command buttons to your forms. You'll see in several places later in this chapter that you need command buttons for some specialized forms (such as a switchboard and a pop-up box). However, you can also use command buttons for actions such as navigating and manipulating records, working with forms and reports, running macros, and even quitting Access.

This section gets you up to speed with adding and configuring command buttons using the Command Button Wizard. Here are the steps to follow to get started with this wizard:

1. In the Form Design view, click the Design tab, make sure the Use Control Wizards button is activated, and then click Button in the Controls group.

2. Move to the form and drag a rectangle to the desired button size. As soon as you release the mouse, Access launches the Command Button Wizard, as shown in Figure 5.4.

Figure 5.4
Use the first wizard dialog box to select the action you want to associate with the button.

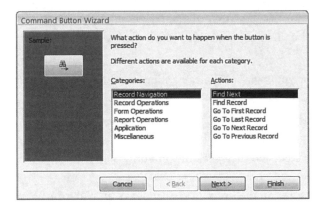

3. A button on a form can perform a number of different actions, which I've summarized in Table 5.1. Select an item in the Categories list and then select an operation in the Actions list. Click Next.

Table 5.1 Actions Available for the Command Button Tool

Action	Description
Record Navigation Category	
Find Next	Navigates to the next record that matches the search settings specified in the most recent Find operation.
Find Record	Displays the Find and Replace dialog box to enable the users to perform a Find or a Find and Replace operation.
Go to First Record	Navigates to the first record in the form's data source.
Go to Last Record	Navigates to the last record in the form's data source.

Action	Description
Go to Next Record	Navigates to the next record in the form's data source.
Go to Previous Record	Navigates to the previous record in the form's data source.

Record Operations Category

Add New Record	Adds a new record to the form's data source.
Delete Record	Deletes the current record from the form's data source.
Duplicate Record	Makes a copy of the current record.
Print Record	Prints the current record.
Save Record	Saves the current record.
Undo Record	Cancels the most recent operation performed on the current record.

Form Operations Category

Apply Form Filter	Filters the current form.
Close Form	Closes the current form.
Edit Form Filter	Displays the Filter window to enable the users to enter filter criteria.
Open Form	Opens a specified form.
Print a Form	Prints a specified form.
Print Current Form	Prints the current form.
Refresh Form Data	Refreshes the form's data source to display the most up-to-date data.

Report Operations Category

Mail Report	Emails a specified report.
Open Report	Opens a specified report.
Preview Report	Displays a specified report in the print preview window.
Print Report	Prints a specified report.
Send Report to File	Sends a specified report to a file (the name and location of which are chosen by the user).

Application Category

Quit Application	Shuts down Microsoft Access.

Miscellaneous Category

Auto Dialer	Displays the AutoDialer utility, which dials the phone number contained in the field that currently has the focus.
Print Table	Prints the data from a specified table.
Run Macro	Launches a specified macro.
Run Query	Launches a specified query.

5

The next step in the Command Button Wizard depends on the action you chose. For example, if you chose the Open Form action, the wizard asks you to specify which form you want the button to open.

The wizard then asks you to choose how the button should appear. You have two choices (click <u>N</u>ext after you've clicked the option you want):

- **<u>T</u>ext**—Choose this option to display a word or phrase on the button. Use the text box provided to enter your text.

- **<u>P</u>icture**—Choose this option to display a picture on the button. Activate the <u>S</u>how All Pictures check box to see a full list of the available pictures.

In the final wizard dialog box, enter a name for the command button and then click <u>F</u>inish to complete the operation.

CASE STUDY

Creating a Switchboard Form

Although there are a number of ways to open a form, you might not want all your forms to be available to novice users. For example, you might not want users to have access to the Forms section of the Navigation pane just in case they accidentally make changes to a form's layout. As an alternative, you can create a separate form—called a *switchboard*—that launches other forms.

A switchboard has no underlying data source. Instead, you populate it with command buttons, as described in the previous section. In most cases, you select the Open Form action (under the Form Operations category) and then select the form that you want to open when the user clicks the button. Note, too, that after you select the form you want to open and click <u>N</u>ext, the Command Button Wizard displays the following options:

- **Open the Form and Find Specific <u>D</u>ata to Display**—This option is designed to display only those records in the other form's underlying data source that are related to the current record. Because your switchboard has no data source, this option does not apply.

- **Open the Form and Show <u>A</u>ll the Records**—Choose this option to display all the records in the form's underlying data source. This is the option to choose if you just want the button to open another form.

Note, too, that it's almost always a good idea to use text on the button face. A caption such as "Open the Customers Form" or "Display Employees" is always easier for users to understand than just a picture.

Of course, a switchboard doesn't have to just open other forms. Here's a short list of actions that are commonly added to switchboards:

- Printing a table (the Print Table action)
- Printing a report (the Print Report action)

- Running a custom macro (the Run Macro action)
- Shutting down Access (the Quit Application action)
- Closing the switchboard (the Close Form action)

Figure 5.5 shows an example of a switchboard form. If you want your switchboard to appear when you start the database, see "Creating a Startup Form," later in this chapter.

Figure 5.5
Use a switchboard to open forms, print tables and reports, run a macro, or even quit Access.

Creating a Form Pop-Up Box or Dialog Box

When you display a form, it becomes just another open window (or tab) in the main Access window. If you have other objects open—tables, queries, forms, reports, and so on—you can switch to them and they appear "on top" of the form you were viewing. This is normal window behavior. However, sometimes this behavior might not be what you want:

- You might want the capability to switch to another window but have your form remain on top at all times. A form that stays on top of other windows but enables users to switch to another window is called a *pop-up*.

- You might want the capability to keep your form on top while preventing users from switching to another window (or even interacting with the Access Ribbon and Navigation pane) until they close your form. This is the same behavior as exhibited by most dialog boxes. A form that stays on top of other windows and doesn't enable users to switch to another window is called a *modal form*.

The next couple of sections show you how to create these forms.

Creating a Pop-Up Form

A pop-up form is useful if you have a control or other data that you want to keep handy for users to view or interact with. For example, you might want to display a calendar control so users can check dates before entering them into another form. You could add a command button to your form (see "Working with Form Command Buttons," earlier in this chapter) and configure the button to open your pop-up form.

→   To learn how to use the ActiveX Calendar control that comes with Office, **see** "Entering Dates Using a Calendar," **p. 71** (Chapter 3)

Follow these steps to convert a form into a pop-up:

1. In Design view, select the form.
2. Choose Design, Property Sheet to display the form's property sheet.
3. In the Other tab, set the `Pop Up` property to `Yes`.
4. Close the property sheet.

Creating a Modal Form

When you work in certain programs, you may come across dialog boxes that don't let you interact with the program until you've dismissed the dialog box. These are called *modal* dialog boxes, and you can apply the same modal feature to your forms, That is, the user won't be able to interact with anything else in Access until he or she has closed the modal form. A modal form is useful for building a dialog box or other form that requires users to deal with the form before moving on to anything else. Follow these steps to convert a regular form into a modal one:

1. In Design view, select the form.
2. Choose Design, Property Sheet to display the form's property sheet.
3. In the Other tab, set the `Modal` property to `Yes`.
4. For a true dialog box look, set the following `Format` properties to `No`:

   ```
   Record Selectors
   Navigation Buttons
   Dividing Lines
   ```
5. Close the property sheet.

> **NOTE**
> The `Modal` property takes precedence over the `Pop Up` property. That is, if you set both properties to `Yes`, the form becomes modal and you can't switch to another window or interact with Access.

> **NOTE**
> If you're creating your modal form from scratch, the best way to begin is to choose Create, More Forms, Modal Dialog.

Using a Custom Form with a Parameter Query

In Chapter 13, "Creating Advanced Queries," you learn how to set up a parameter query that prompts the user for a field criteria value before running the query. Unfortunately, the Enter Parameter Value dialog box that prompts for the parameter value isn't particularly user-friendly. For example, if you want users to type in a customer name, they must type the name exactly as it appears in the associated table, which is just asking for trouble.

➔ For the details on using parameters, **see** "Running Parameter Queries," **p. 302.** (Chapter 13)

A better solution is to design a form that displays the customer names in a combo box or list box. The users can then choose the customer from the list, and Access then uses that selection as the query parameter.

Unfortunately, it isn't possible to get Access to display a custom form in place of the Enter Parameter Value dialog box. However, it *is* possible to do the next best thing: select a value in an open form and use that value as the query parameter.

Creating the Custom Form

Here are some points to bear in mind when constructing your custom form:

- To avoid confusing the users, remove unneeded form elements such as the record selector buttons. In the form's property sheet, set the following Format properties to No:

  ```
  Record Selectors

  Navigation Buttons

  Dividing Lines
  ```

- The form doesn't have to be too fancy. In fact, because you'll be using the form to choose only a single value for the query parameter, you'll most likely want to include just a single combo box or list box on the form (or perhaps an option group, if that better suits your purpose), along with its label.

- If you use a combo box or list box, populate it with the values that you want the users to choose. This is almost always a field from a table or query, although sometimes you might want to specify the values yourself.

- If you use a wizard to set up the combo box or list box, and you populate the list with field values, bear in mind that the wizard assumes the bound list column is the primary key of the field's table. Therefore, you need to display the control's property sheet, select the Data tab, and change the Bound Column property to 2 (assuming the list field is the second one that appears in the Row Source SELECT statement; if not, substitute the appropriate number). See Figure 5.6.

- Add a command button to the form (see Figure 5.6) and set up the button to open the parameter query. (That is, in the first Command Button Wizard dialog box, choose the Miscellaneous category and then choose Run Query.)

5

- Consider changing the name of the control. You'll be using the name in the parameter query, so a meaningful name will make the parameter more readable. To change the name, display the control's property sheet, select the Other tab, and edit the `Name` property.

> **NOTE** In Figure 5.6, the name of the combo box is `cboCompanyName`. The `cbo` part is the standard programmers' prefix for a combo box. Others you can use are `lst` for a list box, `fra` for an option group (a frame), `opt` for an option button, `chk` for a check box, and `txt` for a text box.

- If you want to give the users the capability to enter wildcard characters instead of just choosing a specific value, use a combo box and be sure that its `Limit To List` property (on the property sheet's Data tab) is set to `No`.

- Although it's not shown in Figure 5.6, it's also a good idea to add a Cancel button to the custom form and to configure this button to run the Close Form operation. This gives users a way to bail out of the form without running the query, just in case they launch the form accidentally.

Figure 5.6
A custom form to use with a parameter query.

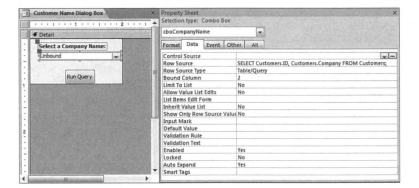

Adjusting the Parameter Query

With the custom form set up to your liking, open the parameter query in Design view. Delete the existing parameter text and replace it with the following:

```
Forms![FormName]![ControlName]
```

Here, replace *FormName* with the name of your custom form and replace *ControlName* with the name of the control that provides the parameter value.

For example, the form shown in Figure 5.6 is named Customer Name Dialog Box, and the combo box control is named `cboCompanyName`. Therefore, the parameter text looks like this, as shown in Figure 5.7:

```
Forms![Customer Name Dialog Box]![cboCompanyName]
```

Figure 5.7
Adjust the parameter
query so that the criteria
reference the control on
the custom form.

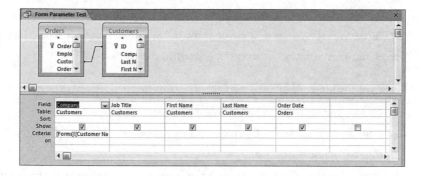

If you give the users the option of including one or more wildcard characters in the parameter value, change the parameter criteria to include the Like operator:

```
Like Forms![FormName]![ControlName]
```

Using the Custom Form and Parameter Query

You're now ready to use the custom form with the parameter query. Here are the steps to follow:

1. Run the custom form.
2. Select or enter a value in the custom form.
3. Run the parameter query.

As you can see in Figure 5.8, Access takes the value in the custom form—in this case, the company name Company D—and uses it as the criteria for the query's Company field.

Figure 5.8
The value chosen in the
custom form is used
as the criteria for the
parameter query.

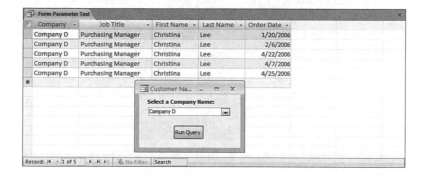

Creating a Startup Form

Displaying a form to the users immediately after they launch the database is often useful. The form can be any of the following:

■ A splash screen that displays the name of the company, department, or project, along with a logo or other image.

- A switchboard form, as described earlier in this chapter.
- A list of instructions that covers how to use the database or what the database contains.
- A summary of news or updates related to the database.

Here are the steps to follow to create a startup form:

1. Create and save the form you want to use.
2. Choose Office, Access Options to open the Access Options dialog box.
3. Click Current Database.
4. In the Display Form list, choose the form you want to appear at startup.
5. If you don't want the users to also have access to the Navigation pane, deactivate the Display Navigation Pane check box.
6. Click OK.
7. When Access warns you that you must restart the database to put the options into effect, click OK and then close and reopen the database.

> **TIP**
>
> Choosing not to display the Navigation pane at startup adds a bit of extra security to your database. However, what if you need to work with the database window yourself? Hold down the Shift key when you start the database to bypass all the startup options.

Creating a PivotChart Form

In Chapter 14, "Creating PivotTable Queries," you learn how to analyze data by displaying it in PivotTable format. (If you've never used a PivotTable before, see Chapter 14 for some background information.) You can also convert a PivotTable into a PivotChart, a data view that works well in a form. Note that Access uses slightly different terminology for a PivotChart than for a PivotTable:

- A PivotTable row field is called a *category field* in a PivotChart.
- A PivotTable column field is called a *series field* in a PivotChart.

Here are the steps to follow to build a PivotChart form:

1. In the Navigation pane, select the table or query that you want to use as the basis of the PivotChart.
2. Choose Create, PivotChart. Access creates a new PivotChart form and displays the field list for the underlying table or query, as shown in Figure 5.9.

Figure 5.9
Use the Create tab's
PivotChart button to
quickly create the skele-
ton of a PivotChart form.

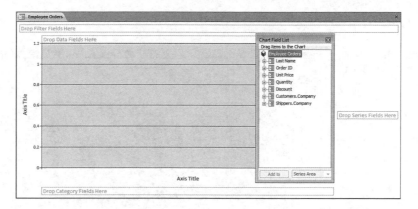

3. In the Chart Field List, click and drag the item you want to use as the category field and drop it on the Drop Category Fields Here area.

4. (Optional) Click and drag the item you want to use as the series field and drop it on the Drop Series Fields Here area.

5. Click and drag the item you want to use as the data field and drop it on the Drop Data Fields Here area.

6. Click and drag the item you want to use as the filter field and drop it on the Drop Filter Fields Here area.

7. Chose Design, Property Sheet to display the property sheet.

8. In the General tab, use the Select list to click Chart Workspace.

9. In the Add group, click the Add Title and Add Legend buttons.

10. In the General tab, use the Select list to choose Title. Display the Format tab and then edit the Caption property to the title you want.

11. In the General tab, use the Select list to choose Value Axis 1 Title. Display the Format tab and then edit the Caption property to the value axis title you want. (In a PivotChart, the value axis displays the data field values.)

12. In the General tab, use the Select list to choose Category Axis 1 Title. Display the Format tab and then edit the Caption property to the category axis title you want. (In a PivotChart, the category axis displays the category field values.)

13. Use the property sheet to format the other chart elements as required.

5

Figure 5.10 shows a completed PivotChart form.

Figure 5.10
A completed PivotChart form.

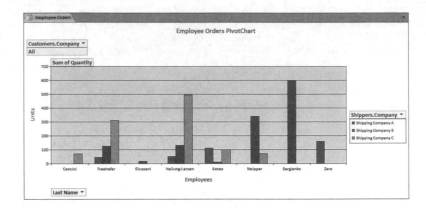

From Here

→   To learn about relational database concepts, **see** "Relational Database Fundamentals," **p. 259**. (Chapter 12)

→   To get the specifics of setting up a relationship between two tables, **see** "Establishing Table Relationships," **p. 267**. (Chapter 12)

→   For the details on using parameters, **see** "Running Parameter Queries," **p. 302** (Chapter 13)

→   To learn more about the Form Wizard, **see** "Creating Simple Forms with the Form Wizard," **p. 12**. (Chapter 1)

→   To get the details on moving, sizing, and performing other control chores, **see** "Manipulating Form Controls," **p. 29**. (Chapter 2)

→   For the specifics of the mortgage calculator mentioned at the beginning of this chapter, **see** "Case Study: Creating a Mortgage Calculator," **p. 46** (Chapter 2)

5

Designing and Customizing Reports

II

IN THIS PART

Creating and Publishing a Report

6

Most of the work you do with Access—whether it's creating tables, entering data, sorting, filtering, or querying—is work that, generally speaking, you do for yourself. It's valuable work, to be sure, but it's really just "behind-the-scenes" stuff. But what happens when it's time for the database equivalent of a coming-out party? That is, what about when you need to show off your data for all to see? When that happens, you need to create a *report*.

A report is a database object that organizes and formats your table or query data to make it presentable and meaningful to other people. With reports, you can organize data into groups; display subtotals and grand totals for appropriate fields; and add lines, graphics, and fonts to put your data in its best light.

Best of all, as you see in this chapter, various Access tools and wizards make it easy to create basic reports. (However, it's also possible to design your own reports from scratch, which you also learn to do in this chapter.)

Creating a Basic Report

By far, the easiest way to create a report is to use the Report command. It lets you create no-frills reports with just a few clicks of the mouse. The Report command—which you can use only on existing tables or queries—is fast and requires no input from you, as the following steps show:

1. In the Navigation window, click the table or query you want to use as the basis for the report.

2. Choose Create, Report.

Access analyzes the selected table or query and then creates a report similar to the one shown in Figure 6.1 for the Northwind Orders table.

> **NOTE** If the table has a field that's used as the basis of a one-to-many relationship with another table and the current table is the "one" side of that relationship, the "many" table's related data is also included in the report. In Figure 6.1, the data in the Employee, Customer, and Ship Via fields all comes from related tables.

Figure 6.1
An Orders table report created with the Report command.

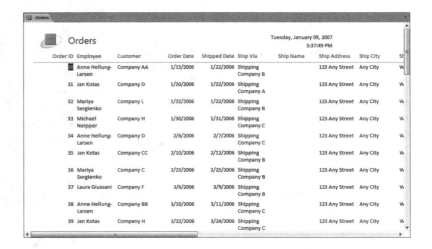

Creating Simple Reports with the Report Wizard

The Report command is a fast way to create a report, but it suffers from a lack of interaction. That is, you have no way of specifying the fields you want to see or the formatting style you want to use. For a bit more control over your reports, you can use the Report Wizard. The Report Wizard is more like a traditional Office wizard: It displays a series of dialog boxes that take you step by step through the entire report-creation process, as described here:

→ The Report Wizard even lets you select fields from multiple tables; **see** "Creating a Report and Subreport with the Report Wizard," **p. 191**. (Chapter 9)

1. In the Navigation pane, click the table or query you want to use as the report record source.

2. Choose Create, Report Wizard. Access displays the first Report Wizard dialog box, shown in Figure 6.2. The Table/Queries list shows the table or query that you chose in step 1.

3. For each field you want to include in the report, click the field in the Available Fields list and click the > button. (If you want to add all the fields, click the >> button.) When you're done, click Next.

Figure 6.2
Use this Report Wizard dialog box to select the table or query and the fields you want to use.

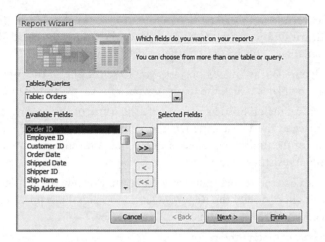

4. The Report Wizard now asks if you want any grouping levels. A *grouping level* is a field on which the report records are grouped. In the Orders table, for example, if you choose Employee ID as the grouping level, the orders are grouped by employee in the report. Click the field you want to use as a grouping level and then click >. Repeat if you want to use other fields as subgroups. Click Next when you're ready to continue.

> **NOTE** You can get more control over the grouping by clicking the Grouping Options button. In the Grouping Intervals dialog box, you can select a custom grouping level for each group-level field. For example, a text field enables you to group according to the first letter, first two letters, and so on; similarly, for a date field, you can group by week, month, quarter, and so on.

5. In the next wizard dialog box, use one or more of the four drop-down lists to select a sort order for the records. For each field, you can also click the toggle button to choose Ascending or Descending.

6. If you want to add calculations to a grouped report, click Summary Options to display the Summary Options dialog box. For any of the displayed fields, activate the Sum, Avg, Min, or Max check boxes to include those calculations in the report. You can also click the following options (click OK after you've made your choices and then click Next):

- **Detail and Summary**—Displays the records associated with each grouping as well as the summary calculations for the group.
- **Summary Only**—Displays only the summary calculations for each group.
- **Calculate Percent of Total for Sums**—Displays the percentage of the total represented by each group.

6

7. Choose the Layout and Orientation you want to use for the report. To ensure that all the fields fit within the width of the page, leave the Adjust the Field <u>W</u>idth So All Fields Fit on a Page check box activated. Click <u>N</u>ext to continue.

8. The next Report Wizard dialog box asks you to select one of the predefined AutoReport templates. Click the template you want to use and then click <u>N</u>ext.

9. The final wizard dialog box lets you modify the name of the report. A suggestion is already in place in the What Title Do You Want for Your Report? text box; it's based on the name of the underlying table or query, but you can enter any name that doesn't conflict with an existing report.

10. If you want to use the report right away, leave the <u>P</u>review the Report option activated. Alternatively, click <u>M</u>odify the Report's Design to open the report in Design view (see the next section, "Creating a Report in Design View").

11. Click <u>F</u>inish to complete the report.

This is the end of the Report Wizard. You can create a sophisticated and professional data entry report in a fraction of the time that it takes to create the report from scratch. This approach isn't as fast as the Report command, but it does give you a bit more flexibility in the customization.

Creating a Report in Design View

Although the Report Wizard is a step up from the Report command in terms of control, the resulting reports still might not satisfy your needs. For example, you might want to build a custom report that mirrors as closely as possible an equivalent paper report. If the Access report resembles the paper report, the person using the report to analyze or review data might feel more comfortable with it and will be less likely to need help interpreting the data.

For maximum report flexibility, you need to use the Report Design view, which gives you total control over the report, including the positioning of the controls, the formatting of the text, the colors, and much more. You can either use the Design view to create a new report from scratch, or you can use the Report Wizard to create a basic report that you then tweak using Design view.

> **NOTE** If you read Chapter 1, "Creating and Using a Form," the following material might give you a strong sense of déjà vu. The reason is that working with forms and reports is almost identical, so most of your hard-worn forms knowledge is directly translatable to report design.

Displaying the Design View

Access reports have a Design view that you can use for your customization chores. How you display this view depends on whether you're dealing with an existing report or a new one.

To open an existing report in Design view, you have two choices:

- If the report isn't open, right-click the report in the Navigation pane and then click <u>D</u>esign View.
- If the report is already open, choose Home, click the lower half of the View split button, and then click <u>D</u>esign View. (Alternatively, click the Design View button on the status bar; see Figure 6.3.)

To start a new report, you have two choices:

- Choose Create, Blank Report; choose Format; click the lower half of the View split button; and then click <u>D</u>esign View.
- Choose Create, Report Design.

Figure 6.3 shows a new, blank report in Design View.

Click to select the report   Report Header/Footer

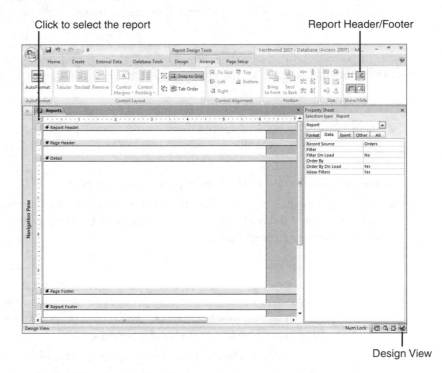

Figure 6.3
Use the Report Design view to design and customize all aspects of your report.

Design View

Changing the Record Source

The fields available to the report depend on the table or query that you've defined as the report's record source. If you've created a blank report, you need to specify the record source yourself. For an existing report, you might want to change the record source to a different table or query. Either way, you follow these steps to change the record source while you're in Design view:

1. Select the report by clicking the report selector button (pointed out in Figure 6.3).
2. Choose Design, Property Sheet. The Property Sheet pane appears.
3. Click the Data tab.
4. Pull down the Record Source list and then click the table or query you want to associate with the report.
5. Choose Design, Property Sheet. The Property Sheet pane disappears.

Understanding the Architecture of Access Reports

As you can see in Figure 6.3, the Design window divides the report into five sections (which are often called *bands* or *layers*). To build useful and attractive reports, you need to understand the function of each section. Here's a summary:

- **Report Header**—This section is used for controls that appear only at the top of the first page. This makes it a good choice for the report title, a company logo, or any other items that you want displayed only at the beginning of the report.

> **NOTE**
> The Report Header and Report Footer sections are not displayed by default in Design view. To see these sections, activate the Arrange, Report Header/Footer toggle button (pointed out in Figure 6.3).

- **Page Header**—This section holds text or other data that appears at the top of each page of the report. (On the first page, the Page Header appears below the Report Header.)
- **Detail**—This section is where the report records are printed.
- **Page Footer**—This section holds text or other data that appears at the bottom of each page of the report. (On the last page, the Page Footer appears below the last record and so above the Report Footer.)

> **TIP**
> You have some control over whether the Page Header and Page Footer appear with the Report Header and Report Footer. Select the report (by clicking the Select Report button pointed out in Figure 6.3) and then choose Design, Property Sheet. In the property sheet's Format tab, choose one of the following values for the Page Header property:
>
> - All Pages—The Page Header appears on all the report pages.
> - Not with Rpt Hdr—The Page Header appears on all the report pages, except the page displaying the Report Header.
> - Not with Rpt Ftr—The Page Header appears on all the report pages, except the page displaying the Report Footer.
> - Not with Rpt Hdr/Ftr—The Page Header appears on all the report pages, except the pages displaying the Report Header and the Report Footer.
>
> Similar values are available for the Page Footer property.

■ **Report Footer**—This section holds text or other data that appears only at the bottom of the last page of the report. It's a good place to add nondata items such as the current date or page numbers.

Understanding Report Controls

Like forms, an Access report can contain three types of controls: bound, unbound, and calculated. The following sections discuss the differences between these types from a report point of view.

Bound Controls (Fields)

Bound controls are used to display data from the report's underlying data source. The term *bound* refers to the fact that the control is tied to a field of a table, query, or SQL SELECT statement. Because report data is not editable, most bound controls are text boxes.

A bound control inherits many of the formatting and text properties defined for the field to which it is bound (for example, Format and Decimal Places). You can change these properties on the report by using the control's property sheet, which you display as follows:

■ Click the control and then choose Design, Property Sheet (or press Alt+Enter).

■ Right-click the control and then click Properties.

See "Adding Fields to the Report," later in this chapter, to learn how to add a bound control to the report.

Unbound Controls

An unbound control is used to convey information to the user. In other words, *unbound* means that the control isn't associated with (bound to) any field.

Here are some examples of using unbound controls:

■ A label for a text box that is used to describe what the text box represents.

■ A line used to separate different sections of the report.

■ A company logo or other graphical effects.

When you add a control to a form when the Control Wizard is activated, the control is automatically unbound.

Calculated Controls

Calculated controls use expressions to derive their data. Expressions are combinations of operators, fields, control names, functions, and constants. Although text boxes are the most common report of calculated controls, any control having the Control Source property can be a calculated control. You can use a calculated control to compute sales tax on a purchase order report, for example.

→ To learn how to build calculated controls, **see** "Adding Calculations to a Report," **p. 161**. (Chapter 8)

Adding Fields to the Report

Here are the steps to follow to add a field (bound control) to your report:

1. Choose Design, Add Existing Fields. Access displays the Field List pane.

2. If the underlying table is related to other tables, you can view those related tables by clicking the Show All Tables link at the bottom of the Field List pane.

3. Double-click the field you want to add to the report.

4. Repeat step 3 until you have added all the fields you need.

After you drop the fields, Access adds controls for each field, and a label control is placed beside each field (see Figure 6.4). The text of the label is the Caption property for the field to which the control is bound.

Figure 6.4
Some fields from the Employees table added to the report.

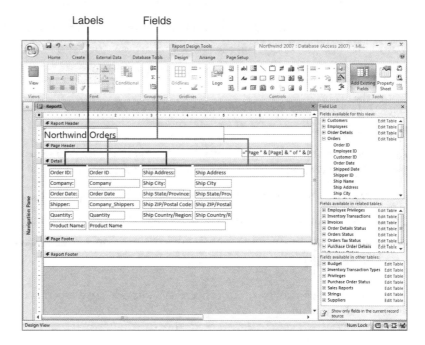

Adding Labels to the Report

A label is a control that displays static text (that is, the user of the report can't edit or copy the text). Labels are most often used to display the name of a field, but they have many other uses, as well:

- The name of an unbound control.
- The report title and, optionally, the subtitle (these should go in the Report Header section).
- Explanatory text (assumptions used in the report, the date and time the report was published, and so on).

As I mentioned earlier, fields come with their own labels. If you want to add a label for another type of control or you just want to add some text to the report, follow these steps:

1. Choose the Design tab.
2. In the Controls group, click Label.
3. Draw the label on the form.
4. Type the label text.
5. Press Enter.

> **TIP** To create a label with multiple lines of text, press Ctrl+Enter at the end of one line to start a new line within the label.

Access assumes that each label must be associated with a control, so if you add a label on its own in the Detail area, Access displays a smart tag to warn you that the label is unassociated. If you're using the label just to display text, you can remove the smart tag by clicking it and then clicking Ignore Error.

If you need to change the label text, you have two choices:

- Click the label to select it and then click the label again to edit the text. Press Enter when you're done.
- Select the label; choose Design, Property Sheet; click the Format tab; and then edit the Caption property.

Adding a Logo

 You can add visual appeal to a report by adding a logo to the Report Header. This will most often be a company logo, but you might also want to use different logos for different projects, teams, or departments. In previous versions of Access, you could insert a logo using the Image control, but you usually had to spend time resizing the resulting image. Access 2007 comes with a separate Logo command that automatically inserts the image into the Report Header section and adjusts the image's dimensions to logo size (usually 0.6 inch square). The resulting image is an Auto_Logo object.

6

Here are the steps to follow to insert a logo:

1. Choose Design, Logo. Access displays the Insert Picture dialog box.
2. Navigate to the folder that contains the image you want to use as a logo.
3. Click the image.
4. Click OK. Access resizes the image and inserts it in the Report Header section.

Adding a Title

 Adding a title to your report is usually a good idea so that users have some idea what the report is used for. You can use a `Label` control to add a title, but Access 2007 comes with a new Title command that automatically inserts an Auto_Title object in the Report Header section.

Here are the steps to follow to insert a title:

1. Choose Title (just to the right of the Logo button). Access adds the Auto_Title object to the Report Header.
2. Type your title. (Note that the Auto_Title box expands automatically as you type your text.)
3. Click outside the title.
4. Move the title to the position you want.

→   For information on moving controls, **see** "Moving Controls," **p. 133**. (this chapter)

Adding Page Numbers to the Report

If your report is only a page or two, you don't need to worry too much about adding page numbers for the printout. For longer reports, however, page numbers are a good idea because they make it easier for the reader to keep track of the pages. Follow these steps to add page numbers to the report:

1. Choose Design, Insert Page Number. Access displays the Page Numbers dialog box, shown in Figure 6.5.

Figure 6.5
Use the Page Numbers dialog box to insert page numbers into your report.

2. In the Format group, activate one of the following options:

   - **Page N**—This option inserts the text Page N on each page, where N is the page number.

   - **Page N of M**—This option inserts the text Page N of M on each page, where N is the page number and M is the total number of pages in the report.

3. In the Position group, activate one of the following options:

   - **Top of Page [Header]**—This option inserts the page number control in the Page Header section.

   - **Bottom of Page [Footer]**—This option inserts the page number control in the Page Footer section.

4. In the Alignment list, select the alignment you want to use for the page number control: Left, Center, or Right. If you select Inside, the page numbers are placed to the left on odd pages and to the right on even pages; if you select Outside, the page numbers are placed to the right on odd pages and to the left on even pages.

5. If you don't want the page numbers to appear on the report's first page, deactivate the Show Number on First Page check box.

6. Click OK. Access adds the page number controls to the report.

7. Move and format the page number controls, if necessary.

Adding the Date and Time to the Report

Including the date and time somewhere on your report is usually a good idea; the Report Header and Report Footer are good locations for the date and time. This information tells the readers when the report was published, so they know at a glance which version of the report they're reading or how old the data is.

Follow these steps to add the date and time to the report:

1. Choose Design, Date & Time. Access displays the Date and Time dialog box.

2. To add the date, leave the Include Date check box activated and then click an option button to choose the desired date format.

3. To add the time, leave the Include Time check box activated and then click an option button to choose the desired date format.

4. Click OK. Access adds the date and/or time controls to the Report Header.

5. Move and format the date and time controls, if necessary.

> **NOTE** Access displays the date and time using the Date() and Time() functions to build calculated controls. This means the values of these controls change every time the report is previewed. This doesn't matter for a printed report, but it might not be what you want in a report distributed electronically. In that case, you need to use a label to enter the date and time manually.

6

Changing the Size of a Report Section

If you find that a report section is either too small to hold all the fields or has too much empty space, you can change the size of the section as follows:

- To adjust the section's height, move the mouse pointer to the bottom edge of the section. Click and drag the edge of the section down (to make the section taller) or up (to make the section smaller).

- To adjust the section's width, move the mouse pointer to the right edge of the section. Click and drag the edge of the section right (to make the section wider) or left (to make the section thinner).

Previewing the Report

After you've added at least one field, you can display the underlying data source in the report by switching to the Print Preview view. You have two choices:

- Choose Design, click the lower half of the View split button, and then click Print Preview.

- In the status bar, click Print Preview.

Figure 6.6 shows the Print Preview tab with a report preview displayed.

Figure 6.6
The report view of the report design shown earlier in Figure 6.4.

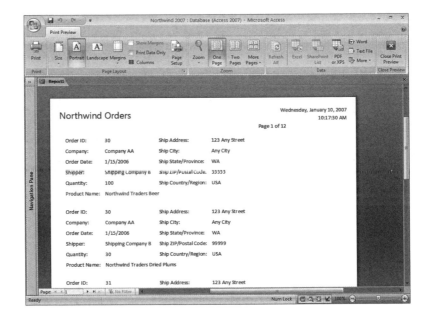

After you have the preview window onscreen, here's a list of the various ways you can view your reports:

- Click the Zoom group's One Page or Two Pages button, or click More Pages and then click the number of pages you want to view.
- Click Zoom and then click a magnification item in the drop-down.
- Click the report to toggle between the 100% and Fit to Window zoom levels.
- Right-click to bring up the shortcut menu, which also contains the Zoom, One Page, and Multiple Pages commands.

When you're done, click Close Print Preview or press Escape.

Assigning an AutoFormat in Design View

You learn later in this chapter how to change control fonts, colors, borders, and other formatting (see "Manipulating Report Controls"). For now, you can do some quick formatting by applying one of the 25 predefined report layouts, called *AutoFormats*. The easiest way to do this is to choose Arrange, AutoFormat and then click an AutoFormat in the gallery that appears.

For more control over the AutoFormat, follow these steps:

1. Choose Arrange, AutoFormat, AutoFormat Wizard to display the AutoFormat dialog box.

2. In the Report AutoFormats list, click the layout you want to use.

3. To control which layout attributes are applied to the report, click Options to display the Attributes to Apply group, shown in Figure 6.7, and then activate or deactivate the following check boxes: Font, Color, and Border.

Figure 6.7
Use this dialog box to choose and configure the AutoFormat you want to use.

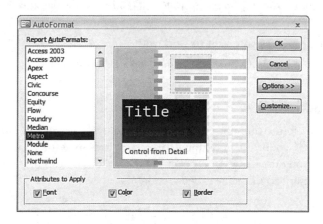

> **NOTE** The default layout used by the AutoReport Wizard is always the most recent layout that you selected in the AutoFormat dialog box.

4. Click the <u>C</u>ustomize button to display the Customize AutoFormat dialog box.

5. Click one of the following three options (click OK when you're done):

   • **Create a New AutoFormat Based on the Report '*Report*'**—Choose this option to create a new AutoFormat template based on the formatting used in the current report (named *Report*).

   • **Update '*AutoFormat*' with Values from the Report '*Report*'**—Choose this option to change the currently selected *AutoFormat* template based on the formatting used in the current report.

   • **Delete '*AutoFormat*'**—Choose this option to delete the currently selected *AutoFormat* template.

6. Click OK.

Working with Report Properties

Any report object comes with a large number of properties that you can work with. Many of them are obscure and can be safely ignored, but the next few sections highlight a few that you might find useful.

To work with the report properties, follow these steps:

1. Select the report by clicking the report selector button, pointed out earlier in Figure 6.3.

2. Choose Design, Property Sheet (or press Alt+Enter) to display the Property Sheet pane.

3. Modify the properties you want to work with.

4. Click the Close button (X) to put the new settings into effect.

Formatting the Background

Most of the report formatting options apply to the controls, as you see later in this chapter. For the report itself, about the only thing you can do is change the look of the background for each section: You can change the background color, or you can display an image as the background, as described in the next two sections.

Setting the Background Color

To change the background color of a report section, follow these steps:

1. Click the section's separator bar to select the section.
2. On the Design tab, click the Fill/Back Color palette (see Figure 6.8) so that it drops down.
3. Click the background color you want.

> **CAUTION**
>
> When choosing a background, make sure the color doesn't clash with the color of the field label text. For example, the default label text color is black, so any dark background can cause a problem. Either use a light color for the background or change the color of the label text.

Figure 6.8
Click the Fill/Back Color palette and then choose the background color you want.

Fill/Back Color palette   Object list

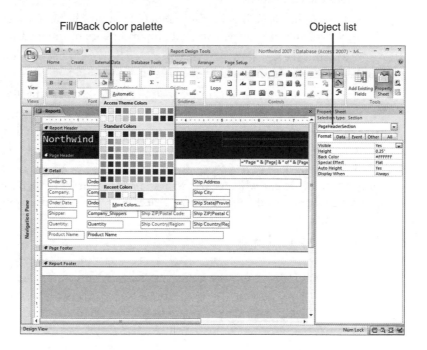

Setting the Background Picture

A simple, solid-color background that contrasts well with the report text (for example, a white or light-colored background with black or dark-colored text) is often the safest bet in a business environment. However, you might feel the need to spice up your report a bit with a more interesting background treatment: an image. Access enables you to use either a single, large image as the background or smaller images that are stretched or tiled to cover the entire report.

Follow these steps to set an image as a report's background:

1. Select the report.

2. Choose Design, Property Sheet to open the Property Sheet pane.

3. Click the Format tab.

4. Click inside the `Picture` property and then click the ellipses (...) button. Access displays the Insert Picture dialog box.

5. Find the file you want to use, click it, and then click OK.

6. Use the `Picture Size Mode` property to choose one of the following settings:

   - `Clip`—The image is displayed using its actual dimensions. If the image is larger than the form, the edges of the image are clipped to fit.

   - `Stretch`—The image is stretched or shrunk vertically and horizontally so that it fills the entire form.

   - `Zoom`—The image is enlarged or reduced until it fills the form either vertically or horizontally; the image's original proportions are maintained.

   - `Stretch Horizontal`—The image is stretched or shrunk horizontally so that it fills the entire form width.

   - `Stretch Vertical`—The image is stretched or shrunk vertically so that it fills the entire form height.

7. Use the `Picture Alignment` property to specify how you want the image aligned within the report.

8. If you selected either `Clip` or `Zoom` as the `Picture Size Mode`, use the `Picture Tiling` property to determine whether you want the image repeated (tiled) across the background so that it fills the entire report. Select `Yes` for tiling; select `No` to display just a single image.

9. Close the property sheet.

> **CAUTION**
>
> As with the background color, be careful which image you choose for the background. A "busy" background can render label text unreadable.

Manipulating Report Controls

When you add a field to a report, Access mostly uses text boxes to display the field data. Whether you stick with the controls that Access suggests or branch out to use other types of controls on your report, your report-building duties are much quicker and of higher quality if you become comfortable manipulating the controls to get them exactly the way you want them. To that end, in this section you learn quite a few useful techniques that you can apply to any control.

Inserting Controls on a Report

As you learned earlier in this chapter, you add bound controls to the report by double-clicking fields in the Field List pane. For unbound controls (or controls that you want to bind to a field later), you need to use the Design tab's Controls group, which contains buttons for all the controls you can add to a report.

Note that many of these controls don't apply to reports. That is, any control designed to edit or add data—including toggle buttons, option groups and buttons, list and combo boxes, and tab controls—either won't appear on the report, or (in the case of list and combo boxes) it will display only the current field data. Therefore, when you're building a report, most of your unbound control chores involve controls that affect the look of the report: labels, images, page breaks, lines, and rectangles.

Here are the basic steps to follow to add a control to the report:

1. In the Design tab's Controls group, click the button you want to use.
2. Move the mouse pointer into the report and position it where you want the top-left corner of the control to appear.
3. Click and drag the mouse pointer. Access displays a dashed border indicating the outline of the control.
4. When the control is the size and shape you want, release the mouse button. Access creates the control and gives it a default name (such as Labeln, where *n* signifies that this is the *n*th check box you've created on this report).

Note that sometimes Access also includes a label beside the control you insert. For example, when you add a text box, Access also inserts a label to the left of the text box.

 TIP If you want to add multiple instances of the same type of control, double-click the appropriate button in the Design tab's Controls group. The button will remain pressed, and you can draw as many instances of the control as you need. When you're done, click the control's button to reset the control.

Selecting Controls

Before you can work with a control, you must select it. For a single control, you select it simply by clicking it. If you prefer to work with multiple controls, Access gives you a number of techniques:

- Hold down the Ctrl key and click each control.
- You also can "lasso" multiple controls by clicking and dragging the mouse. Move the mouse pointer to an empty part of the report, hold down the left button, and click and drag. Access displays a box with a dashed outline, and any control that falls within this box (in whole or in part) is selected.
- To select every control, choose Design, Select All (or press Ctrl+A).

6

To exclude a control from the selection, hold down the Ctrl key and click inside the control.

After you've selected multiple controls, you can set properties for all the controls at once (choose Design, Property Sheet). Note, however, that the Property Sheet pane shows only those properties that are common to all the controls. Not only that, but if you size, move, copy, or delete one of the selected controls (as described in the next few sections), your action applies to all the controls.

Formatting Controls

You saw earlier in this chapter that you can format all the controls on a report by applying one of the predefined AutoFormat layouts. That's an easy way to work, but if the layout isn't quite what you want, or if you want to create your own AutoFormat layout, you need to format the controls manually.

You can format any control by selecting it (you can work with multiple controls, if need be) and using the lists and buttons on the Design tab (see Figure 6.9):

- Use the lists and buttons in the Font group to format the control text as well as the background color of the control.

- Use the lists and buttons on the right side of the Controls group to format the control's outline (the Line Thickness, Line Type, and Line Color lists) and its Special Effect (Flat, Raised, Sunken, and so on).

> **TIP**
>
> After you apply formatting to a particular type of control, you might want Access to use the same formatting on all future controls of the same type that you add to that form. To set up this formatting, click the control with the formatting you want to use, choose Design, and then click the Set Control Defaults button (it's in the Controls group).

Figure 6.9
Use the lists and buttons in the Font and Controls groups to format the selected control.

Adding Conditional Formatting

Access enables you to apply a particular font automatically when a control value meets a specified condition. This is called *conditional formatting*, and how (or even whether) you can take advantage of this feature in a report depends on how you intend to publish the report. For example, if you plan on distributing hard copies created with a black-and-white laser printer, color-based conditions won't appear on the printouts. Bear this in mind when deciding how you want to implement conditional formatting.

Here are the steps to follow:

1. Select the field to which you want the conditional format applied.

2. Choose Design, Conditional. Access displays the Conditional Formatting dialog box, shown in Figure 6.10.

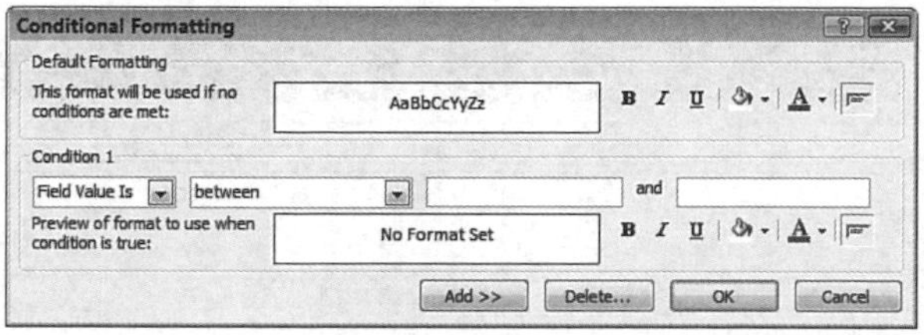

Figure 6.10
Use the Conditional Formatting dialog box to specify font formatting to apply to a control when a specific condition is met.

3. If you want to specify the format to use when the condition is not met, use the formatting buttons in the Default Formatting group.

4. Select the type of condition you want to use:

   • **Field Value Is**—The condition is applied to the current value of the field or unbound control. In this case, you construct the condition by selecting a comparison operator (such as Between or Less Than) in the second list and then entering one or two values (depending on the operator).

   • **Expression Is**—The condition is met when the logical expression you enter returns `True`. For example, if you enter `Date()=#8/23/2007#`, the formatting is applied only on August 23, 2007.

5. Click the formatting buttons to specify the font formatting to apply to the control when the condition is met.

6. If you want to apply another condition, click Add and repeat steps 4 and 5 for the new condition.

7. Click OK.

Sizing Controls

An invisible rectangular frame surrounds each control. When you select a control, Access displays selection handles at the frame's corners and midpoints, as shown in Figure 6.11.

You can resize any control to change its shape or dimensions. The following procedure outlines the steps to work through:

1. Select the object you want to size.

2. Position the mouse pointer over the selection handle you want to move. The pointer changes to a two-headed arrow. To change the size horizontally or vertically, use the appropriate handle on the middle of a side. To change the size in both directions at once, use the appropriate corner handle.

3. Click and drag the handle to the position you want.

4. Release the mouse button. Access redraws the object and adjusts the frame size.

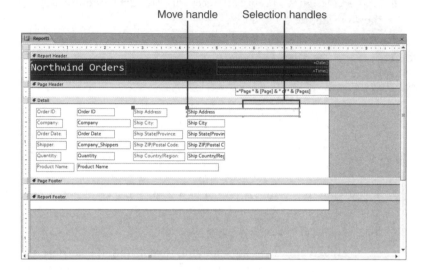

Figure 6.11
Selecting a control displays the control's selection handles.

To reduce some of the drudgery of control sizing, Access also offers a number of automatic sizing techniques. The next few sections give you a quick tour of these techniques.

Sizing to the Grid

When you draw a control on the report, Access normally sizes the control so that it automatically lines up with the nearest grid mark. You can turn off this behavior by deactivating the Format, Snap To Grid command.

If you turn off the Snap To Grid feature, you can still adjust a control's size to the grid manually. To do this, follow these steps:

1. Select the control.

2. Choose Arrange, Size To Grid. Access adjusts the control's frame to the nearest grid marks.

Sizing to the Caption

Access has an annoying habit of not making controls large enough to see the text they contain. This is particularly true when you click and drag fields from the Field List. Instead of sizing the fields or labels manually, you can make a control automatically large enough to display its text by following these steps:

1. Select the control.

2. Choose Arrange, Size To Fit.

Making Controls the Same Size

If you've added similar controls (such as command buttons), your report will look its best if these controls are the same size. Here's the easiest way to get a uniform size height and/or width:

1. Select the controls you want to make the same size.
2. Choose the Arrange tab.
3. In the Size group, click one of the following commands:
   - **Size To Tallest**—Adjusts the height of all the controls to match the height of the tallest control.
   - **Size To Shortest**—Adjusts the height of all the controls to match the height of the shortest control.
   - **Size To Widest**—Adjusts the width of all the controls to match the width of the widest control.
   - **Size To Narrowest**—Adjusts the width of all the controls to match the width of the narrowest control.

Moving Controls

You can move any control to a different part of the report by following these steps:

1. Select the control you want to move.
2. Position the mouse pointer as follows:
   - To move an individual control, place the pointer over the control's frame, although not over a selection handle. When the pointer is positioned correctly, it turns into a four-headed arrow.
   - To move a paired control (that is, a control such as a text box or check box that also comes with a label), place the pointer over the frame of whichever control is selected (again, however, not over a selection handle).
   - To move one control of a paired control, first notice that clicking any control in the pair displays a move handle in the upper-left corner of both controls, as shown earlier in Figure 6.11. Place the pointer over the move handle of the control you want to move. When the pointer is positioned correctly, it turns into a hand with a four-headed arrow.
3. Click and drag the control to the position you want.
4. Release the mouse button. Access redraws the control in the new position.

> **TIP** If you just need to make subtle adjustments to the position of a control, select it and then press an arrow key. Whichever key you press, Access moves the control one grid mark in the arrow's direction. For even more fine-tuned control, hold down the Ctrl key while you press an arrow key. In this case, Access moves the control one pixel in the arrow's direction.

6

As with sizing, Access also boasts quite a collection of commands that can adjust the position of one or more controls automatically. The next few sections give you the rundown.

Aligning to the Grid

If you've turned off the Format menu's Snap To Grid command (which, when activated, causes Access to align moved controls to the grid marks), you can still align to the grid manually:

1. Select the control.
2. Choose Arrange and then click To Grid in the Control Alignment group. Access moves the control to the nearest grid marks.

Aligning Control Edges

Reports look best when the controls are neatly aligned. The simplest way to do this is to use the buttons in the Control Alignment group. These buttons are similar to the Size buttons discussed earlier in that they operate on multiple controls and let you align, say, their left edges.

Note, however, that Access aligns the selected controls with a single *base control*, which is the control that is the farthest positioned in whatever direction you are aligning the controls. For example, if you want to align the controls on their right edges, the base control is the one that is farthest to the right. Here are the steps to follow:

1. Arrange the controls you want to work with so that one of them is the base control.
2. Select the controls you want to work with (including the base control).
3. Choose the Arrange tab.
4. Choose one of the following commands in the Control Alignment group:
    - **Left**—Adjusts the horizontal position of all the selected controls so that they line up on the left edge of the base control.
    - **Right**—Adjusts the horizontal position of all the selected controls so that they line up on the right edge of the base control.
    - **Top**—Adjusts the vertical position of all the selected controls so that they line up on the top edge of the base control.
    - **Bottom**—Adjusts the vertical position of all the selected controls so that they line up on the bottom edge of the base control.

Adjusting the Spacing Between Controls

If you want to make your forms easy to read, the controls shouldn't be crammed together edge to edge, nor should they be too far apart. Again, you can avoid making subtle spacing adjustments manually thanks to a few more Access commands.

To adjust the horizontal spacing between multiple controls, follow these steps:

1. Select the controls.
2. Choose Arrange.
3. Choose one of the following commands in the Position group:

   - **Make Horizontal Spacing Equal**—If you have three or more controls selected, use this command to adjust the horizontal spacing so that it's the same between each control.
   - **Increase Horizontal Spacing**—This command increases the horizontal spacing between each control by one grid mark, relative to the base control.
   - **Decrease Horizontal Spacing**—This command decreases the horizontal spacing between each control by one grid mark, relative to the base control.
   - **Make Vertical Spacing Equal**—If you have three or more controls selected, use this command to adjust the vertical spacing so that it's the same between each control.
   - **Increase Vertical Spacing**—This command increases the vertical spacing between each control by one grid mark, relative to the base control.
   - **Decrease Vertical Spacing**—This command decreases the vertical spacing between each control by one grid mark, relative to the base control.

Grouping Controls

Access lets you create control *groups*. A group is a collection of controls you can format, size, and move—similar to the way you format, size, and move a single control. To group two or more controls, follow these steps:

1. Select the controls you want to include in the group.
2. Choose Arrange, Group.

Access treats a group as a single control with its own frame. To select an entire group, you just need to select one control from the group.

6

To ungroup controls, follow these steps:

1. Select the group.
2. Choose Arrange, Ungroup.

Ordering Overlapped Controls

When you're inserting controls, you usually want to avoid overlapping the controls so that the reader won't be confused and so the captions won't get mixed together. However, sometimes you might want controls to overlap. For example, if you've added two or more picture controls, you might be able to produce interesting effects by superimposing one picture on another.

When you have two controls that overlap, the most recently created control covers part of the other control. The newer control is "in front" of the older one. The overlap order of these controls is called the *Z-order*. (Think of the Z-axis in a three-dimensional graph.)

To change the Z-order, follow these steps:

1. Select one of the overlapping controls.
2. Choose the Arrange tab.
3. In the Position group, click one of the following commands:
    -   **Bring To Front**—Moves the control to the top of the Z-order, which places it in front of every other control.
    -   **Send To Back**—Moves the control to the bottom of the Z-order, which places it behind every other control.

Creating a Report Interactively in Layout View

 The major problem with creating a report in Design view is that you don't see data from the report's record source until you switch to Report view. This means that you often have to switch back and forth to get the layout you prefer and to size the controls properly.

Access 2007 helps you reduce much of this design drudgery by offering a new report view called Layout. This hybrid view shows you the data from the record source but also enables you to change many aspects of the report design. To switch to this view from Design view, choose Design, click the lower half of the View split button, and then click Layout View. (You can also click the Layout View button in the status bar.)

As you can see in Figure 6.12, the report data appears, but you also have access to the Ribbon's Format, Arrange, and Page Setup tabs, which enable you to change the font, add certain controls (such as a logo and title), add fields, apply an AutoFormat, and more.

Figure 6.12
Use Access 2007's new Layout View to modify the report and see its data at the same time.

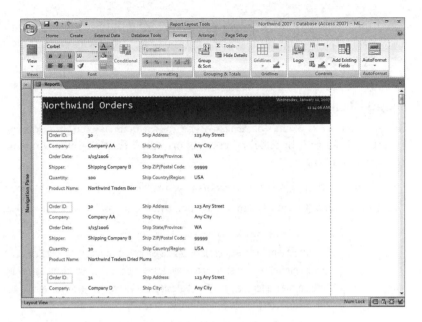

Publishing a Report

With the ever-increasing need to distribute information across the Internet and across platforms, Access offers a number of ways to take reports out of your computer and share them with others. Publishing a report can take many forms, and the next few sections take you through the possibilities.

Publishing on Paper

Printing multiple copies of the report is the standard choice for distributing the report to others. Note that besides setting up the report controls to produce an attractive output, you can also affect the printed output by following these steps:

1. In the Design, Print Preview, or Layout view, choose the Page Setup tab.

2. Use the controls in the Page Layout group to set the page size, orientation (Portrait or Landscape), margins, columns, and so on.

3. For more control over the page layout, click Page Setup to display the Page Setup dialog box.

4. In the Print Options tab's Margins group, use the Top, Bottom, Left, and Right text boxes to specify the page margins. If you activate the Print Data Only check box, Access ignores all the nonbound controls (labels, graphics, and so on) and prints only the report data.

5. In the Page tab, set the page Orientation, choose the paper Size and Source, and set the Printer.

6

6. In the Columns tab, set the number and layout of the report columns.

→ For the specifics of working with report columns, **see** "Creating a Multiple-Column Report," **p. 177.** (Chapter 9)

7. Click OK.

Publishing to Email

The predicted era of the "paperless office" never materialized, but you can move yourself one step closer to it by emailing your report rather than shipping out a hard copy. Here are the steps to follow:

1. Choose Office, E-mail. Access displays the Send Object As dialog box.

2. In the Select Output Format list, click the file format you want to use.

> **NOTE** The Select Output Format list includes the Snapshot Format item. The Report Snapshot format is a special file format that enables the reader to view the report without using Microsoft Access. Instead, the reader uses the Microsoft Snapshot Viewer program. You can find a link to download this program on the following Microsoft page:
>
> support.microsoft.com/kb/175274

3. Click OK.

4. Depending on the format you chose, Access may display a dialog box with further options. If so, choose the options you want and then click OK.

5. Access converts the report to the selected file format and then uses your email program to display a new message window with the report file attached. Fill out the message details (recipient address, subject, and so on).

6. Send the message.

Exporting to Word

If the report needs to be viewed by someone who doesn't have Access but who has Microsoft Office Word, you can export the report to a Rich Text Format (.rtf) file that the other person can open in Word. To do this, follow these steps:

1. Choose External Data, Word. Access displays the Export - RTF File dialog box.

2. Use the File Name text box to enter a path and name for the exported file. (You can also click Browse to choose the destination folder using the File Save dialog box.)

3. If you want to view the resulting RTF document in Word after you're done, click to activate the Open the Destination File After the Export Operation Is Complete check box.

4. Click OK to create the file.

5. Click Close.

After you've saved the file, you can send it to the other person over the network, via email, or on a memory card or recordable CD or DVD.

Exporting to PDF or XPS

What do you do if you don't want to print the report and the person who will be viewing the report doesn't have Access or Word? One possibility is to export the report to a simple text file by choosing External Data and then clicking Text File in the Export group. Follow steps 2–5 from the preceding section to export the report.

The problem with going the text file route is that you lose all your formatting and layout. Fortunately, Office 2007 offers an alternative method that renders your report exactly the way you set it up in Access. This method enables you to export the report to either of the following formats:

■ **PDF**—This is the Portable Document Format, and it's currently the de facto standard for sharing data while preserving its original formatting and layout. Most people have a PDF viewer installed on their computer.

■ **XPS**—This is the new Microsoft file sharing standard and, like PDF, it preserves the original formatting and layout of your report. As I write this, users need Internet Explorer 7 to view XPS documents.

Before you can export your reports to PDF or XPS, you must first install an add-in from Microsoft. Here are the steps to follow:

1. Choose Office, click the arrow beside the Save As command, and then click Find Add-ins for Other File Formats. Access displays a Help topic that features information on the PDF and XPS formats.

2. Click the Install and Use the Publish as PDF or XPS Add-in from Microsoft link.

3. Click the Microsoft Save as PDF or XPS Add-in for 2007 Microsoft Office Programs link. The Office Online page for downloading the add-in appears in your browser.

4. Follow the onscreen instructions for validating your version of Office 2007 and then downloading and installing the add-in.

When the add-in is installed, return to Access and then follow these steps:

1. Choose Office, click the arrow beside the Save As command, and then click the PDF or XPS command. Access displays the Publish as PDF or XPS dialog box.

2. Choose a location and enter a File Name for the file.

3. In the Save as Type list, choose either PDF or XPS Document.

6

4. Click an optimization option:
   - **St̲andard**—Click this option if you're going to print the file or if you're going to distribute the file online and bandwidth isn't a problem.
   - **M̲inimum Size**—Click this option if you're going to distribute the file online and bandwidth is a problem.

5. Click Publi̲sh. Access exports the report to the file format you chose.

From Here

→ To learn how to build calculated controls, **see** "Adding Calculations to a Report," **p. 161** (Chapter 8)

→ For the specifics of working with report columns, **see** "Creating a Multiple-Column Report," **p. 177**. (Chapter 9)

→ To learn how to create subreports (reports that include data from two or more related tables), **see** "Creating a Multiple-Table Report," **p. 189**. (Chapter 9)

→ For the details of using report data in a Word mail merge operation, **see** "Creating a Mail Merge Report," **p. 187**. (Chapter 9)

Designing Effective Business Reports

7

Building a basic report isn't difficult, as you've seen. If you use the Report command or the Report Wizard, you can build a serviceable report with just a few mouse clicks. If you use the Report Design view, Access offers all the tools you need to cobble together a custom design without much fuss. (This is particularly true if you're already familiar with building forms from scratch, because the tools and techniques used in report-building are almost identical to those used in form-building.)

A "serviceable" report might be good enough for your own needs, but in a business environment it's a rare report that's read by just one person. Instead, reports are almost always distributed to multiple readers, which means you need to shoot for a report quality that's higher than merely serviceable.

Fortunately, the techniques required to beautify a report are not complicated and don't require substantial investments of your precious time. As you see in this chapter, you can build attractive and readable reports without hours of tweaking and fussing.

Using Reports in Business

The significance of reports in the business environment is simple: A report is the logical end product of all your hard work—data entry, querying, data analysis, and so on. The report contents represent the "polished" form of the data, and so the report itself should look just as polished. The report is, in a sense, your representative. When you send copies of the report to other people, the report becomes an extension of you and a reflection of your work habits and knowledge.

Taking a few extra minutes now to construct a high-quality report pays off in the long run because doing this makes your data more readable, and it ensures that your readers treat your data with the seriousness it deserves. After all, it's only natural to assume that a sloppy-looking report must contain sloppy data and shoddy conclusions. True, an attractive report isn't automatically an effective one, but it gives your readers one less reason to question the data and one more reason to treat the data with respect.

However, a business report not only must look good, but also must *be* good. There's no point in calling attention to a report that contains inaccurate data or invalid conclusions, or that's aimed at the wrong audience. Before you design any report, always take a step or two back and survey the scene by asking yourself three simple questions: What's in the report? What is the goal of the report? Who will be reading it?

What's in the Report?

Before distributing any report, print out a test copy. Data always looks more "official" on paper rather than onscreen, so a test printout is the best way to view your data dispassionately. Double-check the data to make sure it's accurate. In particular, look for places in the report where you can perform "reality checks." That is, look for numbers or conclusions that you can quickly check against what you know to be true. For example, if your report claims that gross margin for a product is 50% and you know that margins historically run around 10% for similar products, be sure to check your figures. Look for absurd numbers such as negative prices or interest rates.

The content of the report also plays a role in the design of the report. For example, a report that displays invoice data should almost certainly show extended subtotals for each item (units ordered multiplied by the price per unit), freight charges, the order total, and other calculated fields (see Figure 7.1). Similarly, the data often dictates whether the report displays a single record per page or multiple records per page. The former requires a columnar-style report (such as the invoice report shown in Figure 7.1; this is a modified version of the Northwind Invoice report), whereas the latter requires a tabular-style report (as shown in Figure 7.2). Or, if the underlying report table is the "one" side of a one-to-many relationship, you might want to add a subreport that shows the related records from the "many" table.

→ For the details of subreports, **see** "Creating a Multiple-Table Report," **p. 189**. (Chapter 9)

What Is the Goal of the Report?

Reports are rarely built just for the fun of it. In other words, almost every report has a purpose, and establishing that purpose up front is important. Are you just showing raw data? Then you should construct a simple tabular report with field names in the Page Header section for easy reading. Are you using the report as part of a larger data analysis effort? Then you need to determine which data you require and what kinds of summary calculations fit the analysis. Are you trying to persuade your audience of something? Then you need to include those facts and analyses that buttress your position and take into account any objections they might have.

→ For more on placing calculated fields in a report, **see** "Adding Calculations to a Report," **p. 161.** (Chapter 8)

→ To learn about grouping reports, **see** "Sorting and Grouping a Report," **p. 157.** (Chapter 8)

Figure 7.1
An invoice report showing extended prices, subtotal, freight, and overall total.

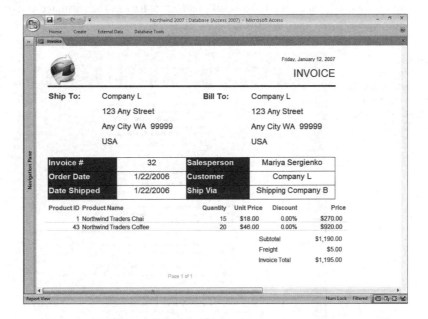

Figure 7.2
This report uses a tabular format to display multiple records per page.

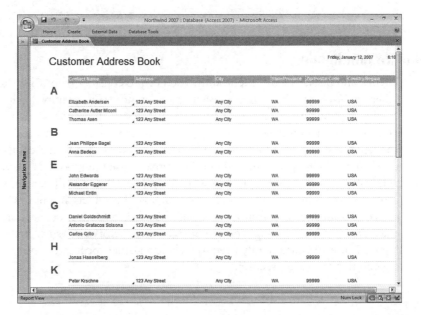

In all these cases, feel free to use the Report Header to state the goal of the report up front. Most people just use the header for the title and publish date, but the header is more flexible than that. For example, consider the Catalog report, shown in Figure 7.3. (This report was imported from an older version of the Northwind sample database.) This text—which appears in the Report Header section of the report—introduces the reader to the catalog and offers some suggested foods, all of which enhances the ultimate goal of the catalog: getting customers to place orders.

Figure 7.3
The Catalog report enhances the goal of the report by including this introductory text in the Report Header.

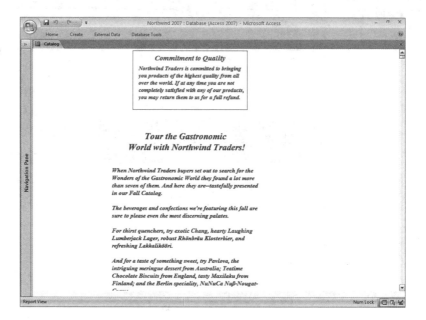

Who Are Your Readers?

Finally, and perhaps most importantly, you need to consider who will read the report. Will other employees in the company use it as a reference? (For example, is it a directory of employee phone extensions?) Then you should design the report so that all readers can find the information they need quickly. Will senior management view the report? Then you need to set up the report so that busy executives can readily access its assumptions and conclusions. Will people throughout the company use the report? If so, you might have to build your report according to corporate design guidelines. Will people outside the company read the report? (For example, it's a catalog of products and prices.) Then you need to put your company's best foot forward and ensure that your report encourages customers to place orders. (For a catalog, you can include introductory text, such as the text shown in Figure 7.3. And you certainly need to include an order form in the back of the catalog—in, say, the Report Footer section.)

Ten Design Guidelines for Business Reports

Answering the three questions from the previous sections is only the first step toward creating a usable business report. The following sections offer a set of 10 guidelines that help you build usable and attractive reports no matter what your goal, data, or readership.

1. Copy Legacy Reports When Practical

If your Access report replaces an existing report that another source produced, such as a mainframe print job, try to make your version mimic its counterpart. The data should be the same, the fields should be in the same order, the sorting and grouping should be identical, and you should include the same summary calculations. This ensures that the report users will have no problems reading and understanding your version, which in turn ensures an easy transition.

This doesn't mean that you can never improve upon a legacy report. If you do make changes that produce a better report, be sure to include a note in the Report Header that details the changes.

Note, too, that it's also a good idea to use fonts, colors, boxes, and lines to make the Access report a carbon copy of the original, if that's practical within the confines of the computer screen (see the discussion of screen resolution in an upcoming section).

2. Give Users What They Need, Then Stop: Part 1

You might have heard the term *PowerPointlessness*, which, in a PowerPoint presentation, refers to any fancy transitions, sounds, and other effects that have no discernible purpose, use, or benefit. It's a despised aspect of many PowerPoint presentations, and it can happen in Access reports, too.

After you've learned the ins and outs of report design, the temptation is to put your hard-won knowledge to good use by adding lots of bells and whistles to each report. Resist this temptation at all costs; nobody likes an overdesigned report.

For example, you see later in this chapter that you can spruce up a drab report with extras such as colors, images, and various special effects. When used judiciously, these goodies can add visual interest to a report. Watch out, though: If you overdo it, your report can easily become a hard-to-read, hard-to-understand mess that distracts the readers. When it comes to report extras, moderation is always the key.

3. Give Users What They Need, Then Stop: Part 2

Depending on the readers and the underlying data source, you might not need to include absolutely every record in the report. If the report shows the top salespeople to determine who gets bonuses or awards, there's probably no point in including every sales rep in the report. If you want to set up a promotion involving your top-selling products, no one wants a report that also includes the worst-selling products. You can avoid including unnecessary records by using a "top *N* values" query as the data source.

→ To learn how to restrict records to the top values, **see** "Returning Only the Top *N* Values," **p. 213**. (Chapter 10)

Also, never show the readers fields that they don't need to see or that have no bearing on the rest of the report data. In general, always assume that your reader is going through a stack of reports (and a pile of other inbox paper) and so only has a limited amount of time to read your report.

Finally, it goes without saying that sensitive data is to be displayed only to those with the authorization to see it.

4. Use Page Numbers

This tip seems like a small thing, but any report that's more than a couple of pages long should always include page numbers, usually in the Page Header or the Page Footer. Page numbers act as a kind of "You Are Here" sign that makes it easier for the readers to navigate the report. Including the total number of pages (for example, Page 2 of 10) also helps the readers by letting them know how big the report is.

5. Use Dates and Times

Another simple addition that helps the readers put the report into context is the date (and, optionally, the time) that the report was prepared or printed. Nobody wants to peruse data that's out of date, and so adding the date in the Report Header or Report Footer ensures the readers of the report's freshness.

Also, if you're planning on publishing multiple versions of the report (say, as your data becomes more complete or more accurate), including the date and time (and possibly a version number in the Report Header) not only enables the readers to work with the latest version, but also gives readers the capability to compare versions to see what has changed.

6. Watch the Field Order

Recall that an Access report based on a legacy report should display the fields in the same order as they appear in the old version. Even if you're not using a legacy report as a model, report fields often have an internal logic. For example, an invoice report should always show the customer information above the report details, and the report details should appear above the order details (see Figure 7.1, earlier in this chapter). Similarly, address fields should always follow the standard street-city-region-country-postal code order. Always examine the underlying data to look for these "natural" field orders and then set up your report accordingly.

7. Watch Your Screen Resolution

If all or most of your readers will view your report onscreen, you need to make sure that they can view it without scrolling horizontally. It's a common design mistake to build a report on a screen with the resolution set at 1,280×1,024 or even 1,600×1,200 and then realize that only part of the report shows up on an 1,024×768 display. You need to determine the lowest screen resolution used by a significant portion of your users and then build your report with your own screen set to that screen area. In most offices today, 1,024×768 is a good design resolution (few people still run at 800×600).

Also, if your users have a uniform screen type—for example, 14-inch laptop screens or 17-inch monitor sizes—be sure to test your report on this screen before deploying it, particularly if your own computer has a significantly larger screen size.

8. Make Report Text Readable

Few things are as frustrating as text that is unreadable. This is particularly true for Access reports where the text is usually there for an important reason (such as naming a field or providing explanatory text). Therefore, take care when you apply font formatting to your reports. See "Enhancing Report Text," later in this chapter, for some pointers on using fonts.

9. Always Sort and/or Group Data

Reports are not meant to be data dumps. After all, if a printout of a table's raw data is all you want, you can simply print the table's datasheet. Most report readers want the data to be organized in some fashion, which means not simply restricting the data (as described earlier), but also taking advantage of the Access sorting and grouping features. Sorting makes it easier for the readers to find the data they need, and grouping enables the readers to analyze the data and look for patterns.

10. Organize the Report Layout

Many reports, especially columnar reports, have groups of related controls. For example, on an invoice report, one group might be the customer's name and address data, another might be overall order data such as the shipping method and payment info, and another might be the order details. You can make report reading much easier if you use visual aids to emphasize these groupings. As you see in the next section, you can use lines, borders, and page breaks to achieve this effect.

Organizing Controls on the Report

A report that holds just three or four fields doesn't require much in the way of organization. You can more or less just plop the fields onto the report, pretty them up a bit, and then move on. However, it's a rare report that contains so few fields. It's much more common for a report to contain 10, 15, even 20 controls, all vying for the user's attention. Tossing all those controls onto the report willy-nilly is definitely not a good idea: People reading the report for the first time are likely to get confused, and busy users might resent the time it takes to determine what's what.

7

Proper control organization doesn't imply anything elaborate. It involves just three principles:

- Grouping related controls together.
- Putting individual controls in a natural order.
- Making it clear which controls belong to which groups.

The first two are a product of the underlying data, as described in the previous section. In the following sections, you learn a few visual aids that can help enclose controls into groups and separate these groups so that users can easily see the overall organization of the report.

Making Good Use of Lines and Rectangles

In the Report Design view, the Design tab's Controls group contains two buttons that create graphic elements on the report: Line and Rectangle. Here's how you use these tools to organize a report's controls:

- Use a rectangle to organize a set of related controls into a group. Place the controls together on the report and then draw the rectangle around them.
- Use a line to separate groups and individual controls. Add a bit of extra space between the bottom (or right) of one control or group and the top (or left) of the next control or group. Then draw the line in this extra space.

> **TIP**
>
> Most people find it a bit tricky to draw a straight line using the standard click-and-drag technique. To ensure a perfectly straight line every time, hold down the Shift key and then click and drag.

In both cases, you click the button in the Controls group and then click and drag on the report to draw the line or rectangle.

Figure 7.4 shows a sample report that uses these techniques.

After you've drawn your line or rectangle, you can use the following Design tab lists to format the graphic:

- **Fill/Back Color (Font group)**—Click a color swatch in this list to set the color of the rectangle's background.

> **TIP**
>
> If you add a rectangle around a set of existing controls and then set the rectangle's background color, the controls will be obscured by the nontransparent background. To fix this problem, select the rectangle and then choose Arrange, Send to Back. This changes the Z-order so that the rectangle is now "behind" the other controls.

Figure 7.4
Use rectangles to orga-
nize related controls into
groups and use lines to
separate individual
controls and groups.

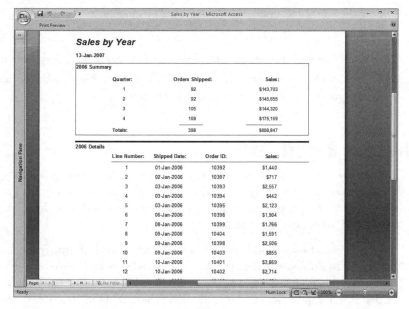

- **Line Thickness (Controls group)**—Click an item in this list to set the width of the line or the rectangle's border.

- **Line Type (Controls group)**—Click an item in this list to set the style (such as dotted or dashed) of the line or the rectangle's border.

- **Line Color (Controls group)**—Click a color swatch in this list to set the color of the line or the rectangle's border.

- **Special Effect (Controls group)**—Click this list and then choose the effect you want to apply to the line or the rectangle's border: Flat, Raised, Sunken, Etched, Shadowed, or Chiseled.

Creating Page Breaks

A page break is an object that tells the printer to start a new page no matter how much of the current page is filled. In the Report Design view, the Controls group includes a Page Break button that enables you to insert a page break anywhere within the report. This capability is useful when you need to break down a particular section into two or more subsec-
tions. For example, you can insert a page break into the Report Header section and thus divide the header into two separate pages. You can use the first page for the report title and possibly the company logo, and you can use the second page to provide the reader with an introduction to the report or instructions for interpreting the report data.

7

Follow these steps to insert a page break into your report:

1. Choose the Design tab.
2. In the Controls group, click the Insert or Remove Page Break button.
3. Click inside the report at the spot where you want the page break to appear. Access displays six dots to mark the page break location.

Enhancing Report Text

Unlike other Access database objects, a report is for the most part nothing but text. With the exception of a few images or lines or rectangles added for beautification or organization, a report *is* text: title, subtitle, page numbers, date and time, introductory remarks, field labels, and, of course, the data itself.

This means that you should set aside a significant parcel of time to work on your report text. That is, don't just accept the Access font defaults and move on to seemingly more important duties such as getting the fields placed just so. The text should be an integral part of the overall report design. After all, nicely formatted characters make the report readable and easy on the eyes, whereas slapdash text formatting can ruin an otherwise successful report.

Text is important because its readability and visual appeal are centered on the four traits that define the "architecture" of each character: typeface, type size, type style, and character spacing. The Report Design view enables you to modify all four of these traits.

→ For a more detailed look at text architecture, **see** "Enhancing Form Text," **p. 86**. (Chapter 4)

Formatting Text

To format a control's text, select it and then use either of the following:

- **The Ribbon**—As pointed out in Figure 7.5, the Design tab's Font group offers six controls for formatting text: Font (that is, the typeface), Font Size, Bold, Italic, Underline, and Font/Fore Color. You can also use the Align Left, Center, and Align Right buttons to align the text within the control.

- **The property sheet**—In a control's property sheet, the Format tab has six text-related properties: Fore Color, Font Name (typeface), Font Size, Font Weight (varieties of boldness), Font Italic, and Font Underline. You can also use the Text Align property to choose the alignment within the control.

Figure 7.5
A report with some
sample text formatting.

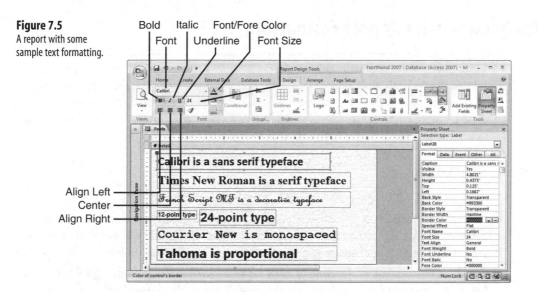

Text Formatting Tips and Guidelines

Access makes it easy to add unique and eye-catching fonts to all your reports. However, some restraint is called for here. Nothing looks worse than—or is as confusing as—a report with too many fonts crammed together. This is known in the trade as the *ransom note look*, and you should avoid it at all costs. Here are a few pointers for keeping your report text looking good:

- Don't make the type size too small. Access defaults to 8-point type, but you can do your users a big favor by bumping up all your text to 10 points.

- Use a larger type size for titles and headings. Report titles (placed in the Report Header section) should stand out from the rest of the text, so use a relatively large type size for them.

- Use a plain, unadorned typeface. A report is no place for fancy, decorative typefaces. A plain typeface, particularly a sans serif typeface such as Calibri, reads best.

- Don't mix typefaces. Try to restrict your typefaces to one, or at most two, per report. If you need various looks, use larger sizes or different styles of the same typeface.

- Make use of bolding. You can make field names and other labels stand out from the report background by formatting them as bold. Avoid other text effects such as italics and underlining.

- Watch the background. For maximum readability, make sure there is significant contrast between the text color and the report's background color. Dark text on a light background is best. Don't use a background image unless it is relatively faint and the text stands out well against it (you might have to use bolding, a larger type size, or a darker text color to achieve this).

7

Applying Fancier Report Formatting

Business reports don't need to be fancy. In fact, in most cases reports should *not* be fancy because a garish or overdone design can distract users. However, that doesn't mean your reports need to be drab, dull affairs. As long as you wield a relatively light touch, there's no reason why you can't use colors, images, and other effects to add visual interest to the report or to apply your company's color scheme or logo to give things an official feel. The rest of this chapter takes you through these nonessential report beautification techniques.

Working with Colors

You've already seen three ways to adjust report colors:

- To adjust the background color of a control, select it and then use the Design tab's Fill/Back Color list (in the Fonts group) to choose a new color. You can also open the control's property sheet and adjust the `Back Color` property on the Format tab.

- To adjust the text color of a control, select it and then use the Design tab's Font Color list (in the Fonts group) to choose a new color. You can also open the control's property sheet and adjust the `Fore Color` property on the Format tab.

- To adjust the line color or the border color of a control, select it and then use the Design tab's Line Color list (in the Controls group) to choose a new color. You can also open the control's property sheet and adjust the `Border Color` property on the Format tab.

Creating a Custom Report Color

The Design tab's lists give you a selection of 40 colors. However, if you use the property sheet, you can also create a custom color. Follow these steps to get started:

1. Select the control you want to work with.
2. In the Design tab, pull down the color list you want to work with and then choose More Colors. Access displays the Color dialog box.
3. Click the Custom tab.
4. Use the Custom tab controls to define the new color.

→ For the details on creating a custom color using the controls in the expanded Color dialog box, **see** "Creating a Custom Color," **p. 89**. (Chapter 4)

5. Click OK.

Using Color Effectively in Reports

Now you know how to apply colors to your reports, but that's only half the battle. Colors that are poorly matched or improperly applied can make a report look worse, not better. This section examines a few basics for effectively using colors in your reports.

With so many colors available, the temptation is to go overboard and use a dozen different hues on each page. However, using too many colors can confuse your users and even cause eye fatigue. Try to stick to two or three colors at most. If you must use more, try to use different shades of two or three hues.

Before finalizing your color scheme, you need to make sure the colors you've selected work well together. For example, blue and black are often difficult to distinguish and green/red combinations clash. Other color combinations to avoid are red/blue, green/blue, and brown/black. On the other hand, color combinations such as red/yellow, gray/red, and blue/yellow go well together, as do contrasting shades of the same color, such as black and gray.

CAUTION

Another good reason to avoid using too much green and red in your worksheets is that approximately 8% of the male population suffers from red-green color blindness.

When selecting colors, think about the psychological impact that your scheme will have on your users. Studies have shown that "cool" colors such as blue and gray evoke a sense of dependability and trust. Use these colors for a more business-like appearance. For reports that require a little more excitement, "warm" colors such as red, yellow, and orange can evoke a festive, fun atmosphere. For a safe, comfortable ambiance, try using brown and yellow. For an environmental touch, use green and brown.

Adding Images to Your Reports

A nice way to spruce up a report is to add an unbound image. This can be a company, department, or project logo; clip art related to the report's purpose; or an image related to the report's underlying data. Access supports all the major graphics formats, so you're free to use images from just about any source (without infringing anyone's copyright, of course).

Follow these steps to add an image to the report:

1. In the Design tab's Controls group, click the Image button.
2. On the report, click and drag to draw a rectangle to contain the image. When you release the mouse button, Access displays the Insert Picture dialog box.
3. Open the folder containing the image you want, click the image file, and then click OK.
4. Resize the image control, as needed.
5. Choose Design, Property Sheet to display the image control's property sheet.
6. Display the Format tab.
7. Use the `Size Mode` property to choose one of the following settings:
   - `Clip`—The image is displayed using its actual dimensions. If the image is larger than the control, the edges of the image are clipped to fit.

7

- Stretch—The image is stretched or shrunk vertically and horizontally so that it fills the entire control.
- Zoom—The image is enlarged or reduced until it fills the control either vertically or horizontally; the image's original proportions are maintained.

8. Use the Picture Alignment property to specify how you want the image aligned within the control.

9. If you selected either Clip or Zoom as the Size Mode, use the Picture Tiling property to determine whether you want the image repeated (tiled) across the background so that it fills the entire control. Select Yes for tiling; select No to display just a single image.

10. Close the property sheet.

Adding Special Effects

Access comes with a palette of six special effects that enable you to display control borders in various interesting ways. The six choices are Flat, Raised, Sunken, Etched, Shadowed, and Chiseled, and they're demonstrated in Figure 7.6. You have two ways to apply these effects to a selected control:

- In the Design tab's Controls group, pull down the Special Effects menu (see Figure 7.6) and then click the effect you want.
- Choose Design, Property Sheet to display the control's property sheet, click the Format tab, and then use the Special Effect property to choose the effect you want.

Figure 7.6
Use the Special Effects menu to create the border effects shown here.

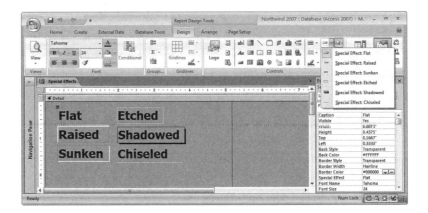

Creating a Shadow Effect for Text

The Shadow effect you saw in the preceding section applies only to control borders. What if you want the same effect with the text in a label? You can do this by following these steps:

1. Add the label to the report, edit the text, and set up the text formatting as needed.
2. With the label selected, choose Design, Line Color, Transparent.
3. With the label selected, pull down the Design tab's Line/Border Color palette and click Transparent.
4. Choose Edit, Duplicate to create a copy of the label.
5. Move the copy of the label so that it is offset slightly from the original (slightly below and slightly to the right is the usual shadow position).

> **T I P**
> If you need to fine-tune the position of the copy, hold down the Ctrl key and press the arrow keys to nudge the label in the direction of the selected key.

6. Choose Design, Font Color and then click a relatively light color for the shadow label (such as light gray).
7. Choose Arrange, Send to Back. Access places the shadow label behind the original label.

Figure 7.7 shows an example of shadowed text.

Figure 7.7
Use a duplicate of a label to create a text shadow effect.

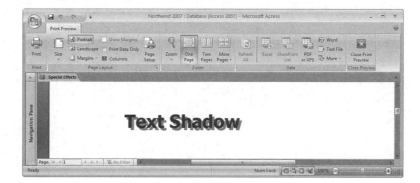

From Here

7

Designing Advanced Reports

8

The Access reporting engine is well designed in the sense that, although it boasts a large number of features and options, most of these features don't get in the way if all you want is a straightforward report. Whether you use the Report command, the Report Wizard, or the Design view, creating a simple report isn't difficult, as I hope the past couple of chapters have shown.

And, when you're ready to take your reports to the next level, the reporting engine is more than willing to accompany you on the trip. However, as you rise in the reporting hierarchy, some of the techniques and features get a little more complicated. Not to worry, though—there's nothing up there that you can't handle, especially if you use this chapter as your guide. Here, you learn about sorting and grouping, adding calculations, launching reports using command buttons and macros, and employing various useful methods for controlling report output.

Sorting and Grouping a Report

The Report Wizard gives you options for sorting the report records as well as grouping the records based on the values in one or more fields. If you need to fine-tune the sorting and grouping options set up through the wizard, or if you're building your report from scratch, you can specify the report's sorting and grouping from the Design view, as explained in the next few sections.

To get started, choose Design, Group & Sort (in the Grouping and Totals group; see Figure 8.1). Access displays the Group, Sort, and Total pane, shown in Figure 8.1.

Group & Sort

Figure 8.1
Use the Group, Sort, and
Total pane to sort the
report records and group
the records based on
the values in one or
more fields.

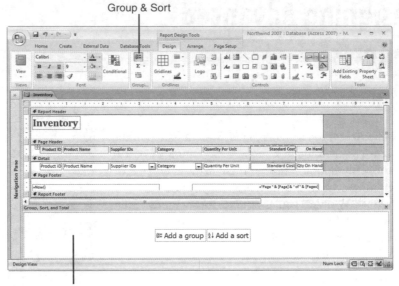

Group, Sort, and Total pane

Setting Up Sorting Options

To use the Group, Sort, and Total pane to define the sort order you want for your report, follow these steps:

1. In the Group, Sort, and Total pane, click Add a Sort. Access adds a Sort By list to the Group, Sort, and Total pane.

2. Use the Sort By list to select the name of the field on which you want to sort. Access adds a Sort Order list to the Group, Sort, and Total pane.

3. Use the Sort Order list to choose either an ascending or descending sort. Note that the name of the sort depends on the field type. For example, for text fields, you see `With A on Top` (an ascending sort) and `With Z on Top` (descending); for numeric fields, you see `From Smallest to Largest` (an ascending sort) and `From Largest to Smallest` (descending)

4. Repeat steps 1–3 to sort the report on other fields, as needed.

Setting Up Grouping Options

A *group* is a collection of related records. In an invoice report, for example, you can create groups of invoices for each customer. This sounds suspiciously like sorting the records, so how is grouping different? The advantage you get with groups is that Access creates two new report sections: a *Group Header* and a *Group Footer*. You can use a header to identify the group and the footer to print summary information about the group. For example, at the bottom of each group, you could print the sum of a particular field or the total number of records in the group (see "Adding Calculations to a Report," later in this chapter).

To group your report, follow these steps:

1. In the Group, Sort, and Total pane, click Add a Group. Access adds a Group On list to the Group, Sort, and Total pane.

2. Use the Group On list to select the field you want to use as the basis of the grouping.

3. Use the Sort Order list to select a sort order for the groups. (Note that this doesn't sort the records *within* the group. If you want sorting within each group, see step 11.)

4. Click More to display a list of properties for the field.

5. Use the Group On list to specify how Access creates the groups:

    • To create a group for each unique value in the field, choose By Entire Value (this is the default).

    • If the field is numeric, click a predefined option, such as By 5s or By 100s. Alternatively, click Custom and then use the Interval text box to enter the numeric value to use as the group basis interval. For example, if you enter 20, the records are grouped in intervals of 20 (such as 1–20, 21–40, and so on) according to the values in the field.

    • If the field is text, choose either By First Character or By First Two Characters. Alternatively, click Custom and then use the Characters text box to enter the number of characters to use as the group basis. For example, when you enter 4, the records are grouped according to the first four letters in the field.

    • If the field contains dates or times, choose one of the various predefined grouping options: By Day, By Week, By Month, By Quarter, or By Year. You can also click Custom and then use the By text box and list to set the number of Minutes, Hours, Days, Weeks, Months, Quarters, or Years to use as the grouping.

6. Use the Totals list to choose either With No Totals or to select the field on which you want the totals to appear for each group. See "Adding Calculations to a Report," later in this chapter, for more details.

7. Use the With Title control to specify a title, which appears in the Group Header section.

8. For the Group Header, choose either With a Header Section or Without a Header Section.

9. For the Group Footer, choose either With a Footer Section or Without a Footer Section.

10. Use the Keep Together list to specify whether you want Access to keep the Group Header and Footer with the group detail on the same page:

    • **Do Not Keep Group Together on One Page**—Choose this item if you don't care about grouping.

- **Keep Whole Group Together on One Page**—Choose this item if you want Access to display the entire group—the Group Header, detail (records), and Group Footer—on the same page. (If this isn't possible, Access ignores this setting.)

- **Keep Header and First Record Together on One Page**—Choose this item if you want Access to display the Group Header on the same page as the first group record. This prevents the Group Header from being *orphaned*, or appearing by itself at the bottom of a page.

11. If you want the records sorted within each group, click Add a Sort and then choose a sort field and sort order.

12. Click the Close button (X) to close the Group, Sort, and Total pane.

Figure 8.2 shows a completed Group, Sort, and Total pane that groups and sorts an Inventory report on the Standard Cost field. Notice that the Design view includes the Group Header and Group Footer sections. (These sections are given the names *FieldName* Header and *FieldName* Footer, where *FieldName* is the name of the field specified in the Group, Sort, and Total pane.)

Figure 8.2
The report's Design view showing the Group, Sort, and Total pane and the Group Header and Group Footer fields.

Group header ⟶

Group footer ⟶

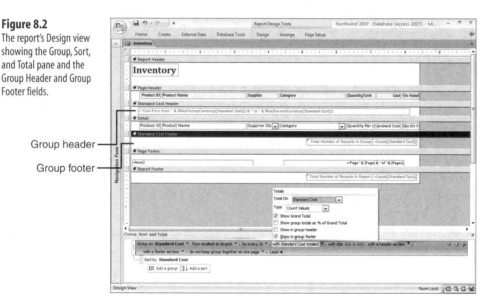

I added a Count Records calculation for the Standard Cost field, and I activated the Show In Group Footer check box to place the total in the Group Footer (see Figure 8.3). Access added the =Count([Standard Cost]) calculated control to the footer, and I added the explanatory text box (Total Number of Records in Group:). In the Group Header, I added a calculated field that displays the minimum and maximum values in the group (using the

Min and Max functions; see "Adding Calculations to a Report," later in this chapter). Figure 8.3 shows the top of the resulting report.

Figure 8.3
A preview of the report shown in Figure 8.2.

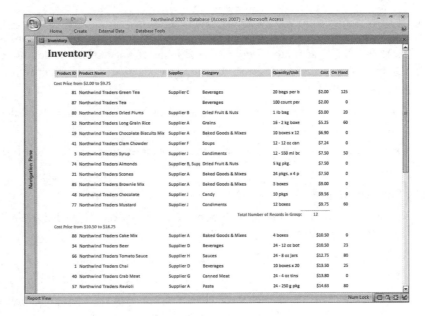

Sorting and Grouping Using an Expression

In the Group, Sort, and Total pane, you saw in the last couple of sections that you use the Field list to choose the field you want to use for sorting and grouping. However, the list also includes an expression option, so it's worth emphasizing here that you can also define your own sorting and grouping expressions. That is, you build an *expression*—a collection of operators, operands, literals, identifiers (field names), and functions—that returns some value for each record. You can then sort and group the report based on the values returned by the expression.

For example, my Inventory report contains the Standard Cost and Qty On Hand fields. Multiplying these figures together gives you an "inventory value" figure. Suppose you want to sort and group the records based on inventory value. Here's the expression to use:

```
=[Standard Cost] * [Qty On Hand]
```

Adding Calculations to a Report

Reports are often used just to display data. For example, it might be enough that an inventory report displays just the in-stock, reorder level, and on-order values for all a company's products. But anyone who uses a report as part of a decision-making process probably wants more than mere data. Such a person likely also needs to *analyze* the data in some way, and most data analysis requires one or more calculations. What were the total sales last quarter? How many days overdue are the unpaid invoices? How many records are in this report?

To answer these and many other questions within a report, you need to add one or more calculations. In the report Design view, the easiest way to add calculations is via the Group, Sort, and Total pane. However, you can also insert calculations by adding text boxes, which you can use as unbound controls that display calculated results. You can use unbound text boxes as follows:

- To display the results of an expression. (See "Using Text Boxes as Calculated Controls," later in this chapter.)
- To accept input values used as part of an expression in another text box.

Using the Totals List

Instead of building a calculation by hand, you can use the Totals list in the Group, Sort, and Total pane. Here are the steps to follow:

1. In the Group, Sort, and Total pane, drop down the Totals list.
2. Use the Total On list to choose the field on which you want to base the calculation.
3. Use the Type list to choose the calculation type: Sum, Average, Count Records, Count Values, Maximum, Minimum, Standard Deviation, or Variance.
4. Activate at least one of the following check boxes:
   - **Show Grand Total**—Activate this check box to add a calculation that applies to the report as a whole. This calculation appears in the Report Footer section.
   - **Show Group Totals as % of Grand Total**—Activate this check box to display the group totals as a percentage of the report total.
   - **Show in Group Header**—Activate this check box to add the calculation to the Group Header.
   - **Show in Group Footer**—Activate this check box to add the calculation to the Group Header
5. Repeat steps 2–4 to add more totals to the report.

Inserting a Text Box

To create a text box, follow these steps:

1. Choose the Design tab.
2. In the Controls group, click Text Box.
3. Draw the text box on the report. Access adds the text box and an associated label.
4. Edit the label text, as necessary.

> **TIP** If the text box is unbound or if it's bound to a Memo field, you can enter multiple lines of text by pressing Ctrl+Enter at the end of one line to start a new line within the text box.

Here are a few useful properties to bear in mind when you use a text box control in a report:

- Format **(Format tab)**—Defines the format used to display the text. You can either select a predefined format (such as General Date or Percent) or enter a format string.

- Decimal Places **(Format tab)**—Defines the number of decimal places to display for numeric values.

- Default Value **(Data tab)**—Specifies text that initially appears inside the text box.

- Name **(Other tab)**—Specifies the name of the text box. For unbound text boxes, this property is important only if you'll be referencing the text box value as part of an expression in another calculated control.

Using Text Boxes as Calculated Controls

In the queries section of the book, Part III, you'll see how to use an expression to build a calculated column that, when you run the query, displays the result of the expression for each record in the query dynaset.

→ For the details on constructing calculated columns in queries, **see** "Setting Up a Calculated Column," **p. 239**. (Chapter 11)

You can do something similar in your reports by setting up a text box to display the results of an expression. This expression can use any of the Access operators, operands, and functions, and it can use the values in both bound and unbound controls.

Here are the steps to follow to create a calculated text box control:

1. Choose the Design tab.
2. In the Controls group, click Text Box.
3. Draw the text box on the report. Access adds the text box and an associated label.
4. Click the text box to select it.
5. Choose Design, Property Sheet to display the control's property sheet. (You can also press Alt+Enter or double-click the control.)
6. Choose the Data tab.
7. Enter the expression in the Control Source property; be sure to begin the expression with an equals sign (=). (If you want to use the Expression Builder, click the ellipsis (…) button beside the Control Source property.)
8. Close the property sheet.

TIP
You can also enter the expression directly into the text box.

NOTE
If you enter a calculation in the Report Header or Report Footer, Access performs the calculation over the entire report. Similarly, if the calculation is in the Page Header or Page Footer, Access uses only those records included in the page; if the calculation is in the Group Header or Group Footer, Access applies the expression to only those records included in the group.

For example, the report in Figure 8.4 contains a number of calculated text box controls.

Calculated text boxes

Figure 8.4
To create a calculated control, enter an expression in an unbound text box (or in its Control Source property).

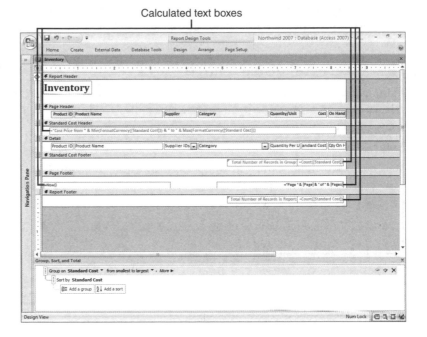

Two of the controls deal with the report grouping. In the Group Header, the text box includes the following expression:

```
="Cost Price from " & Min(FormatCurrency([Standard Cost])) & " to " &
➥Max(FormatCurrency([Standard Cost]))
```

Because this control resides in the Group Header, the expression applies only to those records in the each grouping. In this case, the expression uses the Min and Max functions to specify the range of values within each group.

In the Group Footer (named `Standard Cost Footer` in the figure) and Report Footer sections, a text box includes the expression `=Count([Standard Cost])`, which returns the number of items in the `Standard Cost` field. Access added these automatically when I specified a total for the `Standard Cost` field in the Group, Sort, and Total, pane.

The report in Figure 8.4 also includes two calculated text box controls in the Page Footer section. The text box on the left displays the current date and time using the following expression:

```
=Now()
```

On the right of the Page Footer, a text box displays page number data using the following expression:

```
="Page " & [Page] & " of " & [Pages]
```

Here, the `[Page]` identifier displays the current page number, and the `[Pages]` identifier displays the total number of pages in the report.

CASE STUDY

Creating an Invoice Report

A good example of a report that puts calculations to good use is a customer invoice for an order. Such a report needs to show the extended totals for each item (units order multiplied by unit price, less the discount), the order subtotal (the sum of the extended prices), the tax (a percentage of the subtotal), and the grand total.

Figure 8.5 shows the design of such an invoice. This report uses as its data source Northwind's Invoice Data query, a complex multiple-table query that takes data from a half dozen tables, including Customers, Orders, Order Details, and Products.

The focus in this case study is on the calculated controls that I've embedded in the Invoice report. (The report you see here is a modified version of the Invoice report that comes with the Northwind sample database.) Here's a summary:

- In the Report Header section, the invoice `Date` is generated using the `Date` function, the output of which is displayed in `dd-mmm-yyyy` format using the `Format` function:
  ```
  =Format(Date(), "dd-mmm-yyyy")
  ```
- In the Report Header section, the `Ship To` and `Bill To` areas display the customer's shipping and billing addresses. In both cases, it's ideal to display the address in the following form:
  ```
  City, State/Province Zip/Postal Code
  ```

Figure 8.5
The Invoice report boasts a number of calculated text boxes.

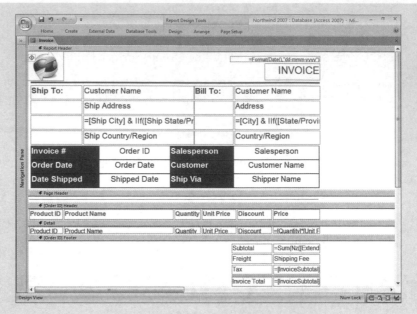

However, not all customers may have a value in the State/Province field, so the report uses an expression that displays this part of the address correctly for all customers (this is the expression in the Ship To area):

```
=[Ship City] & ", " & IIf([Ship State/Province] Is Null, "", ", " &
➡[Ship State/Province]) & " " & [Zip/PostalCode]
```

The IIf function determines whether State/Province is Null. If so, the empty string is displayed; otherwise, a comma, space, and the State/Province value are displayed. A similar expression operates in the Bill To area.

- In the Detail section, the Extended Price calculation uses the following expression:

```
=[Quantity] * [Unit Price] * (1 - [Discount])
```

Note, too, that this text box has its Name property set to ExtendedPrice.

- In the [Order ID] Footer section, the Subtotal text box (actually named InvoiceSubtotal) calculates the invoice subtotal, which is the sum of the extended prices:

```
=Sum([ExtendedPrice])
```

- The invoice tax (assuming 5% tax is charged) is calculated as follows (this text box is named Tax):

```
=[Subtotal] * 0.05
```

- Finally, the grand total is calculated by adding the InvoiceSubtotal calculation and the Tax calculation:

```
=[InvoiceSubtotal] + [Shipping Fee] + [Tax]
```

Figure 8.6 shows a sample invoice in preview mode.

Figure 8.6
The preview of the form shown in Figure 8.5.

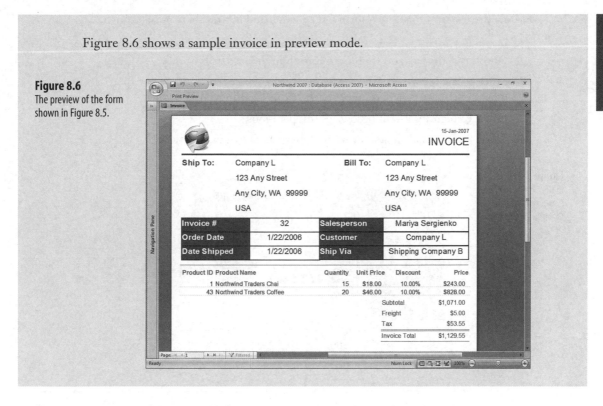

Using Advanced Methods to Launching a Report

You normally launch a report for an onscreen preview either by selecting Print Preview in the Design tab's View menu or by double-clicking the report in the Navigation pane.

If the report is part of a database that you're building for other people in the company to use, however, you might not want them poking around in the Design tab or launching things directly from the Navigation pane. In the following sections, you learn two alternative methods for launching a report—using a command button and a macro—both of which can be used as part of a front end that enables users to access reports safely.

Launching a Report with a Command Button

An Access command button is no different from the command buttons—such as OK and Cancel—that you're used to seeing in Windows and Windows applications. Of course, there is one exception: You can program an Access command button to do your bidding. In this section, you learn how to program a command button to launch a report preview onscreen. Ideally, this command button will be part of a special form, called a *switchboard*, that acts as a front end for the users. You learned how to build a switchboard in Chapter 5, "Creating Specialized Forms."

→ For the specifics on constructing a switchboard, **see** "Case Study: Creating a Switchboard Form," **p. 102**. (Chapter 5)

Follow these steps to modify a form with a command button that runs a report:

1. In the Form Design view, click the Design tab, make sure the Use Control Wizards button is activated, and then click Button in the Controls group.

2. Move to the form and drag a rectangle to the desired button size. As soon as you release the mouse, Access launches the Command Button Wizard.

3. In the Categories list, choose Report Operations.

4. In the Actions list, choose Preview Report, as shown in Figure 8.7.

Figure 8.7
In the Report Operations category, choose the Preview Report action.

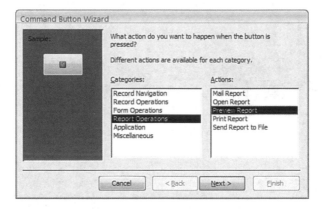

NOTE

The Report Operations category has four other report actions you can choose:

- **Mail Report**—Use this action to initiate sending the report as an email attachment. This is the same as choosing the Office, E-mail command while previewing the report.

- **Open Report**—Use this action to open the report in Report view.

- **Print Report**—Use this action to send the report directly to the printer (that is, the Print dialog box does not appear). This is the same as clicking the Print button in the Print Preview mode.

- **Send Report to File**—Use this action to send the report to a file on the hard disk. The users can choose the file format, location, and name.

---

5. Click Next. Access prompts you to select a report.

6. Choose the report you want to open and then click Next. The wizard asks you to choose how the button should appear.

7. You have two choices (click Next after you've clicked the option you want):

- **Text**—Choose this option to display a word or phrase on the button. Use the text box provided to enter your text.

- **P**icture—Choose this option to display a picture on the button. Activate the **S**how All Pictures check box to see a full list of the available pictures.

8. Enter a name for the command button, if desired.

9. Click **F**inish to complete the operation.

Launching a Report with a Macro

The Preview Report action does only one thing: open a report in Print Preview mode. However, what if you want to perform multiple actions? For example, you might want to open the report, maximize the window, and then display a message to the users. You can't do this using the built-in command button actions, but you can create a custom action by designing your own macro.

> **NOTE**
> A *macro* is a series of actions—such as opening a report, applying a filter, or displaying a message—packaged as a single object. When users run the macro, Access executes each of the defined actions in the order specified within the macro.

In Access you can use macros to automate tasks by building lists of actions that occur in response to events, such as a command button being clicked. You build the list in the order you want these actions to occur. The list can cover all the features available through the menus, as well as some that aren't. By using macros, you can automate the process of importing and exporting data, create buttons that perform complex queries, and perform other useful functions.

Creating the Macro

Unlike, say, programming Visual Basic for Applications code, creating a macro is not difficult. The reason is that Access comes with a finite set of macro actions, and although there are over 50 such actions, only a few are applicable to reports. Therefore, creating a macro is a straightforward process of choosing an action and then configuring the action (using simple lists and text boxes) so that it does exactly what you want.

To get started, choose Create, Macro, M**a**cro. Figure 8.8 shows the Macro window that appears.

Here are the basic steps to follow to build the macro:

1. In the first available Action cell, use the drop-down list to choose the action you want the macro to perform. The arguments that control how the action is performed (if any) appear in the Action Arguments section at the bottom of the Macro window.

2. Use the adjacent Comment cell to enter a brief description of the action.

3. Use the controls in the Action Arguments section to set up the action so that it does what you want.

4. Repeat steps 1–3 to add the other actions you want the macro to run.

5. Save the macro.

6. Test the macro by running it, which you can do by using any of the following methods:

   • Choose Design, Run.

   • In the Macro tab of the Navigation pane, double-click the macro.

   • If your macro depends on having a particular report already open (for example, your macro might close the report), you need to open the appropriate report and choose Database Tools, Run Macro. Access displays the Run Macro dialog box, shown in Figure 8.9. Use the Macro Name list to choose what you want to run and then click OK.

Figure 8.8
The Macro window appears when you launch a new macro.

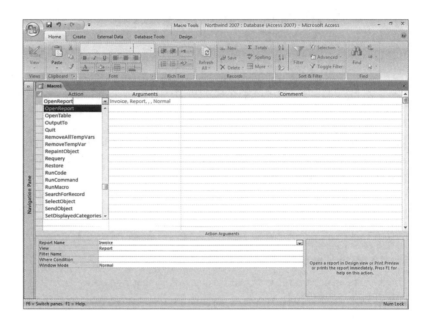

Figure 8.9
If your macro requires an open report, launch the report and then use the Run Macro dialog box to start the macro.

> **TIP**
>
> You can also make one macro run another macro by using the RunMacro action.

Here are some macro actions that are applicable to report scenarios:

`Beep`—Beeps the system's internal speaker.

`Close`—Closes a specified database object. For a report, choose Report in the Object Type argument and then choose the report name in the Object Name argument. You can also use the Save argument to specify whether the report is saved before being closed.

`DeleteObject`—Deletes a specified database object. For a report, choose Report in the Object Type argument and then choose the report name in the Object Name argument.

> **CAUTION**
>
> Use the `DeleteObject` action with extreme caution. Access does *not* display a warning dialog box when it runs this action; instead, it just deletes the object immediately.

`Maximize`—Maximizes the active window.

`Minimize`—Minimizes the active window.

`MoveSize`—Moves and/or sizes the active window. Use the Right and Down arguments to move the window; use the Width and Height arguments to size the window.

`MsgBox`—Displays a message to the users. Use the Message argument to specify the message; use the Beep argument to specify whether Access beeps the system's internal speaker when the dialog box appears; use the Type argument to choose the type of icon to display in the dialog box (Critical, Warning!, and so on); use the Title argument to set the text that appears in the title of the dialog box.

`OpenReport`—Opens the report specified in the Report Name argument. Use the View argument to choose the report view: Print Preview, Design, or Print (see also the `PrintOut` action, which follows). If you want to filter the records, use the Filter Name argument to enter the name of a query or a filter saved as a query. Alternatively, use the Where Condition argument to enter a SQL WHERE expression. Use the Window Mode argument to set the type of window you want the report to appear in: Normal, Hidden, Icon (minimized), or Dialog (the users can't choose any other window or a menu command).

→ In the Where Condition argument, don't include the WHERE keyword; just enter the expression itself. For more information about the SQL SELECT statement's WHERE clause, **see** "The WHERE Clause," **p. 345**. (Chapter 15)

`OutputTo`—Sends the report to a file. For a report, choose Report in the Object Type argument and then choose the report name in the Object Name argument. Use the Output Format argument to select the file format and use Output File to specify the name and location of the file. If you want the file to open automatically in the associated application (for example, a Rich Text Format file opening in Word), set the Auto Start argument to Yes.

PrintOut—Prints the report. Use the Print Range argument to choose All (prints the entire report), Selection (prints only the selected text; this doesn't work with reports because you can't select text when previewing a report); or Pages (prints only a range of pages, as specified by the Page From and Page To arguments). You can also set the print quality, number of copies, and whether Access should collate copies.

Quit—Quits Access. Use the Options argument to determine whether Access saves changed database objects.

Restore—Restores the active window to the size and position it occupied before being maximized or minimized.

Save—Saves a specified database object. For a report, choose Report in the Object Type argument and then choose the report name in the Object Name argument.

SendObject—Sends the specified database object as an email attachment. For a report, choose Report in the Object Type argument and then choose the report name in the Object Name argument. Use the To, Cc, Bcc, Subject, and Message Text arguments to set up the specifics of the email message. If you don't want the users to edit the message before sending it, choose No for the Edit Message argument.

SetValue—Sets the value of a control, field, or property. Use the Item argument to enter the name of the item; use the Expression argument to enter an expression that defines the value of the item (don't precede the expression with an equals sign).

ShowAllRecords—Removes a previously set filter.

Associating the Macro with a Command Button

If you're building a switchboard or other front end for the users, you can program any of the command buttons to run a macro. Here are the steps to follow:

1. Open the Design view for the form you want to work with and then, in the Design tab, make sure the Use Control Wizards button is activated and click the Command Button tool.

2. On the form, drag a rectangle to the desired button size and then release the mouse button. Access launches the Command Button Wizard.

3. In the Categories list, choose Miscellaneous.

4. In the Actions list, choose Run Macro. Click Next.

5. Access prompts you to select a macro. Choose the macro you want to run and then click Next.

6. The wizard asks you to choose how the button should appear. You have two choices (click Next after you've clicked the option you want):

   • **Text**—Choose this option to display a word or phrase on the button. Use the text box provided to enter your text.

   • **Picture**—Choose this option to display a picture on the button. Activate the Show All Pictures check box to see a full list of the available pictures.

7. Enter a name for the command button, if desired, and then click Finish to complete the operation.

Associating the Macro with a Report Event

Access reports support a number of *events*, which are signals triggered when certain events occur. For example, the On Open event is triggered when the users open the report. If you associate a macro with an event, Access runs the macro each time the event fires.

Follow these steps to associate a macro with a report event:

1. Open the report in Design view.
2. Select the report.
3. Choose Design, Property Sheet to display the report's property sheet.
4. Display the Event tab to see a list of the various events that you can use to trigger the macro, as shown in Figure 8.10.

Figure 8.10
Use the Event tab to associate a macro with a particular report event.

5. For the event you want to work with, use the drop-down list to select the macro you want to run.

 TIP   If you need to create a macro from scratch, click the ellipsis (. . .) button to display the Choose Builder dialog box. Select Macro Builder in the list and then click OK to begin building your macro directly.

6. Close the property sheet.

Controlling Report Output

Let's conclude this look at advanced report features by looking at three properties that give you more control over how Access displays the report, particularly at the section level.

Adding Page Breaks After Sections

If you want to make reports more readable, it's often a good idea to start a particular section (such as a grouping) on a new page. Instead of adding a Page Break control, you can force Access to add automatic page breaks by modifying a section's Force New Page property. Follow these steps:

1. Open the report in Design view.
2. Select the section you want to work with.
3. Choose Design, Property Sheet to display the section's property sheet.
4. Display the Format tab.
5. Use the Force New Page list to choose one of the following values:
   - Before Section—Choose this option to force a page break before the section. This ensures that the section begins at the top of a new page.
   - After Section—Choose this option to force a page break after the section. This ensures that the next section begins at the top of a new page.
   - Before & After—Choose this option to force page breaks before and after the section. This ensures that the section appears on a page by itself.
6. Close the property sheet.
7. Print preview the report to confirm that each section is formatted the way you want.

Starting Sections at the Top of a Row or Column

You learn in Chapter 9, "Creating Specialized Reports," that it's possible to configure a report to use multiple columns, where the fields are arranged down and then across (in columns) or across and then down (in rows). You can force Access to start a section at the beginning of a column or row by modifying the section's New Row or Col property. Follow these steps:

➔ For the details on multiple-column reports, **see** "Creating a Multiple-Column Report," **p. 177**. (Chapter 9)

1. Open the report in Design view.
2. Select the section you want to work with.
3. Choose Design, Property Sheet to display the section's property sheet.
4. Display the Format tab.

5. Use the New Row or Col list to choose one of the following values:
   - Before Section—Choose this option to force the section to begin at the top of a new row or column.
   - After Section—Choose this option to force the next section to begin at the top of a new row or column.
   - Before & After—Choose this option to force the section to appear in a new row or column by itself.
6. Close the property sheet.
7. Print preview the report to confirm that each section is formatted the way you want.

Avoiding Widowed Records

A *widow* is a control or field that appears at the top of a new page by itself. In most cases, the report is more readable if you avoid widows and force all the elements of a section to appear together on the page. You can do this by modifying the section's Keep Together property, as shown in the following steps:

1. Open the report in Design view.
2. Select the section you want to work with.
3. Choose Design, Property Sheet to display the section's property sheet.
4. Display the Format tab.
5. In the Keep Together property, choose Yes.
6. Close the property sheet.
7. Print preview the report to verify that each section is formatted the way you want.

From Here

→ For the specifics on constructing a switchboard, **see** "Case Study: Creating a Switchboard Form," **p. 102**. (Chapter 5)

→ For the basics on report design, **see** "Creating a Report in Design View," **p. 116**. (Chapter 6)

→ For a number of techniques for working with controls, **see** "Manipulating Report Controls," **p. 128**. (Chapter 6)

→ For the details on multiple-column reports, **see** "Creating a Multiple-Column Report," **p. 177**. (Chapter 9)

→ For the details on constructing calculated columns in queries, **see** "Setting Up a Calculated Column," **p. 239**. (Chapter 11)

→ For more information about the SQL SELECT statement's WHERE clause, **see** "The WHERE Clause," **p. 345**. (Chapter 15)

Creating Specialized Reports

9

As the natural product of much database work, reports play an important role in business, as I hope the last few chapters have shown. In the computer world, it's axiomatic that the more important a tool is, the more flexible it needs to be. The reason is that the important tools are used by a wide variety of people in a wide variety of circumstances. The more flexible the tool is, the more it can be adapted to suit all these different situations.

The Access reporting engine is a most accommodating tool. Even the reporting tools you've seen so far provide a great deal of flexibility in terms of layout, formatting, and the all-important summary calculations. However, Access reports offer even more pliable tools that enable you to produce an even wider variety of reports. This chapter closes your look at Access reports by showing you how to build five specialized report types: multiple-column, mailing labels, mail merge, multiple-table, and PivotChart.

Creating a Multiple-Column Report

You've seen that a basic report comes in two flavors: tabular, which uses a datasheet-like layout with fields in columns and records in rows; and columnar, which uses a form-like layout with the fields arranged in a single, vertical column for each record. For this reason, the columnar layout is also called the *single-column* layout.

The single-column format is useful when you have wide fields because each field can use up to the entire width of the page. If your fields aren't all that wide, however, the columnar layout is wasteful because you end up with a great deal of whitespace to the right of the fields. The tabular layout can get rid of the whitespace, but it's not as nice looking as the columnar layout.

Instead of compromising, it's possible to get the efficiency of the tabular layout combined with the attractive look of the columnar layout. You can do this by creating a *multiple-column* report that takes the basic columnar format and bends the records so that they now snake through two or more columns (which is why this is sometimes called a *snaked-column* layout).

Setting Up the Report

The multiple-column effect appears only when you preview or print the report. In other words, it's not something that you set up within the Report Design window (that is, by manipulating the position of the fields and field labels). However, that doesn't mean that you can apply the multiple-column layout to any report. When you're building your report, bear in mind that the page is going to be divided into columns, and that the width of each column is the width of the page divided by the number of columns, less the left and right page margins and the amount of space you want between each column.

For example, suppose you want two columns a half-inch apart on a page 8.5 inches wide. Assuming the left and right margins are 1 inch, that leaves 6 inches for the two columns, or 3 inches each. Therefore, when building the report, you need to make sure that no part of the report is wider than 3 inches. (Use the horizontal ruler to monitor the width of the report. If you don't see the ruler, choose the Arrange tab and then click to activate the Ruler toggle button in the Show/Hide group.)

Finally, after your controls are set to the proper width, change the width of the report itself so that it's no wider than the column width you want.

Tweaking the Page Setup

You set up a report to use multiple columns by modifying the Page Setup options. Here are the steps to follow:

1. Choose Page Setup, Page Setup to display the Page Setup dialog box.
2. In the Print Options tab, make note of the left and right margin widths, as given by the values in the Left and Right text boxes. You need these values to calculate the optimal column width.
3. Display the Columns tab.
4. In the Grid Settings group, use the Number of Columns text box to type how many columns you want to use in your report. As shown in Figure 9.1, when you enter a value greater than 1, Access enables the Column Layout group.

Figure 9.1
Use the Columns tab to set up your report to use multiple columns.

5. If you want to include extra space between each record, type the spacing value (in inches) in the Ro̲w Spacing text box.

6. Use the Colu̲mn Spacing text box to specify the amount of space (in inches) to allow between each column.

7. In the Column Size group, the Wi̲dth text box should already be set to the width of your report (assuming the S̲ame As Detail check box is activated). If not, use the Wi̲dth text box to enter the width you want to use for each column. You can also use the H̲eight text box to specify the height of each record.

8. Use the Column Layout group to choose one of the following options:

   • **D̲own, Then Across**—With this option, the records are printed down each column, and the columns run across the page.

   • **Across, The̲n Down**—In this case, the records are printed across each row, and the rows run down the page.

9. Click OK.

10. Preview the report to make sure your columns look the way you want.

→ Remember that you can force Access to start a section at the beginning of a column (or row). For the details, **see** "Starting Sections at the Top of a Row or Column," **p. 174**. (Chapter 8)

Figure 9.2 shows a two-column report with data from the Northwind Customers table. (The Contact Name field combines the First Name and Last Name fields from that table.)

Figure 9.2
An example of a two-column report.

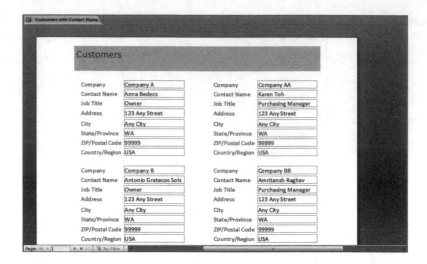

Troubleshooting Multiple Columns

If your columns don't all fit on the page, Access displays the dialog box shown in Figure 9.3.

Figure 9.3
Access displays this dialog box if your columns don't all fit the width of the page.

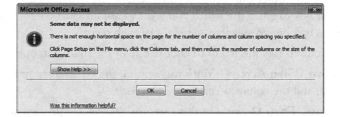

Here are some solutions to try:

■ Reduce the number of columns. For example, if three columns won't fit on the page, try using only two.

■ Reduce the width of each column. In the Columns tab of the Page Setup dialog box, reduce the value of the Width text box in the Column Size group.

■ Reduce the width of your report by reducing the width of the controls and the report itself. If this prevents a field text box from displaying all its data, try increasing the height of the text box to compensate.

■ In the Margins tab of the Page Setup dialog box, reduce the Left and Right values accordingly. The smaller your margins, the more room Access can devote to the columns.

> **CAUTION**
>
> Most printers don't support margins much smaller than about 0.25 inch.

■ In the Page tab of the Page Setup dialog box, choose Landscape instead of Portrait.

CASE STUDY

9

Using Multiple Columns to Reduce Report Page Count

As long as you don't sacrifice readability and sense, a good report goal to bear in mind is minimizing the overall page count. Smaller reports are more likely to be read, and they make it easier for readers to find information. If you'll be printing the report, particularly if you'll be printing a number of copies, reducing page count has the laudable side benefit of being environmentally friendly. You can reduce page count by reducing the font, avoiding page breaks wherever possible, and making sure your groupings don't generate widowed records.

Another easy way to reduce page count is to use multiple columns, which can greatly reduce the amount of whitespace on each page. This case study takes you through a sample report to see just how many pages multiple columns can save.

The study begins with the query shown in Figure 9.4. This query uses data from the old Northwind sample database that shipped with earlier versions of Access. This database has a much larger number of records than the Northwind 2007 database that comes with Access 2007, so it better suits our purposes here. (For example, the old Orders table has 830 records, compared to a mere 48 records in the Northwind 2007 Orders table.) The query combines fields from the Customers, Order Details, Orders, and Employees tables—the `CustomerID` and `OrderDate`—plus two calculated fields called `Employee` (the first and last name of the employee who took each order) and `Order Total` (the sum of the extended prices).

Figure 9.4
This query is used as the data source for the sample report used in this section.

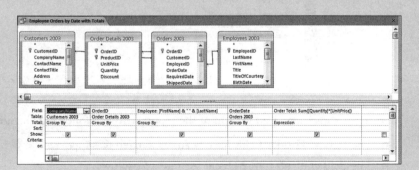

Figure 9.5 shows the initial report, and Figure 9.6 shows the preview. Note that the [Pages] identifier returns 83 as the total page count for the report.

Figure 9.5
The original report.

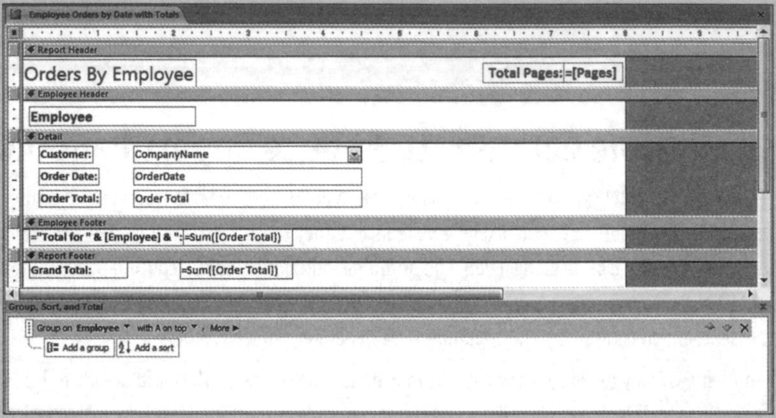

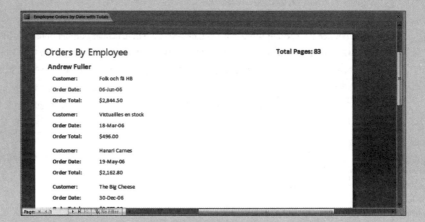

Figure 9.6
The preview of the report shown in Figure 9.5, which produces 83 total pages.

Figure 9.7 shows a revised version of the report with the following changes:

- The Report Header fields have been rearranged to support a thinner report.
- The field controls in the Detail section are narrower.
- The Employee Footer fields have been rearranged to support a thinner report.
- The overall report width has been reduced to 3 inches.
- The page setup has been changed so that the records now appear in two 3-inch columns.

Figure 9.7
A revised version of the report that uses a thinner layout configured into two columns.

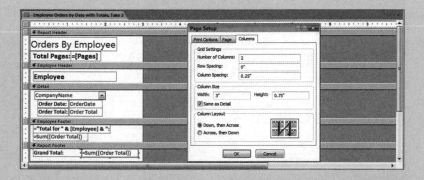

Figure 9.8 shows the preview of the new report. As you can see, the total page count has been cut to much less than half, and is now down to 31 pages.

Figure 9.8
The preview of the report shown in Figure 9.7, which now outputs only 31 total pages.

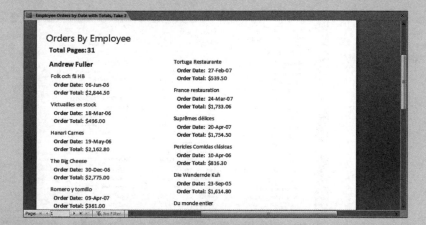

To reduce the page count even further, you can do the following, as shown in Figure 9.9:

- Reduce some of the font sizes.
- Reduce the field widths even further.
- Reduce the overall report width to just 2 inches.
- Configure the report to display three 2-inch columns.

9

Figure 9.9
The final version of the report, configured to use three 2-inch columns.

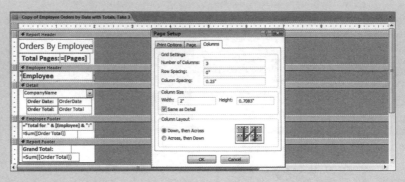

Figure 9.10 shows the preview of the final version of the report, which is now down to 21 pages, about a quarter of its original heft.

Figure 9.10
The preview of the report shown in Figure 9.9, which now produces just 21 total pages.

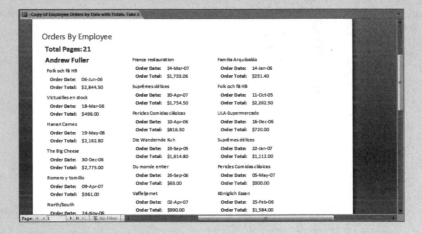

Creating Mailing Labels

When you examine the output of the report shown in Figure 9.10, take out the text in the Report Header and Employee Header sections, and you might be struck by the report's uncanny resemblance to a sheet of mailing labels. You'd be well within your rights to think just that, because a multiple-column layout is exactly how you build a mailing label report in Access. After all, what is a sheet of mailing labels but a collection of stick-ons, each with a specific width and height, repeated in a row-and-column format? What is a multiple-column report? Why, it's the same thing: a collection of records, each with a specific width and height, repeated in a row-and-column format.

So if you want to print mailing labels from a table of address data, you need only use that data as the source of a multiple-column report, where each column is configured to precisely match the width and height of your labels. Of course, you also need to take into account the row and column spacing to match the layout on the mailing label sheet, so some tweaking is required.

Running the Label Wizard

Rather than go through the tedious process of tweaking a report to fit a label sheet, Access provides you with an easier method: the Label Wizard. This wizard takes you step by step through the entire label-making process. It supports all the standard mailing label formats, so the tweaking and guesswork are taken out of the process.

Here are the steps to follow to build a set of mailing labels using the Label Wizard:

1. In the Navigation pane, choose the table or query you want to use as the data source for the report.

2. Choose Create, Labels. Access launches the Label Wizard, as shown in Figure 9.11.

Figure 9.11
Use the initial Label Wizard dialog box to choose the label size you want to use.

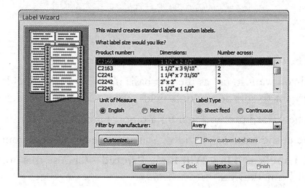

3. Use the What Label Size Would You Like? list to click the label size you want to use. You can also use the following controls to change the displayed labels (to learn how to customize the label size, see "Creating a Custom Label," later in this chapter):

   - **Unit of Measure**—Click either the English or the Metric option.
   - **Label Type**—Click either the Sheet Feed or the Continuous option.
   - **Filter by Manufacturer**—In the drop-down list, click the name of the label manufacturer. (If you don't see the manufacturer listed, choose Avery, because many off-brand labels are manufactured to the Avery standard.)

4. Click Next. The Label Wizard prompts you for font information.

5. Use the Font Name, Font Size, Font Weight, and Text Color controls to choose the font specifics for the label text. You can also choose to italicize and underline the text by activating the Italic and Underline check boxes.

6. Click Next. The wizard asks you to define the layout of the label.

7. Build the label by using the following techniques (see Figure 9.12 for an example):

   - To add a field, click the field name in the Available Fields list and then click >.

- To start a new line in the label, move to the end of the current line and press Enter.
- To add text to the label, position the cursor where you want the text to appear and then type the text.

Figure 9.12
Define the label layout by adding fields, new lines, and text.

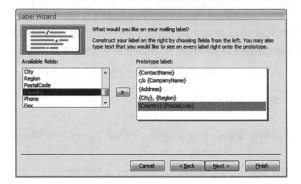

8. Click Next. The wizard prompts you for the report sort order.
9. Click the field you want to use as the sort basis in the Available Fields list and then click >. If you want to sort on multiple fields, repeat in the sort order you want.
10. Click Next. The wizard prompts you for a report name.
11. Type the name in the text box provided. You also need to choose your next action:

    - **See the Labels as They Will Look Printed**—Choose this option to display the report in Print Preview.
    - **Modify the Label Design**—Choose this option to display the report in the Design view.

12. Click Finish.

Figure 9.13 shows a sample report.

Figure 9.13
A report ready to be printed as mailing labels.

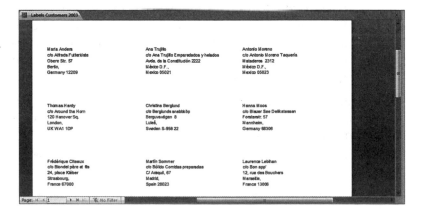

Creating a Custom Label

If the Label Wizard doesn't recognize your mailing labels, or if you need a custom job for some other reason, the wizard enables you to design your own custom label size. Here are the steps to follow:

1. In the Navigation pane, choose the table or query you want to use as the data source for the report.
2. Choose Create, Labels to start the Label Wizard.
3. Click Customize. The wizard displays the New Label Size dialog box.
4. Click New. The New Label dialog box appears.
5. Use the Label Name text box to type a name for the custom label.
6. In the Unit of Measure group, click English or Metric.
7. In the Label Type group, click Sheet Feed or Continuous.
8. In the Orientation group, click Portrait or Landscape.
9. Use the Number Across text box to type the number of columns of labels you require.
10. Use the text boxes in the Enter Label Measurements in Inches/Centimeters area to specify the label dimensions as well as the margin widths, row and column spacing, and other measurements. Figure 9.14 shows an example.
11. Click OK.

Figure 9.14
Use the New Label dialog box to design a custom label size.

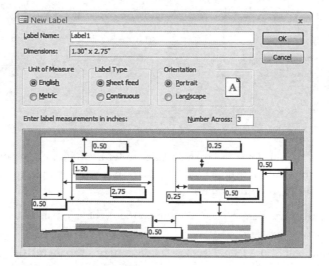

Creating a Mail Merge Report

In Chapter 10, "Creating a Basic Query," you learn how to use an Access query as the data source for the Word Mail Merge Wizard. This wizard takes you through the process of performing a mail merge in Word using the data specified in the query.

→ For the specifics of the Word Mail Merge Wizard, **see** "Case Study: Querying for a Mail Merge," **p. 217**. (Chapter 10)

However, if you don't have Word, or if you'd rather not go through the lengthy steps of the Mail Merge Wizard, you still can set up a mail merge using only the Access reporting engine. The secret lies in judicious use of calculated text boxes. Specifically, you use text boxes to enter not only the text of the form letter, but also the merge fields, which come from the report's underlying data source.

For example, suppose the data source contains a field named `ContactName`, and you want to use the values in this field for the letter's salutation. You can do this in the report by adding an unbound text box in the Detail section and entering into the text box the following formula:

```
="Dear " & [ContactName] & ":"
```

Let's look at a real-world example. Figure 9.15 shows a query that uses fields from the old Northwind database (the one from Access 2003), specifically its Products and Suppliers tables. The calculated column named Reorder compares the `UnitsInStock` value with the `ReorderLevel` value: If `UnitsInStock` is less than or equal to `ReorderLevel`, the formula returns `True`, so this is a product that needs to be reordered. (To make sure you don't reorder a discontinued product, the other criterion is that the `Discontinued` value must be `False`.)

Figure 9.15
This query returns records for those products that need to be reordered, and is used as the data source for the mail merge report.

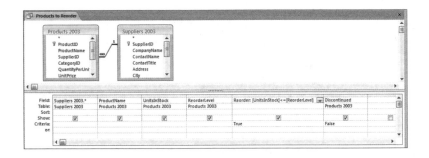

The goal now is to print letters to each supplier to let them know that you want to reorder those products returned by the query. Figure 9.16 shows the completed mail merge report. Here are some notes about this report:

- The top half of the Page Header section contains the company logo, address, title, and current date.

- The second half of the Page Header section contains the merge fields that enter the supplier's contact name, company name, and address. Notice that the merge fields are a mix of unbound text boxes with expressions and regular data fields. You use the calculated controls when you need to customize the output. For example, the following expression inserts a comma and a space between the contact's name and title:
  ```
  =[ContactName] & ", " & [ContactTitle]
  ```

- The Detail section contains the text of the letter. In most cases, the text is interspersed with merge fields and other expressions.

- To ensure that each form letter appears on a separate page, I set the Detail section's `Force New Page` property to `After Section`.

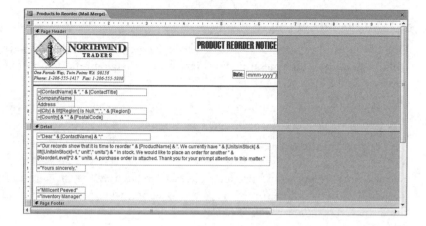

Figure 9.16
This mail merge report uses calculations in unbound text boxes to insert the merge fields into the letter text.

Figure 9.17 shows a sample form letter that appears when you open the report's Print Preview.

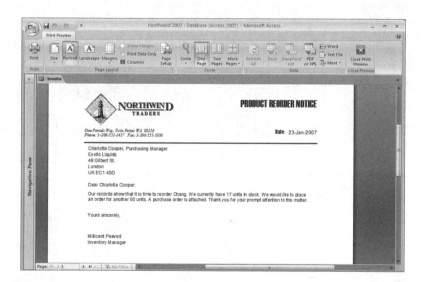

Figure 9.17
A sample form letter created by the mail merge report shown in Figure 9.16.

Creating a Multiple-Table Report

As you've seen in a couple of this chapter's examples, creating a report that uses multiple tables is straightforward. You create a query that includes two or more tables (as detailed in

Chapter 12, "Working with Multiple-Table Queries") and then use that query as the report's data source. However, there's another way that you can use multiple tables with reports: by creating subreports. The next few sections show you various ways to create and work with subreports to build a multiple-table report.

→ For the details of multiple-table queries, **see** "Working with Multiple Tables in a Query," **p. 259.** (Chapter 12)

Understanding Subreports

One of the handiest uses for related tables is to create a report that displays the related data from both tables simultaneously. For example, the Catalog report shown in Figure 9.18 contains data from two sources:

- The top part of the report displays three fields from the old Northwind database's Categories table: `CategoryName`, `Description`, and `Picture`.
- The rest of the report contains records from the Products table.

Because the Categories and Products tables are related by the `CategoryID` field, the products shown are just those for the displayed category; when you move to a different category, the displayed products change accordingly.

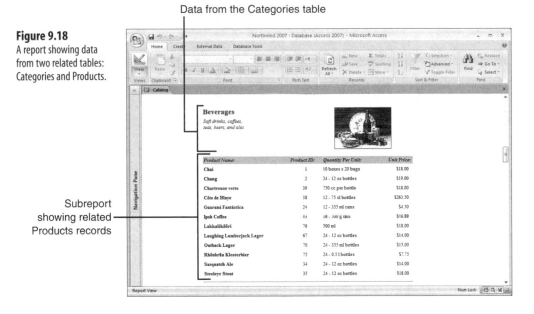

Figure 9.18
A report showing data from two related tables: Categories and Products.

Data from the Categories table

Subreport showing related Products records

This type of report is actually a combination of two separate reports. The regular report fields (in the example, the ones at the top of the page showing the Categories data) are part of the *main report*, and the rest (the Products table data) is called the *subreport*. You can think of a report/subreport combination as a main/detail report or a parent/child report.

Subreports are especially effective at showing dependent records from tables or queries participating in one-to-many relationships. In the preceding example, each item in the Categories table can have many related records in the Products table. Because of this, all subreports are viewed using the tabular layout.

Creating a Report and Subreport with the Report Wizard

In Chapter 6, "Creating and Publishing a Report," you learned how to use the Report Wizard to create basic reports step by step. The Report Wizard is also an easy way to create a report/subreport combination when you're working with multiple tables. Here are the steps to follow:

→ For coverage of the Report Wizard, **see** "Creating Simple Reports with the Report Wizard," **p. 114**. (Chapter 6)

→ When using multiple tables and queries, however, you must have the relationships between those tables and queries established. For more information, **see** "Establishing Table Relationships," **p. 267**. (Chapter 12)

1. In the Navigation pane, click the table or query you want to use for the main report.

2. Choose Create, Report Wizard.

3. In the first of the wizard's dialog boxes, for each field you want to include in the report, click the field in the Available Fields list and click the > button. (If you want to include all the fields, click the >> button.)

4. To add another table or query to the report, click it in the Table/Queries list and then repeat step 3.

5. When you're done adding data sources, click Next.

6. Use the next wizard dialog box (shown in Figure 9.19) to click the table or query that contains the data to be displayed in the main report. Click Next.

Figure 9.19
Use this Report Wizard dialog box to choose which table will be displayed in the main report.

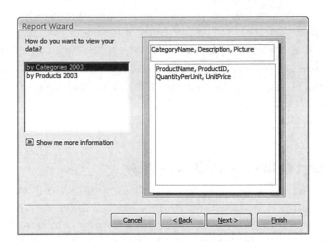

7. The next Report Wizard dialog box asks if you want to add any grouping levels. By default, the report is grouped on the items in the data source used for the main report. Make your changes, if any, and click Next.

8. The wizard then asks if you want to sort the detail records (meaning the subreport records). Choose your field or fields, assign Ascending or Descending to each one, and then click Next.

9. Now the wizard prompts you to choose the report layout, as shown in Figure 9.20. In the sample report, the darker text represents the report headings and the lighter text represents the report data. Choose the layout that you prefer, choose Portrait or Landscape, and then click Next.

Figure 9.20
Use this Report Wizard dialog box to choose the layout of the main report and subreport fields.

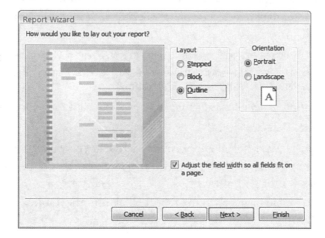

10. The next wizard dialog box asks you to select one of the predefined AutoReport themes. Click the theme you want to use and then click Next.

11. The last wizard dialog box lets you modify the name of the report. A suggestion is already in place, and it's based on the names of the underlying tables for the main report, but you can enter any name that doesn't conflict with an existing report.

12. If you want to use the report right away, leave the Preview the Report option activated. Alternatively, click Modify the Report's Design to open the report in Design view.

13. Click Finish to complete the report. Figure 9.21 shows a sample report created with the Report Wizard.

Creating a Subreport in the Report Design View

If you've already started your report, you can still add a subreport in Design view by using the Subreport control. Access even comes with a handy SubReport Wizard that takes you step by step through the process of setting up the subreport. The next two sections show you how to create a subreport from a table or query and from an existing report.

Figure 9.21
A sample main report/subreport created using the Report Wizard.

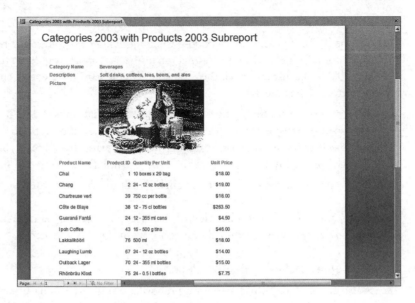

9

Creating a Subreport Using Another Table or Query

If you want to base your subreport on the fields from another table or query, here are the steps to follow to add the subreport using the SubReport Wizard:

1. In the Report Design view, click the Design tab, make sure the Use Control Wizards button is activated and then click the Subform/Subreport button in the Controls group.

2. Draw the subreport on the report. Access launches the SubReport Wizard, as shown in Figure 9.22.

Figure 9.22
The SubReport Wizard makes it easy to add a subreport to an existing report.

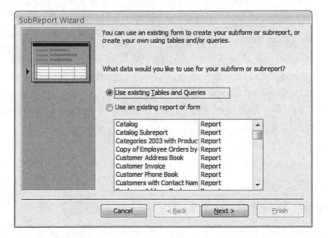

3. Activate the Use Existing Tables and Queries option and click Next.

4. Use the Table/Queries list to choose the underlying data source for the subreport. Then, for each field you want to include in the subreport, highlight the field in the Available Fields list and click the > button. (If you want to select all the fields, click the >> button.) Click Next.

5. Use the next wizard dialog box to choose the field that links the main report and the subreport. As long as the tables are related (which they should be for this to work), Access will establish the correct linking field automatically. (If not, you can always activate the Define My Own option and set up the link fields yourself.) Click Next.

6. Enter a name for the subreport and click Finish to complete your work.

From here, adjust the size and position of the subreport control, as necessary. You might also want to delete the label control that comes with the subreport.

Creating a Subreport Using Another Report

Access also enables you to use an existing report as a subreport. That is, you can draw the subreport control on your report and then embed the existing report within that control. This capability is useful if you have a specific subreport layout in mind and you want to create that layout beforehand.

If you want to base your subreport on an existing report, here are the steps to follow to add the subreport using the SubReport Wizard:

1. Create and save the other report, if you haven't done so already.

2. In the Report Design view, click the Design tab, make sure the Use Control Wizards button is activated, and then click the Subform/Subreport button in the Controls group.

3. Draw the subreport on the report. Access launches the SubReport Wizard.

4. Activate the Use an Existing Report or Form option and use the list provided to select the report you want to use. Click Next.

5. Use the next wizard dialog box to choose the field that links the main report and the subreport. As long as the tables are related (which they should be for this to work), Access will establish the correct linking field automatically. (If not, you can always activate the Define My Own option and set up the link fields yourself.) Click Next.

6. Enter a name for the subreport and click Finish to complete your work.

Again, tweak the size and position of the subreport control, as required.

Creating a PivotChart Report

A PivotChart is an efficient mechanism for summarizing and analyzing complex data. Unfortunately, the Access reporting engine doesn't have a PivotChart view for reports.

However, you still can include a PivotChart as part of a report. The secret is the subreport control, which, as you learned in the previous section, can display an existing report as a subreport. However, the subreport control can also display an existing *form* as a subreport. And, as you learned in Chapter 5, "Creating Specialized Forms," Access forms *do* have a PivotChart view.

→ To learn how to use the Form PivotChart view, **see** "Creating a PivotChart Form," **p. 108.** (Chapter 5)

Therefore, to create a PivotChart report, you first create a PivotChart form and then embed that form into a subreport control. Here are the specific steps to follow:

1. Create and save the PivotChart form, if you haven't done so already.

2. In the Report Design view, click the Design tab, make sure the Use Control Wizards button is activated, and then click the Subform/Subreport button in the Controls group.

3. Draw the subreport on the report. Access launches the SubReport Wizard.

4. Activate the Use an Existing Report or Form option and use the list provided to select the PivotChart form you want to use. Click Next.

5. Use the next wizard dialog box to choose the field that links the main report and the subreport and then click Next.

6. Enter a name for the subreport and click Finish.

7. Adjust the size and position of the subreport control so that the PivotChart is fully visible.

From Here

→ For the specifics on the Word Mail Merge Wizard, **see** "Case Study: Querying for a Mail Merge," **p. 217.** (Chapter 10)

→ For the details on multiple-table queries, **see** "Working with Multiple Tables in a Query," **p. 259.** (Chapter 12)

→ For more information about the relationship between tables, **see** "Establishing Table Relationships," **p. 267.** (Chapter 12)

→ To learn how to use the Form PivotChart view, **see** "Creating a PivotChart Form," **p. 108.** (Chapter 5)

→ For coverage of the Report Wizard, **see** "Creating Simple Reports with the Report Wizard," **p. 114.** (Chapter 6)

→ For the basics on report design, **see** "Creating a Report in Design View," **p. 116.** (Chapter 6)

→ To learn how to force Access to start a section at the beginning of a column (or row), **see** "Starting Sections at the Top of a Row or Column," **p. 174.** (Chapter 8)

Creating Powerful Queries

Creating a Basic Query

10

If you have a large amount of data in a table, it's not often that you'll want or need to work directly with the raw data. Instead, you'll usually work with data that has been massaged in one or both of the following ways:

- The data has been sorted on one or more fields.
- The data has been filtered to show only a relevant subset of the records.

The combination of sorting and filtering is at the heart of one of the most powerful concepts in all of Access: queries. Queries are no great mystery, really. Although the name implies that queries are a sort of question, it's more useful to think of them as *requests*. In the simplest case, a query is a request to see a particular subset of your data in a particular order. For example, showing only those records in a customer table where the country is "Sweden" and the first name is "Sven," sorted by last name, might be a fairly simple query to build. This type of query is known in the trade as a *select query*, and you learn how to build your own select queries in this chapter. (You learn about other query types such as update and delete queries in Chapter 13, "Creating Advanced Queries.")

Sorting Records

Before getting to the specifics of select queries, let's first take a look at the various ways Access enables you to sort a table. Sorting means that you place the records in alphabetical order based on the data in a field (or numerical order if the field contains numeric or currency data). For example, suppose you have a table of customer names and addresses, and you want to see all the customers who are from

California. All you have to do is sort the table by the data in the State field, and all the records with CA in this field appear together.

Sorting on a Single Field

Because sorting is such a common practice, the Access programmers made it easy to perform quick sorts on a single field. To try this, follow these steps:

1. Select the field you want to sort on by clicking within that field on any record.
2. Choose the Home tab.
3. In the Sort & Filter group, choose one of the following commands:

    - **Ascending**—Choose this command to sort on the field in ascending order (A to Z for text fields; smallest to largest for numeric fields; oldest to newest for date and time fields).

    - **Descending**—Choose this command to sort on the field in descending order (from Z to A for text fields; largest to smallest for numeric fields; newest to oldest for date and time fields).

    - **Clear All Sorts**—Choose this command to remove sorting from all fields.

> **TIP**
>
> You can also sort a field directly on the datasheet. Click the drop-down list associated with the field header and then click the sort option you want. Note that the names of the sorting commands vary depending on the field's data type. For example, with an ascending sort, you see Sort A to Z for a text field; Sort Smallest to Largest for a numeric field; and Sort Oldest to Newest for a date or time field.

Sorting on Multiple Fields

Although most of your table sorts will probably be on single fields, sometimes you will have to perform a sort on multiple fields. For example, you might want to sort a table by country and then by postal code within each country. For these more advanced sorts, Access provides the Advanced Filter/Sort tool.

To use this tool, follow these steps:

1. Choose Home, Advanced (in the Sort & Filter group), Advanced Filter/Sort. Access displays the filter window in a new tab.
2. You use the columns in the lower pane to select the fields on which you want to sort. In the Field cell, use the drop-down list to click the field you want to use.
3. In the Sort cell below the field you just chose, use the drop-down list to choose either Ascending or Descending.
4. Repeats steps 2 and 3 to choose other fields you want to include in the sort. Figure 10.1 shows a sort selection in progress.

> **NOTE** Make sure that the order in which you select the fields reflects the sort priority you want to use. For example, if you want to sort by country and then by postal code within each country, select the Country field in the first column and then select the PostalCode field in the second column.

Figure 10.1
Use the filter window to perform sorts on two or more fields.

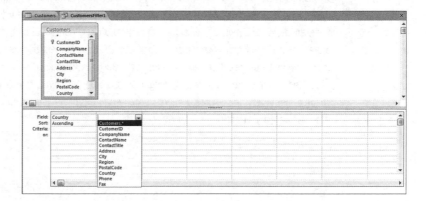

5. When you're done selecting your sort fields, you sort the table by choosing Home, Toggle Filter (in the Sort & Filter group).

To revert the table to its unsorted state, choose Home, Clear All Sorts.

Filtering Table Data

If you've ever been to a large, noisy gathering, you might have been struck by how easily humans can ignore a cacophony of music and voices around them and concentrate on whatever conversation they're having at the time. Our brains somehow filter out the unimportant noise and let in only what we need to hear.

This idea of screening out the unnecessary is exactly what Access filters do. We often want to work with only some of the records in a large table. The other records are just "noise" that we want to somehow tune out. For example, if you have a table of customer invoices, you might want to work with any of the following subsets of the data:

- Only those invoices from a particular customer
- All the overdue invoices
- Every invoice with an amount greater than $1,000

A filter can do all this and more. The idea is that you define the criteria you want to use (such as having the Amount field greater than or equal to 1000), and then, when you filter the table, Access displays only those records that meet the criteria. When you filter a table, the resulting subset of records is called a *dynaset*.

For example, consider the Order Details table shown in Figure 10.2. This is a table of customer purchases and it has, as you can see, more than 2,000 records, so there's plenty of "noise" to filter out.

> **NOTE**
>
> The sample Northwind database that comes with Access 2007 contains tables that, for the most part, have only a small number of records, and most of those records are relatively homogeneous. For example, in the Customers table, the data in the Business Phone, Fax Number, Address, City, State/Province, and Country/Region are the same for all the customers. This pathetic data source is in sharp contrast to the rich set of data found in the Northwind sample data that came with Access 2003 (and earlier). For that reason, I'm going to use the older Northwind sample data for this chapter (and, indeed, the rest of the querying chapters in this book). You can download the sample database from my website:
>
> www.mcfedries.com/Access2007Forms

Figure 10.2
The table of customer purchases has more than 2,000 records.

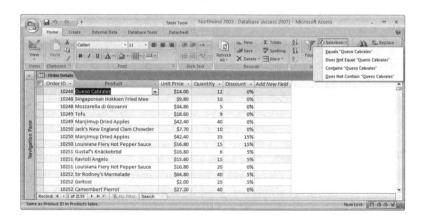

Figure 10.3 shows another view of the same table, in which I've set up a filter to show only a subset of records. In this case, the Product field had to be equal to Queso Cabrales. This view shows all the orders for that particular product. Notice that the dynaset now displays only 38 records, and that Access indicates that a filter is active by changing the interface as follows (see Figure 10.3):

- In the Home tab's Sort & Filter group, the Toggle Filter button is activated.
- A filter icon appears in the field's header.
- The Filtered button appears to the right of the record navigation buttons.
- The word Filtered appears in the status bar.

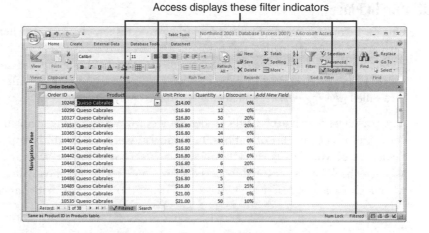

Access displays these filter indicators

Figure 10.3
The same table filtered
to show only one
product's orders.

Filtering by Selection

For simple filters, Access has a Filter by Selection feature. You can select a particular value in a field, and Access then filters the table so that it displays only those records that match the selected value.

Follow these steps to use the Filter by Selection feature:

1. In the table, select the data on which you want to filter the data. In the example just discussed, I selected Queso Cabrales in the Product field (refer to Figure 10.2).
2. Choose Home, Selection (in the Sort & Filter group), Equals *Value*, where *Value* is the value in the cell you chose in step 1 (refer to Figure 10.2).

When you no longer need to work with the filtered list, choose Home, Toggle Filter or click Filtered in the record navigation bar.

Filtering Excluding Selection

An alternative to Filter by Selection is the Filter Excluding Selection feature. Choosing this command filters the table to include every record *except* those that contain the selected value. Here's how it works:

1. In the table, select the data that you want to filter out of the records.
2. Choose Home, Selection, Does Not Equal *Value*, where *Value* is the value in the cell you chose in step 1.

To revert to the unfiltered list, choose Home, Toggle Filter or click Filtered in the record navigation bar.

Filtering in Place

One of the most common filtering operations is to display the records where the data in a particular field equals two or three different values. In the Order Details table, for example, you might want to see those orders where the Product field is Queso Cabrales, Tofu, or Ravioli Angelo. Access 2007 makes this kind of filter easy to build by offering a new feature called *filtering in place*, which enables you to apply filters directly from the datasheet.

The trick here is that each field's header has a downward-pointing arrow that, when you click it, drops down a list of options. In particular, you see a list of the unique values in the field, each of which has a check box beside it, as shown in Figure 10.4 for the Product field. When a check box is activated, Access displays those records that contain that field value; when a check box is deactivated, Access filters out those records that contain that field value.

Figure 10.4
Use a field's drop-down list to filter the table in place.

You use these check boxes as follows:

- If you want to filter out records that contain certain field values, deactivate the check box beside each of those values and then click OK.
- If you want to display records that contain just a few of the field values, first click to deactivate the (Select All) check box, which clears all the check boxes. Now activate the check box beside each value you want to see and then click OK.

To revert to the unfiltered list, drop down the field's list, activate the (Select All) check box, and click OK. (You can also drop down the field's list and click Clear Filter from *Field*, where *Field* is the name of the filtered field.) Alternatively, choose Home, Toggle Filter or click Filtered in the record navigation bar.

Applying Text, Numeric, and Date Filters

In the "Filtering by Selection" section earlier in this chapter, you learned how to apply an Equals filter that matched those records where the value of the current field is equal to the currently selected value. Similarly, in the "Filtering Excluding Selection" section, you learned how to apply a Does Not Equal filter that matched those records where the value of the current field is not equal to the currently selected value.

Access 2007 actually comes with quite a few other built-in filters that give you quite a bit more control over the filtering process. Some of these built-in filters appear in the Selection list (choose Home, Selection; refer to Figure 10.2, earlier in this chapter). To see them all, however, you need to follow these steps:

1. Click the arrow in the header of the field you want to work with to display the field's sorting and filtering options.

2. Click one of the following commands (the one you see depends on the field's data type):

    • **Text Filters**—Displays a list of text-related filter commands, including Begins With, Contains, and Ends With.

    • **Number Filters**—Displays a list of number-related filter commands, including Less Than, Greater Than, and Between.

    • **Date Filters**—Displays a list of date-related commands, including Before, Today, This Month, and Last Quarter (see Figure 10.5).

Figure 10.5
In the field's drop-down list, click the Filters command to see a list of built-in filters for the field's data type.

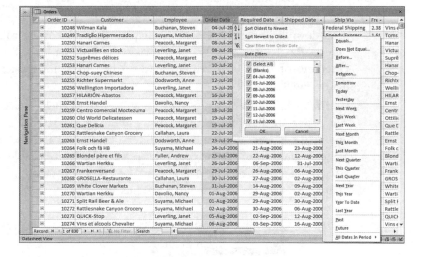

3. Click the filter command you want to use.

4. If the filter requires more data, the Custom Filter dialog box appears. Fill in the value or values required by the filter and then click OK.

To remove the filter, drop down the field's list and click Clear Filter from *Field*, where *Field* is the name of the filtered field. Alternatively, choose Home, Toggle Filter or click Filtered in the record navigation bar.

Filtering by Form

A slightly more advanced filter is one that involves multiple values. These come in two styles:

- And **filter**—In this type of filter, you choose two or more values, and the table is filtered to include only those records that contain *all* the chosen values. For example, you might want to see only those orders where the Product field contains Tofu *and* where the Discount field is empty.

- Or **filter**—In this type of filter, you choose two or more values, and the table is filtered to include only those records that contain *at least one* of the chosen values. For example, you might want to see only those orders where the Product field contains Queso Cabrales *or* Ravioli Angelo.

Note, too, that you can mix and match these filter types.

For these multiple-value filters, Access offers the Filter by Form feature. Here's how it works:

1. Choose Home, Advanced (Sort & Filter group), Filter by Form. Access displays the Filter by Form window in a tab.

2. How you fill in this form depends on the type of filter you want:

    - And **filter**—In this case, in each field you want to include in the filter, use the drop-down list to click the field value upon which the data is to be filtered. In Figure 10.6, for example, I clicked Tofu in the Product list and Is Null in the Discount list. (The Is Null value means Access looks for those records where the field is empty.)

    - Or **filter**—In this case, first use the Look For tab to click a value in the first field you want to include in the filter. Then use the Or tab to click a value in the second field you want to include in the filter. (Access will add a second Or tab, so you can continue to expand your filter as needed.) For example, in the Look For tab, you might click Queso Cabrales in the Product list, and in the Or tab, you might click Ravioli Angelo in the Product list.

Figure 10.6
Use the Filter by Form window to enter the filter values for one or more fields or for one or more values within a single field.

3. Choose Home, Toggle Filter to apply the filter.

To revert the table to its unfiltered state, choose Home, Toggle Filter.

Learning About Filter Criteria

As with sorting, you can create more advanced filters that use multiple fields and calculations. Before I show you how to set up such a filter, let's take a brief look at filter criteria. You use criteria to tell Access what subset of your data you want to see. The basic idea is that you select a field and then enter an *expression* that defines your criteria. In plain English, filters always take the following form:

Show me all records where *field* is *expression*

Here, *field* is the name of the field you want to use, and *expression* defines the criteria you want to apply to the table records. For example, suppose you select the Product field and you enter Queso Cabrales as the criteria expression. Then your filter becomes the following:

Show me all records where Product is "Queso Cabrales"

Similarly, suppose you want to see only those invoices where the Freight amount is greater than $100. In this case, you select the Freight field, and your expression would be > 100 (> is the symbol for "greater than"; see Table 10.1). Here's the English equivalent for this filter:

Show me all records where Freight is greater than 100

This example uses the greater than sign (>) as part of the expression. Access has a number of these symbols (called *operators*) that you can use to add tremendous flexibility to your criteria. Table 10.1 lists the most common ones.

Table 10.1   Operators You Can Use in Criteria Expressions

Symbol	Description
=	Equal to
<	Less than
<=	Less than or equal to
>	Greater than
>=	Greater than or equal to
<>	Not equal to

Here are a few sample expressions and the filters they create (I'm using the Orders table for these examples):

Expression	Field	Description
"Ravioli Angelo"	Product	Displays records where Product is Ravioli Angelo.

Expression	Field	Description
`<> "Tofu"`	`Product`	Displays records where `Product` is not equal to `Tofu`.
`<= "G"`	`Product`	Displays records where `Product` begins with the letters `A` through `G`.
`10250`	`Order ID`	Displays records where `Order ID` is 10250.
`< 10`	`Unit Price`	Displays records where `Unit Price` is less than $10.
`>= 50`	`Quantity`	Displays records where `Quantity` is greater than or equal to 50.
`Null`	`Discount`	Displays records where the `Discount` field is empty.

Here are some notes to keep in mind when entering your criteria expressions:

- If you want your filter to match an exact value, you usually don't have to bother with the equal to operator (=) in your expression. As the preceding examples show, you can simply enter the value itself.

- Although the preceding examples show quotation marks around text, you don't have to bother with these symbols when entering your expressions. Access will kindly add them for you.

→ This section only scratches the surface of criteria expressions. For a more in-depth treatment, **see** "Building Criteria Expressions," **p. 231**. (Chapter 11)

Creating a Filter

With these basics in tow, you're ready to create a criteria-based filter. To get started, choose Home, Advanced (Sort & Filter group), Advanced Filter/<u>S</u>ort. You see a filter window similar to the one shown in Figure 10.7.

Table pane

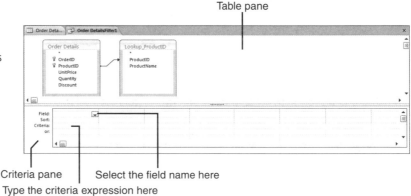

Figure 10.7
You use the filter window to choose the fields and criteria expressions that define how you want to filter the data.

Criteria pane

Select the field name here

Type the criteria expression here

The filter window is divided into two sections:

> **Table pane**—This is the top half of the window. It displays a list box that contains all the fields from your table.
>
> **Criteria pane**—This is the bottom half of the window, and it's where you design your filter.

Adding a Field to the Criteria Grid

After you have the filter window displayed, your first task is to select the field you want to use for your filter. Use one of these techniques:

- Double-click the field name.
- Drag the field name and drop it in the Field box.
- Use the drop-down list in the Field box to select the field.

Entering Criteria and Applying the Filter

The next step is to enter your criteria. In the criteria grid, select the Criteria: line below your field name and type in the criteria. Figure 10.8 shows a filter window set up to display records in the Order Details table whereby the `Quantity` field is greater than or equal to 100. Note, too, that you can also use the `Sort:` line to sort the filtered records.

Figure 10.8
In the filter window, select a field and then enter the criteria below it.

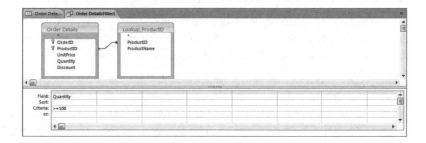

When you're done, you filter the table by choosing Home, Advanced, Apply Filter/Sort. Figure 10.9 shows the resulting filter based on the criteria entered in Figure 10.8.

Figure 10.9
Choose Filter, Apply Filter/Sort to view the table filtered according to the criteria you entered.

Order ID	Product	Unit Price	Quantity	Discount	Add New Field
10286	Steeleye Stout	$14.40	100	0%	
10398	Pâté chinois	$19.20	120	10%	
10451	Pâté chinois	$19.20	120	10%	
10452	Gula Malacca	$15.50	100	5%	
10515	Schoggi Schokolade	$43.90	120	0%	
10549	Rogede sild	$9.50	100	15%	
10588	Singaporean Hokkien Fried Mee	$14.00	100	20%	
10595	Sirop d'érable	$28.50	120	25%	
10607	Alice Mutton	$39.00	100	0%	
10678	Queso Manchego La Pastora	$38.00	100	0%	
10678	Jack's New England Clam Chowder	$9.65	120	0%	
10711	Perth Pasties	$32.80	120	0%	
10713	Rogede sild	$9.50	110	0%	

Record: 1 of 23 · Filtered · Search

10

> **NOTE** You can also use the filter window to create and and or filters:
>
> ■ To create an and filter, use a different column to select the field you want to work with and then enter the criteria for that field. Make sure all your criteria appear on the same line in the design grid.
>
> ■ To create an or filter using the same field, enter the second criteria in the or: line that appears below the Criteria: line. To create an or filter using another field, use a different column to select the field and then enter the second criteria in the or: line below the field.

Working with Queries

Sorts and filters are fine for quick-and-dirty table operations, but they're not very powerful. To really get at the data, you need to use queries, which are similar to the sorting and filtering features, but they're much more powerful. Similar to using filters, you select field names and set up *criteria* that define the records you want to see. However, unlike filters, queries are not simply a different view of the table data. A query is a separate database object that actually *extracts* records from a table and places them in a *dynaset*. As you see later, a dynaset is much like a datasheet, and many of the operations you can perform on a datasheet can also be performed on a dynaset. (Query results are called dynasets because they're dynamic subsets of a table. Here, "dynamic" means that, if you make any changes to the original table, Access updates the query automatically, or vice versa.)

The other major difference between a query and a filter is that you can save queries and then rerun them anytime you like. Filters, on the other hand, are ephemeral: When you close the table, any filters you've defined vanish into thin air.

Other types of queries are more sophisticated. For example, you can set up queries to summarize the data in a table, to find duplicate records, to delete records, and to move records from one database into another. I cover all these kinds of queries in the remaining chapters here in Part III. The rest of this chapter gets you started with some query basics that you need to know.

Creating a Query

As I've said, the result of a query is a dynaset, which looks and acts very much like a table's datasheet. So you might expect that the process of creating a query is similar to that of creating a table, and, in fact, it is. Both processes involve three steps:

1. For a table, you begin by creating a new table object. For a query, you create a new query object.

2. A new table is empty, so you have to define its basic structure by adding fields. New queries are also empty and also need fields to define their structure. The difference, as you'll see, is that the query's fields come from an existing table or tables.

3. In a table, you then need to flesh out the structure by entering data into new records. Queries, too, need records to give them substance. In this case, though, you "enter" records into the query by defining the criteria the query uses to extract records from the underlying table.

The next few sections take you through each of these steps for creating a query.

→ For the details on using two or more tables in a query, **see** "Working with Multiple Tables in a Query," **p. 259**. (Chapter 12)

Creating a New Query Object

To get your query started, follow these steps:

1. Choose Create, Query Design. Access displays the Show Table dialog box.
2. In the Tables tab, click the table you want to use.
3. Click Add.
4. Click Close.

Access creates a new query object and displays the query design window, shown in Figure 10.10. Note, too, that the Access 2007 Ribbon takes on a new Design tab under Query Tools. This window is similar to the filter window you saw earlier in this chapter in that it's divided into two areas:

Table pane—This half of the window displays a list box that displays all the fields from your table. Note that this box is resizable, so you can change the height or width as needed.

Criteria pane—This half of the window is a collection of text boxes (they're called *cells*) where you define the query as described in the next few sections.

Note, too, that you can adjust the relative sizes of both panes by clicking and dragging the horizontal bar that separates them.

Table pane

Figure 10.10
Use the query design window to enter fields, sorting options, and criteria for your query.

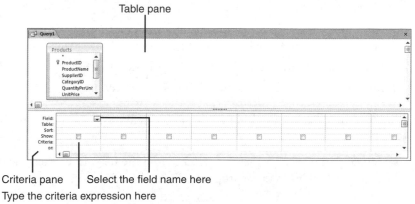

Criteria pane | Select the field name here

Type the criteria expression here

10

Use an External Table in a Query

If you want your query to use a table from another database (called an *external* database), the usual route to take is to first set up the table as a linked table in the current database. For example, if the external data source is an Access database, you'd choose External Data, Access (in the Import group), and then activate the Link to the Data Source by Creating a Linked Table option. The linked table will then appear in the Show Table dialog box when you start your query.

However, if you don't want to use a linked table, you can still use a table from another database. Start a new query and click Close in the Show Tables dialog box. If you don't see the Property Sheet pane (Access displays it by default), choose Design, Property Sheet. In the Property Sheet pane, type the full pathname (or the network path, if the database file is in a shared network folder) of the database file in the `Source Database` property. (If the external database requires extra connection settings, enter them in the `Source Connect Str` field. For example, if another Access database requires a username and password, type `UID=UserID;PWD=Password`, where you replace `UserID` and `Password` with the required values.) Choose Design, Show Table to redisplay the Show Table dialog box to select the table you want to use from the external database.

The criteria pane is also called the *design grid* or sometimes the *QBE grid*. The "QBE" part of QBE grid stands for *query by example*, which is a method that makes it easy to define a query. The idea is that you set up a query by defining an example of what you want each dynaset record to look like. As you'll see in the next few sections, this process involves adding the fields you want to a grid and then setting up criteria for one or more of those fields. The alternative to QBE is SQL—Structured Query Language. Using SQL is a more complex—but also more powerful—method for querying data, and you learn about it later in this book.

→ To get the SQL details, **see** "Querying with SQL Statements," **p. 341**. (Chapter 15)

Selecting the Fields to Include in the Query

After you've created a new query object, it's time to add some structure to it. As I've said, you do this by adding fields from the table associated with the query. The design grid is divided into columns, and you use each column to work with a single field from the table. To choose a field, follow these steps:

1. Click inside the Field cell of the column you want to work with. Access displays a drop-down list in the cell.
2. Use the drop-down list to click the field you want to work with.
3. Repeat steps 1 and 2 to add more fields to the query.

Note, too, that you can also add fields from the field list in the table pane. There are two basic techniques:

■ To add a single field, either double-click it in the field list or click and drag the name from the field list to the appropriate Field cell in the design grid.

■ To add multiple fields, hold down Ctrl, click each field you want, and then click and drag any one of the highlighted fields into a Field cell in the design grid. Access enters each field in its own cell.

If you add a column by mistake, the best approach is to delete it from the design grid to avoid cluttering the dynaset. To do this, click inside the column you want to get rid of and then choose Design, Delete Columns.

> **NOTE** When selecting fields, keep in mind that the order in which you select your fields is the order in which they'll appear in the dynaset. If you add fields in the wrong order, you can fix this easily. First, select the design grid column you want to move by clicking the bar at the top of the column. With the mouse pointer still inside the bar, drag the column left or right to the new location.

10

What about the asterisk (*) that appears at the top of the field list? This is a special symbol that means, in effect, "every field in the table." If you want your query to display every field, the easiest way to do it is to click and drag the asterisk to the design grid and drop it on any Field cell. That way, the only other columns you have to work with in the design grid are those you use to define your criteria.

Entering the Query Criteria

The final step in defining your query is to enter the criteria. Type your expressions directly into the Criteria cells in the design grid and be sure to press Enter when you're done. You can use the same simple criteria I outlined for filters earlier in this chapter. However, I show you more sophisticated criteria in the next chapter.

→ For more detailed coverage of criteria, **see** "Building Criteria Expressions," **p. 231**. (Chapter 11)

Excluding a Field from the Query Results

You'll often add fields to the design grid for criteria purposes only, and you don't want the field to appear in the dynaset. You can exclude any field from the dynaset by clearing the appropriate check box in the field's Show cell. For example, Figure 10.11 shows a query where I'm using the UnitPrice field to look for products that cost more than $25. However, I've already included all the table fields in the dynaset by adding the asterisk to the first column, so I exclude the extra UnitPrice field by clearing its Show check box.

Returning Only the Top *N* Values

You might not need to see every record that satisfies your criteria. For example, in an accounts receivable table, you might be interested in only the overdue invoices that have the highest amounts or are the most overdue. For these situations, you can tell Access to restrict the dynaset to a specified number of records or to a percentage of the total.

Figure 10.11
Clear a column's Show
check box to prevent it
from being displayed in
the dynaset.

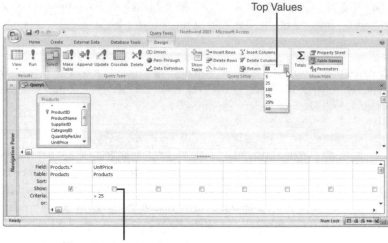

Top Values

Show check box is cleared

You do this by using the Top Values combo box, pointed out in Figure 10.11. You can either type your own value into the box or select a number or percentage value from the list (choose All if you want to see every record).

Setting Field Properties

Any field you include in your query has the same properties as the field has within its table. For example, if a field is set up within the table to display its values using the Currency format, the field will also use the Currency format in the query's dynaset.

This approach works fine in most situations, but sometimes you might prefer to define different field properties for the query results. For example, you might want a column caption other than the field name, or you might want to use a different numeric format. Here are the steps to follow to change a field's properties:

1. In the design grid, click the field you want to work with.
2. Choose Design, Property Sheet to display the Property Sheet pane. (In the pane, the `Selection Type` value should be `Field Properties`.)
3. Use the following properties to customize the field (the properties you see depend on the data type of the field; Figure 10.12 shows the properties for a numeric field):
   - `Description`—The text that appears as the field's column heading in the dynaset.
   - `Format`—The format used to display the field's values.
   - `Decimal Places`—The number of decimal places to display (numeric data types only).
   - `Input Mask`—The input mask to use when entering or editing data in the field.
   - `Caption`—The text that appears in the status bar when any value in the field is selected.

- Smart Tags—Click the ellipsis button (…) to display the Smart Tags dialog box, which enables you to specify one or more smart tags to associate with the field.

4. Close the Field Properties dialog box to put the new settings into effect.

Figure 10.12
You can use the Field Properties dialog box to customize certain aspects of the field for use in the dynaset.

Running the Query

When you have your query set up the way you want, you can run it (that is, display the dynaset) by choosing Design, Run. Figure 10.13 displays the results of the query shown earlier in Figure 10.11.

Figure 10.13
The dynaset produced by the query shown earlier in Figure 10.11.

Design View

As you can see, the dynaset is really just a datasheet. You navigate and format it the same way, and you can even edit the records and add new ones. (Any changes you make are automatically applied to the underlying table.) I discuss these techniques later in this chapter. To return to the query design window, either choose Home and click the top half of the View split button, or click the Design View button in the status bar, pointed out in Figure 10.13.

> **NOTE** When the query is displayed in the datasheet view, you're free to use the commands in the Home tab's Sort & Filter group to filter the dynaset, as described earlier in this chapter. Note that using any of the Sort & Filter commands doesn't affect any of the settings in the query design grid. The filter and sort order are stored separately and are maintained by Access until you remove them.

Querying Notes for Business Users

You'll find yourself needing to query a database for many reasons. For example, you want to work with just a subset of data, or you want to summarize the data in some way (such as by showing field subtotals). But in a business environment, the most common reason for querying is that you need the dynaset in some other context. Here are some typical business querying scenarios:

- You need the dynaset data to display in a report.
- You want other people to view or work with the dynaset.
- You need the dynaset data for another application, such as an Excel worksheet or a Word mail merge.

The common thread here and in most business contexts is that the dynaset isn't an end in itself, but is a means to some further goal. Therefore, you need to keep your ultimate goal—that is, the context in which the dynaset will eventually be used—in mind as you construct your query. Here are some notes that will help your query design decisions:

- When deciding which fields to include in the query, first determine which fields you want to use for the criteria. These are the fields that determine which records you see when you run the query. For example, suppose you have a table of accounts receivable data with a DueDate field and you want your query to show only those invoices that are past their due date. Then you definitely need to include the DueDate field in the query.
- Determine which fields you want to see in the dynaset. When you look at the results of the query, you'll usually want to see more than just the fields you used for the criteria. In the accounts receivable example, you might also want to see the name of the customer, the amount of the invoice, and so on. So you need to include in the query each field you want to see.
- Be careful with the number of fields you display, particularly if you add the asterisk (all fields) "field." Including all the fields in your query is fine for small tables (say, a few

hundred records) because the extra overhead of returning and displaying all the finds won't be noticeable. However, many real-world tables contain thousands or even tens of thousands of records, so your query performance will drag if Access has to process and retrieve every field. This is particularly true in a networked environment where you're using Access as the front end for data that resides on a remote server. It's a good rule in query design to include in the query only those fields you really need.

- Use only fields that are meaningful to the users. Many tables include fields for data such as account numbers, product codes, and employee IDs. These fields are often used as primary keys, so they're a necessary part of the database design, but they're probably meaningless to most users. On the other hand, a user who deals with, say, product codes all day long will be familiar with these values, and they might even mean more to him or her than a long-winded product description field.

- Depending on the number of fields in the dynaset, all the fields might not fit onto the screen, requiring the users to scroll to the right to see them. That's unavoidable in many cases, but make sure that the fields are displayed from left to right in approximate order of importance. That way, the user always sees the most important fields and might not need to scroll if he or she isn't interested in the offscreen fields.

- Certain types of data have a "natural" field order. For example, invoice data might have fields in the following order: invoice number, invoice date, customer name, customer address, and invoice total. When adding your fields to the query, try to preserve this natural order to make it easy for others to read the dynaset data.

- If your data has a date component, you'll usually want to sort the dynaset by date in descending order. This places the newest data at the top of the dynaset.

- If the underlying table has coded or short-form field names, any user who isn't familiar with the names will have a hard time interpreting the resulting dynaset. To make life easier for such users, customize the query fields with natural language column headers and descriptive captions.

CASE STUDY

Querying for a Mail Merge

One common use for queries is to create a dynaset of names and addresses to be used in form letters or address labels. You then use this as the data source for Word's Mail Merge feature. The basic idea behind mail merge is that you set up a main document in which you combine regular text with one or more *fields*, like so:

```
Dear <<FirstName>> <<LastName>>,
```

These fields correspond to fields in the data source. In this example, the data source has a FirstName field and a LastName field. When you merge the main document and the data source, Word creates a new document for each record and fills in the document fields with the appropriate data from each field in the record.

Querying the Customers Table

The Northwind sample database has a Customers table that's suitable for a mail merge operation. For this kind of query, you need to make three design decisions:

- The fields required for the mail merge. You need only those fields that will appear in the address, so you can ignore fields in the Customers table such as `CustomerID` and `Phone`. Here are the fields needed for the mail merge:

  `ContactName`

  `CompanyName`

  `Address`

  `City`

  `Region`

  `Country`

  `PostalCode`

- The customers who receive the mailing. Because business mailings are often tied to specific regions, you usually add some criteria to the query to restrict the dynaset to some geographic area. For example, if you want the mailings to go only to a specific country, you add that country's name as the criteria for the `Country` field.
- The sort order. Bulk mailings get a cheaper rate if the letters are sorted by postal code, so set the `PostalCode` field's Sort cell to `Ascending`.

Figure 10.14 shows the completed query, and Figure 10.15 shows the resulting dynaset.

Figure 10.14
A query that uses the Customers table to create a data source for a mail merge.

Customers Mail Merge Query

Contact Name	Company Name	Address	City	Regic	Count	Postal Coc
Liu Wong	The Cracker Box	55 Grizzly Peak Rd.	Butte	MT	USA	59801
Art Braunschweiger	Split Rail Beer & Ale	P.O. Box 555	Lander	WY	USA	82520
Jose Pavarotti	Save-a-lot Markets	187 Suffolk Ln.	Boise	ID	USA	83720
Paula Wilson	Rattlesnake Canyon Grocery	2817 Milton Dr.	Albuquerque	NM	USA	87110
Jaime Yorres	Let's Stop N Shop	87 Polk St.	San Francisco	CA	USA	94117
Liz Nixon	The Big Cheese	89 Jefferson Way	Portland	OR	USA	97201
Fran Wilson	Lonesome Pine Restaurant	89 Chiaroscuro Rd.	Portland	OR	USA	97219
Howard Snyder	Great Lakes Food Market	2732 Baker Blvd.	Eugene	OR	USA	97403
Yoshi Latimer	Hungry Coyote Import Store	City Center Plaza	Elgin	OR	USA	97827
Helvetius Nagy	Trail's Head Gourmet Provisioner	722 DaVinci Blvd.	Kirkland	WA	USA	98034
Karl Jablonski	White Clover Markets	305 - 14th Ave. S.	Seattle	WA	USA	98128
John Steel	Lazy K Kountry Store	12 Orchestra Terrace	Walla Walla	WA	USA	99362
Rene Phillips	Old World Delicatessen	2743 Bering St.	Anchorage	AK	USA	99508

Record: 1 of 13 No Filter Search

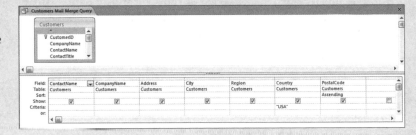

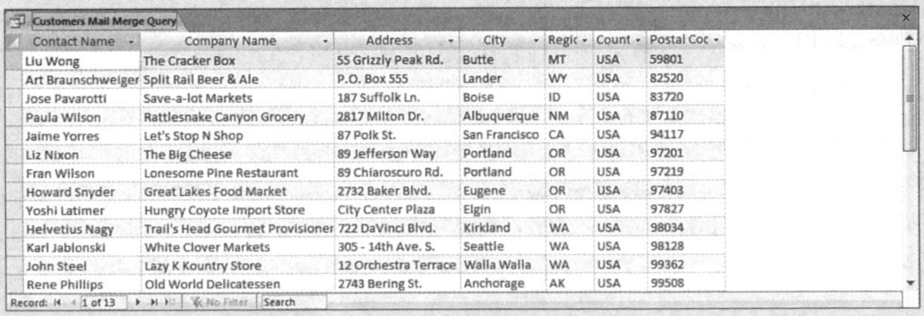

Figure 10.15
The dynaset produced by the mail merge query.

Running the Mail Merge

With your dynaset ready, the next task is to apply the data to a Word mail merge document. Here are the steps to follow:

1. In Access, choose External Data, More (in the Export group), <u>M</u>erge It with Microsoft Office Word. This launches the Microsoft Word Mail Merge Wizard.

2. Click one of the following options and then click OK:

   - **<u>L</u>ink Your Data to an Existing Microsoft Word Document**—Choose this option to link the data to an existing mail merge document. In this case, the wizard displays the Select Microsoft Word Document dialog box so you can pick out the document.

   - **<u>C</u>reate a New Document and Then Link the Data to It**—Choose this option to create a fresh mail merge file in Word. In this case, the wizard starts Microsoft Word so you can create the new document. The rest of these steps assume you chose this option.

3. In the Word document, enter the mail merge document text. When you come to a spot where you need to insert a field placeholder, choose Mailings, Insert Merge Field. Word displays a list of merge fields, as shown in Figure 10.16.

Figure 10.16
Use the Insert Merge Field list to insert a field placeholder into the Word document.

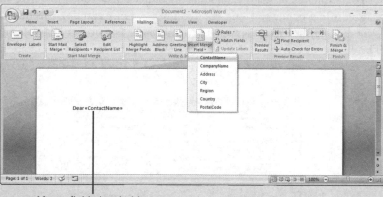

Merge field placeholder

4. Click the field you want to insert. Word inserts the merge field, as shown in Figure 10.16.

5. Repeat steps 3 and 4 until the document is complete.

6. Choose Mailings, Finish & Merge, <u>E</u>dit Individual Documents. Word displays the Merge to New Document dialog box.

7. Click <u>A</u>ll and then click OK. Word creates a new document for each record in the dynaset.

Creating Queries with the Query Wizards

With the Query Wizards, you have access to three other types of queries, and you don't have to mess around with the query design window. The Query Wizards enable you to create each query in the usual step-by-step wizard method that you're probably familiar with.

Follow these steps to get started:

1. Choose Create, Query Wizard. The New Query dialog box appears.
2. Click the wizard you want to use: Crosstab Query Wizard, Find Duplicates Query Wizard, or Find Unmatched Query Wizard.
3. Click OK.

From here, you follow the instructions in each wizard dialog box to create your query. The next three sections describe each of the Query Wizard types.

Creating Crosstab Queries

Crosstab queries take large amounts of complex data and summarize some or all the information into a handy row-and-column format. For example, consider the Sales Promotion Orders table shown in Figure 10.17. This table lists orders taken during a sales promotion. The customer can select any one of four products (copy holder, glare filter, mouse pad, or printer stand) and two promotions (1 free with 10 or extra discount).

Figure 10.17
A table of orders taken during a promotion.

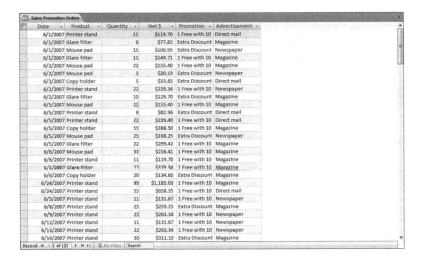

A basic analysis of this table is to calculate how many of each product was ordered for each promotion. With so many orders, determining this number by hand is a nightmare, but a crosstab query like the one shown in Figure 10.18 does the job nicely. In this case, Access took the four unique entries in the Product field and used them as entries in the leftmost column, and it took the two unique entries in the `Promotion` field and used them as headings for the other columns. It then summed the appropriate `Quantity` field values and summarized everything in a nice, neat package.

Figure 10.18
The table data presented as a crosstab query that shows the quantities ordered for each product, broken down by promotion.

Sales Promotion Orders_Crosstab			×
Product ▾	1 Free with 10 ▾	Extra Discount ▾	
Copy holder	792	647	
Glare filter	814	894	
Mouse pad	1705	1655	
Printer stand	638	706	

Record: I4 ◀ 1 of 4 ▶ ▶I ▶ No Filter   Search

Creating a crosstab query is easy thanks to the Access Crosstab Query Wizard. Here are the steps involved:

1. Choose Create, Query Wizard; click Crosstab Query; and then click OK. Access launches the Crosstab Query Wizard.

2. Click the table you want to use and then click <u>N</u>ext.

3. In the Available Fields list, click the field whose unique entries you want to appear in the leftmost column of the query as the row headings. Click > to add the field to the Selected Fields list and then click <u>N</u>ext.

4. Click the field whose unique entries will appear as the headings for the other columns in the query and then click <u>N</u>ext.

5. In the Fields list, click the field to use for the calculations; in the Functions list, click the type of calculation to use (for example, `Sum`, as shown in Figure 10.19). If you want to see a total for each row in the crosstab table, leave the <u>Y</u>es, Include Row Sums check box activated. Click <u>N</u>ext.

Figure 10.19
The Crosstab Query Wizard takes you step by step through the process of creating a crosstab query.

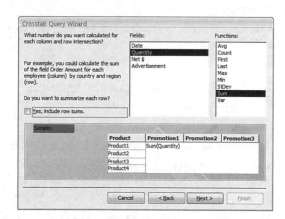

6. Type a name for the query.

7. Click <u>F</u>inish.

Creating Find Duplicates Queries

If you're concerned about having duplicate records in a table, a Find Duplicates query locates them for you. This query displays a list of a table's duplicate entries (if it has any). You can then either edit or delete one or more records to remove the duplication.

The Find Duplicates Query Wizard sets everything up for you by taking you through the following steps:

1. Choose Create, Query Wizard; click Find Duplicates Query; and then click OK. Access launches the Find Duplicates Query Wizard.

2. Click the table you want to use and then click <u>N</u>ext.

3. In the Available Fields list, for each field you want to check for duplicate data, click the field and then click > to add the field to the Duplicate-Value Fields list. When you're done, click <u>N</u>ext.

4. In the Available Fields list, for every other field you want to include in the query, click the field and then click > to add the field to the Additional Query Fields list. When you're done, click <u>N</u>ext.

5. Type a name for the query.

6. Click <u>F</u>inish.

Setting Up a Find Unmatched Query

The Find Unmatched Query Wizard enables you to find records in one table that have no matching entries in another. For example, suppose you have a Products table (with a ProductID field) and an Orders table (also with a ProductID field). This wizard can examine both tables and, using the common ProductID field as a guide, tell you which records in the Products table have no matches in the Orders table. In other words, it gives you a list of the products that have not been ordered.

→ For a Find Unmatched query to work, the two tables must be related on a common field. To learn how to create related tables, **see** "Establishing Table Relationships," **p. 267**. (Chapter 12)

Here's how the wizard works:

1. Choose Create, Query Wizard; click Find Unmatched Query; and then click OK. Access launches the Find Unmatched Query Wizard.

2. Click the table you want to display in the query results and then click <u>N</u>ext.

3. Click the table that contains the related records and then click <u>N</u>ext.

4. If you don't see anything in the Matching Fields box, or if the fields shown are incorrect, specify the matching fields in the two tables by clicking the field name in each list and then clicking <=>. Click <u>N</u>ext.

5. In the Available Fields list, for each other field you want to include in the query, click the field and then click > to add the field to the Selected Fields list. When you're done, click <u>N</u>ext.

6. Enter a name for the query.

7. Click Finish.

Working with a Query Dynaset

When you run a query, the resulting dynaset is displayed in *datasheet view*, whereby the records are displayed in rows and the fields in columns. If you're comfortable working with tables in datasheet view, you don't need to change or learn anything else for the dynaset version because they look and operate identically. Just in case you're not familiar with this view, however, the rest of this chapter gives you a datasheet primer.

Understanding the Datasheet View

Figure 10.20 shows a query opened in the datasheet view and points out the most important features of this screen.

Figure 10.20
When you run a query, the resulting dynaset is displayed in the datasheet view.

The datasheet window has the following features:

- **Fields**—Each column in the datasheet corresponds to a field you added to the design grid.

- **Field names**—These are the buttons at the top of each column. The text is either the name of the field or the field alias, if one exists.

- **Records**—Each row in the datasheet corresponds to a record.

- **Record selectors**—These buttons run down the left side of the window. You use them to select records. They also show icons that give you more information about the record (as described later in this chapter).

- **Record number**—This box tells you which record is currently selected.
- **Field description**—If the field has an associated description, it appears in the status bar as you select each field.
- **Navigation buttons**—These buttons enable you to navigate the dynaset. See "Navigating Records" later in this chapter.

Navigating Fields

To make it easier to enter your data, you need to be familiar with the techniques for navigating the datasheet fields. Using your mouse, you can select a field just by clicking it. If you can't see all your fields, use the horizontal scrollbar to bring them into view.

Using the keyboard, you can use the keys outlined in Table 10.2.

Table 10.2   Keys to Use When Navigating Fields in the Datasheet

Key	Description
Tab or right arrow	Moves to the next field to the right.
Shift+Tab or left arrow	Moves to the previous field to the left.
Home	Moves to the first field.
End	Moves to the last field.
Ctrl+Home	Moves to the first field of the first record.
Ctrl+End	Moves to the last field of the last record.

> **CAUTION**
>
> When you use the keys in Table 10.2 to move into a field that already contains data, Access highlights the data. If you press any key while the field is highlighted, you'll replace the *entire* entry with that keystroke! If this isn't what you want, immediately press Esc to restore the text. To prevent this from happening, you can remove the highlight by clicking inside the field or by pressing F2.

Entering Data

Entering data in Access is, for the most part, straightforward. You just select a field and start typing. Here are a few notes to keep in mind when entering table data:

- If you want to replace an entire field value, you can either type in the correct value (Access automatically replaces the highlighted value with your typing) or press Delete to clear the field.
- If you want to change only one or more characters in a field, press F2 or click inside the field to remove the highlight and then edit the field accordingly.

- If you're editing a field, you can select the entire contents of the cell by pressing F2.

- When you're editing a record, the record selector changes to a pencil icon, as shown in Figure 10.20. This tells you that the record has unsaved changes.

- When entering dates, use the format *mm/dd/yyyyy*, where *mm* is the month number (for example, 12 for December), *dd* is the day, and *yy* is the year. For example, 12/25/2007 is an acceptable date. The date format you end up with depends on the Format property assigned to the field.

- When entering times, use the format *hh:mm:ss*, where *hh* is the hour, *mm* is the minutes, and *ss* is the seconds. Military types can use the 24-hour clock (for example, 16:30:05), and the rest of us can add *am* or *pm* (for example, 4:30:05 pm). Again, the format that's displayed depends on the field's Format property.

> **TIP**
> You can add today's date to a field by pressing Ctrl+; (semicolon). To add the current time, press Ctrl+: (colon).

- When entering a number in a Currency field, don't bother entering a dollar sign ($); Access will add it for you automatically.

- You save the current record by moving to a different record. If you prefer to save the current record and still remain in Edit mode, press Shift+Enter.

Adding More Records

Access always keeps a blank record at the bottom of the table for adding new records (it's the one that has an asterisk in its record selector). The next section tells you how to move around between records, but for now, you can use any of the following methods to select the blank record:

- If you're in the last field of the record directly above the blank record, press Tab.
- Choose Home, New (in the Records group).
- Press Ctrl++ (plus sign).
- Click the New Record button on the navigation bar (see Figure 10.21).

Navigating Records

Navigating a dynaset is straightforward. You can use the up- and down-arrow keys to move up and down through the records, or you can use Page Up and Page Down for larger jumps. If you can see the record you want, you can click it. (You'll usually click whatever field you want to edit.) If you can't see the record, use the vertical scrollbar on the right side of the datasheet window to bring the record into view.

You can also use the five datasheet navigation buttons at the bottom of the window (see Figure 10.21).

Figure 10.21
Use the datasheet window's navigation buttons to navigate the dynaset records.

First record
Previous record
Last record
Next record
New record

You can also choose Home, Go To and then choose one of the commands in the submenu: First, Last, Next, Previous, or New Record.

Selecting a Record

Before you can work with a record, you need to select it:

- To select a single record, click the record selector to the left of the record you want. (You can also move to any field in the record and press Shift+spacebar.)

- To select multiple records, click and drag the mouse pointer over the record selector for each record you want to work with. (From the keyboard, press Shift+spacebar and then press either Shift+up arrow or Shift+down arrow.)

- To select every record, click the blank button in the upper-left corner of the datasheet. (You can also press Ctrl+A.)

Copying a Record

One of the secrets of computer productivity is the maxim "Don't reinvent the wheel." Specifically, if you have to enter a new record that has almost the same data as an existing record, it's much simpler to make a copy of the existing record and then make your changes to the copy.

To copy a record, follow these steps:

1. Select the record you want to copy.

2. Choose Home, Copy (or press Ctrl+C).

3. Choose Home, Paste Append. Access tacks on the record to the end of the table.

Deleting a Record

If you need to delete one or more records from the dynaset (and, therefore, from the underlying table), follow these steps:

1. Select the record or records you want to delete.
2. Choose Home, Delete, Delete Record (or press Delete). Access displays a dialog box telling you how many records will be deleted and asking you to confirm the deletion.
3. Choose Yes.

Formatting the Datasheet

The standard datasheet displayed by Access is serviceable at best. Most people, though, have three major complaints about the default datasheet:

- Some columns are too small to show all the data in a field.
- You can't see all the fields in the datasheet window.
- The characters are a little on the small side, so they're hard to read.

The next few sections show you how to format the datasheet to overcome these problems.

Changing the Datasheet Column Sizes

The default datasheet assigns the same width to every column. Although this standard width might be fine for some fields, for others it's either too large or too small. Fortunately, Access lets you adjust the width of individual columns to suit each field.

The easiest way to do this is to use the mouse. Move the mouse pointer so that it rests on the right edge of the field's column header. The pointer will change to a vertical bar with two arrows protruding from its sides. From here, you have two choices:

- Click and drag the mouse to the left to make the column width smaller, or click and drag it to the right to make the width larger.
- Double-click to size the column width to accommodate the largest field value.

> **TIP**
>
> If you have a field with a large amount of data (a Memo field, for example), it isn't always practical to expand the column width to see all the data. Instead, move to the field and press Shift+F2. Access displays the Zoom dialog box to show you more of your data. If you like, you can also use this dialog box to enter more data or edit the existing data. When you're done, click OK to return to the datasheet.

10

Changing the Datasheet Row Heights

Another way to see more data in each field is to increase the height of each datasheet row (you can't do this for individual rows). As with column widths, the easiest way to do this is to use the mouse.

Position the mouse pointer on the bottom edge of any row selector. The pointer will change into a horizontal bar with arrows sticking out the top and bottom. Click and drag the mouse up to reduce the row height or click and drag it down to increase the row height.

Working with Query Properties

Each query comes with a set of properties that govern many aspects of how the query creates and displays the dynaset. To see these properties, click an empty section of the query design window and then choose Design, Property Sheet (or press Alt+Enter). Access displays the query properties window shown in Figure 10.22.

Figure 10.22
Use the query properties window to customize various aspects of the how the query builds and displays the dynaset.

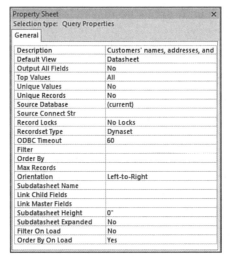

Many of the query properties are designed to modify the appearance or behavior of the datasheet. For example, you can specify whether the user can change the data, and you can change the datasheet orientation so that the fields run from right to left. Here are the properties that affect the datasheet:

- `Default View`—You'll usually want to choose Datasheet here, but you can also choose PivotTable or PivotChart.
- `Output All Fields`—When this property is set to `No`, Access includes in the datasheet only the fields you specify in the design grid. If you change this property to `Yes`, Access outputs all the fields, no matter which ones are specified in the design grid.

- `Top Values`—Use this text box to enter a number or percentage that specifies how many of the highest or lowest (depending on the sort order) values you want displayed. This is the same as entering a value in the Design tab's Top Values combo box.

- `Recordset Type`—Use this list to click the type of recordset that Access creates. If you click Dynaset, users can add, edit, and delete data; if you choose Snapshot, users can only view the data. (The Dynaset [Inconsistent Updates] item is not recommended.)

- `Filter`—Use this text box to define a filter for the data. If you add a filter using the datasheet view (by using the filtering commands in the Home tab's Sort & Filter group), the resulting filter is stored in the `Filter` property.

- `Order By`—Use this text box to enter one or more field names (separated by commas) that define the sort order in the datasheet. If you specify a sort order using the datasheet view (by using the sorting commands in the Home tab's Sort & Filter group), the resulting sort order is stored in the `Order By` property.

- `Orientation`—Use this property to determine how the fields are arranged in the datasheet. If you click Left-to-Right (the default), the fields appear from left to right as they appear in the design grid; if you click Right-to-Left, the fields appear from right to left in the order they appear in the design grid (the leftmost field in the design grid appears on the far right of the datasheet, the next field in the design grid appears second from the right, and so on).

Many of the rest of these properties are obscure and so are of interest only to professional database designers and programmers. However, some of the others are useful in a business environment, and you learn about them over the next few chapters.

From Here

➜ For a more in-depth treatment of criteria expressions, **see** "Building Criteria Expressions," **p. 231**. (Chapter 11)

➜ To learn how to create related tables, **see** "Establishing Table Relationships," **p. 267**. (Chapter 12)

➜ For the details on using two or more tables in a query, **see** "Working with Multiple Tables in a Query," **p. 259**. (Chapter 12)

➜ To get the details on SQL, **see** "Querying with SQL Statements," **p. 341**. (Chapter 15)

10

Building Criteria Expressions

The heart of any query is its criteria. They are a set of expressions that determine the records that appear in the dynaset. In this chapter, you go beyond the simple criteria that you learned about in Chapter 1, "Creating and Using a Form," and examine more complex examples that enable you to unleash the full power of Access queries.

The queries you've seen so far are simple filters that use literal values to select matching table records. To create more advanced queries, however, you have to go beyond literals and construct full-fledged *expressions* that combine operators, functions, and field names with literal values. Access applies the result of the expression to the field in which it was entered in the query design grid, and only those records that match the result are included in the dynaset.

All query expressions have the same general structure. They contain one or more *operands*—which can be literal values (such as 123 or "USA" or #8/23/2005#), *identifiers* (names of Access objects), or functions—separated by one or more *operators*—the symbols that combine the operands in some way, such as the plus sign (+) and the greater than sign (>).

Most criteria expressions are logical formulas that, when applied to each record in the table, return True or False. The dynaset contains only those records for which the expression returned True. In fact, you can see that even criteria that use simple literal values are also expressions (albeit not very sophisticated ones). For example, suppose you have a `Customer` field in the design grid and you enter **Barney's Beanery** as the criterion. This is equivalent to the following logical formula:

```
Customer = "Barney's Beanery"
```

Access constructs the dynaset by applying this formula to each record in the table and selecting only those records for which it returns `True` (that is, those records where the value in the `Customer` field is equal to `"Barney's Beanery"`).

Using Operands in Criteria Expressions

As mentioned in the preceding section, your criteria expressions will make use of three types of operands: literals, identifiers, and functions.

Literals

A *literal* is a value that you enter directly. Access recognizes four types of literals:

- **Text literal**—This is a series of one or more characters, surrounded by quotation marks, that represent a string value. You can combine one or more text literals by using the concatenation operator (&). The following are all text literals:
  ```
  "Canada"
  "Sales Manager"
  "Nancy" & " " & "Davolio"
  ```

- **Numeric literal**—This is a series of one or more digits—along with a sign and decimal point, if required—that represent a number.

- **Date/time literal**—This is a date, a time, or a combination of date and time, surrounded by pound signs (#).

- **Constant**—This is a logical value—`True` or `False`—or the `Null`. The latter is most often used to test for a field that doesn't contain a value.

Identifiers

In Access queries, an identifier is a field name from the query's underlying table, surrounded by square brackets. In the Products table, for example, if you want to refer to the `ReorderLevel` field in an expression, you use the following operand:

```
[ReorderLevel]
```

 TIP You don't need to include the square brackets when entering an identifier because Access will add them for you. In fact, it's good practice *not* to include the square brackets because this gives you a simple way to guard against misspelling field names. If you enter a field name correctly, Access will recognize the name and add the square brackets; if you don't see the brackets after you move out of the cell, it means you misspelled the field name.

Functions

A *function* is a built-in expression that, usually, takes one or more input values—called *arguments*—and processes those values to return a result. For example, the Sum function returns the sum of its arguments. If you apply it to a field, it returns the sum of the field's values, as in this example:

```
Sum([UnitsInStock])
```

→ For a closer look at Sum and many other Access functions, **see** "Using the Built-In Functions," **p. 241**. (this chapter)

Using Operators in Criteria Expressions

Access has a few dozen operators you can include in your expressions. The four types of operators—comparison, logical, arithmetic, and miscellaneous—are covered in the next few sections.

Comparison Operators

You use comparison operators to compare field values to a literal, a function result, or to a value in another field. Table 11.1 lists Access's comparison operators.

Table 11.1 Comparison Operators for Criteria Expressions

Operator	General Form	Description
=	= *Value*	Matches records whereby the field value is equal to *Value*.
<>	<> *Value*	Matches records whereby the field value is not equal to *Value*.
>	> *Value*	Matches records whereby the field value is greater than *Value*.
>=	>= *Value*	Matches records whereby the field value is greater than or equal to *Value*.
<	< *Value*	Matches records whereby the field value is less than *Value*.
<=	<= *Value*	Matches records whereby the field value is less than or equal to *Value*.

For example, the Northwind database's Products table has a UnitsInStock field. If you want your query to return just those products that are out of stock, you enter the following expression in the Criteria cell for the UnitsInStock field (see Figures 11.1 and 11.2):

```
=0
```

> **NOTE**
> As I mentioned in Chapter 10, "Creating a Basic Query," I'm going to use the older (Access 2003) Northwind sample data for the querying chapters. You can download the sample database from my website:
>
> www.mcfedries.com/Access2007Forms

11

Figure 11.1
To see which items in the Products table are currently out of stock, add the expression =0 to the Criteria cell of the UnitsInStock field.

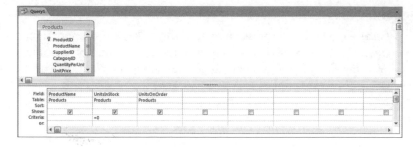

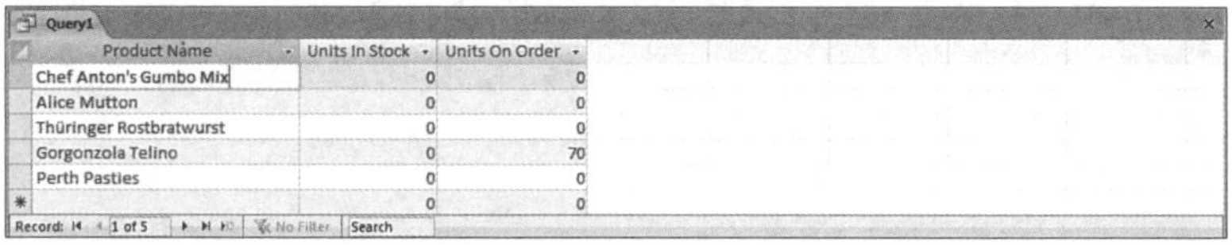

Figure 11.2
The dynaset produced by the query in Figure 11.1.

You'll mostly use the comparison operators on numeric or date fields, but you can also use them on text fields. For example, if you want to return from Northwind's Customers table just those records with company names that begin with the letters A, B, or C, you enter the following expression into the CompanyName field's Criteria cell:

<"D"

Arithmetic Operators

You use the arithmetic operators shown in Table 11.2 to perform various math operations on a field.

Table 11.2   Arithmetic Operators for Criteria Expressions

Operator	General Form	Description
+	*Value1* + *Value2*	Adds *Value1* and *Value2*.
-	*Value1* - *Value2*	Subtracts *Value2* from *Value1*.
- (unary)	-*Value*	Changes the sign of *Value*.
*	*Value1* * *Value2*	Multiplies *Value1* and *Value2*.
/	*Value1* / *Value2*	Divides *Value1* by *Value2*.
\	*Value1* \ *Value2*	Divides *Value1* by *Value2* and rounds the result to the nearest integer (this is called *integer division*).
^	*Value1* ^ *Value2*	Raises *Value1* to the exponent *Value2*.
Mod	*Value1* Mod *Value2*	Divides *Value1* by *Value2* and returns the remainder.

For example, suppose you have a sales history table with UnitSales2005 and UnitSales2006 fields. To find all the records where the unit sales in 2006 were at least 10% higher than those in 2005, you add the UnitSales2006 field to the design grid and enter the following expression in the Criteria cell:

```
>=[UnitSales2005]*1.1
```

The Like **Operator**

If you need to allow for multiple spellings in a text field, or if you're not sure how to spell a word you want to use, the *wildcard characters* can help. There are two wildcards: the question mark (?) substitutes for a single character, and the asterisk (*) substitutes for a group of characters. You use them in combination with the Like operator, as shown in Table 11.3.

Table 11.3   The Like **Operator for Criteria Expressions**

Example	Description
Like "Re?d"	Matches records where the field value is Reid, Read, reed, and so on.
Like "M?"	Matches records where the field value is MA, MD, ME, and so on.
Like "R*"	Matches records where the field value begins with R.
Like "*office*"	Matches records where the field value contains the word office.
Like "12/*/2007"	Matches records where the field value is any date in December 2007.

The Between...And **Operator**

If you need to select records where a field value lies between two other values, use the Between...And operator. For example, suppose you want to see all the invoices where the invoice number is between (and includes) 123000 and 124000. Here's the expression you enter in the invoice number field's Criteria cell:

```
Between 123000 And 124000
```

You can use this operator for numbers, dates, and even text.

The In **Operator**

You use the In operator to match records whereby the specified field value is one of a set of values. For example, suppose you want to return a dynaset that contains only those records where the Region field equals NY, CA, TX, IN, or ME. Here's the expression to use:

```
In("NY","CA","TX","IN","ME")
```

The Is Null **Operator**

What do you do if you want to select records where a certain field is empty? For example, an invoice table might have a Date Paid field where, if this field is empty, it means the invoice hasn't been paid yet. For these challenges, Access provides the Is Null operator.

11

Entering this operator by itself in a field's Criteria cell selects only those records whereby the field is empty.

To select records when a particular field is *not* empty, use the Is Not Null operator.

Compound Criteria and the Logical Operators

For many criteria, a single expression just doesn't do the job. For example, in the query shown in Figure 11.1, I selected all the records in the Products table with no inventory by adding the UnitsInStock field to the design grid and entering =0 in this field's Criteria cell.

That approach works, but what if you want to select only the out-of-stock products that haven't been reordered? For queries like these, you need to set up *compound criteria* where you enter either multiple expressions for the same field or multiple expressions for different fields. The following sections cover the two basic types of multiple criteria: And criteria and Or criteria.

Entering And Criteria

You use And criteria when you want to select records that satisfy two or more different expressions. So given *expression1* and *expression2*, a record appears in the dynaset only if it satisfies both *expression1* and *expression2* (which is why they're called And criteria).

Let's look at an example. Suppose you want to display all products with no inventory (UnitsInStock=0) *and* that have not yet been reordered (UnitsOnOrder=0). In this case, you add both the UnitsInStock and UnitsOnOrder fields to the design grid and enter =0 into the Criteria cells for each field, as shown in Figure 11.3.

Figure 11.3
When you enter two expressions in the same row of the design grid, you create an And criterion.

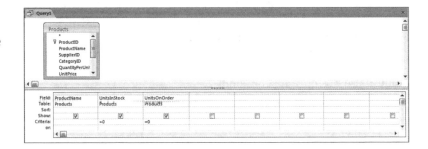

Entering Or Criteria

With Or criteria, you want to display records that satisfy one expression *or* another. If the record satisfies either expression (or both), it appears in the query results; if it satisfies neither expression, it's left out of the results. (Again, you're allowed to use more than two expressions if necessary. No matter how many expressions you use, a record appears in the query results only if it satisfies at least *one* of the expressions.)

Again, an example will help clarify this usage. Suppose you want to select products with an inventory greater than or equal to 100 (`UnitsInStock>=100`) *or* where the number of units on order is greater than or equal to 100 (`UnitsOnOrder>=100`). In this case, you add both the `UnitsInStock` and `UnitsOnOrder` fields to the design grid and enter the criteria expressions *on separate lines* in the design grid (that's why the or appears under `Criteria` in the grid). Figure 11.4 shows how you set up such a query.

Figure 11.4
To use Or criterion for different fields, enter the expressions on separate lines in the design grid.

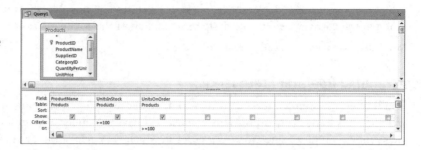

> **NOTE**
> If necessary, you can set up Or criteria using a single field. For example, suppose you want to select those products with no inventory (`UnitsInStock=0`) *or* those products with more than 100 units in stock (`UnitsInStock>=100`). To set this up, you add the `UnitsInStock` field to the design grid, enter `=0` in the Criteria cell, and then enter `>=100` in the or cell below it.

Using the Logical Operators

You use the logical operators to combine or modify `True`/`False` expressions. Table 11.4 summarizes Access's logical operators.

Table 11.4   Logical Operators for Criteria Expressions

Operator	General Form	Description
And	*Expr1* And *Expr2*	Matches records when both *Expr1* and *Expr2* are True.
Or	*Expr1* Or *Expr2*	Matches records when at least one of *Expr1* and *Expr2* is True.
Not	Not *Expr*	Matches records when *Expr* is not True.
Xor	*Expr1* Xor *Expr2*	Matches records when only one of *Expr1* and *Expr2* is True (Xor stands for *exclusive Or*).
Eqv	*Expr1* Eqv *Expr2*	Matches records when both *Expr1* and *Expr2* are True or both *Expr1* and *Expr2* are False (Eqv stands for *equivalence*).
Imp	*Expr1* Imp *Expr2*	Matches records when *Expr2* is True or when *Expr1* is False and *Expr2* is False (Imp stands for *implication*).

The And and Or operators let you create compound criteria using a single expression. For example, suppose you want to match all the records in your Products table where the UnitsInStock field is either 0 or greater than or equal to 100. The following expression does the job:

```
=0 Or >=100
```

The Not operator looks for records that *don't* match a particular logical expression. In a table of customer data, for example, if you want to find all non-North American customers, you add the Country field to the design grid and enter the following expression:

```
Not 'USA' And Not 'Canada' And Not 'Mexico'
```

Understanding Operator Precedence

You'll often use simple expressions that contain just two values and a single operator. In practice, however, many expressions you use will have a number of values and operators. In these more complex expressions, the order in which the calculations are performed becomes crucial. For example, consider the expression 3+5^2. If you calculate from left to right, the answer you get is 64 (3+5 equals 8 and 8^2 equals 64). However, if you perform the exponentiation first and then the addition, the result is 28 (5^2 equals 25 and 3+25 equals 28). As this example shows, a single expression can produce multiple answers depending on the order in which you perform the calculations.

To control this problem, Access evaluates an expression according to a predefined *order of precedence*. This order of precedence lets Access calculate an expression unambiguously by determining which part of the expression it calculates first, which part second, and so on.

The order of precedence that Access uses is determined by the various expression operators I outlined earlier in this chapter. Table 11.5 summarizes the complete order of precedence used by Access.

Table 11.5 The Order of Precedence for Operators

Operator	Operation	Order of Precedence
^	Exponentiation	First
-	Negation	Second
* and /	Multiplication and division	Third
\	Integer division	Fourth
Mod	Modulus	Fifth
+ and -	Addition and subtraction	Sixth
&	Concatenation	Seventh
= < > <= >= <>	Comparison	Eighth
And Eqv Imp Or Xor Not	Logical	Ninth

From this table, you can see that Access performs exponentiation before addition. Therefore, the correct answer for the expression 3+5^2 (just discussed) is 28.

Notice, as well, that some operators in Table 11.5 have the same order of precedence (for example, multiplication and division). This means that it doesn't matter in which order these operators are evaluated (although Access always evaluates them from left to right).

Note that you can override the order of precedence by using parentheses. Terms inside parentheses are always calculated first; terms outside parentheses are calculated sequentially (according to the order of precedence). For example, consider the expression (3+5)^2. In this case, Access performs the addition within the parentheses first and then performs the exponentiation, giving the result of 64.

Setting Up a Calculated Column

Most queries simply display the raw data for the fields included in the design grid, probably filtered by some criteria. In a business environment, however, you often need to perform some kind of analysis on the dynaset. To do that, you need to introduce calculations into your query by creating what is called a *calculated column*. This is a column in the dynaset where the "field" is an expression and the field values are the results of the expression for each record.

With calculated columns, you can create extremely sophisticated queries that use the full power of Access's expression-building features. Here are just a few examples:

- Suppose you have a table of products with a UnitPrice field and you want to display a new column that shows the unit price for each product plus a 5% increase. You can do that by creating a calculated column based on the following expression:
  `[UnitPrice] * 1.05`

- Suppose you have a table of orders with a UnitPrice field and a Quantity field and want a new column that shows the order total. You can do that by creating a calculated column based on this expression:
  `[UnitPrice] * [Quantity]`

- Suppose you have a table of employees with FirstName and LastName fields and you want to see the names combined. You can do that by basing a calculated column on the following expression:

  `[FirstName] & " " & [LastName]`

The expression you use for a calculated column can be any combination of operator, identifier, and literal values, and there are many built-in functions you can use.

Building a calculated column is straightforward: Instead of specifying a field name when adding a column to the dynaset, you enter an expression. You type the expression directly into the column header in the design grid using the following general form:

`ColumnName:expression`

11

Here, `ColumnName` is the name you want to use for the calculated column, and `expression` is the calculation.

> **TIP**
>
> Calculated column expressions are routinely quite long, which means you won't see the entire expression in the Field cell. One solution is to widen the column to fit the length of the expression. Alternatively, click anywhere inside the expression and press Shift+F2 to display the expression inside the Zoom window.

Calculating Inventory Value

The Northwind database's Products table, for example, contains both a `UnitsInStock` field and a `UnitPrice` field. The *inventory value* is the quantity in stock multiplied by the price of the product. You can set up a calculated column to show the inventory value by entering the following expression as the header of a new column in the design grid, as shown in Figure 11.5 (see Figure 11.6 for the resulting dynaset):

```
Inventory Value:[UnitsInStock]*[UnitPrice]
```

Figure 11.5
This query includes a calculated column that derives its values by multiplying the `UnitsInStock` field by the `UnitPrice` field.

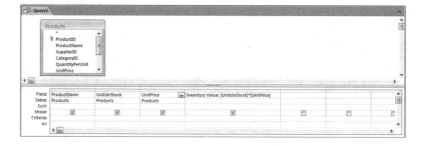

Figure 11.6
The calculated column named Inventory Value contains the results of the expression `[UnitsInStock]*[UnitPrice]`.

> **NOTE**
>
> Keep in mind that you can always use a calculated column for filtering the dynaset. In other words, you can use the calculated column's Criteria cell to enter a criteria expression. For example, if you want to see those products where the inventory value is greater than $3,000, you enter `>3000` in the Criteria cell of the calculated column.

Calculating Discounted Product Totals

As another example, Northwind's Order Details table contains data for orders, including the Quantity, UnitPrice, and Discount for each product ordered. To get the discounted total for a product, you multiply the Quantity by the UnitPrice and then subtract the percentage discount. Here's a calculated column expression that returns this discounted product total:

```
Discounted Total:[UnitPrice] * [Quantity] * (1 - [Discount])
```

Figure 11.7 shows the calculated column, and Figure 11.8 shows the resulting dynaset (the calculated column was set up to use the Currency format).

Figure 11.7
This orders query includes a calculated column that derives its values by multiplying the quantity by the price and then subtracting the discount.

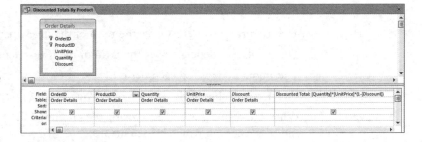

Figure 11.8
The calculated column named Discounted Total contains the results of the expression.

Using the Built-In Functions

Functions are built-in expressions that Access makes available to you. They enable you to beef up your criteria expressions with powerful constructs that can manipulate text and dates and even perform sophisticated math and financial calculations.

Every function has the same basic form:

```
Function(argument1, argument2, ...)
```

The *Function* part is the name of the function. The items that appear within the parentheses and separated by commas are the function *arguments*. The arguments are the function's inputs—the data it uses to perform its calculations. With respect to arguments, functions come in two flavors:

- **No arguments**—Many functions don't require any arguments at all. For example, the Now function returns the current date and time and doesn't require arguments.

- **One or more arguments**—Most functions accept at least one argument, and some accept as many as 9 or 10 arguments. These arguments fall into two categories: required and optional. The required arguments must appear between the parentheses; otherwise, the formula will generate an error. You use the optional arguments only if your formula needs them. To make optional arguments stand out, I put them inside square brackets.

Let's look at an example. The FV function determines the future value of a regular investment based on three required arguments and two optional ones:

```
FV(rate, nper, pmt[, pv][, type])
```

rate	The fixed rate of interest over the term of the investment.
nper	The number of deposits over the term of the investment.
pmt	The amount deposited each period.
pv	The present value of the investment. The default value is 0.
type	When the deposits are due (0 for the beginning of the period; 1 for the end of the period, which is the default).

The preceding is called the function *syntax*, and there are three conventions at work here and throughout the rest of this book:

- *Italic type* indicates a placeholder. That is, when you use the function, you replace the placeholder with an actual value.

- Arguments surrounded by square brackets are optional.

- All other arguments are required.

 TIP

One common problem when using functions is an error caused by misspelling the function name. To guard against this, always enter function names entirely in lowercase letters. If you type the function name correctly, Access will recognize the name and convert it to its correct case (in all Access functions, at least the first letter is capitalized). If Access doesn't convert the name's case, it means you misspelled it.

For each argument placeholder, you substitute an appropriate value. For example, in the FV() function, you substitute *rate* with a decimal value between 0 and 1, *nper* with an integer, and *pmt* with a dollar amount. Arguments can take any of the following forms:

- Literal alphanumeric values
- Expressions
- Results of other functions

Using Text Functions

In Access, *text* is any collection of alphanumeric characters that isn't a numeric value, a date or time value, a logical value, or an expression that returns any of these values. Text literals and fields formatted as text are all obviously text values, but so are any values surrounded by quotation marks. Text values are also called *strings*, and I use both terms interchangeably in this book.

The built-in text functions enable you to perform fairly powerful operations on strings. With these functions, you can convert numbers to strings, change lowercase letters to uppercase (and vice versa), compare two strings, and more. Table 11.6 summarizes the built-in Access text functions.

> **NOTE**
> The function tables in this chapter are not meant to be exhaustive. I skip some obscure functions as well as some optional function arguments. To get the details of any function, use the Expression Builder (discussed later in this chapter). That is, highlight the function in the Expression Builder window and then choose Help.

Table 11.6   The Access Text Functions

Function	What It Returns
Asc(*string*)	The ANSI character code of the first letter in *string*. For example, the following expression returns 97: Asc("a")
Chr(*charcode*)	The character that corresponds to the ANSI code given by *charcode*. For example, the following expression returns the string a: Chr(97)
Format(*expression*[,*format*])	Formats *expression* according to the specified *format* string. For example, the following expression returns the string August 23, 2007: Format(#8/23/2007#, "mmmm dd, yyyy")
InStr([*start*],*string1*,*string2*)	The character position of *string2* in *string1*, from the beginning of the string (or at *start*). For example, the following expression returns 4: InStr("Let's Stop N Shop","'")
InStrRev([*start*],*string1*,*string2*)	The character position of *string2* in *string1*, from the end of the string (or at *start*). For example, the following expression returns 17: InStrRev("Let's Stop N Shop","p")

continues

Table 11.6 Continued

Function	What It Returns
LCase(*string*)	The *string* converted to lowercase. For example, the following expression returns the string sasquatch ale: LCase("Sasquatch Ale")
Left(*string,length*)	The leftmost *length* characters from *string*. For example, the following expression returns the string Boston: Left("Boston Crab Meat", 6)
Len(*string*)	The number of characters in *string*. For example, the following expression returns 17: Len("Let's Stop N Shop")
LTrim(*string*)	A string without the leading spaces in *string*. For example, the following expression returns the string Sasquatch Ale: LTrim(" Sasquatch Ale")
Mid(*string,start,length*)	*length* characters from *string* beginning at *start*. For example, the following expression returns the string Crab: Mid("Boston Crab Meat", 8, 4)
Replace(*string, find, replace*)	A string in which the text *find* has been replaced by the text *replace* in *string*. For example, the following expression returns the string Sasquatch Lager: Replace("Sasquatch Ale", "Ale", "Lager")
Right(*string*)	The rightmost *length* characters from *string*. For example, the following expression returns the string Meat: Right("Boston Crab Meat", 4)
RTrim(*string*)	A string without the trailing spaces in *string*. For example, the following expression returns the string Sasquatch Ale: RTrim("Sasquatch Ale ")
Space(*number*)	A string with *number* spaces. For example, the following expression returns a string with 10 spaces: Space(10)
StrComp(*string1,string2*)	An integer indicating the result of comparing *string1* and *string2*. (Returns -1 if *string1* < *string2*; 0 if *string1* = *string2*; 1 if *string1* > *string2*.) For example, the following expression returns -1: StrComp("Chai","Chang")

Function	What It Returns
StrReverse(*string*)	A string in which the characters are reversed from those in *string*. For example, the following expression returns the string arukI: StrReverse("Ikura")
Trim(*string*)	A string without the leading and trailing spaces in *string*. For example, the following expression returns the string Sasquatch Ale: Trim(" Sasquatch Ale ")
UCase(*string*)	The *string* converted to uppercase. For example, the following expression returns the string SASQUATCH ALE: UCase("Sasquatch Ale")

Extracting a First Name or Last Name

The Northwind database's Suppliers table has a ContactName field that includes the first and last names of the supplier contacts. This often happens in databases, and it's handy to know how to extract the first name and last name from such a field. (For example, you might need to sort the data based on the last name.) The Access text functions enable you to do this.

In the Suppliers table, the first and last names are separated by a space, so the trick here is first to use the InStr function to locate the space. From there, you can use the Left function to extract the first name or the Right function to extract the last name.

For the first name, you use the following expression:

```
Left([ContactName], InStr([ContactName], " ") - 1)
```

Notice how the formula subtracts 1 from the InStr result to avoid including the space in the extracted substring. You can use this expression in more general circumstances to extract the first word of any multiword string.

For the last name, you need to build a similar formula using the Right function:

```
Right([ContactName], Len([ContactName]) - InStr([ContactName], " "))
```

To extract the correct number of letters, the expression takes the length of the original field value and subtracts the position of the space. You can use this formula in more general circumstances to extract the second word in any two-word string.

Figure 11.9 shows a query with two calculated columns—one for the first name and one for the last name—and Figure 11.10 shows the resulting dynaset.

Figure 11.9 This query includes calculated columns that extract the first name and last name from the `ContactName` field.

Contact Name	First Name	Last Name
Charlotte Cooper	Charlotte	Cooper
Shelley Burke	Shelley	Burke
Regina Murphy	Regina	Murphy
Yoshi Nagase	Yoshi	Nagase
Antonio del Valle Saavedra	Antonio	del Valle Saavedra
Mayumi Ohno	Mayumi	Ohno
Ian Devling	Ian	Devling
Peter Wilson	Peter	Wilson
Lars Peterson	Lars	Peterson
Carlos Diaz	Carlos	Diaz
Petra Winkler	Petra	Winkler
Martin Bein	Martin	Bein
Sven Petersen	Sven	Petersen
Elio Rossi	Elio	Rossi

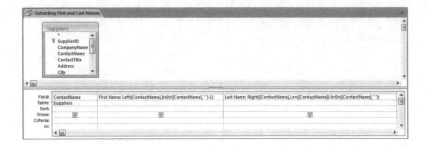

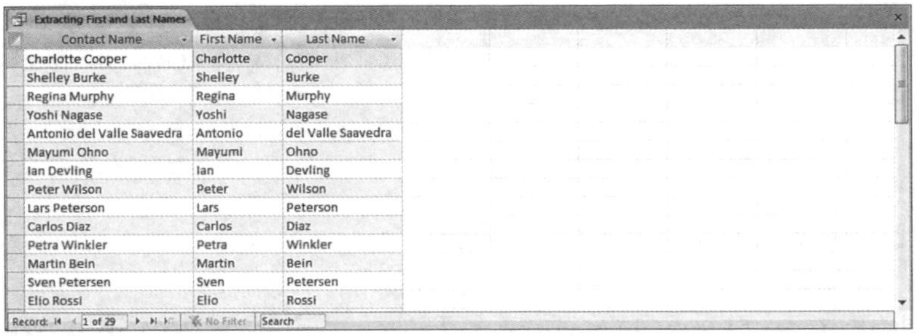

Figure 11.10 The calculated columns named First Name and Last Name contain the results of the expressions.

Formatting Words with Proper Case

Mainframe or downloaded data often comes formatted entirely in uppercase letters. If you want to use this data in a report, you'll probably want to convert some of it to *proper* case, whereby just the first letter of the word is uppercase. Here's an expression that does this using a field named `FirstName`:

```
UCase(Left([FirstName],1)) & LCase(Right([FirstName],Len([FirstName])-1))
```

The leftmost character is extracted, and the `UCase` function is applied to it (although this isn't technically necessary if the field is already all-uppercase). Then the `Right` function extracts the rest of the field, and the `LCase` function converts those characters to lowercase.

Using Date and Time Functions

The date and time functions enable you to convert dates and times to serial numbers and perform operations on those numbers. For example, you can calculate how far apart two dates are, or you can extract the day or month from a specified date. For operands in date expressions, you can use either the result of a date function or a date literal. For the latter, you enclose the date in pound signs, like so:

```
#8/23/2007#
```

When you're working with dates, it helps to remember that Access works with dates internally as *serial numbers*. Specifically, Access uses December 30, 1899, as an arbitrary starting point and then represents subsequent dates as the number of days that have passed since then. So, for example, the date serial number for December 31, 1899, is 1; January 1, 1900, is 2; and so on. Table 11.7 displays some sample date serial numbers.

Table 11.7   Examples of Date Serial Numbers

Serial Number	Date
366	December 31, 1900
16229	June 6, 1944
39317	August 23, 2007

Similarly, Access also uses serial numbers to represent times internally. In this case, though, Access expresses time as a fraction of the 24-hour day to get a number between 0 and 1. The starting point, midnight, is given the value 0, noon is 0.5, and so on. Table 11.8 displays some sample time serial numbers.

Table 11.8   Examples of Time Serial Numbers

Serial Number	Time
0.25	6:00:00 AM
0.375	9:00:00 AM
0.70833	5:00:00 PM
.99999	11:59:59 PM

You can combine the two types of serial numbers. For example, 39317.5 represents 12 noon on August 23, 2007.

The advantage of using serial numbers in this way is that it makes calculations involving dates and times very easy. Because a date or time is really just a number, any mathematical operation you can perform on a number can also be performed on a date. This capability is invaluable for procedures that track delivery times, monitor accounts receivable or accounts payable aging, calculate invoice discount dates, and so on.

Access also comes equipped with quite a few date and time functions. Table 11.9 summarizes them all.

Table 11.9   The Access Date and Time Functions

Function	Returns
CDate(date)	The date string converted into a date value. For example, the following expression returns the date 8/23/2007: CDate("August 23, 2007")
Date()	The current system date.

continues

Table 11.9   Continued

Function	Returns
DateAdd(*interval*,*number*,*date*)	A date that is *number intervals* from the specified *date*. For example, the following expression returns the date December 23, 2007: DateAdd("m",4,#8/23/2007#)
DateDiff(*interval*,*date1*,*date2*)	The difference between *date1* and *date2* based on the specified *interval*. For example, the following expression returns 22: DateDiff("d",#8/1/2007#,#8/23/2007#)
DatePart(*interval*,*date*)	The part (day, month, and so on) of *date* specified by *interval*. For example, the following expression returns 5 (Thursday): DatePart("w",#8/23/2007#)
DateSerial(*year*,*month*,*day*)	A date serial number for the specified *year*, *month*, and *day*. For example, the following expression returns the serial number of the date August 23, 2007: DateSerial(2007,8,23)
DateValue(*date*)	The *date* string converted to a date value. For example, the following expression returns the date 8/23/2007: DateValue("August 23, 2007")
Day(*date*)	The day of the month given by *date*. For example, the following expression returns 23: Day(#8/23/2007#)
Hour(*time*)	The hour component of *time*. For example, the following expression returns 14: Hour(#2:30:45 PM#)
IsDate(*expression*)	True if *expression* is a date; False, otherwise. For example, the following expression returns True: IsDate(#0/23/2007#)
Minute(*time*)	The minute component of *time*. For example, the following expression returns 30: Minute(#2:30:45 PM#)
Month(*date*)	The month component of *date*. For example, the following expression returns 8: Month(#8/23/2007#)
MonthName(*month*)	The name of the month represented by the integer value *month*. For example, the following expression returns the string August: MonthName(Month(#8/23/2007#))

Function	Returns
Now()	The current system date and time.
Second(*time*)	The second component of *time*. For example, the following expression returns 45: Second(#2:30:45 PM#)
Time()	The current system time.
TimeSerial(*hour,minute,second*)	A time serial number for the specified *hour*, *minute*, and *second*. For example, the following expression returns the serial number for 2:30:45 PM: TimeSerial(14,30,45)
TimeValue(*time*)	The *time* string converted to a time serial number. For example, the following expression returns the serial number for 2:30:45 PM: TimeValue("2:30:45 PM")
Weekday(*date*)	The day of the week, as a number, associated with *date*. For example, the following expression returns 5 (Thursday): WeekDay(#8/23/2007#)
WeekdayName(*weekday*)	The name of the day of the week represented by the integer value *weekday*. For example, the following expression returns the string Thursday: WeekdayName(WeekDay(#8/23/2007#))
Year(*date*)	The year component of *date*. For example, the following expression returns 2007: Year(#8/23/2007#)

Calculating a Person's Age

The Northwind's Employees table contains a BirthDate field with a date that represents the date of birth of each employee. Suppose you want to know the current age of each employee. To calculate a person's age, you might think the following formula would do the job:

```
Year(Date()) - Year([BirthDate])
```

This formula works only if the person's birthday has already passed this year. If he or she hasn't had a birthday yet, this formula reports the age as being one year greater than it really is.

To solve this problem, you need to take into account whether the person's birthday has passed. To see how to do this, first check out the following logical expression:

```
DateSerial(Year(Date()), Month([BirthDate]), Day(BirthDate)) > Date()
```

This expression uses `DateSerial` to return the person's birthday for this year, and this is compared with today's date. If the birthday is greater, the expression returns logical `True`, which is equivalent to –1; if it isn't, the expression returns logical `False`, which is equivalent to 0. In other words, you can get the person's true age by adding the result of the logical expression from the original formula, like so:

```
Year(Date()) - Year([BirthDate]) +
➥(DateSerial(Year(Date()), Month([BirthDate]), Day(BirthDate)) > Date())
```

Figure 11.11 shows a query that uses this expression as the basis of a calculated column, and Figure 11.12 shows the resulting dynaset.

Figure 11.11
This query includes a calculated column that calculates employee ages given a `BirthDate` field.

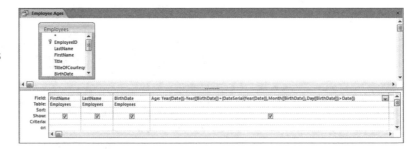

Figure 11.12
The calculated column named Age contains the results of the expression.

Calculating How Long Someone Has Been Employed

If you have a table that specifies when an employee was hired, you can use the `DateDiff` function to calculate how many years each person has been employed with the company. For example, the Northwind Employees table has a `HireDate` field that contains the date on which each employee was hired. To determine the number of years of service, use the following expression:

```
DateDiff("yyyy"[,HireDate],Date())
```

Here, the yyyy string for the *interval* argument tells Access to return the number of years (rounded up to the next highest year). The `DateDiff` function's *interval* argument accepts the values shown in Table 11.10.

Table 11.10	Acceptable Values for the DateDiff Function's *interval* Argument
Interval	**Date/Time Units**
yyyy	Years
y	Days of the year
q	Quarters
m	Months
ww	Calendar weeks
w	Weeks
d	Days
h	Hours
n	Minutes
s	Seconds

Using Math Functions

Queries based on purely mathematical expressions don't come up often in business environments, but Access does come with a few built-in math functions in case you need them. Table 11.11 lists the built-in Access mathematical functions.

Table 11.11	The Access Math Functions
Function	**Returns**
Abs(*number*)	The absolute value of *number*. For example, the following expression returns 5: Abs(-5)
Atn(*number*)	The arctangent of *number*.
Cos(*number*)	The cosine of *number*.
Exp(*number*)	*e* (the base of the natural logarithm) raised to the power of *number*.
Fix(*number*)	The integer portion of *number*. If *number* is negative, Fix returns the first negative integer greater than or equal to *number*. For example, the following expression returns -5: Fix(-5.2)
Int(*number*)	The integer portion of *number*. If *number* is negative, Int returns the first negative integer less than or equal to *number*. For example, the following expression returns -6: Int(-5.2)
Log(*number*)	The natural logarithm of *number*.

continues

Table 11.11   The Access Math Functions

Function	Returns
Rnd([*number*])	A random number greater than or equal to 0 and less than 1. You use the optional *number* as a "seed" value, as follows: *number* — *Generates* Less than 0 — The same number every time (varies with *number*). Equal to 0 — The most recently generated number. Greater than 0 — The next random number in the sequence (this is the default).
Round(*number*[, *places*])	The *number* rounded to the specified number of decimal *places*. For example, the following expression returns 5.3: Round(5.29,1)
Sgn(*number*)	An integer that represents the sign of *number*: *number* — *Returns* Less than 0 — -1 Equal to 0 — 0 Greater than 0 — 1
Sin(*number*)	The sine of *number*.
Sqr(*number*)	The square root of *number*.
Tan(*number*)	The tangent of *number*.

Generating Random Numbers Between Two Values

The Rnd function returns a random number that is greater than or equal to 0 and less than 1. Rnd is often useful by itself (for example, it's perfect for generating random time values). However, you'll most often use it in an expression to generate random numbers between two values.

In the simplest case, if you want to generate random numbers greater than or equal to 0 and less than *n*, use the following expression:

```
Rnd * n
```

For example, the following formula generates a random number between 0 and 30:

```
=Rnd() * 30
```

The more complex case is when you want random numbers greater than or equal to some number *m* and less than some number *n*. Here's the expression to use for this case:

```
Rnd() * (n - m) + m
```

For example, the following formula produces a random number greater than or equal to 100 and less than 200:

```
=Rnd() * (200 - 100) + 100
```

When you're using Rnd in a calculated column, Access generates the same random number for every record unless you provide the function with a different seed value for each record. You can avoid this situation if the table has a numeric field with unique values, such as an AutoNumber field or a numeric primary key field. In this case, you use the field identifier as the seed value. For example, the following expression generates random numbers using the numbers in the EmployeeID field as seed values:

```
Rnd([EmployeeID])
```

Generating Random *N*-Digit Numbers

It's often useful to create random numbers with a specific number of digits. For example, you might want to generate a random six-digit account number for new customers, or you might need a random eight-digit number for a temporary filename.

The procedure for this is to start with the general formula from the previous section and apply the Int function to ensure an integer result:

```
Int(Rnd() * (n - m) + m)
```

In this case, however, you set n equal to 10^n and you set m equal to 10^{n-1}:

```
Int(Rnd() * (10ⁿ - 10ⁿ⁻¹) + 10ⁿ⁻¹)
```

For example, if you need a random eight-digit number, this formula becomes the following:

```
Int(Rnd() * (100000000 - 10000000) + 10000000)
```

This generates random numbers greater than or equal to 10000000 and less than or equal to 99999999. (Again, remember to specify a field-based seed value if you need to generate a unique random number for each record.)

Using Financial Functions

Access has quite a few built-in financial functions that enable you to calculate, for example, the monthly payment for a loan, the future value of an annuity, or the yearly depreciation of an asset.

Although the financial functions use many arguments, the following list covers the arguments you'll see most frequently:

rate	The fixed rate of interest over the term of the loan or investment.
nper	The number of payments or deposit periods over the term of the loan or investment.
pmt	The periodic payment or deposit.

11

pv	The present value of the loan (the principal) or the initial deposit in an investment.
fv	The future value of the loan or investment.
type	The type of payment or deposit. Use 0 (the default) for end-of-period payments or deposits and 1 for beginning-of-period payments or deposits.

For most financial functions, the following rules apply:

■ The underlying unit of both the interest rate and the period must be the same. For example, if the *rate* is the annual interest rate, you must express *nper* in years. Similarly, if you have a monthly interest rate, you must express *nper* in months.

■ You enter money you receive as a positive quantity, and you enter money you pay as a negative quantity. For example, you always enter the loan principal as a positive number because it's money you receive from the bank.

■ The *nper* argument is always a positive integer quantity.

Table 11.12 lists all the Access financial functions.

Table 11.12 The Access Financial Functions

Function	Returns
DDB(*cost,salvage,life,period*)	The depreciation of an asset in a specified *period* given its initial *cost*, *salvage* value, and useful *life*, using the double-declining balance method.
FV(*rate,nper,pmt*[,*pv*][,*type*])	The future value of an investment or loan.
IPmt(*rate,per,nper,pv*[,*fv*][,*type*])	The interest payment for a specified period of a loan.
IRR(*values*[,*guess*])	The internal rate of return for a series of cash flows.
MIRR(*values,finance_rate,reinvest_rate*)	The modified internal rate of return for a series of periodic cash flows.
NPer(*rate,pmt,pv*[,*fv*][,*type*])	The number of periods for an investment or loan.
NPV(*rate,value1,value2...*)	The net present value of an investment based on a series of cash flows and a discount rate.
Pmt(*rate,nper,pv*[,*fv*][,*type*])	The periodic payment for a loan or investment.
PPmt(*rate,per,nper,pv*[,*fv*][,*type*])	The principal payment for a specified period of a loan.
PV(*rate,nper,pmt*[,*fv*][,*type*])	The present value of an investment.

Function	Returns
Rate(*nper*,*pmt*,*pv*[,*fv*][,*type*])	The periodic interest rate for a loan or investment.
SLN(*cost*,*salvage*,*life*)	The straight-line depreciation of an asset over one period given its initial *cost*, *salvage* value, and useful *life*.
SYD(*cost*,*salvage*,*life*,*period*)	The sum-of-years' digits depreciation of an asset in a specified *period* given its initial *cost*, *salvage* value, and useful *life*.

Creating a Mortgage Payment Calculator

You probably don't think of Access when you think about building any kind of "calculator," but you can build a rudimentary financial calculating device using an expression that takes advantage of the financial functions. As an example, this section shows you a query that calculates a monthly mortgage payment given a mortgage rate, term, and principal.

Calculating a loan payment is the job of the Pmt function. The first step is to create a table that includes five fields, one for each argument in the Pmt function: *rate*, *nper*, *pv*, *fv*, and *type*. When that's done, you create a query with this table as the source data. Assuming *rate* is the annual interest rate and *nper* is the number of years in the mortgage term, you include in this query a calculated column based on the following expression:

```
Pmt([rate]/12,[nper]*12,[pv],[fv],[type])
```

Note that in this expression the square brackets indicate that the arguments are fields. (So don't confuse this with the square brackets used to indicate optional arguments in the function's syntax.) Figure 11.13 shows a query that uses this expression as the basis of a calculated column, and Figure 11.14 shows the resulting dynaset. Access updates the Monthly Payment value as soon as you change any value in the record (even if you just move to another field in the same record).

Figure 11.13
This query includes a calculated column that uses the Pmt function to determine the monthly mortgage payment using field values as the function arguments.

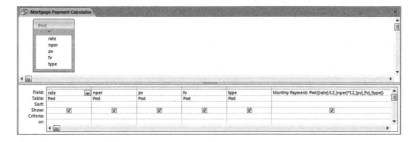

11

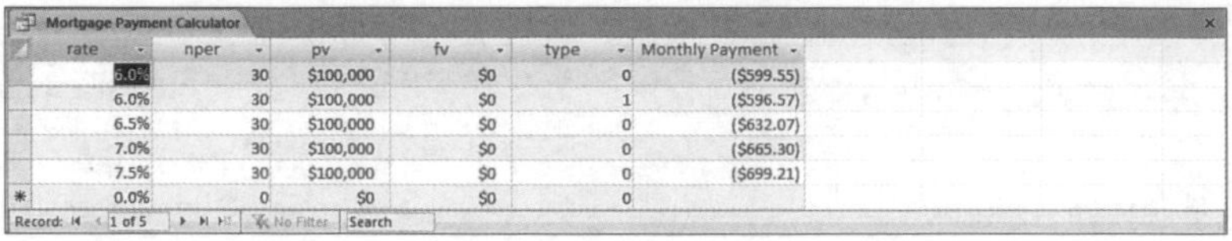

Figure 11.14
The calculated column
named Monthly Payment
contains the results of
the expression.

rate	nper	pv	fv	type	Monthly Payment
6.0%	30	$100,000	$0	0	($599.55)
6.0%	30	$100,000	$0	1	($596.57)
6.5%	30	$100,000	$0	0	($632.07)
7.0%	30	$100,000	$0	0	($665.30)
7.5%	30	$100,000	$0	0	($699.21)
0.0%	0	$0	$0	0	

Record: H ◄ 1 of 5 ► H ►I 🔍 No Filter Search

Working with the Expression Builder

Access doesn't provide much help when you type an expression into a Field cell or Criteria
cell. It doesn't provide function syntax; it doesn't match parentheses (as, say, Excel does
when entering formulas); it doesn't give you an easy way to pick out field names; and its
error messages can be distressingly vague.

There isn't much that you can do about the vague error messages, but Access does come
with a tool that can ease some of the burden of expression building. The tool is called,
appropriately, *Expression Builder*, and it works according to the following steps:

1. Click the Field or Criteria cell in which you want to enter the expression.
2. Choose Design, Builder. Access displays the Expression Builder window.
3. Enter some or all of the expression in the large text box.
4. To add an operator to the expression, place the cursor where you want the operator to
   appear. Then either click an operator button or click the Operators category and then
   double-click the operator you want.
5. To add a database object to the expression, place the cursor where you want the object
   to appear, use the categories (Tables, Queries, and so on) to find the object, and then
   double-click the object you want.
6. To add a function to the expression, place the cursor where you want the function to
   appear; open the Functions, Built-In Function branch; click the function type; and then
   double-click the function you want. Figure 11.15 shows the Expression Builder with
   the Pmt function added to the expression. Be sure to replace each argument placeholder
   with an actual operand.
7. Repeats steps 4–6 as necessary to complete the expression.
8. Click OK.

Figure 11.15
Use the Expression
Builder to add text,
operators, database
objects, and functions
to an expression.

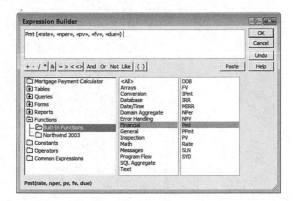

From Here

→ To learn how to use an expression in a calculated form control, **see** "Using Text Boxes as Calculated Controls," **p. 44**. (Chapter 2)

→ For an example of a financial function, **see** "Case Study: Creating a Mortgage Calculator," **p. 46**. (Chapter 2)

→ You'll use expressions quite a bit when you create totals queries; **see** "Creating a Totals Query," **p. 287**. (Chapter 13)

→ To learn about the IIf and Switch functions, **see** "Creating Queries That Make Decisions," **p. 296**. (Chapter 13)

11

Working with Multiple-Table Queries

Most database applications (and *all* well-designed database applications) store their information in multiple tables. Although most of these tables have nothing to do with each other (for example, tables of customer information and employee payroll data), it's likely that at least some of the tables do contain related information (such as tables of customer information and customer orders).

Working with multiple, related tables in a query presents you with two challenges: You need to design your database so that the related data is accessible, and you need to set up links between the tables so that the related information can be retrieved and worked with quickly and easily in the query design window. This chapter tackles both challenges and shows you how to exploit the full multiple-table powers of Access.

Relational Database Fundamentals

Why do you need to worry about multiple tables, anyway? Isn't it easier to work with one large table instead of two or three medium-sized ones? To answer these questions and demonstrate the problems that arise when you ignore relational database models, take a look at a simple example: a table of sales leads.

The Pitfalls of a Nonrelational Design

Table 12.1 outlines the structure of a simple table (named Leads) that stores data on sales leads.

Table 12.1   The Structure of a Simple Sales Leads Table (Leads)

Field	Description
LeadID	The primary key.
Jones, Ann	The contact's first name.
LastName	The contact's last name.
Company	The company that the contact works for.
Address	The company's address.
City	The company's city.
State	The company's state.
Zip	The company's ZIP code.
Phone	The contact's phone number.
Fax	The contact's fax number.
Source	Where the lead came from.
Notes	Notes or comments related to the sales lead.

This structure works fine until you need to add two or more leads from the same company (a not-uncommon occurrence). In this case, you end up with repeating information in the Company, Address, City, and State fields. (The Zip field also repeats, as do, in some cases, the Phone, Fax, and Source fields.)

All this repetition makes the table unnecessarily large, which is bad enough, but it also creates three major problems:

■ During data entry, the repeated information must be entered for each lead from the same company.

■ Entering the same data repeatedly increases the chances of entering that data either incorrectly (due to typos and other errors) or inconsistently (for example, entering "St." in one field and "Street" in another).

■ If any of the repeated information changes (such as the company's name or address), each corresponding record must be changed.

One way to eliminate the repetition and solve the data entry and maintenance inefficiencies is to change the table's focus. As it stands, each record in the table identifies a specific contact in a company. But it's the company information that repeats, so it makes some sense to allow only one record per company. You can then include separate fields for each sales lead within the company. The new structure might look something like the one shown in Table 12.2.

Table 12.2   A Revised, Company-Centered Structure of the Sales Leads Table

Field	Description
LeadID	The primary key.
Company	The company's name.
Address	The company's address.
City	The company's city.
State	The company's state.
Zip	The company's ZIP code.
Phone	The company's phone number.
Fax	The company's fax number.
First_1	The first name of contact #1.
Last_1	The last name of contact #1.
Source_1	Where the lead for contact #1 came from.
Notes_1	Notes or comments related to contact #1.
First_2	The first name of contact #2.
Last_2	The last name of contact #2.
Source_2	Where the lead for contact #2 came from.
Notes_2	Notes or comments related to contact #2.
First_3	The first name of contact #3.
Last_3	The last name of contact #3.
Source_3	Where the lead for contact #3 came from.
Notes_3	Notes or comments related to contact #3.

In this setup, the company information appears only once, and the contact-specific data (I'm assuming this involves only the first name, last name, source, and notes) appears in separate field groups (for example, First_1, Last_1, Source_1, and Notes_1). This setup solves the earlier problems, but at the cost of a new dilemma: The structure as it stands will hold only three sales leads per company. Of course, it's entirely conceivable that a large firm might have more than three contacts—perhaps even dozens. This raises two unpleasant difficulties:

- If you run out of repeating groups of contact fields, new ones must be added. Although this might not be a problem for the database designer, most data entry clerks generally don't have access to the table design (nor should they).

- Empty fields take up as much disk real estate as full ones, so making room for, say, a dozen contacts from one company means that all the records that have only one or two contacts have huge amounts of wasted space.

How a Relational Design Can Help

To solve the twin problems of repetition between records and repeated field groups within records, you need to turn to the relational database model. This model was developed by Dr. Edgar Codd of IBM in the early 1970s. It was based on a complex relational algebra theory, so the pure form of the rules and requirements for a true relational database setup is quite complicated and decidedly impractical for business applications. The next few sections look at a simplified version of the model.

Step 1: Separate the Data

After you know which fields you need to include in your database application, the first step in setting up a relational database is to divide these fields into separate tables where the "theme" of each table is unique. In technical terms, each table must be composed of only entities (that is, records) from a single *entity class*.

For example, the table of sales leads you saw earlier dealt with data that had two entity classes: the contacts and the companies for which they worked. Every one of the problems encountered with that table can be traced to the fact that we were trying to combine two entity classes into a single table. So the first step toward a relational solution is to create separate tables for each class of data. Table 12.3 shows the table structure of the contact data (the Contacts table), and Table 12.4 shows the structure of the company information (the Companies table). Note, in particular, that both tables include a primary key field.

Table 12.3   The Structure of the Contacts Table

Field	Description
ContactID	The primary key.
FirstName	The contact's first name.
LastName	The contact's last name.
Phone	The contact's phone number.
Fax	The contact's fax number.
Source	Where the lead came from
Notes	Notes or comments related to the sales lead.

Table 12.4   The Structure of the Companies Table

Field	Description
CompanyID	The primary key.
CompanyName	The company's name.
Address	The company's address.
City	The company's city.

Field	Description
State	The company's state.
Zip	The company's ZIP code.
Phone	The company's phone number (main switchboard).

Step 2: Add Foreign Keys to the Tables

At first glance, separating the tables seems self-defeating because, if you've done the job properly, the two tables will have nothing in common. So the second step in this relational design is to define the commonality between the tables.

In the sales leads example, what is the common ground between the Contacts and Companies tables? It's that every one of the leads in the Contacts table works for a specific firm in the Companies table. So what's needed is some way of relating the appropriate information in Companies to each record in Contacts (without, of course, the inefficiency of simply cramming all the data into a single table, as we tried earlier).

The way you do this in relational database design is to establish a field that is common to both tables. You can then use this common field to set up a link between the two tables. The field you use must satisfy three conditions:

- It must not have the same name as an existing field in the other table.
- It must uniquely identify each record in the other table.
- To save space and reduce data entry errors, it must be the smallest field that satisfies the two preceding conditions.

In the sales leads example, you need to add a field to the Contacts table that establishes a link to the appropriate record in the Companies table. The CompanyName field uniquely identifies each firm, but it's too large to be of use. The Phone field is also a unique identifier and is smaller, but the Contacts table already has a Phone field. The best solution is to use CompanyID, the Companies table's primary key field. Table 12.5 shows the revised structure of the Contacts table that includes the CompanyID field.

Table 12.5 The Final Structure of the Contacts Table

Field	Description
ContactID	The primary key.
CompanyID	The Companies table foreign key.
FirstName	The contact's first name.
LastName	The contact's last name.
Phone	The contact's phone number.

continues

12

Table 12.5	**Continued**
Field	**Description**
Fax	The contact's fax number.
Source	Where the lead came from.
Notes	Notes or comments related to the sales lead.

When a table includes a primary key field from a related database, the field is called a *foreign key*. Foreign keys are the secret to successful relational database design.

Step 3: Establish a Link Between the Related Tables

After you have your foreign keys inserted into your tables, the final step in designing your relational model is to establish a link between the two tables. This step is covered in detail later in this chapter (see "Establishing Table Relationships").

Types of Relational Models

Depending on the data you're working with, you can set up one of several relational database models. In each of these models, however, you need to differentiate between a *child* table (also called a *dependent* table or a *controlled* table) and a *parent* table (also called a *primary* table or a *controlling* table). The child table is the one that is dependent on the parent table to fill in the definition of its records. The Contacts table, for example, is a child table because it is dependent on the Companies table for the company information associated with each person.

The One-to-Many Model

The most common relational model is one where a single record in the parent table relates to multiple records in the child table. This is called a *one-to-many* relationship. The sales leads example is a one-to-many relation because one record in the Companies table can relate to many records in the Contacts table (in other words, you can have multiple sales contacts from the same firm). In these models, the "many" table is the one where you add the foreign key.

Another example of a one-to-many relationship is an application that tracks accounts-receivable invoices. You need one table for the invoice data (Invoices) and another for the customer data (Customers). In this case, one customer can place many orders, so Customers is the parent table, Invoices is the child table, and the common field is the Customer table's primary key.

The One-to-One Model

If your data requires that one record in the parent table be related to only one record in the child table, you have a *one-to-one* model. The most common use of one-to-one relations is to create separate entity classes to enhance security. In a hospital, for example, each patient's data is a single entity class, but it makes sense to create separate tables for the patient's basic information (such as the name, address, and so on) and his or her medical history. This setup enables you to add extra levels of security to the confidential medical data (such as a password). The two tables then become related based on a common `PatientID` key field.

Another example of a one-to-one model is employee data. You separate the less-sensitive information such as job title and startup date into one table, and restricted information such as salary and commissions into a second table. If each employee has a unique identification number, you use that number to set up a relationship between the two tables.

Note that in a one-to-one model, the concepts of *child* and *parent* tables are interchangeable. Each table relies on the other to form the complete picture of each patient or employee.

The Many-to-Many Model

In some cases, you might have data in which many records in one table can relate to many records in another table. This is called a *many-to-many* relationship. In this case, there is no direct way to establish a common field between the two tables. To see why, let's look at an example from a pared-down accounts-receivable application.

Table 12.6 shows the simplified structure of an Invoices table. It includes a primary key—`InvoiceID`—as well as a foreign key—`CustomerID`—from a separate table of customer information (which I ignore in this example).

Table 12.6   The Structure of an Invoices Table

Field	Description
InvoiceID	The primary key.
CustomerID	The foreign key from a table of customer data.

Table 12.7 shows the stripped-down structure of a table of product information. It includes a primary key field—`ProductID`—and a description field—`Product`.

Table 12.7   The Structure of a Products Table

Field	Description
ProductID	The primary key.
Product	The product description.

12

The idea here is that a given product can appear in many invoices, and any given invoice can contain many products. This is a many-to-many relationship, and it implies that *both* tables are parents (or, to put it another way, neither table is directly dependent on the other). But relational theory says that a child table is needed to establish a common field. In this case, the solution is to set up a third table—called a *relation table*—that is the child of both the original tables. In the ongoing example, the relation table contains the detail data for each invoice. Table 12.8 shows the structure of such a table. As you can see, the table includes foreign keys from both Invoices (`InvoiceID`) and Products (`ProductID`), as well as a `Quantity` field.

Table 12.8   The Structure of a Table of Invoice Detail Data

Field	Description
DetailID	The primary key.
InvoiceID	The foreign key from the Invoices table.
ProductID	The foreign key from the Products table.
Quantity	The quantity ordered.

Enforcing Referential Integrity

Database applications that work with multiple, related tables need to enforce *referential integrity rules*. These rules ensure that related tables remain in a consistent state relative to each other. In the sales leads application, for example, suppose the Companies table includes an entry for "ACME Coyote Supplies" and that the Contacts table contains three leads who work for ACME. What would happen if you deleted the ACME Coyote Supplies record from the Companies table? Well, the three records in the Contacts table would no longer be related to any record in the Companies table. Child records without corresponding records in the parent table are called, appropriately enough, *orphans*. This situation leaves your tables in an inconsistent state, which can have unpredictable consequences. For example, certain types of queries may fail because Access can't properly relate the underlying tables.

Preventing orphaned records is what is meant by enforcing referential integrity. You need to watch out for two situations:

- Deleting a parent table record that has related records in a child table.
- Adding a child table record that isn't related to a record in the parent table (either because the common field contains no value or because it contains a value that doesn't correspond to any record in the parent table).

Establishing Table Relationships

Now that you know the theory behind the relational model, you can turn your attention to creating and working with related tables in queries. The first step, however, is to establish the relationship between the two tables, which is what this section is all about.

To get started, choose Database Tools, Relationships. You'll see the Relationships window, which will be similar to the one shown in Figure 12.1.

> **NOTE**
> As I mentioned in Chapter 10, "Creating a Basic Query," I'm going to use the older (Access 2003) Northwind sample data for the querying chapters. You can download the sample database from my website:
>
> www.mcfedries.com/Access2007Forms

Figure 12.1
You use the Relationships window to establish relations between tables.

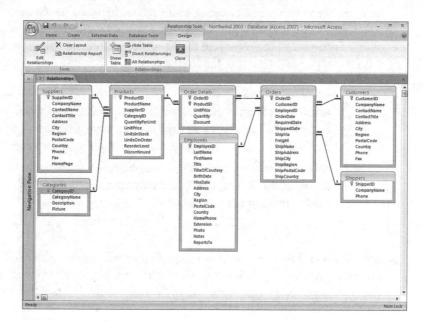

Understanding Join Lines

Because the Northwind sample database is well designed, all the tables are related to each other in one way or another. You can tell this by observing the lines that connect each table in the Relationships window. These lines are called *join lines*. As you can see in Figure 12.1, the join line connects the two fields that contain the related information. For example, the Suppliers and Products tables are joined on the common SupplierID field. In this case, SupplierID is the primary key field for the Suppliers table, and it appears as a foreign key in the Products table. This lets you relate any product to its corresponding supplier data.

The symbols attached to the join lines tell you the type of relation. In the join between the Suppliers and Products tables, for example, the Suppliers side of the join line has a 1, and the Products side of the line has an infinity symbol (?). This stands for "many," so you interpret this join as a one-to-many relation.

Identifying Join Types

Access lets you set up four kinds of joins:

- **Inner join**—An *inner join* includes only those records in which the related fields in the two tables match each other exactly (which is why this type of join is often called an *equijoin*). This is the most common type of join.

- **Outer join**—An *outer join* includes every record from one of the tables and only those records from the other table in which the related fields match each other exactly. In the sales leads example, it's possible that there might be companies for which no contacts have yet been established. Creating an inner join between the Company and Contacts tables shows you only those firms that have existing contacts. However, setting up an outer join shows *all* the records in the Companies table, including those in which there is no corresponding record in the Contacts table.

> **NOTE**
>
> An outer join is also called a *left-outer join*. To see why, consider a one-to-many relation. Here, the "left" side is the "one" table, and the "right" side is the "many" table. So this type of join includes every record from the "one" (left) side and only those matching records from the "many" (right) side.
>
> You use the term *left-outer join* when you need to differentiate it from a *right-outer join*. In a one-to-many relation, this type of join includes every record from the "many" (right) side and only those matching records from the "one" (left) side.

- **Self-join**—A *self-join* is a join on a second copy of the same table. Self-joins are handy for tables that include different fields with the same type of information. For example, the Northwind Employees table has an `EmployeeID` field that lists the identification number of each employee. The same table also includes a `ReportsTo` field that lists the identification number of the employee's manager. To display the name of each employee's manager, you use a second copy of the Employees table and join the `EmployeeID` and `ReportsTo` fields.

- **Theta join**—A *theta join* is created when the data in two fields from two tables is related via some comparison operator other than equals (=). For example, a *not-equal join* relates data using the not-equal operator (<>). For example, suppose you want to compare the unit price data in Northwind's Order Details table with the unit price data in the Products table. Specifically, you want to see those orders where the unit price on the order differs from the unit price of the product. In this case, you look for records where the `[Order Details].UnitPrice` field is not equal to the `[Products].UnitPrice` field.

Adding Tables to the Relationships Window

If you need to establish a new relationship between two tables, your first order of business is to add the tables to the Relationships window. Here are the steps to follow:

1. Under Relationship Tools, choose Design, Show Table to display the Show Table dialog box, shown in Figure 12.2.

Figure 12.2
Use this dialog box to add tables to the Relationships window.

2. Click the table you want to add. (You can also build queries based on existing queries; see "Nesting Queries Within Queries," later in this chapter.)
3. Click <u>A</u>dd. Access adds the table to the Relationships window.
4. Repeat steps 2 and 3 to add more tables.
5. Click <u>C</u>lose to return to the Relationships window.

Joining Tables

To create a join between two tables (or a self-join between two copies of the same table), use the mouse to click and drag one of the related fields and drop it on the other. Here are the specific steps:

1. Add the tables you want to join.
2. Arrange the table boxes so that in each box you can see the fields you want to use for the join.
3. Click and drag the related field from one table and drop it on the related field in the other table. Access displays the Edit Relationships dialog box, shown in Figure 12.3.
4. The grid should show the names of the fields in each table that you want to relate. If not, use the drop-down list in one or both cells to click the correct field or fields.

Figure 12.3
Access displays the Edit Relationships dialog box when you click and drag a related field from one table and drop it on another.

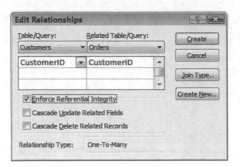

5. If you want Access to enforce referential integrity rules on this relation, click the Enforce Referential Integrity check box. If you do this, two other check boxes become active:

   - **Cascade Update Related Fields**—If you click this check box and then make changes to a primary key value in the parent table, Access updates the new key value for all related records in all child tables. For example, if you change a CompanyID value in the Companies table, all related records in the Contacts table have their CompanyID fields updated automatically.

   - **Cascade Delete Related Fields**—If you activate this check box and then delete a record from the parent table, all related records in all child tables are also deleted. For example, if you delete a record from the Companies table, all records in the Contacts table that have the same CompanyID as the deleted record are also deleted.

6. To set the type of join, click Join Type to display the Join Properties dialog box, shown in Figure 12.4. Here, option 1 corresponds to an inner join, option 2 corresponds to a left-outer join, and option 3 corresponds to a right-outer join. After you've clicked the option you want, click OK to return to the Edit Relationships dialog box.

Figure 12.4
Use the Join Properties dialog box to establish the type of join.

7. Click Create. Access establishes the relationship and displays a join line between the two fields.

Editing a Relationship

If you need to make changes to a relationship, Access lets you edit the relation parameters from within the Relationships window. For the relation you want to adjust, click the join line for the two fields and then choose Design, Edit Relationships (you can also double-click the join line or right-click the join line and choose Edit Relationship from the shortcut menu). Access displays the Edit Relationships dialog box so that you can make your changes.

Removing a Join

If you no longer need a join, you can remove it by clicking the join line and pressing Delete, or by right-clicking the join line and then clicking Delete. When Access asks you to confirm the deletion, click Yes.

Working with Multiple Tables in a Query

With a properly constructed relational database model, you'll end up with fields that don't make much sense by themselves. For example, the Northwind database has an Order Details table that includes a `ProductID` field—a foreign key from the Products table. This field contains only numbers and therefore by itself is meaningless to an observer.

The idea behind a multiple-table query is to *join* related tables and by doing so create a dynaset that replaces meaningless data (such as a product ID) with meaningful data (such as a product name).

The good news is that after you've established a relationship between two tables, Access handles everything else behind the scenes, so working with multiple tables isn't much harder than working with single tables.

Adding Multiple Tables to a Query

To add multiple tables to a query, follow these steps:

1. Display the Show Table dialog box. You have two choices:
   - If you're starting a new query, choose Create, Query Design.
   - If you're already in the query design window, choose Design, Show Table.
2. Click the table name and then choose Add.
3. Repeat step 2 to add other tables, as necessary.
4. Click Close.

12

As you can see in Figure 12.5, Access displays join lines between related tables.

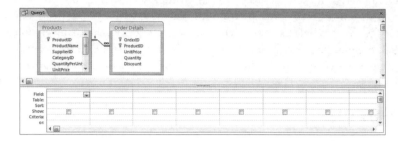

Figure 12.5
When you add multiple, related tables to the query design window, Access automatically displays the join lines for the related fields.

Adding Fields from Multiple Tables

With your tables added to the query design window, adding fields to the query is only slightly different than adding them for a single-table query:

■ You can still add any field by clicking and dragging it from the table pane to one of the Field cells in the design grid.

■ When you choose a field directly from a Field drop-down list, note that the field names are preceded by the table name (for example, `Products.SupplierID`).

■ To lessen the clutter in the Field cells, first use the Table cell to choose the table that contains the field you want. After you do this, the list in the corresponding Field cell will display only the fields from the selected table.

From here, you can set up the query criteria, sorting, top *N* values, and calculated columns exactly as you can with a single-table query. Figure 12.6 shows a query based on the Products, Order Details, and Orders tables. The query shows the `SupplierID`, `ProductName`, and `UnitsInStock` (from Products), the `Quantity` (from Order Details), and `OrderDate` (from Orders), and a Left In Stock calculated column that subtracts the `Quantity` from the `UnitsInStock`. The dynaset will contain just those orders from January 7, 2007, and is sorted on the Left In Stock calculated column. Figure 12.7 shows the resulting dynaset.

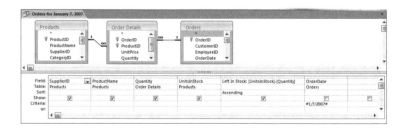

Figure 12.6
A query with three related tables that includes fields from all the tables.

12

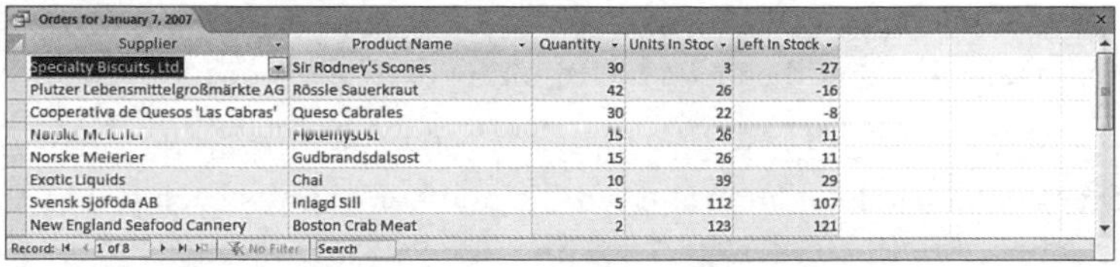

Figure 12.7
The dynaset returned by the multiple-table query shown in Figure 12.6.

Supplier		Product Name	Quantity	Units In Stoc	Left In Stock
Specialty Biscuits, Ltd.		Sir Rodney's Scones	30	3	-27
Plutzer Lebensmittelgroßmärkte AG		Rössle Sauerkraut	42	26	-16
Cooperativa de Quesos 'Las Cabras'		Queso Cabrales	30	22	-8
Norske Meierier		Flotemysost	15	26	11
Norske Meierier		Gudbrandsdalost	15	26	11
Exotic Liquids		Chai	10	39	29
Svensk Sjöföda AB		Inlagd Sill	5	112	107
New England Seafood Cannery		Boston Crab Meat	2	123	121

> **NOTE** In the query shown in Figure 12.6, the Products and Orders tables are said to have an *indirect relationship*. That is, they're related to each other, but only via the Order Details table. Note that it's possible to construct a query that includes fields only from Products and Orders, but you must still include the Order Details table in the query design to allow Access to set up the indirect relationship.

The only thing you have to watch out for is dealing with tables that each have a field with the same name. For example, both the Order Details table and the Products table have a `UnitPrice` field. To differentiate between them in, say, an expression for a calculated column, you need to preface the field name with the table name, like so:

`[Table Name].[FieldName]`

For example, consider the formula that calculates the `ExtendedPrice` field in the Order Details Extended query. The idea behind this formula is to multiply the unit price times the quantity ordered and subtract the discount. Here's the formula:

`[Order Details].[UnitPrice]*[Quantity]*(1-[Discount])`

To differentiate between the `UnitPrice` field in the Order Details table and the `UnitPrice` field in the Products table, the formula uses the term `[Order Details].[UnitPrice]`, as shown in Figure 12.8.

Figure 12.8
When the tables in a multiple-table query share a common field name, precede the field name with the table name in an expression.

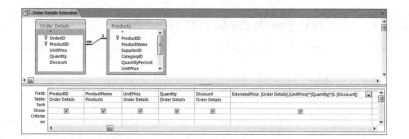

Nesting Queries Within Queries

In the previous section, I showed you how to add multiple tables to a query, but there's no reason why you can't also add other queries to the table pane. After all, the Show Table dialog box has a Queries tab that lists all your saved queries, so you can add them to the query design as easily as you add a table. When you nest one query inside another, Access runs the nested query first and then uses the resulting dynaset to produce the rest of the query.

For example, in the Orders for January 7, 2007, query from the previous section, the Left In Stock calculated column returned the number of units each product had left in stock after subtracting the order quantity. Suppose you then wanted a new query that checked for those products with a negative Left In Stock value and returned the appropriate supplier data so that the product can be reordered.

To do this, you begin by adding both the Suppliers table and the Orders for January 7, 2007, query to the query design window. As you can see in Figure 12.9, Access automatically sets up a temporary relation between the common `SupplierID` fields (because `SupplierID` is the primary key of the Suppliers table). The rest of the query is created in the usual way, and the result is shown in Figure 12.10.

Figure 12.9
You can nest one query inside another, and Access will set up a temporary relation based on a common field.

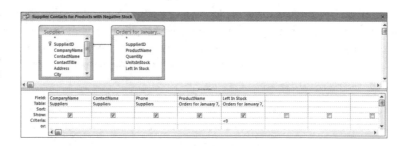

Figure 12.10
The dynaset produced by the query in Figure 12.9.

Joining Tables Within the Query Design Window

As you've seen, Access recognizes existing relationships in multiple-table queries and will also set up a temporary relationship if the common field is a primary key in one of the tables.

In other cases, you can have fields with common or similar data, but there's no existing relationship and Access doesn't set up a temporary relationship. For example, both Northwind's Customers and Suppliers tables have a `City` field. How can you create an inner join on this common field (to, say, see which customers and suppliers are located in the same city)?

You can do this by creating a temporary relationship. After you've added the tables to the query design window's table pane, click and drag the field from one table and drop it on the related field in the other table. Access displays a temporary join line between the fields, as shown in Figure 12.11.

Figure 12.11
To create a temporary relationship by hand, click and drag the field from one table and drop it on the related field in the other table.

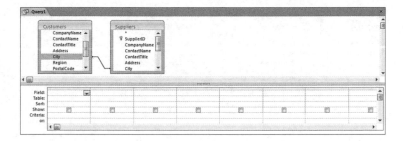

Creating Other Types of Joins

So far, you've worked only with inner joins, which is as it should be because inner joins are by far the most common, particularly in a business environment. However, the three other types of joins—outer, self, and theta—can also come in handy and are discussed in the next three sections.

Creating Outer Joins

An outer join is one where *all* the records in one table are included in the dynaset regardless of whether there are matching records in the other table. For example, suppose you're dealing with Northwind's Customers and Orders tables, which are related on the common CustomerID field. An inner join between these tables shows only those customers who have placed orders. By contrast, an outer join on the Customers table displays all the records from that table, even customers who have never placed an order.

There are two types of outer joins:

- **Left-outer join**—This join displays all the records from the "left" table. For example, in tables with a one-to-many relationship, the left-outer join displays all the records from the "one" table.

- **Right-outer join**—This join displays all the records from the "right" table. For example, in tables with a one-to-many relationship, the left-outer join displays all the records from the "many" table.

To set the type of outer join, follow these steps:

1. Add the tables to the query design window.
2. Create the relationship between the tables, if one doesn't exist.
3. Double-click the join line, or right-click the join line and then click Join Properties. Access displays the Join Properties dialog box, shown in Figure 12.12.
4. Option 1 creates an inner join. To change to an outer join, click either 2 (for a left-outer join) or 3 (for a right-outer join).
5. Click OK.

12

Figure 12.12
Use the Join Properties dialog box to select the type of join you want.

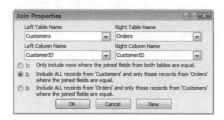

Using Outer Joins to Find Records Without Matching Records in a Related Table

The most common use for outer joins is to look for records in one table that don't have a matching record in some related table. For example, you can look for records in the Customers table that have no corresponding records in the Orders table; this tells you which customers have not yet placed an order. Similarly, you can look for records in the Products table that have no corresponding records in the Categories table; this tells you that you have a data entry problem because all products should have a category.

As a general rule, to see only those records without matching records in a related table, do one of the following:

- To see records in the parent table without matching records in the child table, create a left-outer join and filter the dynaset by adding Is Null as the criterion for the common field in the child table.

- To see orphan records in the child table (that is, records in the child table without any corresponding records in the parent table), create a right-outer join and filter the dynaset by adding Is Null as the criterion for the common field in the parent table.

The next two sections take you through examples of these techniques.

Finding Customers Without Matching Orders

Suppose, for example, you want to see a list of customers who haven't yet placed an order. This means you want to join the Customers table and the Order table, which are related on the CustomerID field. You start by displaying all the Customers. This means, because Customers is the parent of Orders, you need to create a left-outer join. Figure 12.13 shows the query setup, including the fact that option 2 (left-outer join) is chosen in the Join Properties dialog box. Figure 12.14 shows the resulting dynaset.

In Figure 12.14, notice that the first two records in the Customer field are blank. This tells you that these are the records in Customers that have no matching records in Orders, meaning they haven't yet placed any orders. Therefore, instead of displaying all the records, filter the dynaset to show only those where the CustomerID field of the Orders table is equal to Null. Figure 12.15 shows the revised query that adds this criterion.

Figure 12.13
A query set up for a left-outer join between the Customers and Orders tables.

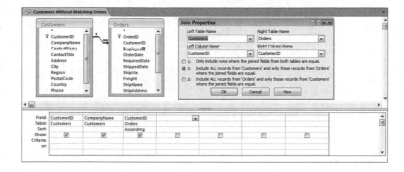

Figure 12.14
The dynaset created by the query in Figure 12.13.

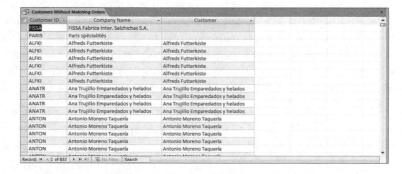

Figure 12.15
To see only those customers without matching orders, add the expression `Is Null` to the `Orders.CustomerID` field.

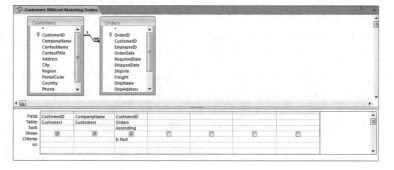

Finding Products Without an Assigned Category

In the Products table, each record should have been assigned an item from the Categories table. To make sure, you can build a query that looks for those Products without a matching category. This process requires joining the Products table and the Categories table, which are related via the `CategoryID` field. Because Products is a child of Categories, you need to create a right-outer join. You then add the `CategoryID` field from the Categories table and filter it using the `Is Null` criterion, as shown in Figure 12.16.

Figure 12.16
To find those products without an assigned category, create a right-outer join and filter the `Categories`. `CategoryID` field using the `Is Null` expression.

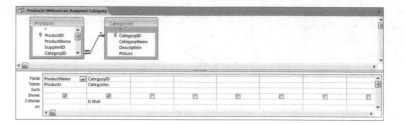

Creating Self-Joins

Database tables are sometimes *self-referential*, which means they contain a field with data that points to another field in the same table. A good example is the Northwind Employees table, which includes an `EmployeeID` field, the primary key that contains the employee identification numbers. The Employees table also contains the `ReportsTo` field, which contains the identification number of the person each employee reports to. In other words, each value in the `ReportsTo` field will have a corresponding value in the `EmployeeID` field.

If you want to know, say, which employees have people reporting to them, you need to create a self-join—a table joined to itself—on the Employees table. Creating a self-join involves the following steps:

1. Start a new query and add the table (Employees in this case) *twice*.
2. Create a temporary join by clicking and dragging the field that contains the data (`EmployeeID`) to the field that contains the subset of the data (`ReportsTo`).
3. Add the fields you want to use for the query to the design grid and then set up your criteria, sorting, and other query elements.
4. For a self-join to work properly, you need to tell Access to return only unique values in the query. To do this, click an empty spot inside the query design window and then choose Design, Property Sheet (or press Alt+Enter). In the Property Sheet pane, click `Yes` in the `Unique Values` list and then close the window.

→ For more information about the `Unique Values` property, **see** "Creating a Unique Values Query," **p. 280**. (this chapter)

Figure 12.17 shows a self-join on the Employees table, and Figure 12.18 shows the resulting dynaset, which displays the employees who have people reporting to them.

Figure 12.17
A query set up for a self-join on the Employees table.

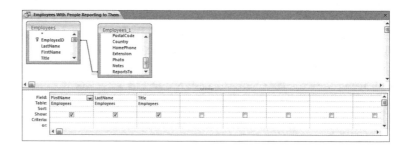

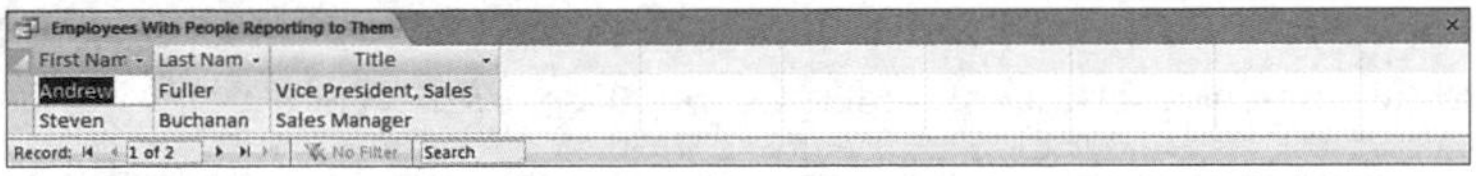

Figure 12.18
The dynaset created
by the query in
Figure 12.17.

Creating Theta Joins

The joins you've seen so far have all worked on the premise that the join is based on the equality between two fields. In an inner join, for example, you see only records where the joined fields from both tables are equal; similarly, in an outer join, you see all the records from one table, but only those records from the second table where the joined fields are equal.

In business, however, you sometimes need a join that's based on fields that are unequal. For example, Northwind's Customers table has a `CompanyName` field, and its Orders table has a `ShipName` field. In most cases, these values should be the same; that is, if a customer places an order, that order should be sent to that company. If the shipping name isn't the same as the customer name, it might mean either that the order was sent to the wrong company or that the company name is wrong in one table or the other. (It's also possible that the order is correct and that the customer asked for the shipment to be sent to a different ship address.)

To check into this type of scenario, you need a *not-equal join* that joins two tables and shows only those records where the joined fields from both tables are not equal—for example, joining the Customers and Orders tables based on whether the `CompanyName` and `ShipName` fields are not equal.

Here's the procedure to follow to create a not-equal join:

1. Start a new query and add the tables you want to work with (such as Customers and Orders).
2. If no relation exists between the tables, create a temporary join by clicking and dragging the appropriate field from one table and dropping it on the related field in the other table.
3. Add the fields you want to use for the query to the design grid and then set up your criteria, sorting, and other query elements. Be sure to include the fields on which the not-equal join will be based (such as `CompanyName` from the Customers table and `ShipName` from the Orders table).
4. In the Criteria cell of the field for which you want to check for not-equal values (such as the Orders table's `ShipName` field), enter a comparison formula using the following general form:

   `<>[RelatedTable].[JoinedField]`

   Here, `RelatedTable` is the name of the other table in the query, and `JoinedField` is the field from the other table that is joined to the current field. Here's an example for the `Orders.ShipName` field:

   `<>[Customers].[CompanyName]`

12

Figure 12.19 shows a not-equal join between the Customers table and the Orders table, with the not-equal criterion added for the `Orders.ShipName` field. Figure 12.20 shows the resulting dynaset, which displays the orders where the shipping name is different from the customer name. Notice that query has caught two subtle errors:

- For the customer "Galeria del gastrónomo," the accent is in the wrong place in the `ShipName` field ("Galeria del gastronómo").

- For the customer "Wolski Zajazd," the `CompanyName` field has two spaces between "Wolski" and "Zajazd."

Figure 12.19
A query set up for a not-equal join on the Customers and Orders table to look for orders where the `ShipName` is not equal to the `CompanyName`.

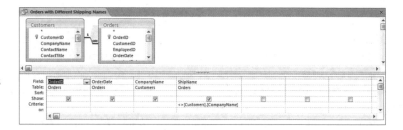

Figure 12.20
The dynaset created by the query in Figure 12.19.

Creating a Unique Values Query

Most business data—dealing as it does with unique customers, suppliers, products, shippers, and employees—is stored in tables that are designed to prevent duplicate records. In most cases, preventing duplicates is a straightforward matter of adding a primary key field (such as a customer account number or employee ID number), which, by definition, does not allow duplicate values. You can also add an index to any field and specify the `Yes (No Duplicates)` option in the table design window's `Indexed` property.

However, some tables are set up to allow duplicate values. For example, consider a simple table that contains only employee names and the dates on which they took customer orders. A single employee can take more than one order on a given day, so that table will have multiple records with the same data.

It's also not unusual for a query to return a dynaset that contains duplicate data. For example, suppose you put together a multiple-table query using Northwind's Employees, Orders, and Shippers tables. If you include the Orders table's OrderID in the query, there will be no duplicate records in the dynaset because OrderID is the primary key of the Orders table. However, if you don't include the OrderID field, the dynaset will have duplicate records. Figure 12.21 shows such a dynaset, and you can see that the two highlighted records are the same.

Figure 12.21
This query combines the Employees, Orders, and Shippers tables and, because the OrderID primary key is not part of the dynaset, the result contains duplicate records.

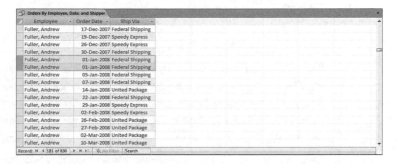

If your multiple-table dynaset is returning what appear to be duplicate records, or if you're working with a single table that contains duplicate records, you can tell Access to include only unique records in the result. You do this by specifying that Access first examine the dynaset data to look for records that have *the same values in all the dynaset fields* and then display only the first of those records. Because the determination whether a record is a duplicate is based on the field values, Access calls this a *unique values* query.

Follow these steps to create a unique values query:

1. Start a new query and add the tables you want to work with.
2. Add the fields you want to use for the query to the design grid and then set up your criteria, sorting, and other query elements.
3. Click an empty spot inside the query design window and then choose Design, Property Sheet (or press Alt+Enter). In the Property Sheet pane, click Yes in the Unique Values list and then close the window.

When you run the query, Access will display only unique records in the dynaset. In Figure 12.22, for example, you can see that only one of the duplicate records highlighted in Figure 12.21 appears in this unique values version of the query.

12

Orders By Employee, Date, and Shipper

Employee	Order Date	Ship Via
Fuller, Andrew	17-Dec-2007	Federal Shipping
Fuller, Andrew	19-Dec-2007	Speedy Express
Fuller, Andrew	26-Dec-2007	Speedy Express
Fuller, Andrew	30-Dec-2007	Federal Shipping
Fuller, Andrew	01-Jan-2008	Federal Shipping
Fuller, Andrew	05-Jan-2008	Federal Shipping
Fuller, Andrew	07-Jan-2008	Federal Shipping
Fuller, Andrew	14-Jan-2008	United Package
Fuller, Andrew	22-Jan-2008	Federal Shipping
Fuller, Andrew	29-Jan-2008	Speedy Express
Fuller, Andrew	02-Feb-2008	Speedy Express
Fuller, Andrew	26-Feb-2008	United Package
Fuller, Andrew	27-Feb-2008	United Package
Fuller, Andrew	02-Mar-2008	United Package
Fuller, Andrew	10-Mar-2008	United Package
Fuller, Andrew	13-Mar-2008	Federal Shipping

Record: 176 of 812 No Filter Search

Figure 12.22
This query is the same as the one in Figure 12.21, except that the `Unique Values` property has been set to `Yes`, thus eliminating the duplicate records in the dynaset.

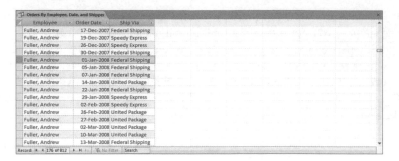

> **NOTE**
>
> What about the `Unique Records` property in the Property Sheet pane? This setting isn't all that useful because it applies only to a very limited case. Suppose you have two tables that are joined via a one-to-many relationship. By definition, data from the "one" table can appear multiple times in the "many" table. So if you then set up a query that uses both tables but includes only fields from the "one" table, there's a good chance the dynaset will display duplicate records.
>
> (Why might you add two tables to a query and then not include any fields from one of the tables in the dynaset? The most common reason is that you're using one or more fields from the second table to enter the criteria for the query, but you don't need to see those fields in the result.)
>
> To suppress the display of duplicate records from the "one" table, change the value of the `Unique Records` property to `Yes`.

12

CASE STUDY

Drilling Down to the Order Details

You might know that Access has the welcome capability to view data contained in another, related table from within the table datasheet. In Figure 12.23, for example, you can see that the Customers table also includes a column of plus signs (+) on the left. Clicking a plus sign displays a new datasheet—called a *subdatasheet*—that, in this case, contains that customer's data from the Orders table (see Figure 12.24).

Customers

Customer I	Company Name	Contact Name	Contact Title	Address
ALFKI	Alfreds Futterkiste	Maria Anders	Sales Representative	Obere Str. 57
ANATR	Ana Trujillo Emparedados y helados	Ana Trujillo	Owner	Avda. de la Constitución 2222
ANTON	Antonio Moreno Taquería	Antonio Moreno	Owner	Mataderos 2312
AROUT	Around the Horn	Thomas Hardy	Sales Representative	120 Hanover Sq.
BERGS	Berglunds snabbköp	Christina Berglund	Order Administrator	Berguvsvägen 8
BLAUS	Blauer See Delikatessen	Hanna Moos	Sales Representative	Forsterstr. 57
BLONP	Blondel père et fils	Frédérique Citeaux	Marketing Manager	24, place Kléber
BOLID	Bólido Comidas preparadas	Martín Sommer	Owner	C/ Araquil, 67
BONAP	Bon app'	Laurence Lebihan	Owner	12, rue des Bouchers
BOTTM	Bottom-Dollar Markets	Elizabeth Lincoln	Accounting Manager	23 Tsawassen Blvd.
BSBEV	B's Beverages	Victoria Ashworth	Sales Representative	Fauntleroy Circus
CACTU	Cactus Comidas para llevar	Patricio Simpson	Sales Agent	Cerrito 333
CENTC	Centro comercial Moctezuma	Francisco Chang	Marketing Manager	Sierras de Granada 9993
CHOPS	Chop-suey Chinese	Yang Wang	Owner	Hauptstr. 29
COMMI	Comércio Mineiro	Pedro Afonso	Sales Associate	Av. dos Lusíadas, 23
CONSH	Consolidated Holdings	Elizabeth Brown	Sales Representative	Berkeley Gardens

Record: 1 of 91 No Filter Search

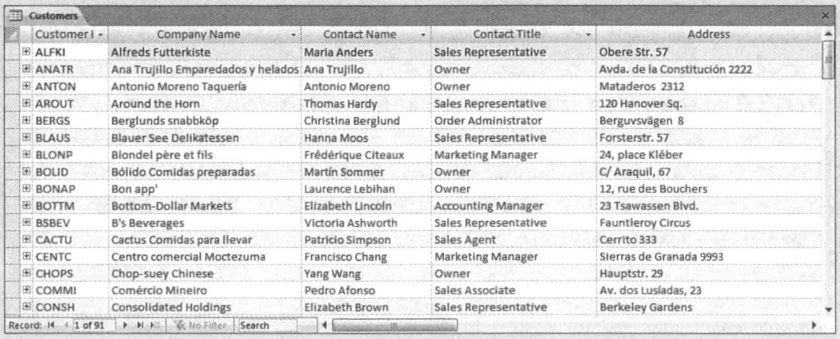

Figure 12.23
When you view certain tables in the datasheet view, the leftmost column will contain a plus sign (+) for each record.

Figure 12.24
Clicking a plus sign displays a subdatasheet showing the related data from another table.

Access sets up this subdatasheet capability whenever you establish a relationship between two tables. The Customers and Orders tables have a one-to-many relationship on the `CustomerID` field, so clicking a customer's plus sign displays the related records from the Orders table.

Notice, too, that the Orders subdatasheet also has a column of plus signs. Orders has a one-to-many relation with the Order Details table on the `OrderID` field. So clicking the plus sign beside an order displays the related details, as shown in Figure 12.25.

Figure 12.25
Clicking a plus sign in the Orders subdatasheet displays another sub-datasheet that contains the related order details.

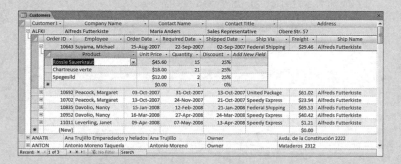

The subdatasheet is a great feature, but it suffers from the same problems inherent in all table-based datasheet views: The subdatasheet might show more fields than you need to see, and it might not show fields you want to see (such as the extended price in the order details).

You can solve these problems by using query-based subdatasheets. Because the subdatasheets display data from a query dynaset, you can configure the query to display the data any way you want and even include calculated columns.

To demonstrate the power and flexibility of query-based subdatasheets, this case study remakes the Customers-Orders-Order Details example to create a more useful way of drilling down into a customer's order details.

12

Adding a Subdatasheet to a Query

Before getting to the details of the case study, you need to know how to add a subdatasheet to a query. Datasheets and subdatasheets have the same parent-to-child relationship as linked tables. Here are the steps to follow:

1. In the query design window, click an empty spot and then choose Design, Property Sheet (or press Alt+Enter). Access displays the Property Sheet pane.

2. In the `Subdatasheet Name` property, use the list to click the name of the table or query you want to use as the basis for the subdatasheet.

3. In the Link Child Fields box, enter the name of a field from the child table or query (the object you chose in the `Subdatasheet Name` list). This must be the field that will be related to a field in the parent (which is, in this case, the dynaset created by the query).

4. In the `Link Master Fields` property, type the name of a field from the parent query. This must be the field that will be related to the field you entered in step 3.

5. (Optional) Use the `Subdatasheet Height` box property to type the maximum height (in inches) of the subdatasheet. If you type **0**, Access displays all the records in the subdatasheet.

6. When the `Subdatasheet Expanded` property is set to `No`, Access hides all the subdatasheets, and you need to click the plus signs (+) to see them. If you prefer that Access display all the subdatasheets automatically, change this property to `Yes`. Figure 12.26 shows an example of the Query Properties dialog box with these fields filled in.

7. Close the window.

Figure 12.26
To add a subdatasheet to a query, fill in the `Subdatasheet Name`, `Link Child Fields`, and `Link Master Fields` properties.

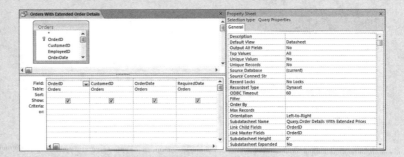

Working with Query Subdatasheets

The secret to working with query-based subdatasheets is to work from the bottom up. That is, you begin with the lowest level of data and create a query that displays the data in exactly the way you want. Then you move up to the next level, which will be a query based on a table that has a common field (or, at least, a relatable field) with the first table. Repeat this process until you get to the topmost query.

For example, in the Customers-Orders-Order Details case, you proceed as follows:

1. Create a query based on the Order Details table. In this case study, I created a query named Order Details With Extended Prices that shows not only the details such as product, price, quantity, and discount, but also the *extended price* for each product, which is given by a calculated column based on the following expression, as shown in Figure 12.27:

```
[UnitPrice] * [Quantity] * (1 - [Discount])
```

Figure 12.27
The query forms the lowest level of the drill-down: the Order Details with an Extended Price calculated column.

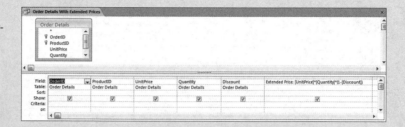

2. Create a query based on the Orders table and include the Order Details With Extended Prices query as a sub-datasheet (as described previously) related on the `OrderID` field. For the case study, I named this new query Orders With Extended Order Details.

3. Create a query based on the Customers table and include the Orders With Extended Order Details query as a sub-datasheet related on the `CustomerID` field, as shown in Figure 12.28.

Figure 12.28
The query based on the Customers table also has a subdatasheet that is used with the Orders With Extended Order Details query.

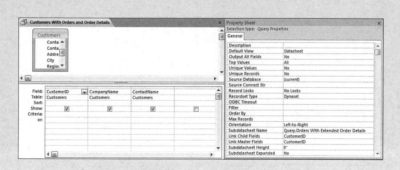

Figure 12.29 shows the resulting Customers query with displayed subdatasheets for the Orders With Extended Order Details query and the Order Details With Extended Prices query.

Figure 12.29
Drilling down from the Customers-based query to the Orders With Extended Order Details query and to the Order Details With Extended Prices query.

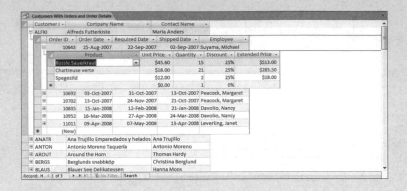

From Here

→ To learn how to use multiple tables in a form, **see** "Creating a Multiple-Table Form," **p. 95**. (Chapter 5)

→ To learn how to use multiple tables in a report, **see** "Creating a Multiple-Table Report," **p. 189**. (Chapter 9)

→ For the details on creating multiple-table queries using SQL, **see** "Using SQL with Multiple-Table Queries," **p. 346** (Chapter 15)

12

Creating Advanced Queries

13

The query techniques you studied in the first three chapters of the book add powerful new weapons to your Access arsenal. From expressions to functions to multiple-table setups, you've seen that you can perform some sophisticated and powerful querying. So when I tell you that this chapter covers "advanced" queries, am I talking about obscure features that will be rarely used in a business environment? Are these complex techniques that require a math degree to comprehend? The answer is a firm "No" on both counts. The queries you'll see in this chapter are "advanced" only in the sense that they'll advance your knowledge of how to get the most out of Access querying for your business needs.

Creating a Totals Query

A totals query includes a column that performs an aggregate operation—such as summing or averaging—on the values of a particular field. A totals query derives either a single value for the entire dynaset or several values for the records that have been grouped within the dynaset. Table 13.1 outlines the aggregate operations you can use for your totals queries.

Table 13.1	Aggregate Operations Available for Totals Queries
Operation	**Purpose**
Group By	Groups the records according to the unique values in the field.
Sum	Sums the values in the field.
Avg	Averages the values in the field.
Min	Returns the smallest value in the field.
Max	Returns the largest value in the field.
Count	Counts the number of values in the field.
StDev	Calculates the standard deviation of the values in the field.
Var	Calculates the variance of the values in the field.
First	Returns the first value in the field.
Last	Returns the last value in the field.
Expression	Returns a custom total based on an expression in a calculated column.
Where	Tells Access to use the field's criteria to filter the records before calculating the totals.

The next few sections show you how to use these operations in your queries.

Displaying the Total Row in the Design Grid

Before you can work with the aggregate operations, you need to choose Design, Totals (in the Show/Hide group). As shown in Figure 13.1, Access adds the Total row to the design grid, and each Total cell contains a list of the aggregate operations.

Totals button

Figure 13.1
Choose Design, Totals to display the Total row in the query design grid.

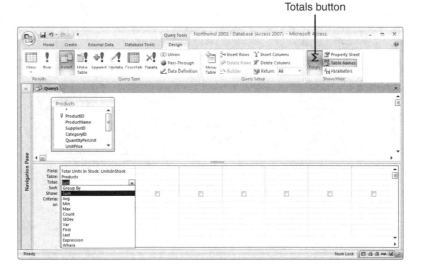

> NOTE
> As I mentioned in Chapter 10, "Creating a Basic Query," I'm going to use the older (Access 2003) Northwind sample data for the querying chapters. You can download the sample database from my website:
>
> www.mcfedries.com/Access2007Forms

Setting Up a Totals Query on a Single Field

In the simplest totals query case, you can apply one of the mathematical aggregate operations to a single field. Access will then display just the mathematical result for that field. The following steps are required to create a totals query on a single field:

1. Display the Total row, if it's not already displayed.

2. In the field's Total cell, use the drop-down list to click the function you want to use.

3. If you want to restrict the records involved in the aggregate operation, enter the appropriate expression in the field's Criteria cell.

4. (Optional) In the dynaset, Access displays `OperationOfFieldName` in the field header, where `Operation` is the aggregate operation you chose in step 2 and `FieldName` is the name of the field you're working with. If you'd rather see a more readable name, change the Field cell to the following, where `FieldName` is the name you want to use (see Figure 13.1 for an example):

   `Field Alias:FieldName`

5. Run the query.

Figure 13.2 shows the result when the `Sum` aggregate operation is applied to the `UnitsInStock` field of Northwind's Products table. As you can see, the datasheet consists of a single cell that shows the result of the aggregate operation.

Figure 13.2
The datasheet shows only the result of the calculation applied to the single field.

Setting Up a Totals Query on Multiple Fields

If you want to see more data in the totals query, you can add more fields:

- Add other fields and apply any mathematical aggregate operation to each field.

- Add other copies of the same field and apply different mathematical aggregate operations to each field.

Note, however, that you can add only fields to which you want to apply an aggregate operation; you can't add nonaggregate fields to the query.

Figure 13.3 shows a query with five columns. They include a Count of the ProductID field, Sum of the UnitsInStock field, and three operations on the UnitPrice field—Max, Min, and Avg. Figure 13.4 shows the result.

Figure 13.3
A totals query showing five aggregate operations on three fields.

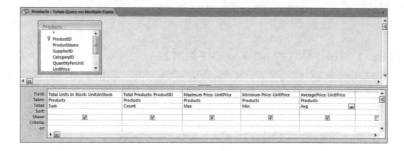

Figure 13.4
The result of the totals query shown in Figure 13.3.

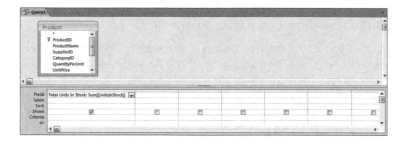

Filtering the Records Before Calculating Totals

I mentioned earlier that you can add criteria to any of the aggregate columns and Access will perform the operation on only the records that match the criteria. What if you want to filter the table based on a field that isn't part of any aggregate operation? You can't include a nonaggregate field in the query results, but it *is* possible to use a nonaggregate field to filter the records. Here are the steps to follow:

1. Add the nonaggregate field to the query design grid.
2. Clear the field's Show check box.
3. In the field's Total cell, drop down the list and click Where.
4. Add the required expression to the field's Criteria cell.

In this case, Access filters the records based on the criteria and *then* performs the aggregate operation.

For example, in the query shown earlier in Figure 13.3, suppose you want to run the aggregate operations on only those products in the Beverages category. To do this, you add the Categories table to the query and then set up the CategoryName field with the Where operation and the criteria "Beverages", as shown in Figure 13.5. Figure 13.6 shows the results for the filtered records.

Figure 13.5
A totals query that uses the Where operation to filter the records before performing the other aggregate operations.

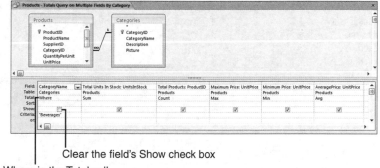

Clear the field's Show check box

Choose Where in the Total cell

Figure 13.6
The result of the totals query shown in Figure 13.5.

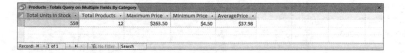

Creating a Totals Query for Groups of Records

In its basic guise, a totals query shows a single total for all the records in a table (or all the records in a subset of the table, depending on whether the query includes criteria). Suppose, however, that you prefer to see that total broken out into subtotals. For example, instead of a simple sum on the UnitsInStock field, how about seeing the sum of the orders grouped by category?

Grouping your totals requires just two steps:

1. Add the field you want to use for the groupings to the design grid.
2. In the field's Total cell, drop down the list and click Group By.

Note, too, that in most cases you'll probably want to see the group names in the results, so you should activate the grouped field's Show check box.

Figure 13.7 shows the query from Figure 13.5 changed so that the CategoryName field is now set up with the Group By operation. Running this query produces the result shown in Figure 13.8. As you can see, Access groups the entries in the Category Name column and displays subtotals for each group.

Grouping on Multiple Fields

You can extend this technique to derive totals for more specific groups. The general idea is that as you apply the Group By operation to more fields, Access groups the records from left to right.

13

Figure 13.7
To group your totals, add the field used for the grouping and click `Group By` in the Total cell.

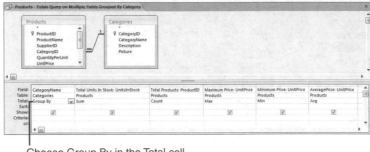

Choose Group By in the Total cell

Figure 13.8
Access groups the records and displays subtotals for each group.

Category Nam •	Total Units In Stock •	Total Products •	Maximum Price •	Minimum Price •	AveragePrice •
Beverages	559	12	$263.50	$4.50	$37.98
Condiments	507	12	$43.90	$10.00	$23.06
Confections	361	12	$81.00	$9.50	$26.49
Dairy Products	393	10	$55.00	$2.50	$28.73
Grains/Cereals	308	7	$38.00	$7.00	$20.25
Meat/Poultry	165	6	$123.79	$7.45	$54.01
Produce	100	5	$53.00	$10.00	$32.37
Seafood	701	12	$62.50	$6.00	$20.68

For example, suppose you want to see subtotals for each supplier within the categories. You can do this by adding the Suppliers table to the query, adding the `SupplierName` field to the right of the `CategoryName` field, and clicking `Group By` in the Total cell. Figure 13.9 shows the revised query, and Figure 13.10 shows the result. Access creates the groups from left to right, so the records are first grouped by Category and then by Supplier.

Figure 13.9
You can refine your groupings by applying the `Group By` operation to more fields, where the grouping occurs from left to right.

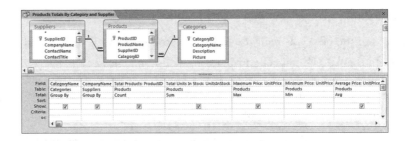

Figure 13.10
The dynaset produced by the query in Figure 13.9.

Category Name •	Company Name •	Total Products •	Total Units In Stock •	Maximum Price •	Minimum Price •	Average Price •
Beverages	Aux joyeux ecclésiastiques	2	86	$263.50	$18.00	$140.75
Beverages	Bigfoot Breweries	3	183	$18.00	$14.00	$15.33
Beverages	Exotic Liquids	2	56	$19.00	$18.00	$18.50
Beverages	Karkki Oy	1	57	$18.00	$18.00	$18.00
Beverages	Leka Trading	1	17	$46.00	$46.00	$46.00
Beverages	Pavlova, Ltd.	1	15	$15.00	$15.00	$15.00
Beverages	Plutzer Lebensmittelgroßmärkt	1	125	$7.75	$7.75	$7.75
Beverages	Refrescos Americanas LTDA	1	20	$4.50	$4.50	$4.50
Condiments	Exotic Liquids	1	13	$10.00	$10.00	$10.00
Condiments	Forêts d'érables	1	113	$28.50	$28.50	$28.50
Condiments	Grandma Kelly's Homestead	2	126	$40.00	$25.00	$32.50
Condiments	Leka Trading	1	27	$19.45	$19.45	$19.45
Condiments	Mayumi's	1	39	$15.50	$15.50	$15.50
Condiments	New Orleans Cajun Delights	4	133	$22.00	$17.00	$20.35
Condiments	Pavlova, Ltd.	1	24	$43.90	$43.90	$43.90
Condiments	Plutzer Lebensmittelgroßmärkt	1	32	$13.00	$13.00	$13.00
Confections	Forêts d'érables	1	17	$49.30	$49.30	$49.30
Confections	Heli Süßwaren GmbH & Co. KG	3	140	$43.90	$14.00	$29.71
Confections	Karkki Oy	2	75	$20.00	$16.25	$18.13

Record: I◄ ◄ 1 of 49 ► ►I ►   No Filter   Search

Creating a Totals Query Using a Calculated Field

So far, you've seen aggregate operations applied to regular table fields. However, you can also apply them to calculated fields. For example, you've seen how to use the following expression in the Northwind Order Details table to calculate the extended price of an item given its unit price, quantity, and discount percentage:

```
[UnitPrice] * [Quantity] * (1 - [Discount])
```

This gives you the total charge per product, but what if you want to know the total charge for the entire invoice? You can calculate this by applying the Sum operation to the calculated field that's based on the previous expression. Also, because Order Details usually includes a number of records for each invoice, you need to group the records by the unique OrderID field to get the per-invoice total. Figure 13.11 shows a query with this setup, and Figure 13.12 shows the results. (For good measure, the query also displays the customer and order date from the joined Orders table and displays the total units in each order.)

Figure 13.11
To calculate the total charge for each invoice, apply the Sum operation to the calculated Extended Price field and group the Order Details records by OrderID.

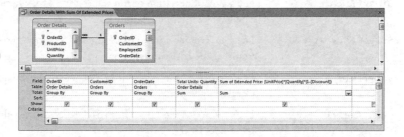

Figure 13.12
The dynaset produced by the query in Figure 13.11.

Order ID	Customer	Order Date	Total Units	Sum of Extended Price
10248	Wilman Kala	04-Jul-2006	27	$440.00
10249	Tradição Hipermercados	05-Jul-2006	49	$1,863.40
10250	Hanari Carnes	08-Jul-2006	60	$1,552.60
10251	Victuailles en stock	08-Jul-2006	41	$654.06
10252	Suprêmes délices	09-Jul-2006	105	$3,597.90
10253	Hanari Carnes	10-Jul-2006	102	$1,444.80
10254	Chop-suey Chinese	11-Jul-2006	57	$556.62
10255	Richter Supermarkt	12-Jul-2006	110	$2,490.50
10256	Wellington Importadora	15-Jul-2006	27	$517.80
10257	HILARIÓN-Abastos	16-Jul-2006	46	$1,119.90
10258	Ernst Handel	17-Jul-2006	121	$1,614.88
10259	Centro comercial Moctezuma	18-Jul-2006	11	$100.80
10260	Old World Delicatessen	19-Jul-2006	102	$1,504.65

Record: 1 of 830 — No Filter — Search

NOTE
If you apply an aggregate operation to a calculated field in the manner shown in Figure 13.11 and then close and reopen the query, you'll see that Access has changed the calculated field by "moving" the aggregate operation into the field's expression and changing the Total cell to Expression. Access has converted the totals query so that it uses an aggregate *function*. See the next section for an explanation of the aggregate functions.

13

Creating a Totals Query Using Aggregate Functions

The collection of Access built-in functions also includes a category called *SQL Aggregate* that includes all the mathematical aggregate operations. There are nine aggregate functions in all, as shown in Table 13.2.

Table 13.2	Aggregate Functions Available for Totals Queries
Function	**Returns**
Avg(*field*)	The average of the values in *field*.
Sum(*field*)	The sum of the values in *field*.
Min(*field*)	The smallest value in *field*.
Max(*field*)	The largest value in *field*.
Count(*field*)	The number of values in *field*.
StDev(*field*)	The standard deviation of the values in *field*, where those values are a sample of a larger population.
StDevP(*field*)	The standard deviation of the values in *field*, where those values represent the entire population.
Var(*field*)	The variance of the values in *field*, where those values are a sample of a larger population.
VarP(*field*)	The variance of the values in *field*, where those values represent the entire population.

The most straightforward way to use an aggregate function is to apply it to a single field using an expression in the Field cell instead of entering an operation in the Total cell. For example, instead of clicking Sum in the Total cell of the UnitsInStock field, you can use the expression in the Field cell (see Figure 13.13):

```
Sum([UnitsInStock])
```

Figure 13.13
This query uses the Sum function to calculate the sum of the UnitsInStock field without using the Total row.

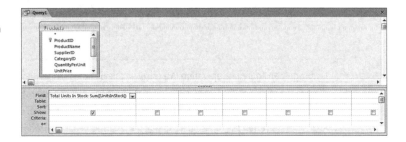

The advantage here is that you don't need to display the Total row, so your query is a little less cluttered. (In fact, you *must* turn off the totals to use this method; otherwise, Access will convert the Sum function to a Sum aggregate operation.)

You can also include in the query other calculated fields that use aggregate functions. For example, if you also want to know the maximum unit price, you can create a second calculated field that uses the following aggregate expression:

```
Max([UnitPrice])
```

You might also be thinking that the aggregate functions might make excellent choices for building criteria expressions. For example, if you wanted to see those products in which the unit price was greater than the average unit price, would an expression such as `>Avg([UnitPrice])` do the trick? Unfortunately, it won't, because Access will generate an error if you try to do this. What you need to do instead is create a *subquery* that returns the average, and you can then use the comparison expression on that result. I explain this in detail in Chapter 15, "Querying with SQL Statements."

→   To learn how to create subqueries, **see** "Using SQL to Create Subqueries," **p. 354**. (Chapter 15)

Combining Aggregate Functions and Totals

The problem with using the aggregate functions without the Total row is that there's no function that's equivalent to the `Group By` operation, so you can't group the records. If you need to use the `Group By` operation, or if you want to filter the records before the aggregate calculation by using the `Where` operation, you need to use the Totals feature.

This means you can't apply the aggregate functions on a single field, because Access will just convert the function to an operation in the Total row. However, it does mean that you're free to create *custom totals*. These are totals that you create yourself by building expressions that combine one or more aggregate functions with the other query operators and operands. This is a calculated field, so you enter the expression in the Field cell. Note, too, that you must also choose `Expression` in the Total cell. Figure 13.14 shows the query from Figure 13.11 converted to use the following aggregate function expression:

```
Sum([UnitPrice] * [Quantity] * (1 - [Discount]))
```

Figure 13.14
The Sum of Extended Price calculated field uses the Sum function in the Field cell and `Expression` in the Total cell.

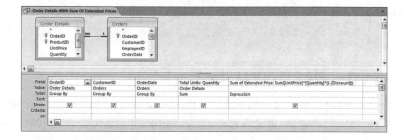

Calculating Units Left In Stock

If you manage inventory, you always need to know how many units of each product you have left in stock. You might take a physical inventory once or twice a year, but in between these counts you still need to keep tabs on the stock in case you need to reorder. The easiest way to do that is to take the existing number of units in stock and subtract the day's order quantities. The result is the number of units left in stock. Figure 13.15 shows a query set up to make this calculation using the Northwind sample database.

Figure 13.15
This query uses a custom total to calculate the number of units left in stock after subtracting a day's orders from the current inventory.

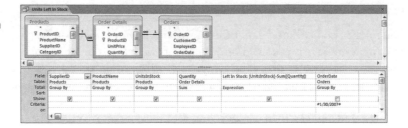

Here are some features of this query to note:

- Just in case a reorder is necessary, the records are grouped first by SupplierID and then by ProductName (both from the Products table).

- The query also includes the UnitsInStock field and the Sum of the Quantity field from Order Details.

- The Left In Stock calculated field is set up with the Expression operation in the Total cell and uses the following expression in the Field cell to create a custom total:
  [UnitsInStock] - Sum([Quantity])

- The records are filtered to include only those orders from a specific date, using the Where operation applied to the nonaggregate OrderDate field.

Figure 13.16 shows the results.

Figure 13.16
The dynaset produced by the query in Figure 13.16.

Supplier	Product Name	Units In Stock	SumOfQuantity	Left In Stock
Pavlova, Ltd.	Alice Mutton	0	95	-95
Specialty Biscuits, Ltd.	Sir Rodney's Scones	3	50	-47
New England Seafood Cannery	Boston Crab Meat	123	50	73
Zaanse Snoepfabriek	Zaanse koeken	36	30	6
Pasta Buttini s.r.l.	Gnocchi di nonna Alice	21	30	-9
Gai pâturage	Raclette Courdavault	79	70	9

Record: 1 of 6 — No Filter — Search

Creating Queries That Make Decisions

The queries that you've seen so far in this book have been used to perform one or more of the following tasks: sorting, filtering, and calculating. This is what most business queries do, and you've seen that Access offers some slick techniques and features that enable you to create very powerful and useful sorts, filters, and calculations.

But queries are also useful analytical tools that can be pressed into service to help you make decisions. For example, the query from the preceding section returned the number of units left in stock. If you see a negative number returned, obviously a product is going to be backordered, so you need to contact the supplier right away. However, some products also have a specified *reorder level*, which is the minimum number of units that need to be in stock before the product is reordered. So instead of waiting for the stock to get to 0 (or less), you might need to reorder when it gets down to 25 units or 10 units.

A logical approach here would be to add the ReorderLevel field to the query and then compare the Units Left In Stock calculation with the reorder level. If the number of units remaining is less than or equal to the reorder level, you need to reorder the product; otherwise, you do nothing.

This approach will work, but it suffers from two drawbacks:

- It can be tedious and time-consuming if you have a lot of products.
- It's easy to make a mistake one way or the other (that is, to reorder a product that has sufficient stock or to miss reordering a product that is below the reorder threshold).

Making Decisions with the IIf Function

The solution to both problems is to get Access to make the decision for you. One of the secrets to this is a handy function called IIf (which you read as "Inline If"). Here's the syntax:

```
IIf(logical_test, value_if_true, value_if_false)
```

logical_test	A logical expression; that is, an expression that returns True or False.
value_if_true	The value returned by the function if *logical_test* evaluates to True.
value_if_false	The value returned by the function if *logical_test* evaluates to False.

Let's start with a simple example:

```
IIf([UnitsInStock]) = 0, "Reorder", "Don't reorder")
```

The logical test is the expression [UnitsInStock] = 0. If this returns True, the function returns the string value "Reorder"; otherwise, it returns the string value "Don't reorder". The idea is that you use this function as the expression for a calculated field, as shown in Figure 13.17. This creates a field that, when you run the query, displays either "Reorder" or "Don't Reorder" for each product, as shown in Figure 13.18.

13

Figure 13.17
This query uses the IIf function to test whether the UnitsInStock field is 0.

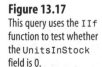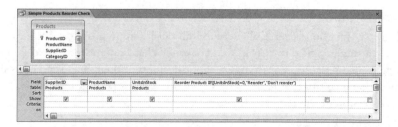

Figure 13.18
The dynaset produced by the query in Figure 13.17.

Supplier	Product Name	Units In Stock	Reorder Product
Exotic Liquids	Chai	39	Don't reorder
Exotic Liquids	Chang	17	Don't reorder
Exotic Liquids	Aniseed Syrup	13	Don't reorder
New Orleans Cajun Delights	Chef Anton's Cajun Seasoning	53	Don't reorder
New Orleans Cajun Delights	Chef Anton's Gumbo Mix	0	Reorder
Grandma Kelly's Homestead	Grandma's Boysenberry Spread	120	Don't reorder
Grandma Kelly's Homestead	Uncle Bob's Organic Dried Pears	15	Don't reorder
Grandma Kelly's Homestead	Northwoods Cranberry Sauce	6	Don't reorder
Tokyo Traders	Mishi Kobe Niku	29	Don't reorder
Tokyo Traders	Ikura	31	Don't reorder
Cooperativa de Quesos 'Las Cabras'	Queso Cabrales	22	Don't reorder
Cooperativa de Quesos 'Las Cabras'	Queso Manchego La Pastora	86	Don't reorder
Mayumi's	Konbu	24	Don't reorder
Mayumi's	Tofu	35	Don't reorder
Mayumi's	Genen Shouyu	39	Don't reorder
Pavlova, Ltd.	Pavlova	29	Don't reorder
Pavlova, Ltd.	Alice Mutton	0	Reorder
Pavlova, Ltd.	Carnarvon Tigers	42	Don't reorder

Record: 1 of 77 | No Filter | Search

Determining Whether Stock Needs to Be Reordered

A more realistic example takes into account the day's orders by subtracting them from the current stock and then comparing the result with the product's reorder level:

```
IIf([UnitsInStock] - Sum([Quantity]) <= [ReorderLevel], "Yes", "No")
```

If the units left in stock are less than or equal to the reorder level, the function returns the string `"Yes"`; otherwise, it returns `"No"`. As you can see in Figure 13.19, I've used this expression as the basis for the calculated `Reorder` field, and I've also set the field's criteria to `"Yes"` so that the query returns the records only for those products that need ordering, as shown in Figure 13.20.

Figure 13.19
This query uses the `IIf` function to test whether the number of units left in stock is at or below the reorder level.

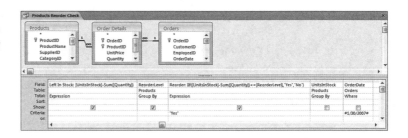

Figure 13.20
The dynaset produced by the query in Figure 13.19.

Supplier	Product Name	Left In Stock	Reorder Level	Reorder
Pavlova, Ltd.	Alice Mutton	-95	0	Yes
Specialty Biscuits, Ltd.	Sir Rodney's Scones	-47	5	Yes
Pasta Buttini s.r.l.	Gnocchi di nonna Alice	-9	30	Yes

Record: 1 of 3 | No Filter | Search

Combining `IIf` with `And` and `Or`

The `IIf` function is certainly very useful, but it's limited by the fact that it can perform only a single logical test. You can get around that limitation to a certain extent by using the `And` or `Or` operators. For example, suppose an order qualifies for a bonus discount only if the total quantity is at least 50 units *and* the order total is at least $1,000. Here's a simplified version of the required logical test:

```
If Quantity >= 50 And Total >= 1000
```

Here's an actual IIf function that tests for this:

```
IIf(Sum([Quantity]) >= 50 And
➥Sum([UnitPrice] * [Quantity] * (1 - [Discount])) >= 1000, 0.05, 0)
```

Similarly, suppose an order qualifies for a bonus discount only if the total quantity is at least 50 units *or* the order total is at least $1,000. Here's an IIf function that tests for this:

```
IIf(Sum([Quantity]) >= 50 Or
➥Sum([UnitPrice] * [Quantity] * (1 - [Discount])) >= 1000, 0.05, 0)
```

Making Decisions with the Switch Function

Using IIf with And and Or is a powerful idea, but you're still really performing only a single logical test and then returning one of two values depending on whether the result is True or False.

For more complex situations, you need a tool that can run multiple tests and return multiple values depending on the result. Fortunately, Access comes with just the thing—the Switch function:

```
Switch(test1, value1[,test2, value2, ...])
```

test1	A logical expression; that is, an expression that returns True or False.
value1	The value returned by the function if *test1* evaluates to True.
test2	A logical expression; that is, an expression that returns True or False.
value2	The value returned by the function if *test2* evaluates to True.

> **NOTE** If all of the logical tests in a Switch function return False, the function returns Null.
>
> For example, Northwind's Shippers table lists three shipping compa-

nies: Speedy Express (ShipperID = 1), United Package (ShipperID = 2), and Federal Shipping (ShipperID = 3). Suppose that each company charges based on the total value of an order, and the charges are, respectively, 5%, 10%, and 15%. The freight charge formula will look something like this:

```
Total * Shipping Charge
```

Calculating the Shipping Charge portion is a perfect task for the Switch function:

```
Switch([ShipperID] = 1, .05, [ShipperID] = 2, .1, [ShipperID] = 3, .15)
```

If ShipperID is 1 (Speedy Express), the function returns .05; if ShipperID is 2 (United Package), the function returns .1; if ShipperID is 3 (Federal Shipping), the function returns .15.

13

CASE STUDY

Calculating a Customer Discount Rate

In transactions between businesses, the supplier will almost always offer the customer a discount off the list price of an item. In publishing, for example, the publisher might offer a bookstore a 40% discount, meaning that a book with a $10 list price is sold to the bookstore for $6.

This case study involves the Northwind Order Details table, which comes with a `Discount` field. However, we can only surmise what conditions are in place in the fictional Northwind world to determine the numbers in that field. Let's suppose, instead, that you want to add a "bonus" discount to the orders. This case study shows you how to use the `IIf` and `Switch` functions to calculate simple and complex discount rates.

Calculating a Simple Discount Rate

A "simple" discount rate is one where the rate is applied only if the order meets some predetermined threshold. For this case study, you'll offer an extra 5% discount for any order in which the total quantity is at least 50 units.

In other words, if the total of an order's `Quantity` field is greater than or equal to 50, return a bonus discount of 5%; otherwise, return nothing (or a bonus discount of 0%). Here's an `IIf` function expression that does this:

```
IIf(Sum([Quantity]) >= 50, 0.05, 0)
```

Figure 13.21 shows this expression at work in a query, and Figure 13.22 shows the results.

Figure 13.21
This query uses the `IIf` function to determine whether an order qualifies for a bonus discount.

Order Details Bonus Discount

Order ID	Customer	Total Units	Bonus Discount
10248	Wilman Kala	27	0.00%
10249	Tradição Hipermercados	49	0.00%
10250	Hanari Carnes	60	5.00%
10251	Victuailles en stock	41	0.00%
10252	Suprêmes délices	105	5.00%
10253	Hanari Carnes	102	5.00%
10254	Chop-suey Chinese	57	5.00%
10255	Richter Supermarkt	110	5.00%
10256	Wellington Importadora	27	0.00%
10257	HILARIÓN-Abastos	46	0.00%
10258	Ernst Handel	121	5.00%
10259	Centro comercial Moctezuma	11	0.00%
10260	Old World Delicatessen	102	5.00%

Record: 1 of 830 No Filter Search

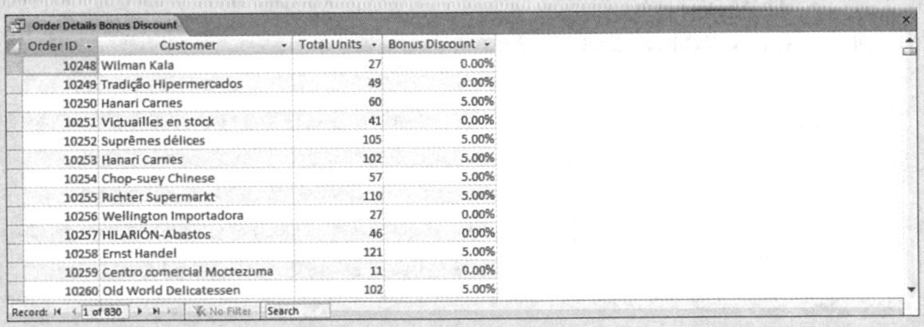

Figure 13.22
The dynaset produced by the query in Figure 13.21.

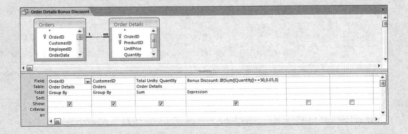

Of course, you really want to use this "decision" to recalculate the final total of the invoice, which means taking the extended invoice total and, if the customer qualifies for the bonus discount, reducing the total by another 5% (or whatever). Recall the formula for calculating the extended total for an invoice:

```
Sum([UnitPrice] * [Quantity] * (1 - [Discount]))
```

In Northwind, the value in the `Discount` field is applied per product, not on the invoice total. Therefore, to include the bonus discount in the calculation, you need to multiply this sum by one minus the bonus discount:

```
Sum([UnitPrice] * [Quantity] * (1 - [Discount])) * (1 -
➡IIf(Sum([Quantity]) >= 50, 0.05, 0))
```

If the order qualifies for the bonus discount, the extended sum is reduced by 5%; otherwise, it stays the same. Figure 13.23 shows a query that implements this formula, and Figure 13.24 shows the results.

Figure 13.23
This query uses the `IIf` function to determine whether an order qualifies for a bonus discount and then applies that discount to the extended order total.

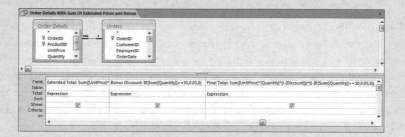

Figure 13.24
The dynaset produced by the query in Figure 13.23.

Calculating a Complex Discount Rate

In business-to-business transactions, the discount given to a customer is often on a sliding scale. For example, a bookstore might get a 40% discount for orders under 100 copies, a 45% discount for orders between 100 and 1,000 copies, and a 50% discount for orders over 1,000 copies. The `IIf` function doesn't handle these "complex" discount rate calculations well, but it's easy for the `Switch` function:

```
Switch(Sum([Quantity]) < 100, .4, Sum([Quantity]) < 1000, .45,
➡Sum([Quantity]) >= 100, .5)
```

13

Let's try this idea on the bonus discount calculation for the Order Details table. Let's say that customers get a bonus 5% discount for orders between 50 and 75 units, a bonus 10% discount for orders between 75 and 100 units, and a bonus 15% discount for orders of at least 100 units. Here's a `Switch` function that can handle this:

```
Switch(Sum([Quantity]) >= 50 And Sum([Quantity]) < 75, 0.05,
Sum([Quantity]) >= 75 And Sum([Quantity]) < 100, 0.1,
Sum([Quantity]) >= 100, 0.15)
```

Running Parameter Queries

Building a query is usually a get-it-right-and-then-forget-it proposition. That is, after you have your query returning the correct dynaset, you usually don't have to worry about the query design any longer. The data that appears in the dynaset might change as the records in the underlying tables are added, deleted, and edited, but the query itself remains static.

However, in certain situations the query itself undergoes regular change. For example, you saw earlier (refer to Figure 13.15) that you can use aggregate operations to determine how many units of each product remained after processing a certain day's orders. That query used a specific date as the criteria for the OrderDate field. If you want to see the results using another date, you need to edit the criteria. If you used a query like this often, you might eventually find that it's a real pain to constantly have to open the query design window, edit the query criteria, and then run the query.

To avoid this kind of hassle, you can set up such a query as a *parameter query*. This means that the query doesn't use a specific criteria expression for a certain field (or fields). Instead, you set up the field so that Access prompts you to enter the criteria when you run the query.

Note, however, that the parameter can accept only literal values such as strings, numbers, dates, times, and logical values. You can't enter an expression as the parameter value.

→ You can create more sophisticated parameter queries by building dialog box-like forms to accept user input. To learn how to do this, **see** "Creating a Form Pop-Up Box or Dialog Box," **p. 103**. (Chapter 5)

Creating a Simple Query Parameter

Here are the steps to follow to create a basic parameter query:

1. Start a new query and add the table or tables you want to work with.

2. Add the fields you want to use for the query to the design grid.

3. In the Criteria cell of the field for which you want to prompt for a parameter, enter the prompt text, surrounded by square brackets. For example, if you want to prompt the users to enter a last name, you type something like this in the cell:
   `[Enter the last name you want to work with:]`

4. Set up the other criteria and the rest of your query elements.

Figure 13.25 shows a Products and Categories query with the following parameter prompt in the `CategoryName` field:

[Enter the product category you want to work with:]

Figure 13.25
This query prompts for a parameter to use as the criteria for the `CategoryName` field.

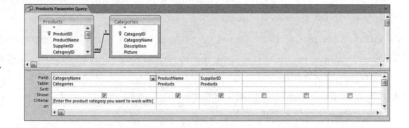

When you run the query, Access displays the Enter Parameter Value dialog box, as shown in Figure 13.26. Notice that the dialog box prompt text is exactly the same as the text entered in the Criteria (minus the square brackets).

Figure 13.26
When you run the query, Access uses the Enter Parameter Value dialog box.

You use the text box to enter the value to use as the criteria (double-check your typing to make sure your entry is accurate) and then click OK. (If you click Cancel, Access returns you to the query design window without running the query.) Figure 13.27 shows the dynaset that results when Beverages is entered as the criteria.

Figure 13.27
The dynaset that results when the criteria entered in Figure 13.26 is applied to the query in Figure 13.25.

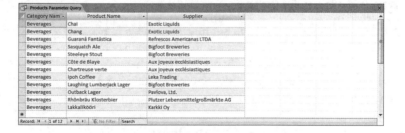

NOTE
You can specify more than one parameter in a single query. Access will display a separate Enter Parameter Value dialog box for each parameter.

Specifying the Parameter Data Type

Access assumes that the parameter values you enter are text. If you want to use other data types, you need to tell Access which data you prefer to use. Here are the steps to follow:

1. If you already have a parameter prompt text in the query, click inside the Criteria cell that contains the prompt text.

2. Choose Design, Parameters. Access displays the Query Parameters dialog box.

3. Enter the prompt text (without the square brackets) in the first available text box in the Parameter column.

4. Use the Data Type list to the right of the text box to choose the data type you want for the parameter (see Figure 13.28).

5. Repeat steps 3 and 4 for other parameters you want to enter.

6. Click OK.

Figure 13.28
To specify the data type of your parameters, choose Design, Parameters to enter the parameter prompt and data type in the Query Parameters dialog box.

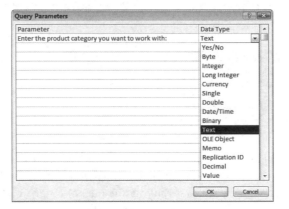

Running Action Queries

All the queries you've worked with to date have been *select queries*. A select query is one in which Access uses the query criteria to select the matching rows from a table or join. However, Access has several other query types that are designed to perform actions on the data, such as changing values, adding records, deleting records, and writing records to a new table. These so-called *action queries* are the subject of the next four sections.

Modifying Table Data with an Update Query

Access, like many programs, has a Replace command that enables you to substitute one piece of text for another either in certain records or throughout a table. Although this command often comes in handy, it simply can't handle some jobs. For example, what if you want to replace the contents of a field with a new value, but only for records that meet certain criteria? Or what if your table includes price data and you want to increase all the prices by 5%?

For these tasks, you need a more sophisticated tool: an *update query*. Unlike a select query, which displays only a subset of the table, an update query actually makes changes to the table data. The idea is that you select a field to work with, specify the new field value, set up some criteria (this is optional), and then run the query. Access flashes through the table and changes the field entries to the new value. If you enter criteria, only records that match the criteria are updated.

To create and run an update query, follow these steps:

1. Create a select query that includes the field (or fields) you want to update and the field (or fields) you'll need for the criteria. (Remember, criteria are optional for an update query. If you leave them out, Access updates every record in the table.)

2. When the select query is complete, run it to make sure the criteria are working properly.

> **CAUTION**
>
> Update queries can save you a great deal of time, but they must be approached with caution. After you run an update query, Access offers no direct method for undoing the operation. Therefore, *always* start off with a select query to make sure your criteria are doing what they're supposed to do. If your data is particularly precious, consider making a temporary copy of the table before running the update query. (To copy a table, click it in the Navigation pane, press Ctrl+C, and then press Ctrl+V. In the Paste Table As dialog box, edit the Table <u>N</u>ame (if desired) for the backup table, make sure the Structure and <u>D</u>ata option is clicked, and then click OK.)

3. Convert the query to an update query by choosing Design, Update. Access removes the Sort and Show rows from the design grid and replaces them with an Update To row, as shown in Figure 13.29.

Update button

Figure 13.29
When you convert a select query to an update query, Access replaces the design grid's Sort and Show rows with an Update To row.

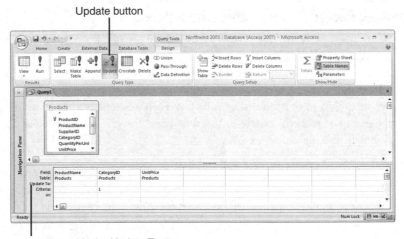

Access adds the Update To row

4. In the Update To cell for the field you want to change, enter the new value.

5. Choose Design, Run. Access displays a dialog box to tell you how many rows (records) will be updated.

6. Click <u>Y</u>es to perform the update.

After you see what update queries can do, you'll wonder how you ever got along without them. For example, one common table chore is changing prices and, in a large table, it's a drudgery most of us can live without. However, if you're increasing prices by a certain percentage, you can automate the whole process with an update query.

In Northwind's Products table, suppose you want to increase each value in the UnitPrice field by 5%. To handle this in an update query, you add the UnitPrice field to the design grid and then enter the following expression in the Update To cell:

```
[UnitPrice] * 1.05
```

This expression tells Access that you want every UnitPrice field entry increased by 5%. You can also set up criteria to gain even more control over the update. Figure 13.30 shows an update query that raises the UnitPrice field by 5%, but only for those records where the CategoryID field is 1.

Figure 13.30
This update query increases the UnitPrice values by 5% for those products where CategoryID equals 1.

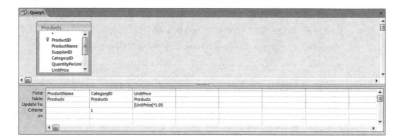

Removing Records from a Table with a Delete Query

If you need to delete one or two records from a table, it's easy enough just to select each record and choose <u>E</u>dit, Delete <u>R</u>ecord. But what if you have a large chunk of records to get rid of? For example, you might want to clean out an Orders table by deleting any old orders that were placed before a certain date. Or you might want to delete records for products that have been discontinued. In both examples, you can set up criteria to identify the group of records to delete. You then enter the criteria in a delete query, and Access will delete all the matching records.

Follow these steps to create and run a delete query:

1. Create a select query that includes the asterisk "field" (the asterisk represents the entire table) and any field you need for your deletion criteria.

2. Enter the criteria and then run the select query to make sure the query is picking out the correct records.

3. Convert the select query to a delete query by choosing Design, Delete. Access replaces the design grid's Sort and Show rows with a Delete row. The asterisk field will display From in the Delete cell, and each criteria field will display Where in the Delete cell. Figure 13.31 shows a delete query for the Products table that removes all the records where the Discontinued field is set to True.

Delete button

Figure 13.31
A delete query uses the asterisk field and any fields you need for your criteria.

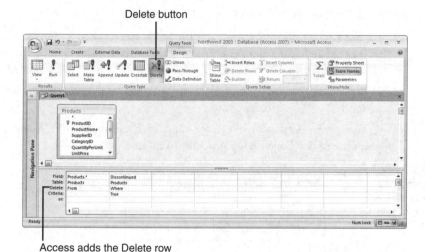

Access adds the Delete row

4. Choose Design, Run. Access analyzes the criteria and then displays a dialog box telling you how many records you'll be deleting.

5. Click Yes to proceed with the deletion.

> **CAUTION**
>
> If anything, the delete query is even more dangerous than the update query because the records you delete are gone for good and nothing can bring them back. Again, by setting up and running a select query first, you can easily avoid wiping out anything important. (Remember, too, that you can always make a temporary copy of any table that contains particularly important data.)

Creating New Tables with Make-Table Queries

The results of select queries are called *dynasets* because they're dynamic subsets of the table data. When I say "dynamic," I mean that if you edit the query records, the corresponding records in the table also change. Similarly, if you edit the table, Access changes the query records automatically.

This behavior is usually welcome because at least you know you're always working with the most up-to-date information. However, there might be the odd time when this is not the behavior you want. For example, at the end of the month or the end of the fiscal year, you might want some of your tables to be "frozen" while you tie things up for month- or year-end (this applies particularly to tables that track invoices).

Instead of letting the new work pile up until the table can be released, Access lets you create a table from an existing one. You can then use the new table for your month-end duties, so the old table doesn't need to be held up. You do this by using a *make-table* query.

Here are the steps to follow to create and run a make-table query:

1. Create a select query that includes the fields you want to include in the new table as well as the field (or fields) you need for the criteria. (The criteria are optional for a make-table query. If you leave them out, Access includes every record in the new table.)

2. When the select query is complete, run it to make sure the criteria are working properly.

3. Convert the query to a make-table query by choosing Design, Make Table. Access displays the Make Table dialog box, shown in Figure 13.32.

Figure 13.32
Use the Make Table dialog box to define your new table.

4. Use the Table Name text box to type the name you want to use for the new table.

5. To create the table in the same database, click Current Database. If you prefer to add the table to an external database, click Another Database and type the path and filename of the database in the File Name text box (or click Browse to locate the database file using a dialog box).

6. Click OK.

7. Choose Design, Run. Access displays a dialog box to tell you how many rows (records) will be added to the new table.

8. Click Yes to create the new table.

> **TIP**
>
> You can create powerful queries by combining make-table queries and parameter queries. For example, suppose each month you want to see the orders processed in the previous month. Assuming the order dates are in a field named OrderDate, you could create a make table query and add a calculated field defined by the expression Month([OrderDate]). You could then set up this field with a parameter prompt such as [Enter the month:]. Each time you run the query, you're prompted to specify the month and Access then copies the orders from that month into the other table.

Adding Records to a Table with an Append Query

Instead of creating an entirely new table, you might prefer to add records from one table to an existing table. You can accomplish this by using an *append query*.

Follow these steps to create and run an append query:

1. Create a select query that includes the fields you want to include in the appended records as well as the field (or fields) you need for the criteria. (The criteria are optional for an append query. If you leave them out, Access appends every record to the other table.)

2. When the select query is complete, run it to make sure the criteria are working properly.

3. Convert the query to an append query by choosing Design, Append. Access displays the Append dialog box, which is identical to the Make Table dialog box shown in Figure 13.32.

4. Use the Table Name text box to type the name of the table to which you want the records appended.

5. If the other table is in the same database, click Current Database. If the other table is in an external database, click Another Database and enter the path and filename of the database in the File Name text box (or click Browse to locate the database file using a dialog box).

6. Click OK. Access adds an Append To row to the design grid.

7. For each field in the design grid, use the Append To cell to choose the field in the other table to use for the append operation.

> **NOTE**
> If you add the asterisk field to the design grid, its Append To cell will show the name of the other table. In this case, if you add other fields for criteria purposes, make sure these fields have their Append To cells blank.

8. Choose Design, Run. Access displays a dialog box to tell you how many rows (records) will be appended to the table.

9. Click Yes to append the records.

From Here

→ You can create more sophisticated parameter queries by building dialog box-like forms to accept user input. To learn how to do this, **see** "Creating a Form Pop-Up Box or Dialog Box," **p. 103**. (Chapter 5)

→ To learn how to create subqueries, **see** "Using SQL to Create Subqueries," **p. 354**. (Chapter 15)

13

Creating PivotTable Queries

14

It's not unusual for Access tables to contain hundreds or even thousands of records. Analyzing that much data can be a nightmare without the right kinds of tools. To help you, Access offers a powerful data-analysis tool called a *PivotTable*. This tool enables you to summarize hundreds of records in a concise tabular format. You can then manipulate the layout of the table to see different views of your data. This chapter introduces you to PivotTable queries and shows you various ways to use them with your own data.

What Is a PivotTable?

To understand PivotTables, you need to see how they fit in with Access's other database-analysis features. Database analysis has several levels of complexity. The simplest level involves the basic lookup and retrieval of information. For example, if you have a database that lists the company sales reps and their territory sales, you can use a datasheet or form to search for a specific rep and to look up the sales in that rep's territory.

The next level of complexity involves more sophisticated lookup and retrieval techniques based on the querying tools you've seen in the previous chapters, particularly the use of totals and calculated fields. For example, suppose that each sales territory is part of a larger region, and you want to know the total sales in the eastern region. You can either subtotal by region or set up your criteria to match all territories in the eastern region and use the Sum function to get the total. To get more specific information, such as total eastern region sales in the second quarter, you just add the appropriate conditions to your criteria.

The next level of database analysis applies a single question to multiple variables. For example, if the company in the preceding example has four regions, you might want to see separate totals for each region broken down by quarter. One solution is to set up four different queries that use the Sum function. But what if there were a dozen regions? Or a hundred? Ideally, you need some way of summarizing the database information into a "sales table" that has a row for each region and a column for each quarter. This is exactly what PivotTables do. With Access's PivotTable Wizard, you can create your own tables with just a few mouse clicks. And if you prefer to visualize your data, Access can also create a PivotChart, which is just the PivotTable data displayed in chart form.

How PivotTables Work

In the simplest case, PivotTables work by summarizing the data in one field (called a *data field*) and breaking it down according to the data in another field. The unique values in the second field (called the *row field*) become the row headings. For example, Figure 14.1 shows a table of sales by sales representatives. With a PivotTable, you can summarize the numbers in the Sales field (the data field) and break them down by Region (the row field). Figure 14.2 shows the resulting PivotTable query. Notice how Access uses the four unique items in the Region field (East, West, Midwest, and South) as row headings.

You can further break down your data by specifying a third field (called the *column field*) to use for column headings. Figure 14.3 shows the resulting PivotTable with the four unique items in the Quarter field (1st, 2nd, 3rd, and 4th) used to create the columns.

Figure 14.1
A database of sales by
sales representatives.

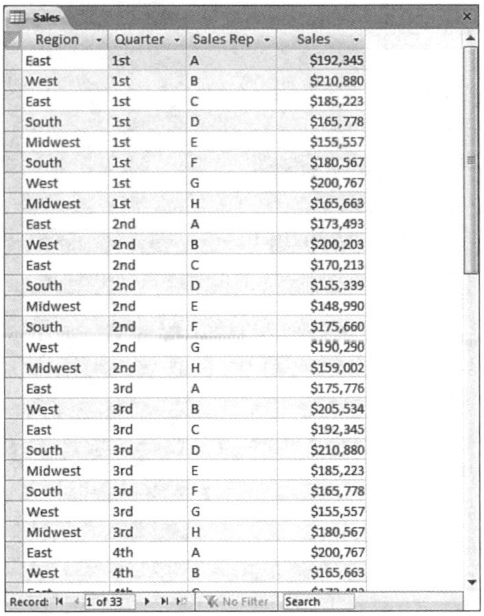

Region	Quarter	Sales Rep	Sales
East	1st	A	$192,345
West	1st	B	$210,880
East	1st	C	$185,223
South	1st	D	$165,778
Midwest	1st	E	$155,557
South	1st	F	$180,567
West	1st	G	$200,767
Midwest	1st	H	$165,663
East	2nd	A	$173,493
West	2nd	B	$200,203
East	2nd	C	$170,213
South	2nd	D	$155,339
Midwest	2nd	E	$148,990
South	2nd	F	$175,660
West	2nd	G	$190,290
Midwest	2nd	H	$159,002
East	3rd	A	$175,776
West	3rd	B	$205,534
East	3rd	C	$192,345
South	3rd	D	$210,880
Midwest	3rd	E	$185,223
South	3rd	F	$165,778
West	3rd	G	$155,557
Midwest	3rd	H	$180,567
East	4th	A	$200,767
West	4th	B	$165,663

Region	Sum of Sales
East	$1,463,655
Midwest	$1,540,875
South	$1,409,544
West	$1,477,884
Grand Total	$5,891,958

Figure 14.2
A PivotTable query showing total sales by region.

Region	1st Sum of Sales	2nd Sum of Sales	3rd Sum of Sales	4th Sum of Sales	Grand Total Sum of Sales
East	$377,568	$343,706	$368,121	$374,260	$1,463,655
Midwest	$321,220	$307,992	$365,790	$545,873	$1,540,875
South	$346,345	$330,999	$376,658	$355,542	$1,409,544
West	$411,647	$390,493	$361,091	$314,653	$1,477,884
Grand Total	$1,456,780	$1,373,190	$1,471,660	$1,590,328	$5,891,958

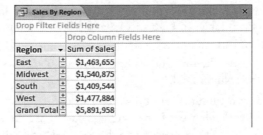

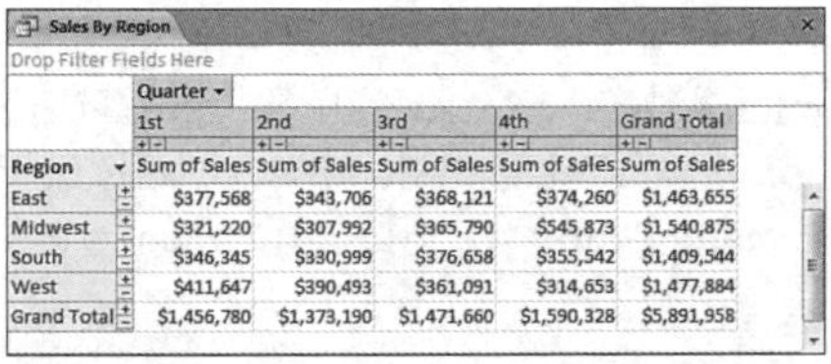

Figure 14.3
A PivotTable showing sales by region for each quarter.

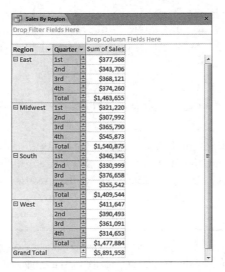

The big news with PivotTables is the "pivoting" feature. If you want to see different views of your data, you can, for example, drag the column field over to the row field area, as shown in Figure 14.4. The result, as you can see, is that the table shows each region as the main row category, with the quarters as regional subcategories.

Region	Quarter	Sum of Sales
East	1st	$377,568
	2nd	$343,706
	3rd	$368,121
	4th	$374,260
	Total	$1,463,655
Midwest	1st	$321,220
	2nd	$307,992
	3rd	$365,790
	4th	$545,873
	Total	$1,540,875
South	1st	$346,345
	2nd	$330,999
	3rd	$376,658
	4th	$355,542
	Total	$1,409,544
West	1st	$411,647
	2nd	$390,493
	3rd	$361,091
	4th	$314,653
	Total	$1,477,884
Grand Total		$5,891,958

Figure 14.4
You can drag row or column fields to "pivot" the data and get a different view.

Some PivotTable Terms

Pivot tables have their own terminology, so here's a quick glossary of some terms you need to become familiar with:

Field—A category of data, such as `Region`, `Quarter`, or `Sales`.

Item—An element in a field.

Row field—A field with a limited set of distinct text, numeric, or date values to use as row headings in the PivotTable. In Figures 14.2 and 14.3, Region is the row field.

Column field—A field with a limited set of distinct text, numeric, or date values to use as column headings for the PivotTable. In the PivotTable shown in Figure 14.3, the Quarter field is the column field.

Filter field—A field with a limited set of distinct text, numeric, or date values that you use to filter the PivotTable view. For example, you can use the Sales Rep field to create separate filters for each rep. Selecting a different sales rep filters the table to show data only for that person.

Data field—A field that contains the data you want to summarize in the table. Access recognizes two types of data fields: totals and details. A totals field performs an operation (such as sum, count, or average, and so on) on the data; a details field displays the raw data.

Layout—The overall arrangement of fields and items in the PivotTable.

In Access, PivotTables are implemented as a "view" of the underlying data. The next few sections show you how to display and manipulate the PivotTable view.

Creating a One-Dimensional PivotTable

The simplest kind of PivotTable is one that combines either a row field or a column field with a data field. This capability is useful if you want to group the data according to the unique values in the row or column field and see either the data field details or totals.

Display Data Field Details

Here are the steps to follow to create a one-dimensional PivotTable that shows the data field details:

1. Build a select query that defines the fields and records you want to use for the PivotTable. Make sure you run the query to ensure that it's returning the correct records and fields. Figure 14.5 shows the select query that I use as an example over the next few sections, and Figure 14.6 shows the resulting dynaset.

> **NOTE**
> When constructing your query, make sure that at least one of the fields contains "groupable" data. That is, the field contains data with a limited number of distinct text, numeric, or date values. In the Employee Orders query shown in Figure 14.6, the LastName field is perfect for a PivotTable because, despite having hundreds of items, it has only nine distinct values (Buchanan, Callahan, Davolio, and so on).

NOTE As I mentioned in Chapter 10, "Creating a Basic Query," I'm going to use the older (Access 2003) Northwind sample data for the querying chapters. You can download the sample database from my website:

www.mcfedries.com/Access2007Forms

Figure 14.5

In Access, PivotTables are views of the underlying data, such as this query.

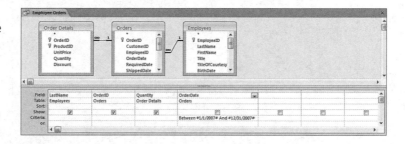

Figure 14.6

The dynaset generated by the query shown in Figure 14.5.

Last Nam	Order ID	Quantity
Davolio	10400	21
Davolio	10400	35
Davolio	10400	30
Davolio	10401	18
Davolio	10401	70
Davolio	10401	20
Davolio	10401	60
Callahan	10402	60
Callahan	10402	65
Peacock	10403	21
Peacock	10403	70
Fuller	10404	30
Fuller	10404	40
Fuller	10404	30
Davolio	10405	50
King	10406	10
King	10406	30

Record: 1 of 1059   No Filter   Search

2. In the query's Design view or Datasheet view, choose the Home tab, click the lower half of the View split button, and then click PivotTable View. Access displays an empty PivotTable view as well as the Design tab under PivotTable Tools, as shown in Figure 14.7.

3. In the PivotTable Field List, click the field you want to use as the row or column field. (If you don't see the PivotTable Field List, choose Design, Field List.)

4. In the drop-down list at the bottom of the PivotTable Field List, lick either Row Area or Column Area.

5. Click Add To. Access adds the field to the PivotTable's row area or column area.

6. In the PivotTable Field List, click the field you want to use as the details data field.

7. In the drop-down list, choose Detail Data.

8. Click Add To. Access adds the field to the PivotTable's detail area.

14

Field List button   Field List

Figure 14.7
The first time you choose
Home, View, PivotTable
View for a query, Access
displays an empty
PivotTable view similar
to this one.

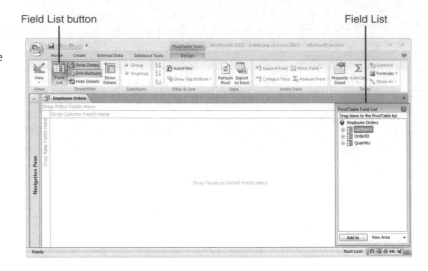

> **TIP** Another way to add a row or column field is to click and drag the field and drop it on either the Drop Row Fields Here label or the Drop Column Fields Here label. For a details data field, you can also click and drag the field and drop it on the Drop Totals or Details Fields Here label.

Figure 14.8 shows a PivotTable where the LastName field is the row field and the Quantity field is used as the details data field.

Figure 14.8
In this PivotTable view,
the Quantity field is
displayed as a details
data field.

Displaying the Sum of the Data Field Values

If you want to go beyond the data detail and see the sum of the data field values for each row or column field item, you need to add a totals data field, as described in the following steps:

1. Build a select query that defines the fields and records you want to use for the PivotTable. Make sure you run the query to ensure that it's returning the correct records and fields.

2. In the query's Design view or Datasheet view, choose the Home tab, click the lower half of the View split button, and then click Pivot Table View.

3. Add the row or column field, if you haven't done so already.

4. In the PivotTable Field List, click the field you want to use as the totals data field.

5. In the drop-down list, choose Data Area.

6. Click Add To.

In Figure 14.9, the Quantity is used as both the details data field and the totals data field. The LastName field is set up as a column field this time because this usually makes it easier to differentiate the details and totals. Notice, too, that the PivotTable Field List also has a new Totals item that includes Sum of Quantity, which represents the totals data field just added.

> **TIP**
> If you want to change your PivotTable to use a column field instead of a row field, you don't have to start from scratch. Instead, click the field name in the PivotTable Field List, choose Column Area in the drop-down list, and click Add To. (Alternatively, click and drag the current row field and drop it in the Drop Column Fields Here area.) Follow the reverse procedure if you want to convert a column field to a row field.

Details

Figure 14.9
In this PivotTable view, the Quantity field is displayed as both a details field and a totals data field.

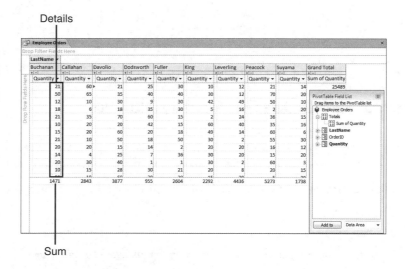

Sum

Hiding and Showing the Data Details

If your PivotTable contains both details and totals, you can switch between hiding the details (and, therefore, showing just the totals) and showing the details.

To do this for the entire PivotTable, use the following Design tab commands:

- **Hide Details**—Choose this command to hide the details for the entire PivotTable.
- **Show Details**—Choose this command to show the details for the entire PivotTable.

If you want to hide or show details only for a particular item in the row or column field, use the Show/Hide Details buttons (see Figure 14.10) associated with each item:

- Click the minus sign (–) to hide the item's details.
- Click the plus sign (+) to show the item's details.

Figure 14.10
The details of the Buchanan column have been hidden.

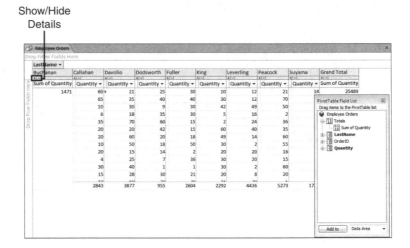

Inserting an AutoCalc Data Field Summary Calculation

The only problem with adding a totals data field is that you can use it only as a sum of the detail values. If you want to perform other calculations, you need to use an AutoCalc data field, which enables you to choose one of the nine available summary functions.

Follow these steps to insert an AutoCalc data field into the PivotTable:

1. In the PivotTable, click the data field caption.
2. Choose Design, AutoCalc.
3. In the submenu, choose one of the commands listed in Table 14.1.

Table 14.1   The AutoCalc Data Field Summary Commands

Command	Description
<u>S</u>um	Totals the values for the data field.
<u>C</u>ount	Counts the values for the data field.
<u>Mi</u>n	Returns the smallest value for the data field.
Ma<u>x</u>	Returns the largest value for the data field.
<u>A</u>verage	Computes the average of the values for the data field.
Standard <u>D</u>eviation	Computes the standard deviation of the values for the data field, treated as a sample.
<u>V</u>ariance	Computes the variance of the values for the data field, treated as a sample.
Standard Deviation <u>P</u>opulation	Computes the standard deviation of the values for the data field, treated as a population.
Va<u>r</u>iance Population	Computes the variance of the values for the data field, treated as a population.

Figure 14.11 shows a PivotTable with five AutoCalc summaries for the Quantity field: Sum, Count, Min, Max, and Average. The details are hidden to show just the summary fields.

> **CAUTION**
>
> When you hide details as shown in Figure 14.11, Access disables the Design tab's AutoCalc list. If you need to add more calculations to the data field, first choose Design, Show Details to redisplay the details.

AutoCalc button

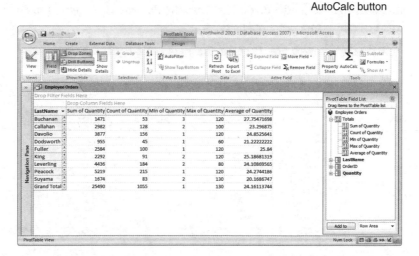

Figure 14.11
In this PivotTable view, the Quantity field has AutoCalc summaries for Sum, Count, Min, Max, and Average.

Changing the AutoCalc Calculation Type

By default, the value displayed by an AutoCalc summary applies to the current row or column item. In some cases, you might want to view the result with respect to the rest of the data. For example, you might want to know what percentage the current item's sum is with respect to the grand total of all the items' sums. Follow these steps to change the calculation type for an AutoCalc summary:

1. In the PivotTable, click any value in the AutoCalc summary you want to work with.
2. Choose Design, Show As.
3. In the submenu, choose one of the commands listed in Table 14.2.

Table 14.2   The AutoCalc Calculation Type Commands

Command	Description
Normal	Displays the summary with respect to the row or column item (the default).
Percent of Row Total	Displays the summary as a percentage of the total of the values in the current row.
Percent of Column Total	Displays the summary as a percentage of the total of the values in the current column.
Percent of Parent Row Item	Displays the summary as a percentage of the total of the values in the PivotTable's row field.
Percent of Parent Column Item	Displays the summary as a percentage of the total of the values in the PivotTable's column field.
Percent of Grand Total	Displays the summary as a percentage of the PivotTable's grand total.

Figure 14.12 shows the PivotTable with the Percent of Column Total command applied to the Sum of Quantity AutoCalc field.

Figure 14.12
The PivotTable with the Percent of Column Total calculation type applied to the Sum of Quantity field.

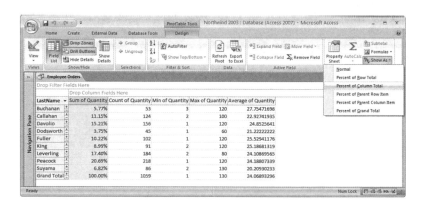

If you want to see an actual value in a field that's displayed as a percentage, hover the mouse
pointer over the value. After a second or two, a banner appears that displays the value.

Creating a Calculated Field

You learned back in Chapter 11, "Building Criteria Expressions," that you can create calculated columns that display the results of an expression. You're free to use these calculated columns as field values in a PivotTable. However, if your query doesn't have a calculated column, or if you want only a particular calculation to appear in the PivotTable view, Access enables you to create a calculated detail or total field.

→ To learn about adding calculated columns to queries, **see** "Setting Up a Calculated Column," **p. 239**. (Chapter 11)

Here are the steps to follow to add a calculated field:

1. If the expression used by the calculated detail field requires one or more table fields, return to Design view and make sure those fields are added to the select query.

2. In the PivotTable view, choose Design, Formulas and then choose either Create Calculated Total or Create Calculated Detail Field. Access displays the Properties dialog box with the Calculation tab selected (see Figure 14.14).

3. Use the Name text box to type the name you want to use for the field.

4. Use the large text box to type your expression. You can use the same operators, literals, and identifiers that you learned about in Chapter 11. If you're not sure which fields are available, select the one you want from the drop-down list and then click Insert Reference To.

5. Click Change. Access adds the calculated field to the PivotTable.

Figure 14.13 shows an updated version of the Employee Orders query that now includes the UnitPrice and Discount fields from the Order Details table. Figure 14.14 shows both the Calculation tab with an expression that defines the discounted price for each item and the resulting Discounted Price field added to the PivotTable.

Figure 14.13
A revised version of the Employee Orders query with the UnitPrice and Discount fields added.

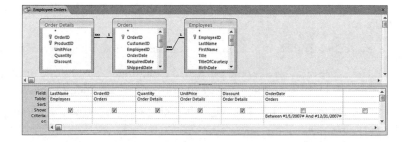

Figure 14.14
The calculated
`Discounted Price`
field as it appears in the
Calculation tab and the
PivotTable.

Removing a PivotTable Field

If you add a field and decide later that you no longer need it in the PivotTable, you can
remove it by using either of the following techniques:

- **For any field**—Click and drag the field caption and drop it outside the PivotTable
  view window.
- **For AutoCalc and calculated fields only**—In the PivotTable Field List, right-click
  the field name and then click <u>D</u>elete.

Creating a Multiple-Field One-Dimensional PivotTable

Having a single row or column field is useful for grouping the data on that field, either as
the detail or as a summary calculation. But often a single row or column doesn't provide
enough information. For example, in the PivotTable shown in Figure 14.14, after we went
to all that trouble to create a calculated field for the discounted price, the PivotTable detail
still shows just the discounted price for each item in the orders. It would be nice to know
more:

- Which order are you dealing with?
- What's the total dollar amount for each order?

You can answer both questions by adding a second row field for, in this case, the `OrderID`
field.

Here are the general steps to follow to add a second field to an area of the PivotTable:

1. If the expression used by the calculated detail field requires one or more table fields,
   return to Design view and make sure those fields are added to the select query.
2. In the PivotTable Field List, click the field you want to add.
3. In the drop-down list, choose the PivotTable area you want to use.
4. Click <u>A</u>dd To.

14

Figure 14.15 shows the Employee Order PivotTable with `Order ID` added as a second row field. Notice how the Discounted Price items are now broken down by order. And because I added a sum field for the Discounted Price data, the PivotTable also shows the total for each order.

Figure 14.15
The Employee Orders PivotTable with `Order ID` added as a second row field.

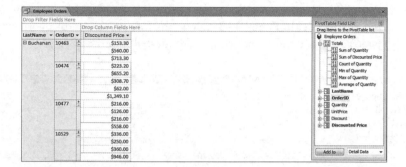

If you just want to see the totals for each order, click the `OrderID` field header and then choose Design, Hide Details. Figure 14.16 shows the result.

Figure 14.16
Hiding the details for the `OrderID` field displays only the Discounted Price totals for each order.

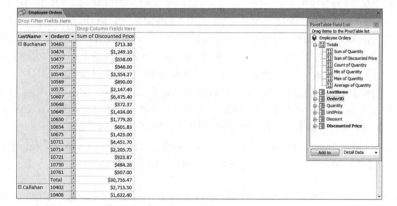

Creating a Two-Dimensional PivotTable

A one-dimensional PivotTable approaches the data from a single viewpoint. In the examples you've seen so far, the Employee table's `LastName` field provided a focus for examining data such as units ordered and the discounted price. When you look at the totals for this data, the PivotTable makes it easy to compare the employees' order-taking performance over the year.

The beauty of PivotTables, however, is that you don't have to focus on just one aspect of the data. Instead, you can add a second viewpoint that breaks down the existing data into its component parts. For example, you might want to see a breakdown of which shipping company was used for each order. You do this in a PivotTable by defining both a row field and a column field.

Here are the steps to follow to create such a two-dimensional PivotTable:

1. Build a select query that defines the fields and records you want to use for the PivotTable. Make sure you run the query to ensure that it's returning the correct records and fields. Figure 14.17 shows the Employee Orders query with the Shippers table added and the CompanyName field inserted into the query.

Figure 14.17
The updated Employee Orders query with the Shippers table and CompanyName field added.

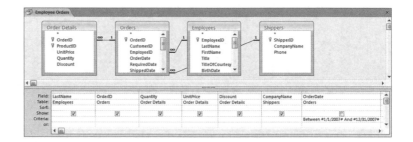

2. In the query's Design view or Datasheet view, choose the Home tab, click the lower half of the View split button, and then click PivotTable View.

3. In the PivotTable Field List, click the field you want to use as the row field, use the drop-down list to choose Row Area, and then click Add To. (Alternatively, click and drag the field and drop it on the Drop Row Fields Here label.)

4. In the PivotTable Field List, click the field you want to use as the column field, use the drop-down list to choose Column Area, and then click Add To. (Alternatively, click and drag the field and drop it on the Drop Column Fields Here label.)

5. In the PivotTable Field List, click the field you want to use as the data field, use the drop-down list to choose either Detail Data or Data Area, and then click Add To.

Figure 14.18 shows a PivotTable where the LastName and OrderID fields are the row fields, the CompanyName field is the column field, and the calculated Discount Price field is used as the details data field.

Analyzing Customer Orders by Product Category

Two-dimensional PivotTables enable you to examine one element of your data with respect to another. Depending on the data—remember, this extends to all your related tables, not just the data in a single table—you can bring together and analyze data that is otherwise inaccessible.

In the Northwind sample database, for example, you won't find two pieces of data less distantly related than the Customers table and the Categories table. To get from the former to the latter, you link Customers to the Orders table (common field: `CustomerID`), and then the Order Details table (common field: `OrderID`), the Products table (common field: `ProductID`), and finally the Categories table (common field: `CategoryID`).

		CompanyName			
		Federal Shipping	Speedy Express	United Package	Grand Total
LastName	OrderID	Sum of Discounted Price	Sum of Discounted Price	Sum of Discounted Price	Sum of Discounted Price
Buchanan	10463	$713.30			$713.30
	10474			$1,249.10	$1,249.10
	10477			$558.00	$558.00
	10529			$946.00	$946.00
	10549		$3,554.27		$3,554.27
	10569		$890.00		$890.00
	10575		$2,147.40		$2,147.40
	10607		$6,475.40		$6,475.40
	10648			$372.37	$372.37
	10649	$1,434.00			$1,434.00
	10650	$1,779.20			$1,779.20
	10654		$601.83		$601.83
	10675			$1,423.00	$1,423.00
	10711			$4,451.70	$4,451.70
	10714	$2,205.75			$2,205.75
	10721	$923.87			$923.87
	10730		$484.26		$484.26
	10761			$507.00	$507.00
	Total	$7,056.12	$14,153.17	$9,507.17	$30,716.47
Callahan	10399	$1,765.60			$1,765.60
	10402			$2,713.50	$2,713.50

Figure 14.18
This two-dimensional PivotTable view uses both row fields and a column field.

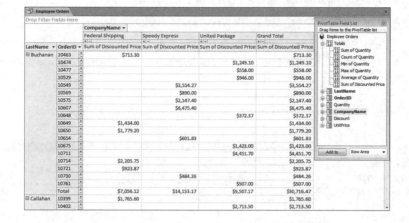

Figure 14.19 shows a query that uses these relationships to display the company name and the company's orders with the category name, order quantity, and discounted total. (Also, the `OrderDate` field is used to restrict the orders to those placed in 2007.) Figure 14.20 shows the resulting dynaset.

Figure 14.19
A query that links the Customers and Categories tables.

Company Name	Order ID	Category Name	Quantity	Discounted Total
Alfreds Futterkiste	10643	Beverages	21	$283.50
Alfreds Futterkiste	10643	Produce	15	$513.00
Alfreds Futterkiste	10643	Seafood	2	$18.00
Alfreds Futterkiste	10692	Condiments	20	$878.00
Alfreds Futterkiste	10702	Beverages	15	$270.00
Alfreds Futterkiste	10702	Condiments	6	$60.00
Ana Trujillo Emparedados y helados	10625	Dairy Products	10	$340.00
Ana Trujillo Emparedados y helados	10625	Grains/Cereals	5	$70.00
Ana Trujillo Emparedados y helados	10625	Produce	3	$69.75
Ana Trujillo Emparedados y helados	10759	Dairy Products	10	$320.00
Antonio Moreno Taquería	10507	Beverages	15	$586.50
Antonio Moreno Taquería	10507	Confections	15	$162.56
Antonio Moreno Taquería	10535	Dairy Products	15	$742.50
Antonio Moreno Taquería	10535	Dairy Products	50	$945.00

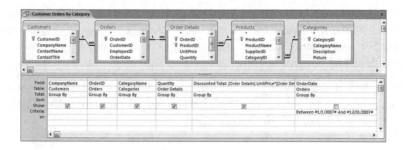

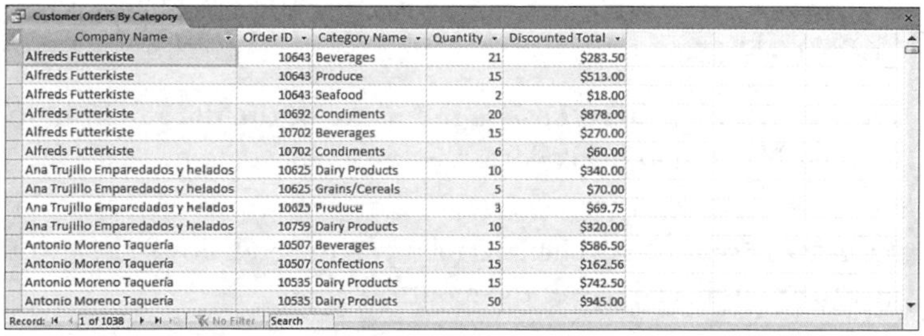

Figure 14.20
The dynaset produced by the query in Figure 14.19.

14

It would be interesting to get a sense of what each customer ordered in each product category, both in terms of units ordered and total dollars ordered. This is most efficiently done with a two-dimensional PivotTable with the following layout:

- The `CategoryName` field is the PivotTable's row field.
- The `CompanyName` field is the PivotTable's column field.
- The `Quantity` and `Discounted Total` fields are used as detail data fields.
- The AutoCalc `Sum` operation is applied to both the `Quantity` and `Discounted Total` fields.

Figure 14.21 shows the resulting PivotTable, with detail hidden.

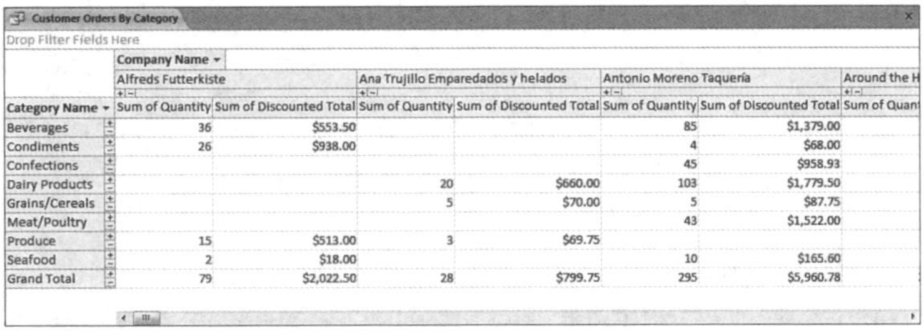

Customer Orders By Category

Drop Filter Fields Here

Company Name	Alfreds Futterkiste		Ana Trujillo Emparedados y helados		Antonio Moreno Taquería		Around the H
Category Name	Sum of Quantity	Sum of Discounted Total	Sum of Quantity	Sum of Discounted Total	Sum of Quantity	Sum of Discounted Total	Sum of Quan
Beverages	36	$553.50			85	$1,379.00	
Condiments	26	$938.00			4	$68.00	
Confections					45	$958.93	
Dairy Products			20	$660.00	103	$1,779.50	
Grains/Cereals			5	$70.00	5	$87.75	
Meat/Poultry					43	$1,522.00	
Produce	15	$513.00	3	$69.75			
Seafood	2	$18.00			10	$165.60	
Grand Total	79	$2,022.50	28	$799.75	295	$5,960.78	

Figure 14.21
A two-dimensional PivotTable showing the sum of `Quantity` and `Discounted Total` for each customer, broken down by product category.

Adding a Temporal Dimension to the PivotTable

Two-dimensional PivotTables are particularly useful when the second dimension is time. For example, you might want to summarize the orders taken by employees each quarter to look for performance drop-offs, or you might need to summarize customer orders by month to look for trends in the data.

In an Access PivotTable, you have two choices for using dates as row or column fields: using the built-in features or creating your own custom date fields. The next two sections give you the details of both approaches.

Working with the Built-In PivotTable Date Features

If you include a date field in your query, Access automatically adds two new items to the PivotTable Field List:

- ***Field* By Week (where *Field* is the name of the date field in the query)**—This item enables you to break down the PivotTable data by year, week, and day of the week.
- ***Field* By Month**—This item enables you to break down the PivotTable data by year, quarter, month, and day of the month.

14

For example, Figure 14.22 shows the Employee Orders by Date query that displays the employee name, the three fields used to calculate the discounted total (UnitPrice, Quantity, and Discount), and the OrderDate.

Figure 14.22
To use the built-in PivotTable date features, be sure to include a date field in your query, such as the OrderDate field shown here.

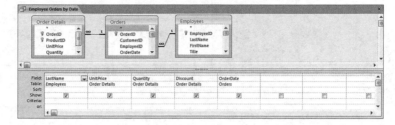

Figure 14.23 shows a PivotTable view of this query, which has the following layout:

■ The LastName field is the row field.

■ The detail data field is a calculated field that derives the discounted total for each order; this field uses an AutoCalc Sum operation and the details have been hidden.

■ The Order Date By Week field is the column field.

Figure 14.23
A two-dimensional PivotTable that uses the automatically generated Order Date By Week field as the column field.

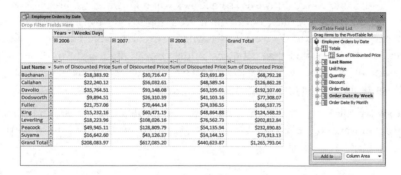

As you can see, using Order Date By Week at first displays the years associated with the underlying date field—in this case, 2006, 2007, and 2008. You can manipulate the dates as follows:

■ Click the plus sign (+) beside a year value to display the weeks of that year (as numbers from 1 to 52).

■ Click the plus sign (+) beside a week value to display the days of that week (Monday through Friday).

■ If applicable for your data, you can continue clicking plus signs to expand the data even further to a day's hours, minutes, and seconds.

14

Figure 14.24 shows the column field expanded to show the weeks for 2007 and the days of the week for week 1.

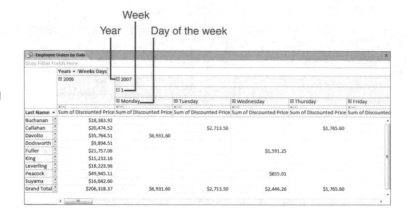

Figure 14.24
The column field expanded to show the weeks for 2007 and the days of the week for week 1.

Adding Custom Date Fields

The built-in PivotTable date features are certainly useful and can save you lots of time if they suit your needs. However, sometimes you might want to break down data by date using some other format. For example, you might want to view product orders as they occur on the days of the week to see whether some products are more likely to be ordered on, say, Friday rather than Monday. Similarly, you might want to break down employee orders by quarter, but your fiscal year isn't the same as the calendar year. (The built-in PivotTable date features display quarters for the calendar year only.)

To solve these problems, you need to create calculated query columns that return the values you want to use in your PivotTable. The next two sections illustrate this by taking you through two examples.

Viewing Product Orders by Day of the Week

Are your customers more likely to order certain products on certain days of the week? This is a tough question to answer using a regular select query that combines Northwind's Orders, Order Details, and Products tables. You can get closer to the answer by creating a calculated column that displays only the day of the week associated with the OrderDate field:

```
Format([OrderDate], "dddd")
```

Using the dddd format string tells access to return the day of the week (Monday, Tuesday, and so on). Figure 14.25 shows a query that includes such a calculated field (named Day of the Week) as well as the Product's table's ProductName field and the Order Details table's Quantity field. Figure 14.26 shows the resulting dynaset.

Figure 14.25
A query that generates the day of the week for each order date.

Product Orders by Day of the Week

Product Name	Day of the We	Quantity
Chai	Wednesday	45
Chai	Wednesday	18
Chai	Friday	20
Chai	Tuesday	15
Chai	Tuesday	12
Chai	Wednesday	15
Chai	Friday	10
Chai	Wednesday	24
Chai	Wednesday	15
Chai	Monday	40
Chai	Wednesday	8
Chai	Wednesday	10
Chai	Thursday	20
Chai	Tuesday	3
Chai	Wednesday	6
Chai	Monday	25
Chai	Monday	15
Chai	Monday	35
Chai	Wednesday	30
Chai	Wednesday	5

Record: 1 of 2155 No Filter Search

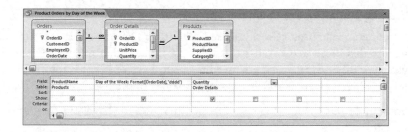

Figure 14.26
The records displayed by the query shown in Figure 14.25.

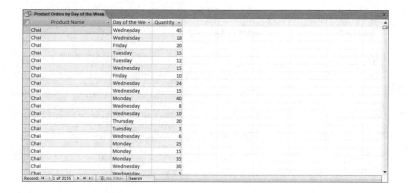

To make sense of this data, you need to display it in a PivotTable view that has the following layout:

- The `ProductName` field is the row field.
- The calculated `Day of the Week` field is the column field.
- The quantity field is the detail data field with an AutoCalc `Sum` operation applied and details hidden.

Figure 14.27 shows a PivotTable with such a layout.

Product Orders by Day of the Week

Drop Filter Fields Here

	Day of the Week				
	Monday	Tuesday	Wednesday	Thursday	Friday
Product Name	Sum of Quantity	Sum of Quantity	Sum of Quantity	Sum of Quantity	Sum of Quantity
Alice Mutton	146	355	254	123	100
Aniseed Syrup	50	64	108	56	50
Boston Crab Meat	329	113	461	106	94
Camembert Pierrot	452	440	524	161	
Carnarvon Tigers	18	214	252	55	
Chai	225	190	255	128	30
Chang	276	254	348	179	
Chartreuse verte	377	33	208	175	
Chef Anton's Cajun Seasoning	23	121	218	91	
Chef Anton's Gumbo Mix	65	20	93	120	
Chocolade		23	115		
Côte de Blaye	143	215	25	240	
Escargots de Bourgogne	182	180	100	72	
Filo Mix	126	164	182	28	
Fløtemysost	254	367	336	100	
Geitost	163	228	276	58	30
Genen Shouyu	22	75	25		

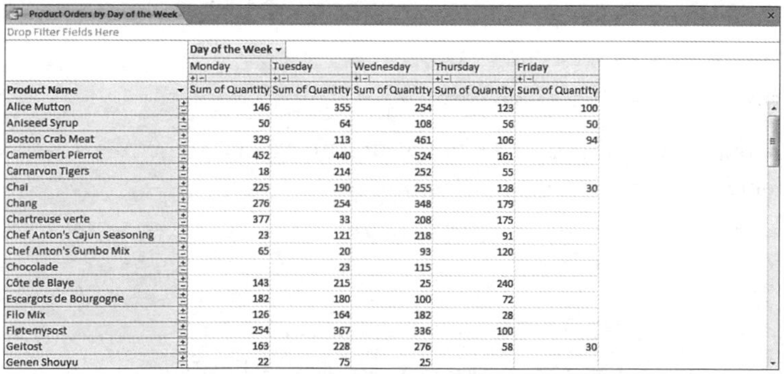

Figure 14.27
A two-dimensional PivotTable that uses a calculated query field to display products orders by day of the week.

14

Viewing Employee Orders by Custom Quarter

If your company uses a fiscal year end other than December 31, the built-in PivotTable date feature that displays quarters won't be of use because that feature works only by calendar year. For other fiscal years, you need to create a custom expression that calculates the quarter in which a given date falls given the first day of the fiscal year.

You can do this by building an expression that uses the `DateDiff` function:

```
DATEDIFF(interval, date1, date2 [,firstdayofweek] [,firstweekof year])
```

`interval`	The date unit used in the result:

Interval	**What It Returns**
yyyy	The number of years between *date1* and *date2*.
q	The number of quarters between *date1* and *date2*.
m	The number of months between *date1* and *date2*.
d	The number of days between *date1* and *date2*.
w	The number of weekdays between *date1* and *date2*.
ww	The number of weeks between *date1* and *date2*.
h	The number of hours between *date1* and *date2*.
n	The number of minutes between *date1* and *date2*.
s	The number of seconds between *date1* and *date2*.

`date1`	The starting date.
`date2`	The ending date.
`firstdayofweek`	A constant that specifies the first day of the week. Use 1 for Sunday (this is the default), 2 for Monday, and so on.
`firstweekofyear`	A constant that specifies the first week or the year. Use 1 for the week that includes January 1 (this is the default); use 2 for the first week that has at least four days in the new year; use 3 for the first full week of the new year.

Suppose your fiscal year begins on April 1, 2007. The following expression returns the quarter in which a given date falls:

```
DateDiff("q", #4/1/2007#, date) + 1
```

Note that you need to add one to the `DateDiff` result to get the actual quarter number. For example, the following expression returns 2:

```
DateDiff("q", #4/1/2007#, #8/23/2007#) + 1
```

14

CAUTION

The `DateDiff` formula works only with dates that fall within the fiscal year.

Let's put this expression to work with the Northwind data to look at employee performance per quarter. Assume the Northwind fiscal year runs from April 1, 2007, to March 31, 2008. Figure 14.28 shows a query that uses the Orders, Order Details, and Employees tables. The calculated `Quarter` field uses the `DateDiff` expression to return the quarter in which each order falls, and the `OrderDate` field restricts the records to just those that fall within the fiscal year. Figure 14.29 shows the resulting dynaset.

Figure 14.28
A query that calculates the custom quarter number for each order date.

Last Nam	Quantity	Quarter	Order Date
Leverling	50	1	26-Jun-2007
Leverling	4	1	27-Jun-2007
Leverling	14	1	27-Jun-2007
Fuller	10	1	27-Jun-2007
Fuller	24	1	27-Jun-2007
Fuller	10	1	27-Jun-2007
Peacock	50	1	29-Jun-2007
King	15	2	02-Jul-2007
Dodsworth	4	2	02-Jul-2007
Davolio	6	2	02-Jul-2007
Davolio	20	2	02-Jul-2007
Davolio	20	2	02-Jul-2007
Fuller	40	2	03-Jul-2007

Record: 1 of 1260

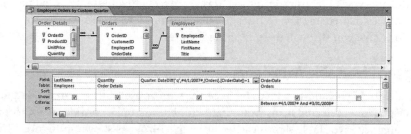

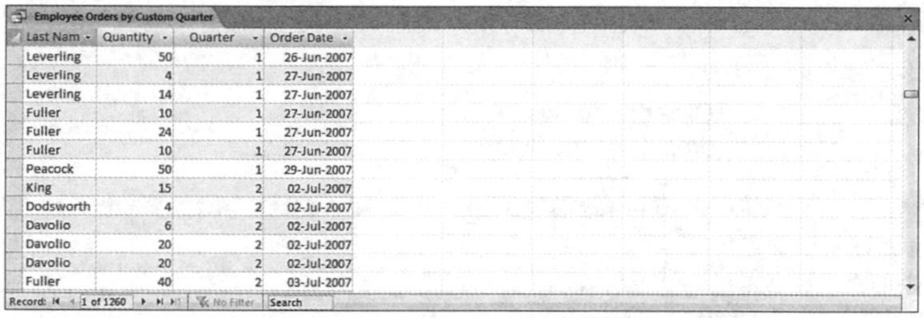

Figure 14.29
The dynaset produced by the query in Figure 14.28.

Figure 14.30 shows a PivotTable view of the query that uses the following layout:

- The `LastName` field is the row field.
- The calculated `Quarter` field is the column field.
- The quantity field is the detail data field with an AutoCalc `Sum` operation applied and details hidden.

Employee Orders by Custom Quarter

Drop Filter Fields Here

Last Name	1 Sum of Quantity	2 Sum of Quantity	3 Sum of Quantity	4 Sum of Quantity	Grand Total Sum of Quantity
Buchanan	370	471	442	777	2,060
Callahan	423	521	889	1,398	3,231
Davolio	617	1,215	1,298	1,315	4,445
Dodsworth	221	129	394	851	1,595
Fuller	912	738	517	1,041	3,208
King	571	984	153	900	2,608
Leverling	1,161	564	1,575	1,985	5,285
Peacock	951	1,314	1,200	1,675	5,140
Suyama	485	211	722	578	1,996
Grand Total	5,711	6,147	7,190	10,520	29,568

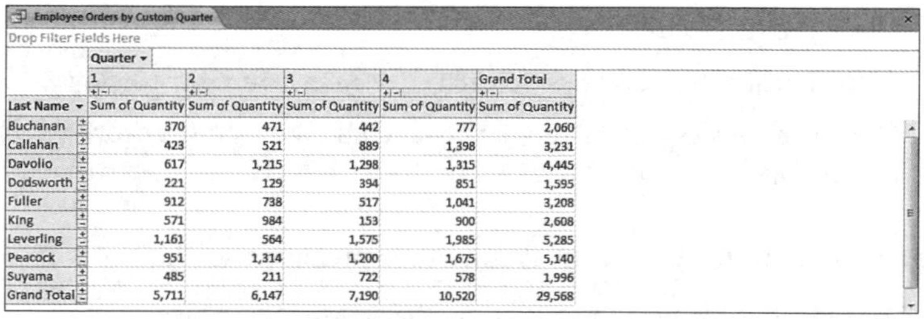

Figure 14.30
A two-dimensional PivotTable that uses a calculated query field to display employee orders by quarter.

14

Filtering a PivotTable

PivotTables are a great way to bring a large table down to size. However, even a PivotTable might still give you too much information. In the Northwind database, for example, the Customers table has more than 90 records, which is still a sizable amount of data to display as a row or column field in a PivotTable. To truly narrow the focus of your PivotTables, you need to *filter* the data to show just the items you need to see. Of course, you can do this at the query level by using criteria. However, Access PivotTables also come with a number of features that enable you to filter the items while viewing the PivotTable. The next four sections take you through these filtering features.

Using the PivotTable AutoFilters

Each field you add to a PivotTable comes with an AutoFilter feature that enables you to display only selected items from that field. For example, consider the Customer Order By Category PivotTable shown earlier in Figure 14.21. As shown in Figure 14.31, the Company Name and Category Name field captions are actually drop-down lists. You use these lists to choose which items in each field you want to see in the PivotTable.

Click the arrows to
drop down the lists

Figure 14.31
Each field caption in a PivotTable contains a drop-down list of the unique items in that field.

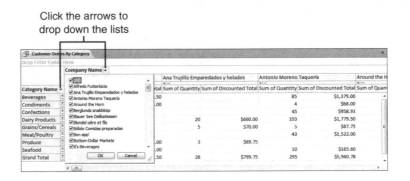

Here are the steps to follow to filter a PivotTable using an AutoFilter list:

1. Drop down the AutoFilter list for the field you want to filter.
2. Clear the (All) check box.
3. Activate the check box beside each field item you want to view.
4. Click OK. Access filters the data to include only those records that match the activated field items.

When you want to remove the AutoFilter, you have two choices:

- Activate the (All) check box in the field's AutoFilter list.
- Choose Design, AutoFilter.

Displaying Only the Top or Bottom Items

Another way to filter the PivotTable data is to show only the extreme values in the table. For example, given the Products Orders by Day of the Week PivotTable shown earlier in Figure 14.27, you might want to know the top 10 products in terms of units sold, or you might want to see the bottom 5 products.

Before setting this up, you need to decide whether you want to filter based on the grand total of the field or on a single value in a field:

- To filter based on the grand total, make sure the PivotTable is displaying the Grand Total field.

> **NOTE**
> You toggle a field's Grand Total item on and off by clicking the field's caption to select the field and then choosing the Design, Subtotal command.

- To filter based on a single value in a field, use that field's AutoFilter list to display only the value you want to use.

With that done, follow these general steps to display the top or bottom values in a PivotTable:

1. Click the field caption to select that field.
2. Choose Design, Show Top/Bottom.
3. Choose one of the following commands:
   - **Show Only the <u>T</u>op**—Choose this command to return the top values.
   - **Show Only the <u>B</u>ottom**—Choose this command to return the bottom values.
4. In the submenu that appears, you have three choices:
   - Choose a specific number (such as 1, 2, or 5).
   - Choose a specific percentage (such as 5%, 10%, or 25%).
   - Choose <u>O</u>ther to display the Properties dialog box with the Filter and Group tab displayed, as shown in Figure 14.32. The Filtering group offers three controls for specifying a custom top or bottom filter:

     <u>D</u>isplay The—Choose either Top or Bottom.

     Ite<u>m</u>s—Choose a number from the list or type a number into the box. If this number represents a percentage, activate the % check box.

14

> Viewing the top or bottom percentages is useful when you need to analyze data across divisions, regions, or departments where the actual numbers are wildly different. By comparing percentages, you can easily find the top (or bottom) performers without having to factor in the differences in the actual values.

Based **On**—Use this list to choose the data field on which the calculation will be based.

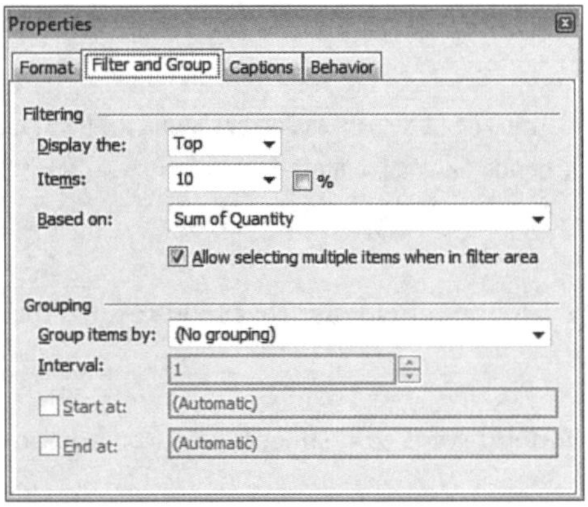

Figure 14.32
Use the controls in the Filtering group to specify a custom top or bottom filter for your PivotTable.

For example, suppose you want to filter the Products Orders by Day of the Week PivotTable to show the top 10 products for Monday. To do this, you use AutoFilter on the Day of the Week field to show only the Monday item, and then you choose Design, Show Top/Bottom, Show Only the <u>T</u>op, <u>1</u>0. Figure 14.33 shows the resulting PivotTable.

Figure 14.33
This PivotTable shows the top 10 products in terms of unit sales on Monday.

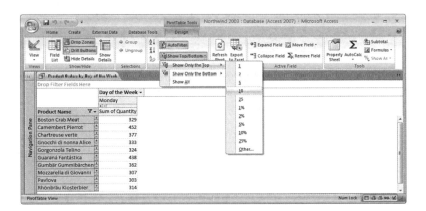

To revert to viewing all the items, you have two choices:

- Choose Design, Show Top/Bottom, Show <u>A</u>ll.
- Choose Design, AutoFilter.

Grouping Field Items

Another way you can filter items is to organize them into groups. For example, you might want to combine customers based on the first letter of the company name, or you might want to group a date field by month or quarter.

Here are the steps to follow to group a field's items:

1. Right-click the caption of the field you want to work with and then click <u>P</u>roperties. Access displays the Properties dialog box.

2. Click the Filter and Group tab.

3. Use the controls in the Grouping section to set up the group. How you do this depends on the data type of the field:

   - **Text**—In the Group Items By list, choose Prefix Characters. Use the Interval spin box to specify the number of characters at the start of each item to use for the grouping. For example, if you choose an interval of 1, Access groups the field items based on the first letter; if you choose 2, Access groups the items based on the first two letters.

   - **Numeric**—In the Group Items By list, choose Numeric Interval. Use the Interval spin box to enter the size of the grouping interval (for example, entering 5 combines 1–5, 6–10, and so on). Use the Start At box to specify the starting point (that is, the first item will be every number up to but not including the Start At value). Use the End At box to specify the ending point (that is, the last item will be every number after but not including the End At value).

   - **Date**—In the Group Items By list, choose one of the following: Years, Quarters, Months, Weeks, Days, Hours, Minutes, or Seconds. Use the Interval spin box to enter the size of the date interval. For example, if you chose Months and you entered 2 as the interval, Access groups the items into two-month ranges. Use the Start At and End At boxes to enter the starting and ending dates for the items to include in the grouping.

To remove the grouping, display the Properties dialog box once again, click the Filter and Group tab, and then choose (No Grouping) in the Group Items By list.

Adding a Filter Field

The final way you can filter a PivotTable is to add a filter field to the PivotTable layout. This creates a kind of third dimension PivotTable because the filter field will be different than the row and column fields. For example, the Products Orders by Day of the Week

14

PivotTable (see Figure 14.27) uses ProductName as the row field and Day of the Week as the column field. Suppose you want to filter the data to show only those products from a specific category, such as Beverages? To do that, you need to add a third nondata field: a filter field.

Filter fields filter your data the same way criteria do. When you include a filter field in your PivotTable, Access creates a drop-down list that contains the unique items from the field. You use these items to filter the list and display just the data associated with the selected filter field values. (This is also known as *slicing* the data. Think of a scientist examining a cross section of some tissue or a mineral.)

To filter the PivotTable, follow these steps:

1. Add the field you want to use as the filter to the query, if you haven't already done this.
2. In the PivotTable view, display the PivotTable Field List, click the field you want to use as the filter, select Filter Area in the drop-down list, and click <u>A</u>dd To.
3. Drop down the filter field list.
4. Clear the (All) check box.
5. Activate the check box beside each filter field item you want to view (see Figure 14.34).
6. Click OK. Access filters the data to include only those records that match the filter field item and then updates the table.

When you want to remove the filter, activate the (All) check box.

Figure 14.34
Activate the check box beside each item in the filter field that you want to view.

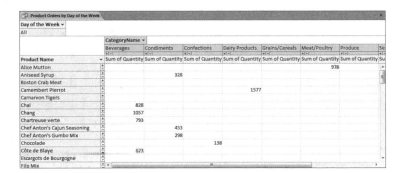

Pivoting a PivotTable

In their most basic form, PivotTables consolidate large amounts of complex data into a comprehensive, readable summary. But the real beauty of PivotTables is how they enable you to view your data from different angles. You can see the numbers in an entirely different way simply by dragging fields to different table locations. This is called *pivoting*.

PivotTables pivot because the data area acts as a kind of fulcrum around which you can move row, column, and filter fields. There are two main pivoting actions you can perform:

- You can move a field to a different area of the PivotTable. For example, you can move a filter field into the row field area.
- You can change the field order within an area. If you have two row fields, for example, you can reverse their position in the table.

The next couple of sections show you how to use data pivoting to change the table view.

Moving a Field to a Different Area

Just because you created a PivotTable with particular captions in the row, column, and filter fields, that doesn't mean you have to leave these captions where they are. Keep in mind that the row, column, and filter fields are only facets of your data. By their very nature (that is, fields with a limited set of distinct text, numeric, or date items), these fields can change places with each other to enable you to view your data in different ways. So if the PivotTable doesn't show your data in quite the way you want, you can easily move any of the row, column, or filter fields to a different area of the table.

For example, the PivotTable view shown earlier in Figure 14.34 shows the product sales by day of the week. You can filter the data using the `Category Name` field, but suppose you want to see the quantities by category and you want to filter everything by day of the week. In other words, you want to see the `Category Name` field as a column field and the `Day of the Week` field as a filter field.

To do this, use your mouse to click and drag the `Category Name` filter field caption into the column field drop area, and then click and drag the `Day of the Week` column field caption into the filter field drop area. Figure 14.35 shows the PivotTable view with the `Category Name` and `Day of the Week` fields reversed.

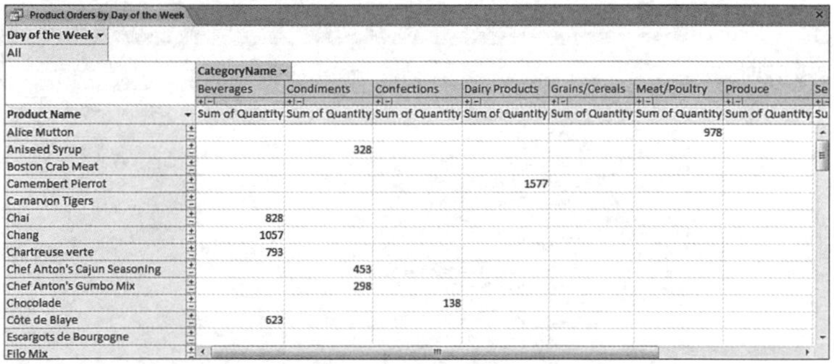

Figure 14.35
You can move a field into a different drop zone by dragging the field caption and dropping it in the zone.

Changing the Field Order

In the same way that you can take a three-dimensional object and rotate it in space to see different sides and facets, so too can you rotate a three-dimensional PivotTable to see different views of your data. Rotating means that you take a multiple-field area in the PivotTable and change the order of the fields.

For example, consider the PivotTable shown in Figure 14.36. This layout breaks down each product by the day of the week on which the order was placed and displays the Quantity by CustomerID. For the row area, you can think of the Product Name items as the main categories and the Day of the Week items as the subcategories.

Figure 14.36
This PivotTable view has two row fields.

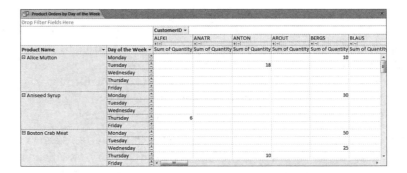

Suppose, instead, that you prefer to focus on the Day of the Week field and view the various Product Names as subcategories. You can do this just by changing the order of the field captions within the row area. Use your mouse to click and drag the Day of the Week caption and drop it to the left of the Product Name caption. (Or you can click and drag the Product Name caption and drop it to the right of the Day of the Week caption.) As you can see in Figure 14.37, the table now breaks down each day of the week by product name.

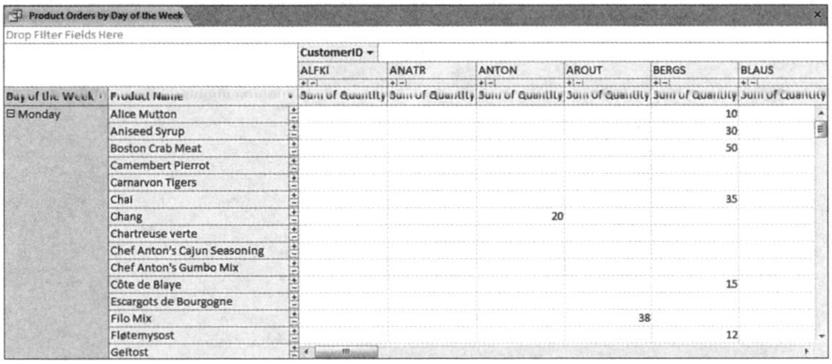

Figure 14.37
You can "rotate" the table by moving field captions within an area.

Formatting a PivotTable

For your final PivotTable chore, you look at the various ways you can format the table to make it look its best. You can format the PivotTable's colors, fonts, numeric formats, alignment, and more.

There are two methods you can use to format the PivotTable's cells:

- Click any cell in the field you want to work with and then use the buttons and lists in the Home tab.

- Right-click any item in a field and then click Properties. In the Properties dialog box, use the controls in the Format tab (see Figure 14.38) to change the field's font, colors, and other formatting.

Figure 14.38
Use either the toolbar or the Format tab to format a field's cells.

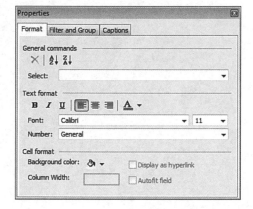

If you just want to format a field's caption, right-click the caption, click Properties, and then use the Captions tab to format or change the caption text.

From Here

→ To learn how to add a PivotChart (a chart representation of a PivotTable) to a form, **see** "Creating a PivotChart Form," **p. 108**. (Chapter 5)

→ To learn how to insert a PivotChart in a report, **see** "Creating a PivotChart Report," **p. 194**. (Chapter 9)

→ For information on creating calculated query columns, **see** "Setting Up a Calculated Column," **p. 239**. (Chapter 11)

→ For more details about the Access functions you can use in your expressions, **see** "Using the Built-In Functions," **p. 241**. (Chapter 11)

→ In a relational database, PivotTable queries almost always require linked multiple tables. To learn how to create multiple-table queries, **see** "Working with Multiple Tables in a Query," **p. 271**. (Chapter 12)

14

Querying with SQL Statements

15

When you build an Access query, what you're really doing is building a Structured Query Language (SQL) statement. In other words, the Query Design view is just a front end to help you construct an SQL (pronounced *ESS-kew-ell*, although many people say it as *SEE-kwul*) statement without having to know anything about SQL syntax.

Fortunately, in a business context the majority of query needs are adequately fulfilled using the Design view (or even one of the query wizards), so business users don't often need to learn SQL. However, some aspects of querying are difficult or impossible to perform without going "under the hood" to write or edit an SQL statement. For example, often you need to include the results of some other query as a "table" in a second query. Instead of going to the trouble of creating the initial query, you can include the dynaset directly into the second query as a "subquery." However, the only way to do that is to use an SQL statement. Also, certain types of theta joins require modifying the SQL statement. Finally, SQL is also a valuable troubleshooting tool if your query isn't returning the result set you expected.

This chapter tells you how to use SQL. You learn the basic syntax for select and action queries, and you learn how to create subqueries, theta joins, and other SQL-only queries.

Viewing the SQL Statement

Before getting to the SQL specifics, let's first see how the Design view and the underlying SQL are related. Figure 15.1 shows a basic query using the

Northwind database's Customers table. The query displays the CompanyName and ContactName fields, and the criterion "USA" is applied to the Country field.

> **NOTE**
>
> As I mentioned in Chapter 10, "Creating a Basic Query," I'm going to use the older (Access 2003) Northwind sample data for the querying chapters. You can download the sample database from my website:
>
>   www.mcfedries.com/Access2007Forms

Figure 15.1
A simple query on the Customers table.

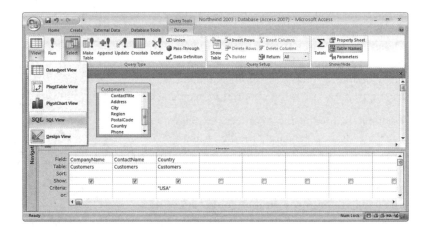

To view the underlying SQL statement for this query, choose the Design tab, click the bottom half of the View split button, and then click SQL View (see Figure 15.1). Figure 15.2 shows the SQL statement created by the query shown in Figure 15.1. Editing this statement changes how the query appears in the Design view, and modifying the Design view changes the SQL statement.

Figure 15.2
The SQL statement generated by the query shown in Figure 15.1.

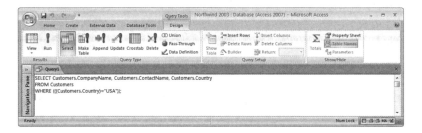

Using SQL to Perform a Select Query

As you've seen, the most basic type of query is the select query that returns records from one or more tables based on the fields you choose and the criteria you apply to those fields. This is called a *select* query not only because you use it to select certain records, but also because it's based on the SQL language's SELECT statement (refer to Figure 15.2). SELECT is the SQL "verb" that you'll see and work with most often, so the following sections give you a detailed look at its syntax.

Understanding the SELECT Statement

The SELECT statement is used to create a dynaset based on the tables, fields, criteria, and other clauses specified in the statement. Here's the basic syntax of the SELECT statement:

```
SELECT [ALL | DISTINCT | DISTINCTROW] [TOP n [PERCENT]] select_list
FROM table_name
WHERE criteria
ORDER BY field_list [ASC | DESC];
```

SELECT ... select list	The field names included in the query. If a field name includes a space, surround the name with square brackets ([and]).
FROM table_name	The table included in the query. If a table name includes a space, surround the name with square brackets ([and]).
WHERE criteria	The criteria applied to one or more fields.
ORDER BY field_list	The sort order of the dynaset.

The next few sections take you through the details of the SELECT, FROM, WHERE, and ORDER BY keywords.

> **TIP**
> If you want to include all a table's fields in the query, the easiest way is to use an asterisk (*) in place of specific field names as the select_list argument.

The SELECT Verb

All SQL SELECT statements begin with the SELECT keyword. In the simplest case, SELECT is followed by the select_list, which is a list of field names, separated by commas. To relate this to the Query Design view, specifying a field in the select_list is the same as adding the field to the criteria pane and leaving the field's Show cell check box activated.

When Access generates the SQL statement based on the existing query design, it always precedes each field name with the table name, separated by a dot, as in this example:

```
SELECT Customers.CompanyName, Customers.ContactName
```

However, if you're building your SQL statement from scratch, in most cases you don't need to include the table name:

```
SELECT CompanyName, ContactName
```

> ┌─ C A U T I O N ───
> You must include the table names only when you're working with a multiple-table query and a field
> name you're using with SELECT exists in more than one table. In this case, you have to specify the
> table name; otherwise, Access generates an error. For more details on multiple-table SQL SELECT
> statements, see "Using SQL with Multiple-Table Queries," later in this chapter.

If a field name includes a space, you need to surround the name with square brackets:

```
SELECT [Company Name], [Contact Name]
```

The SELECT keyword supports three optional modifiers—called *predicates* in SQL:

- ALL—This tells Access to return all the records specified by the rest of the statement. This is the default.

- DISTINCT—This tells Access to look for records that contain duplicate data in the fields specified by the *select_list* argument and then to display only the first of those records in the dynaset. Adding the DISTINCT predicate is the same as setting the query's Unique Values property to Yes.

- DISTINCTROW—This tells Access to look for records that contain duplicate data in *all* the fields in the underlying table (not just the ones included in the query) and then to display only the first of those records in the dynaset. Adding the DISTINCTROW predicate is the same as setting the query's Unique Records property to Yes.

The SELECT keyword also supports the optional TOP *n* [PERCENT] predicate, which tells Access to return only the first *n* selected records in the dynaset. For example, the following returns the first 10 records:

```
SELECT TOP 10 CompanyName, ContactName
```

If you include the PERCENT modifier, Access returns only the first *n* percent of the selected records:

```
SELECT TOP 5 PERCENT CompanyName, ContactName
```

Using the TOP *n* [PERCENT] predicate is the same as selecting a number or percentage in the query Design tab's Top Values list.

The FROM **Clause**

An SQL statement won't work until you combine the SELECT portion with at least the FROM clause, which specifies the name of the underlying table (or query):

```
SELECT CompanyName, ContactName
FROM Customers;
```

Adding the FROM clause is the same as specifying the table name in the Table cells of the Query Design view's criteria grid.

The WHERE **Clause**

A SELECT statement that includes just the FROM clause returns all the records from the under-lying table (unless you include a SELECT predicate such as DISTINCT or TOP). The real meat of a query is the criteria you use to filter the resulting dynaset. In SQL, you specify the criteria by including the WHERE clause:

```
WHERE criteria
```

Here, criteria is a valid Access expression, which usually takes the following general form:

```
WHERE field_name operator value
```

In this case, field_name is the name of the field to which the criteria are applied, operator is any operator (such as =, <>, or Like), and value is the value (literal, function result, and so on) to apply to the field.

For example, if you want to view only those customers whose Country field contains USA, you use the following statement:

```
SELECT CompanyName, ContactName
FROM Customers
WHERE Country = "USA";
```

Adding the WHERE clause is the same as specifying an expression in a field's Criteria cell in the Query Design view.

> **NOTE** You'll notice in this chapter that all my SQL statements end with a semicolon (;). This is an old habit of mine, and it comes from the fact that some database systems enable you to run multiple SQL statements at a time. In such cases, you use the semicolon to designate the end of each statement. Access can only run one SQL statement at a time, which means it doesn't require a semicolon at the end of a SQL statement, so feel free to leave it off. However, Access *does* add a semicolon to the SQL statements that it generates automatically when you build a query in Design view. Why? Probably because some people use Access to generate SQL statements that they then paste into other sys-tems, so including semicolons can prevent problems if the other system requires them.

The ORDER BY **Clause**

The ORDER BY clause specifies the field or fields used to sort the resulting dynaset:

```
ORDER BY field_list [ASC | DESC]
```

An ascending sort is the default, so you don't need to include the ASC predicate; use the DESC predicate when you want a descending sort.

For example, to sort the Customers query on the City field and then the CompanyName field, you use the following:

```
SELECT CompanyName, ContactName
FROM Customers
WHERE Country = "USA"
ORDER BY City, CompanyName;
```

Adding the ORDER BY clause is the same as choosing either Ascending or Descending in a field's Sort cell in the Query Design view.

Using SQL with Multiple-Table Queries

When you use two related tables in a query, Access creates a join between the tables based on a common field. Recall from Chapter 12, "Working with Multiple-Table Queries," that there are four join types: inner, outer (both left and right), self, and theta. You can create all four join types using SQL and, as you'll see a bit later, certain theta joins can only be built using SQL.

→ For more information about joins, **see** "Understanding Join Lines," **p. 267**. (Chapter 12)

Using SQL to Create Inner Joins

To create an inner join on two tables, use the following version of the FROM clause:

```
FROM table1 INNER JOIN table2 ON table1.field = table2.field
```

Here, *table1* and *table2* are the names of the two tables you want to join. In a one-to-many relationship, *table1* is the "one" table and *table2* is the "many" table. Also, *table1.field* and *table2.field* are the common fields in each table.

For example, the following SELECT statement sets up an inner join on Northwind's Orders and Order Details tables:

```
SELECT Orders.OrderID, Orders.CustomerID, [Order Details].Quantity
FROM Orders
INNER JOIN [Order Details] ON Orders.OrderID = [Order Details].OrderID;
```

Things start to get complicated when you have three or more related tables in a query. SQL handles this by creating inner joins on inner joins. For example, here's the general syntax for a three-table query:

```
FROM table1 INNER JOIN (table2 INNER JOIN table3 ON
table1.field1 = table2.field1) ON table1.field2 = table3.field2
```

For example, here's an SQL statement that sets up an inner join on the Products, Orders, and Order Details tables:

```
3ELECT Orders.OrderID, Products.ProductName, [Order Details].Quantity
FROM Products INNER JOIN (Orders INNER JOIN [Order Details]
ON Orders.OrderID = [Order Details].OrderID)
ON Products.ProductID = [Order Details].ProductID;
```

The complexity of such statements means that you're almost always better off just adding the related table to the Query Design view and letting Access build the SQL for you. If you then need to tweak the SQL, you can choose Design, click the lower half o the View split button, and then choose SQL View.

Using SQL to Create Outer Joins

When you use SQL to create an outer join—a join that includes every record from one of the tables and only those records from the other table in which the related fields match each other exactly—you need to differentiate between the two types of outer join—left and right.

In a one-to-many relationship, a left-outer join includes every record from the "one" (left) side and only those matching records from the "many" (right) side. In SQL, you specify a left-outer join in the following general way:

```
FROM table1 LEFT JOIN table2 ON table1.field = table2.field
```

For example, suppose you want to see a list of all customers who haven't yet placed an order. In the Northwind database, the Customers table is in a one-to-many relationship with the Orders table. The idea is to return all the records from the Customers table and the matching records from Orders table (so it must be a left-outer join) and then look for those "extra" records where the Orders table's `CustomerID` field is `Null`. The following `SELECT` statement sets up a left-outer join on the Customers and Orders tables and returns those where `Orders.CustomerID` is `Null`:

```
SELECT Customers.CompanyName
FROM Customers
LEFT JOIN Orders ON Customers.CustomerID = Orders.CustomerID
WHERE Orders.CustomerID Is Null;
```

A right-outer join includes every record from the "many" (right) side and only those matching records from the "one" (left) side. Here's the general SQL syntax for a right-outer join:

```
FROM table1 RIGHT JOIN table2 ON table1.field = table2.field
```

For example, suppose you want to return a list of products that have not been assigned a category. The Categories table is in a one-to-many relationship with the Products table. You need to return all the records from the Products table and just the matching records from the Categories table (so it must be a right-outer join) and then look for those records where `Categories.CategoryID` is `Null`. Here's a `SELECT` statement that does this:

```
SELECT Products.ProductName
FROM Categories
RIGHT JOIN Products ON Categories.CategoryID = Products.CategoryID
WHERE Categories.CategoryID Is Null;
```

Using SQL to Create Self-Joins

A self-join is an inner join on a second copy of the same table. In the Query Design view, you add a second copy of the table and then set up a join between by relating one field with another field that contains the same type of information.

```
FROM table INNER JOIN table AS table_alias ON table.field1 = table_alias.field2
```

This is just an inner join, except that the second table is the first table used with an *alias*, a name that's different from the one used by the original table.

For example, the Northwind Employees table has an `EmployeeID` field that lists the identification number of each employee, as well as a `ReportsTo` field that lists the identification number of the employee's manager. If you want to see the records of those employees who have people reporting to them, you use a second copy of the Employees table and join the

`EmployeeID` and `ReportsTo` fields:

```
SELECT DISTINCT Employees.FirstName, Employees.LastName
FROM Employees INNER JOIN
Employees AS Employees2 ON Employees.EmployeeID = Employees2.ReportTo;
```

Using SQL to Create Theta Joins

A theta join is an inner join created when the data in two fields from two tables is related via some comparison operator other than equals (=). For example, a *not-equal join* relates data using the not-equal operator (<>).

For example, suppose you want to see those orders where the unit price on the order differs from the unit price of the product. In this case, you not only join the tables on the related `ProductID` fields, but you also add a not-equal join on the `UnitPrice` fields. Here's a `SELECT` statement that does this:

```
SELECT [Order Details].OrderID,Products.Productname,
➥[Order Details].UnitPrice,Products.UnitPrice
FROM Products INNER JOIN [Order Details] ON
Products.ProductID = [Order Details].ProductID AND
[Order Details].UnitPrice <> Products.UnitPrice;
```

Figure 15.3 shows the resulting dynaset.

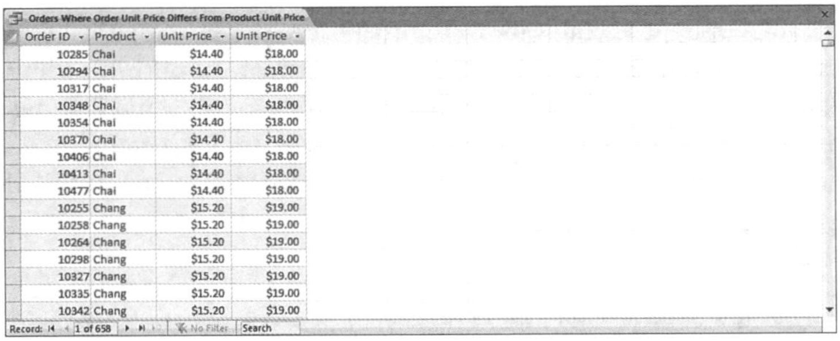
Orders Where Order Unit Price Differs From Product Unit Price

Order ID	Product	Unit Price	Unit Price
10285	Chai	$14.40	$18.00
10294	Chai	$14.40	$18.00
10317	Chai	$14.40	$18.00
10348	Chai	$14.40	$18.00
10354	Chai	$14.40	$18.00
10370	Chai	$14.40	$18.00
10406	Chai	$14.40	$18.00
10413	Chai	$14.40	$18.00
10477	Chai	$14.40	$18.00
10255	Chang	$15.20	$19.00
10258	Chang	$15.20	$19.00
10264	Chang	$15.20	$19.00
10298	Chang	$15.20	$19.00
10327	Chang	$15.20	$19.00
10335	Chang	$15.20	$19.00
10342	Chang	$15.20	$19.00

Figure 15.3
The results of an SQL not-equal join that returns orders where the unit price on the order differs from the unit price of the product.

> **CAUTION**
>
> After you add the not-equal join to the SQL statement, Access no longer has any way to display the query in the Design View because the latter has no equivalent of a not-equal join. If you try to switch to Design view, Access displays an error message and then returns you to the SQL view.

Finding Customers Where the Ship Address Is Different from the Customer Address

As another example of a theta join, suppose you want to extract from the Orders table those records where the shipping address is different from the address specified in the Customers table. To do this, you need to join Customers and Order on the related

`CustomerID` field, and you need to create a not-equal join on the Orders table's `ShipAddress` field and the Customers table's `Address` field. Here's a `SELECT` statement that does this:

```
SELECT DISTINCT Customers.CompanyName,Orders.ShipAddress,Customers.Address
FROM Customers INNER JOIN Orders ON
Customers.CustomerID = Orders.CustomerID AND
Orders.ShipAddress <> Customer.Address;
```

Figure 15.4 shows the dynaset that results.

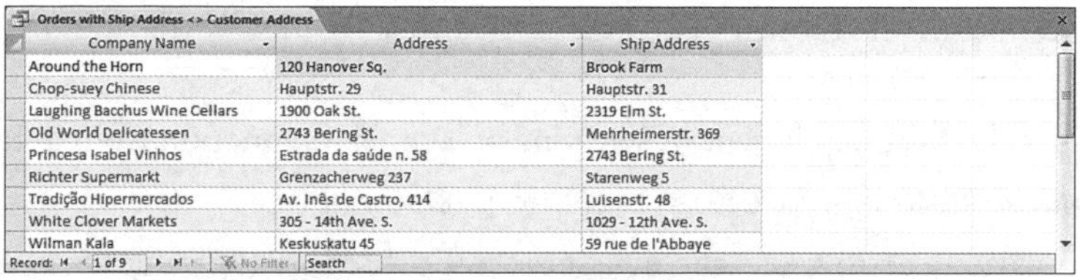

Orders with Ship Address <> Customer Address

Company Name	Address	Ship Address
Around the Horn	120 Hanover Sq.	Brook Farm
Chop-suey Chinese	Hauptstr. 29	Hauptstr. 31
Laughing Bacchus Wine Cellars	1900 Oak St.	2319 Elm St.
Old World Delicatessen	2743 Bering St.	Mehrheimerstr. 369
Princesa Isabel Vinhos	Estrada da saúde n. 58	2743 Bering St.
Richter Supermarkt	Grenzacherweg 237	Starenweg 5
Tradição Hipermercados	Av. Inês de Castro, 414	Luisenstr. 48
White Clover Markets	305 - 14th Ave. S.	1029 - 12th Ave. S.
Wilman Kala	Keskuskatu 45	59 rue de l'Abbaye

Record: 1 of 9 No Filter Search

Figure 15.4
The results of an SQL not-equal join that returns orders where the shipping address is different from the customer address.

Adding a Calculated Column to the `SELECT` Statement

To include a calculated column as part of a `SELECT` statement, you add the expression directly into the *`select_list`* argument and also include an alias for the column's name:

```
SELECT expression AS alias
```

➔ For the details of calculated columns, **see** "Setting Up a Calculated Column," **p. 239**. (Chapter 11)

For example, the following `SELECT` statement calculates the extended price using the Order Details table's `UnitPrice`, `Quantity`, and `Discount` fields and displays the results in a column named Extended Price:

```
SELECT OrderID, ProductID, UnitPrice, Quantity, Discount,
[UnitPrice]*[Quantity]*(1-[Discount]) AS [Extended Price]
FROM [Order Details];
```

Figure 15.5 shows the dynaset that Access generates.

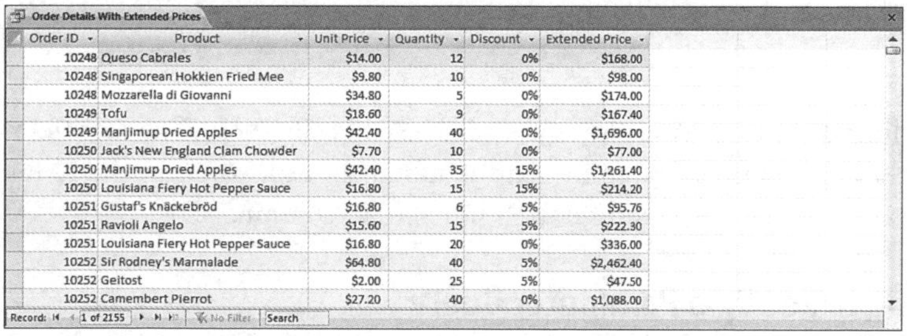

Order Details With Extended Prices

Order ID	Product	Unit Price	Quantity	Discount	Extended Price
10248	Queso Cabrales	$14.00	12	0%	$168.00
10248	Singaporean Hokkien Fried Mee	$9.80	10	0%	$98.00
10248	Mozzarella di Giovanni	$34.80	5	0%	$174.00
10249	Tofu	$18.60	9	0%	$167.40
10249	Manjimup Dried Apples	$42.40	40	0%	$1,696.00
10250	Jack's New England Clam Chowder	$7.70	10	0%	$77.00
10250	Manjimup Dried Apples	$42.40	35	15%	$1,261.40
10250	Louisiana Fiery Hot Pepper Sauce	$16.80	15	15%	$214.20
10251	Gustaf's Knäckebröd	$16.80	6	5%	$95.76
10251	Ravioli Angelo	$15.60	15	5%	$222.30
10251	Louisiana Fiery Hot Pepper Sauce	$16.80	20	0%	$336.00
10252	Sir Rodney's Marmalade	$64.80	40	5%	$2,462.40
10252	Geitost	$2.00	25	5%	$47.50
10252	Camembert Pierrot	$27.20	40	0%	$1,088.00

Record: 1 of 2155 No Filter Search

Figure 15.5
For a calculated column, insert an expression directly into the `select_list` and supply an alias for the column.

Using SQL to Total and Group Records

Including totals in your SQL statement is similar to including calculated columns. That is, you add the aggregate function expression to the *select_list* and specify an alias for the column:

```
SELECT aggregate_function(field) AS alias
```

For example, if you want to return the sum of the Products table's UnitsInStock field, you use the following SELECT statement:

```
SELECT Sum(UnitsInStock) AS [Total In Stock]
FROM Products;
```

This is the SQL equivalent of selecting an aggregate function from a field's Total column.

→ To learn about totals queries, **see** "Creating a Totals Query," **p. 287**. (Chapter 13)

If you also need to group the dynaset records based on the values in one or more fields, add the GROUP BY clause to the SELECT statement:

```
GROUP BY field_list [HAVING aggregate_function(field) criteria]
```

Here, *field_list* is the list of fields to use for the groupings. Use the optional HAVING clause when you want to apply criteria to a totals column.

For example, suppose you want the sum of the Products table's UnitsInStock field grouped by CategoryID, and you want to see only those categories where the sum is greater than 300. Here's a SELECT statement that does this (see Figure 15.6 for the results):

```
SELECT Sum(UnitsInStock) AS [Total In Stock], CategoryID
FROM Products
GROUP BY CategoryID
HAVING Sum(UnitsInStock) > 300;
```

Figure 15.6
The dynaset produced by an SQL statement that uses a totals column and the GROUP BY and HAVING clauses.

Adding the GROUP BY clause is the same as choosing Group By in a field's Total cell. Adding the HAVING clause is the equivalent of adding an expression to the Criteria cell of a field that has an aggregate function selected in its Total column.

Using SQL to Set Up a Parameter Query

If you want Access to prompt you to enter a parameter for a field, enter the prompt text in the WHERE clause:

```
WHERE field = [prompt_text]
```

→ For the full details on parameter queries, **see** "Running Parameter Queries," **p. 302**. (Chapter 13)

For example, the following SELECT statement prompts the user for a value to use as the criteria for the Products table's CategoryName field:

```
SELECT CategoryName, ProductName
FROM Categories
INNER JOIN Products ON Categories.CategoryID = Products.CategoryID
WHERE CategoryName = [Enter the product category:];
```

The Full SQL SELECT Syntax

For reference, here's the full syntax of the SELECT statement, as discussed in this section:

```
SELECT [ALL | DISTINCT | DISTINCTROW] [TOP n [PERCENT]] select_list
aggregate_function(field) AS alias
FROM table1
[[INNER | LEFT | RIGHT] JOIN table2 ON join_criteria]
WHERE criteria
GROUP BY field_list [HAVING aggregate_function(field) criteria]
ORDER BY field_list [ASC | DESC];
```

SELECT ... select list	The field names included in the query.
aggregate_function(field) AS alias	A totals column that uses the specified aggregate_function.
FROM table1	The main table included in the query.
INNER	LEFT	RIGHT JOIN table2	The table related to table1.
ON join_criteria	The criteria that specify the join between table1 and table2.
WHERE criteria	The criteria applied to one or more fields.
GROUP BY field_list	The fields used to group the records.
HAVING aggregate_function(field) criteria	The criteria applied to the totals column.
ORDER BY field_list	The sort order of the dynaset.

Using SQL to Perform Action Queries

Back in Chapter 13, "Creating Advanced Queries," you learned how to work with queries that performed some action on the data in the underlying table. These so-called *action queries* come in four varieties: update, delete, make-table, and append. You can perform all four types using SQL statements, as the following sections show.

→ To learn more about action queries, **see** "Running Action Queries," **p. 304**. (Chapter 13)

> **CAUTION**
>
> Remember that action queries such as update and delete are dangerous because they make irreversible changes to the underlying data. Exercise caution by setting up and running a SELECT query first to make sure you're working with the correct data. You should also consider making a temporary copy of any table that contains particularly important data. (Click the table in the Navigation pane, press Ctrl+C, and then press Ctrl+V. In the Paste Table As dialog box, edit the Table Name for the backup table, make sure the Structure and Data option is clicked, and then click OK.)

Using SQL to Perform an Update Query

An update query modifies the values in one or more fields and optionally restricts the scope of the updating to those records that satisfy some criteria. In SQL, you build an update query by using the UPDATE verb to construct a statement with the following syntax:

```
UPDATE table
SET field1=value1 [,field2=value2…]
[WHERE criteria];
```

UPDATE *table*	The table that contains the data you want to update.
SET *field1=value1* [,*field2=value2…*]	The new values you want to assign to the specified fields.
WHERE *criteria*	The criteria that define which records will be updated.

For example, in Northwind's Products table, suppose you want to increase the values in the UnitPrice field by 5% for the Beverages category (CategoryID = 1). This is the same as multiplying the current UnitPrice values by 1.05, so the UPDATE statement looks like this:

```
UPDATE Products
SET UnitPrice = [UnitPrice]*1.05
WHERE CategoryID = 1;
```

This is the same as using the Design view to choose Query, Update Query and then entering the following expression in the Update To cell of the UnitPrice field:

```
[UnitPrice] * 1.05
```

Using SQL to Perform a Delete Query

A delete query removes records from a table and optionally restricts the scope of the deletion to those records that satisfy some criteria. If you don't include criteria, Access deletes every record in the specified table.

In SQL, you build a delete query by using the DELETE verb to construct a statement with the following syntax:

```
DELETE
FROM table
[WHERE criteria];
```

FROM *table*	The table that contains the records you want to delete.
WHERE *criteria*	The criteria that define which records will be deleted.

For example, if you want to delete those records in the Products table where the SupplierID value is 1, you use the following SQL statement:

```
DELETE
FROM Products
WHERE SupplierID=1;
```

Using SQL to Perform a Make-Table Query

A make-table query takes one or more fields from a table, optionally filters the records using criteria, and then inserts the resulting records into a new table. In SQL, you build a make-table query using the SELECT verb with the INTO predicate:

```
SELECT [ALL | DISTINCT] select_list
INTO table2
FROM table1
[WHERE criteria];
```

SELECT [ALL | DISTINCT] *select list*	The fields to include in the new table.
INTO *table2*	The name of the new table.
FROM *table1*	The table that contains the records you want to include into the new table.
WHERE *criteria*	The criteria that define which records will be included in the new table.

For example, if you want to create a new table named Orders From 2007 and insert into it those records from the Orders table that were placed in 2007, the following SQL statement does the job (note the pound signs [#] around the dates, which are required by Access even in SQL statements):

```
SELECT *
INTO [Orders From 2007]
FROM Orders
WHERE OrderDate Between #1/1/2007# And #12/31/2007#;
```

Using SQL to Perform an Append Query

An append query takes records from an existing table and inserts them into another existing table. In SQL, you build an append query using the INSERT INTO verb:

```
INSERT INTO table2 (append_list)
SELECT [ALL | DISTINCT] select_list
FROM table1
[WHERE criteria];
```

INSERT INTO *table2 (append_list)*	The name of the table into which you want the records appended.
(append_list)	The fields in *table2* that correspond to the *select_list* fields from *table1*.
SELECT [ALL | DISTINCT] *select list*	The field names of the data to be appended into *table2*.
FROM *table1*	The table that contains the records you want to append to *table2*.
WHERE *criteria*	The criteria that define which records will be appended in *table2*.

For example, suppose the supplier named "Exotic Liquids" also becomes a customer. Because Northwind's Suppliers and Customers tables have a number of fields in common, you can save some work by taking the Exotic Liquids record from the Suppliers table and appending it to the Customers table. Here's an SQL statement that does this:

```
INSERT INTO Customers (CustomerID, CompanyName, ContactName,
ContactTitle, Address, City, Region, PostalCode, Country, Phone, Fax)
SELECT SupplierID, CompanyName, ContactName,
ContactTitle, Address, City, Region, PostalCode, Country, Phone, Fax
FROM Suppliers
WHERE CompanyName="Exotic Liquids";
```

Using SQL to Create Subqueries

For most nonprogrammers who attempt to learn SQL, the subject becomes immediately worthwhile when they learn about *subqueries*: the capability to include a query dynasct as the criteria for another query. This powerful feature enables you to perform many otherwise difficult or even impossible query tasks.

Suppose, for example, you want to analyze Northwind's Products table to find out which products have a UnitPrice value that's greater than the average unit price. You know you can calculate the average unit price by using a totals query with the field expression Avg(UnitPrice). But how do you get that answer into a second query so that you can compare all the UnitPrice values with the result to see which ones are greater than the average? That sounds like a tall order, but it's actually fairly straightforward if you use a subquery.

To see why, let's first take a general look at subqueries. You can define a subquery as an SQL SELECT statement that is included in a regular select query in one of two ways:

- As part of an expression that defines a calculated field. In this case you use a totals query that returns a value and then use that value within the expression.
- As the criteria for a field. In this case, you can use any type of SELECT statement.

The next few sections run you through the specifics of these methods and provide some examples.

Using a Subquery to Define a Field

The following SELECT statement implements a totals query that returns the average of the values in the Product's table's UnitPrice field:

```
SELECT Avg(UnitPrice) From Products
```

If you want to use this value as a field in a query, you enter it in the Field cell, surrounded by parentheses, as shown in Figure 15.7. Figure 15.8 shows the resulting dynaset.

Figure 15.7
You can use a SELECT statement that defines a totals query as the expression that defines a calculated field.

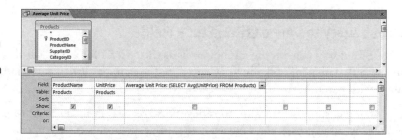

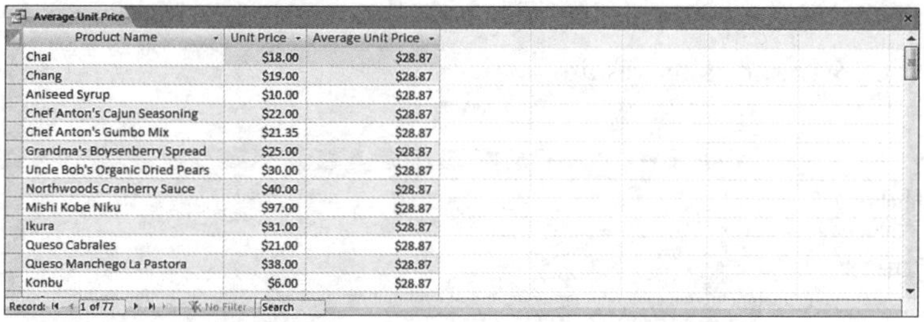

Figure 15.8
The results of the query defined in Figure 15.7.

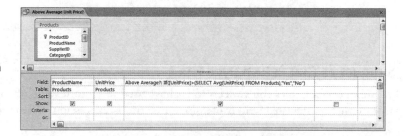

Determining Whether a Unit Price Is Greater Than the Average

A more common scenario is to include the totals query result as part of a larger expression. For example, you might want to compare each product's UnitPrice and compare that with the average: If it's greater, return Yes; otherwise, return No. Here's an expression that does this:

```
IIf([UnitPrice]>(SELECT Avg(UnitPrice) FROM Products), "Yes", "No")
```

Figure 15.9 shows a query that uses this expression, and Figure 15.10 shows the results.

Figure 15.9
In this example, the SELECT totals query is used as part of a larger expression that defines a calculated field.

Figure 15.10
The results of the query defined in Figure 15.9.

Using a Subquery to Define Criteria for a Field

The second way you can use a subquery is as the criteria for a field. In this case, you add the SELECT statement to the field's Criteria cell. Again, be sure to surround the SELECT statement with parentheses.

For example, suppose you want to return those records in the Products field that have a UnitPrice value greater than the average unit price. In this case, you enter the following into the Criteria cell of the UnitPrice field, as shown in Figure 15.11:

```
>(SELECT Avg(UnitPrice) From Products)
```

Figure 15.12 shows the results.

Figure 15.11
You can also filter records by including a subquery in a field's Criteria cell.

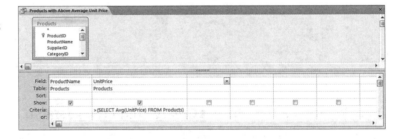

Figure 15.12
The results of the query defined in Figure 15.11.

Using Subqueries That Return Dynasets

The subquery examples you've seen so far have used the return value of a totals query as part of either a calculated field expression or a criteria expression. When you're building criteria, however, you can also use regular SELECT subqueries that return dynasets. You then apply the following special predicates or predicate expressions to get the dynaset you want:

In	Returns those records in which the value of a particular field is in a set of values for another table's field returned by a SELECT subquery.
Not In	Returns those records in which the value of a particular field is not in a set of values for another table's field returned by a SELECT subquery.
= | <> | < | <= | > | >= Any	Returns those records where the comparison operation is True for at least one of the values returned by the subquery.
= | <> | < | <= | > | >= All	Returns those records where the comparison operation is True for all the values returned by the subquery.

The next couple of sections take you through some examples.

In **Predicate: Customers Who Have Placed Orders**

As an example of the In predicate, suppose you want to return a dynaset that includes all those customers who placed at least one order in a particular month. You can do this by first creating a subquery that returns the CustomerID values for all those records in the Orders table that were placed in the month in question. For example, here's a SELECT subquery that returns the CustomerID values for customers who placed an order in January 2007:

```
SELECT CustomerID FROM Orders
WHERE OrderDate Between #1/1/2007# And #1/31/2007#
```

Now, in the Query Design view, apply the In predicate to this subquery in the Criteria cell for the Customers table's CustomerID field, as shown in Figure 15.13. Figure 15.14 shows the resulting dynaset.

Figure 15.13
Using the In predicate to match field values with the values returned by the subquery in the field's Criteria cell.

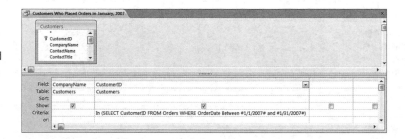

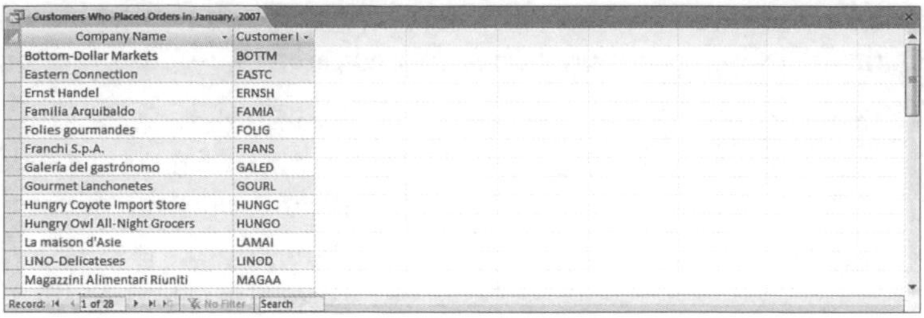

Figure 15.14
The results of the query
defined in Figure 15.13.

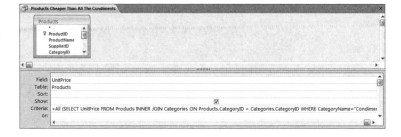

If you're interested in seeing those customers who did *not* place an order in January 2007, you use the Not In predicate, instead:

```
Not In (SELECT CustomerID FROM Orders
➥WHERE OrderDate Between #1/1/2007# And #1/31/2007#)
```

All Predicate: Products Cheaper Than All the Condiments

As an example of the All predicate, suppose you want to return a list of products that have a UnitPrice value that's cheaper than all the UnitPrice values in the Condiments category. You do this by first setting up a SELECT subquery that joins Products and Categories and then returns the UnitPrice values for just the Condiments category:

```
SELECT Products.UnitPrice FROM Products
INNER JOIN Categories ON Products.CategoryID = Categories.CategoryID
WHERE CategoryName="Condiments"
```

In the Query Design view, apply the < All predicate expression to this subquery in the Criteria cell for the Products table's UnitPrice field:

```
< All (SELECT Products.UnitPrice FROM Products INNER JOIN Categories
➥ON Products.CategoryID = Categories.CategoryID
➥WHERE CategoryName="Condiments")
```

Figure 15.15 shows the query design, and Figure 15.16 shows the results.

Figure 15.15
Using the < All predi-
cate expression to match
field values with the
values returned by the
subquery in the field's
Criteria cell.

Products Cheaper Than All The Condiments

Product Name	Unit Pric
Konbu	$6.00
Teatime Chocolate Biscuits	$9.20
Tunnbröd	$9.00
Guaraná Fantástica	$4.50
Geitost	$2.50
Jack's New England Clam Chowder	$9.65
Røgede sild	$9.50
Zaanse koeken	$9.50
Filo Mix	$7.00
Tourtière	$7.45
Rhönbräu Klosterbier	$7.75
*	$0.00

Record: 1 of 11 No Filter Search

Figure 15.16
The results of the query defined in Figure 15.15.

Using SQL to Create Union Queries

A union query is another SQL-only entity. It enables you to combine the dynasets of two or more `SELECT` statements into a single dynaset. Here's the general syntax:

```
SELECT statement1
UNION SELECT statement2
[UNION SELECT statement3...]
ORDER BY field_list [ASC | DESC];
```

`SELECT` *statement1*	The SQL `SELECT` statement that defines the first dynaset that you want to include in the union.
`SELECT` *statement2*	The SQL `SELECT` statement that defines the second dynaset that you want to include in the union.
`SELECT` *statement3...*	The SQL `SELECT` statements that define the other dynasets that you want to include in the union.
`ORDER BY` *field_list*	The sort order of the final dynaset.

For example, suppose you want to create a dynaset that includes all the companies in three Northwind tables—Customers, Shippers, and Suppliers—and you want the dynaset to have the following fields:

`CompanyID`—This new field will hold the `CustomerID`, `ShipperID`, and `SupplierID` values.

`CompanyName` and `Phone`—These are the two fields that all three tables have in common.

`CompanyType`—This new field will contain one of the following values, as appropriate: `Customer`, `Shipper`, or `Supplier`.

Here's the SQL statement that creates this union query:

```
SELECT CustomerID AS CompanyID, CompanyName, Phone,
"Customer" AS CompanyType FROM Customers
UNION SELECT ShipperID, CompanyName, Phone, "Shipper" FROM Shippers
UNION SELECT SupplierID, CompanyName, Phone, "Supplier" FROM Suppliers
ORDER BY CompanyName
```

Figure 15.17 shows the resulting dynaset.

Figure 15.17
The results of the union query.

From Here

→ For the details of calculated columns, **see** "Setting Up a Calculated Column," **p. 239**. (Chapter 11)

→ For more information about joins, **see** "Understanding Join Lines," **p. 267**. (Chapter 12)

→ To learn about totals queries, **see** "Creating a Totals Query," **p. 287**. (Chapter 13)

→ For the full details on parameter queries, **see** "Running Parameter Queries," **p. 302**. (Chapter 13)

→ To learn more about action queries, **see** "Running Action Queries," **p. 304**. (Chapter 13)

INDEX